Dictionary of Media and Jour...

Dictionary
of
Media and Journalism

—TV, Radio, Print and Internet—

Edited by

Chandrakant P. Singh PhD

Indian Institute of Mass Communication (IIMC)
New Delhi

ik

I.K. International Pvt. Ltd.

New Delhi • Mumbai • Bangalore

© 2004 Chandrakant P. Singh

ISBN 81-88237-08-6 (Hardbound)
ISBN 81-88237-13-2 (Paperback)

Published by Krishan Makhijani for I.K. International Pvt. Ltd., S-25, Green Park Extension, Uphaar Cinema Market, New Delhi 110 016. Typeset and printed at Rekha Printers Pvt. Ltd., Okhla Industrial Area, Phase-II, New Delhi 110 020.

Dedicated
to
Babooji (father), Iya (mother),
Sangeeta (my wife)
and
sons Anu, Tanu and Manu

Foreword

The need for a dictionary dealing with media and journalism is justified, as it becomes a useful reference tool for students, scholars and others. It enhances the understanding of the users to pursue their enquiry.

A comprehensive listing spanning a range of journalism and media activities has been attempted. The author intends to "empower the media and journalism students to understand not only the nuances of the medium in which they are trained but other media which have a bearing on their professional life".

With his practical experience and current assignment as a faculty, Dr. C.P. Singh is in a position to understand the requirements of the users, particularly the students. His attempt to compile the dictionary by including nearly 4000 terms and concepts is timely in the context of proliferation of journalism and mass communication institutions which are in need of teaching and reference material. Some of us engaged in writing about the profession may find it useful to probe the background and explanation for some of the terms we use. In certain cases words used in a particular sequence gain currency and over a period of time we may find it difficult to trace the origin and context in which the usage began. Dictionaries serve functions in this sense.

I welcome this attempt and hope that the users go beyond mere understanding of the terms and concepts and use them appropriately in their work. The etymological aspects of the terms apart, consistent scholarship and serious work in our area would definitely strengthen and improve professionalism in journalism and mass communication. This is a novel attempt and responses to this work will hopefully spur many others to take the cue and make meaningful contributions.

It is gratifying to note that a young colleague from our Institute has taken up this challenging task and I sincerely hope that it will be a useful reference manual for us engaged in this discipline.

March 2004

B.P. Sanjay
Director, IIMC, Delhi

Preface

ORDER OUT OF CHAOS

At a time when the society is witnessing a media and communication revolution and the synergy between different media is being considered very important, the need for a multi-media dictionary for students, professionals and researchers need not be overemphasized.

What is This Book About?

- Being first of its kind, it includes key as well as related concepts and terms (e.g. those originating from advertising, time-selling, circulation, production and PR) that mass communication & journalism students need to know as part of their syllabus.
- It also includes terms that journalists and other media professionals come across in their day-to-day operations while interacting with other departments (circulation, marketing, time selling etc.) within the same media organization.
- Terms specific to a country or a region are properly contextualised. For example, *Dark Edition* meaning newspaper edition brought out for places distant from the place of its production centre, is used only in India, Pakistan and Bangladesh. Likewise, there are similar/same terms having different meanings the UK and the USA.

What is This Not?

Uniqueness of this work lies in the fact that it tries to link academic and professional needs with experience. But this is its weakness as well. Many of the concepts you might like to understand in their historical contexts, have been given a very neutral treatment. For example, if you want to look for the term *newspaper*, the book will give you a very standard and neutral definition of what a newspaper is, not its historical development over the last two and a half centuries.

Also, generally most of the things relating to history of media and journalism are kept out of the ambit of the book to make it more handy and useful. This is for those who are grappling with the present to make their future better.

Break-up of Terms and Concepts

Over 4000 key concepts and related terms have been grouped into four major categories:

TV & Radio:	1150-1200
Internet, Information and Communication Technologies:	1150-1200
Newspaper, Magazine, Printing & Publishing:	1350-1400
Related terms (advertising & PR, media marketing, management, e-commerce, etc.):	300-350

Why This Dictionary?

- The objective is to empower the media and journalism students to understand not only the nuances of the medium in which they are trained but all other media which have a bearing on their professional life.
- It may also serve as an effective tool for promoting better intra-medium as well as inter-departmental understanding (circulation, advertising, time-selling, PR) that is increasingly becoming crucial for the growth of a news and media organization in a multi-media environment.
- All this has the potential of turning the media professionals and journalists into change agents who are always ready to go an extra mile to strengthen the brand image of the organization they work for. This is reinforced by the new mantra of business of all kinds: *'Your brand is as good as your people'*.

Target Audiences

- Over 50 university departments and more than 100 colleges all over India are offering courses in Journalism & Mass Communication. In addition, about 500 privately run institutes have come up to take care of the demand of the media savvy generation. In Delhi alone, there are over 40 such institutes and colleges.

- Not to be left out of the race and to meet the demands of their students, who want to go in the media sector, even management schools have started teaching media basics.
- Media professionals of all hues who intend to better upon their knowledge of other departments within the same media organization and also those who want to have a reasonably good idea of convergence induced newsroom lingo may find this dictionary useful. It can also benefit those who want to leapfrog to say TV from print but don't have exposure to basic concepts of the television as a medium.
- Social science students who want to venture into media related research would also find this dictionary handy and useful.

A Bold Assumption

It contains a body of concepts and terms that may be of help in the understanding of media, mass communication and journalism. In addition to its core areas—media and journalism—the book also draws upon various disciplines, especially media marketing, advertising, public relations, management, theatre, film, sociology, information and communication technologies, etc. The underlying current being an academic and professional craving for connecting these apparently unconnected things that are impacting radio, TV, print and Internet as vehicles of mass communication, and journalism as a profession. In this context, the very title 'Dictionary of Media and Journalism' is a bold assumption of sorts as many of the concepts and terms themselves are evolving fast.

Limitations

Since this is largely a work by an individual, limitations are many. To name the prime limitation, everything is looked at from the perspective of one person who moved straight from university classrooms to a journalism school and remained in the industry for over a decade before defecting to journalism teaching. No wonder you find yourself trapped by a person who is capitalizing to the hit on his journalistic license of being the jack of all (read many) trades and master of none.

This dictionary comes at a time when the mass media are undergoing revolutionary changes and so is the profession of journalism. The changes are so profound that boundaries are getting blurred thanks to convergence of media vehicles at one platform that is

Internet which is lending ever-increasing interactivity to all media channles. All this has portends of making uncertain very concepts of media, mass communication and journalism.

Does this mean that one should wait till the debates over the concepts are settled or venture to make the best out of the uncertainty through a better understanding of those changes? The editor risks taking the latter view. If you also want to enjoy finding out an order out of chaos (that media scene in general and a newsroom in particular is) you are welcome.

How to Use This Book

- all entires are alphabetized by letter so that multiple-word terms are treated as single words;
- abbreviations and acronyms are used as entries in cases where they are more commonly understood than full terms. For example, HDTV is more commonly used than High Definition Television, and so the explanation is given under HDTV;
- where a term has several meanings, various meanings have been given;
- for the sake of brevity, explanation or definition of an entry may require the use of one or more than one term. In such cases, the terms are italicized meaning thereby that you can see them as cross references in the form of independent entries to have a better understanding of the original entry;
- wherever required, illustrations have been given, especially to make clear such concepts as close-up, medium shot, long shot, extreme close-up, extreme long shot, etc. In such cases, you may benefit more by having a look of all the related illustrations; and,
- in case of many entries, you are advised to look for several other related terms and concepts mentioned in italics at the end of the standard definition or explanation. This is for those who may want to have a fuller understanding of the original entry.

March, 2004 **Chandrakant P. Singh**
IIMC, Delhi

Acknowledgement

Working on a books of this kind presupposes drawing upon diverse sources directly and indirectly and benefiting from the experiences and services of a good number of people—professionals, academicians and friends, over an extended period. I started working on this book in November 1997 and it is likely that I miss on some of them. I would gratefully acknowledge them as and when such lapses are brought to my notice.

Foremost among the people who have inspired me into taking up this work and provided all help at their command are:

Mr. B. Sreedharanath, a Times School of Journalism alumnus and brilliant copywriter based in Hyderabad;

Dr. S. P. Gupta, Chairman, Indian Archaeological Society, Delhi;

Mr. Alok Mehta, Editor, Outlook Saptahik, Delhi;

Mr. Tabrez Ahmad, E-commerce Consultant, Federation of Chambers of Commerce and Industry (FICCI), Delhi;

Ms. Praveen Malhotra, Career Consultant & Director, Vision Books, Delhi;

Mr. Aseem Bhatnagar and Ms. Harjeet K. Gill, Software Professionals;

Mr. Ashwini Gaddoo, a Film Maker;

Mohammad Shahbaz, a Mumbai-based Cartoonist and Script Writer;

Mr. Ramsubramanian, Senior Librarian, Indian Institute of Mass Communication (IIMC), Delhi;

Mr. Siddhi Vishwakarma and Ms. Madhuri Singh, Journalists, Sahara Samay;

Mr. Ramlal Khanna, Assistant Editor, Career Economy Magazine;

Mr. Sudhir Goel, Senior Documentation Officer, IIMC;

Ms. Megha Prasad and Ms. Anshu Joshi,, student and project assistant respectively, IIMC;

Mr. Suresh Kumar, Sub-Editor, online edition of Hindi Daily Dainik Jagaran, Delhi.

Mr. Ashok Ogra, Formerly Vice-President, Programming (South Asia), Discovery Channel.

I need to pay special gratitude to a budding caricaturist: Sumant Anurag, a class V student, DAV Public School, Delhi, who made most of the initial illustrations for the dictionary.

I want to thank the following without whose persistent support and faith in me this book would not have seen the light of the day:

Mrs. Jewari Devi, my mother; Ms Sanjeeta Kumari, my wife, Sumant, Sushant and Sumit, my sons; Anita Chaudhary, my sister-in-law, and her daughter Megha; Mrs. Nirmala Dubey and Mrs. Gayatri Chaudhary, my sisters; Anee, my niece; my friends—Mr. Satyanand Roy, branch Manager, Spectrum Business Support Ltd., Kolkata; Mr. G.K. Singh, Director, Telecom Department, Delhi; Ms. Anita Kanungo, Formerly Principal Correspondent, The Hindustan Times, Delhi; Dr. Deodatta Poddar, Jaipur Golden Hospital; Ms. Uma, Lecturer, Delhi University; and Mr. Manish Kumar, Ph. D. Scholar, Delhi University.

Over the last eight years or so, I consulted dozens of books on mass communication, journalism, information & communiction technologies and other sources. Most of these have been listed in the extended references given at the end and which, I urge you to read as an extension of my acknowledgements. Those omitted inadvertently would be given due credit in future editions.

I would like to thank Prof. B.P. Sanjay, Director, IIMC, who facilitated the acquisition of a wide variety of books and other resources that I wanted to consult, and also for writing a context-setting foreword to the dictionary. May thanks are also due to IIMC staff for having happily extended all the facilities without which this book would not have seen the light of the day.

It would be only in the fitness of things to bow to *Rahu-Ketus* (evil forces) to have allowed me to complete my work at the cost of theirs.

Finally, I want to thank the students of journalism and mass communication, especially those at IIMC, who continue to be my best teachers, and Mr. Kishan Makhijani and Mr. Beenu Bhalla of I.K. International Pvt. Ltd., their handling of the project in a professional manner.

Chandrakant P. Singh

Contents

Aa

ABC ▶ (i) American Broadcasting Company; (ii) Australian Broadcasting Corporation; (iii) Audit Bureau of Circulations; an autonomous body with regional and national publishers, advertisers, news agencies, and advertising agencies as its members; a source of authoritative figures of newspaper's and magazine's net sale over specified periods, this is important as advertising rates are related to circulation figures.

ABNI ▶ Asia Business News International.

Above-the-line cost ▶ Expenditure under the producer's control in addition to fixed overheads (below-the-line).

AB-roll ▶ This is a hold over from film. This refers to footage that is coming from a second player (i.e. B-roll), as the footage from the first player (i.e. A-roll) is being edited on to the recorder. Here both the shots are together, i.e. one is superimposed over the other. This is normally not used in hard news stories. However, in feature stories, say, on fashion or entertainment, this is common.

Absolute privilege ▶ The right of legislators, government officers and judges to speak without threat of libel when acting officially.

Access broadcasting ▶ Radio and TV programmes in which editorial decisions are made by the contributor, not by professional staff.

Access channel ▶ Channel used on a cable TV system whereby citizens may produce TV programmes to be shown to the community (different from local origination).

Access number ▶ The telephone number dialed by the modem that lets a computer communicate with an online service or Internet Service Provider (ISP).

Access time ▶ (i) Interval between the selection of a computer function and its appearance on the screen. (ii) In television programming, time segment in Eastern and Pacific time zones from 7:30 P.M. to 8:00 P.M., just prior to *prime time* Monday through Saturday. On Sundays, prime time is extended one hour to include access time. See also *daypart*.

Account executive (AE) ▶ (i) Member of staff of an advertising agency dealing with clients and preparing advertisements. (ii) An ad and PR executive of an agency, who represents a client within that agency and coordinates the agency's services for the client.

Accountability ► The question of who controls media professionals and who has the power to punish them for their ethical/professional lapses. The professionals are accountable to corporate owners, editors, news councils, internal censors, and citizen's groups as well as their own conscience.

Accreditation ► Certification by an industry association or a government agency. For example, senior journalists or those with good journalistic credentials are accredited by the state government public relations departments or the PIB (Press Information Bureau) of the government fo India. Journalists so accredited get certain privileges in terms of access to various ministires and the press briefings by them.

Achromatic ► In TV, it refrs to video shots lacking colour; neutral tonal values (white, grays, black) without distinct hue.

Acoustic ► The environment that surrounds and affects any given sound, particularly when making a recording. Acoustics: the science of sound, the way sound behaves.

Acoustic screen ► Free-standing movable screen designed to create special acoustic effects or prevent unwanted sound reaching a particular microphone. Its one side is soft and absorbent while the other is hard and reflective.

Across-the-board ► A programme scheduled to be broadcast at the same time, on the same radio or television station, for five consecutive days every week (usually Monday through Friday). The name derives from the fact that a weekday programme schedule is sometimes referred to as the board. Across-the-board pro-grammes target the same audience every day and are considered excellent vehicles for advertisers indenting to reach their current or prospective customers in the belief that frequent repetition of commercials will best sell their products. Across-the-board programming is also known as strip *programming*, because the programme fills in a strip in the broadcast schedule.

Action ► (i) A general term for performance, movement. Usually begins on hand-cue from floor manager (FM) and a cue can be taken from light, sound, action or monitor pictures. (ii) Order to begin movement in filming, as in "Lights, camera, action".

Action Accelerators ► See *Cutaways*.

Action shot ➤ (i) Photograph showing someone or something in motion. (ii) See also *moving shot*.

Active desktop ➤ A feature you use to make Web pages your desktop wallpaper.

Active satellite ➤ A satellite equip-ped to receive signals and to relay its own signals back to earth.

ActiveX ➤ It is a model for writing programmes. ActiveX technology is used to make interactive web pages that look and behave like computer programme, rather than static pages. With ActiveX, users can ask or answer questions, use push buttons, and interact in other ways with the web page.

Actuality ➤ (i) A recording of someone speaking (a newsmaker), or of an event, used in radio news bulletins or similar output; a reporter's voice-piece is not in itself actuality, neither is any recording made for fictional or dramatic purposes.
(ii) Actuality programme of feature made without accompanying narrative or commentary.

Actual malice ➤ Legal term meaning that the defendent knowingly or recklessly published a false item.

Ad alley ➤ (US) Section of composing room where advertisements are assembled.

A/D converter ➤ Analogue-to-digital converter, it creates a digital output from an analogue input, e.g., a conventional microphone recording on minidisc.

Add ➤ Written on copy to be added at end of story already set or subbed and sent to printer (see *insert*).

Ad dummy ➤ The blank sets of newspaper or magazine pages of an edition with the shapes and positions of advertisements marked in; also on screen. Sometimes also called *scheme*.

Address ➤ It refers to the location of a file on the Internet or any computer. You can use addresses to find files on the Internet and your computer. Internet addresses are also known as URLs (*Uniform Resource Locators*). See also *address bar*.

Address bar ➤ A method of opening files that are on the Internet or your computer. When you type an address in the address bar, you open the file at that address. See also *AutoComplete*.

Ad/Ed ratio ➤ The ratio of advertising to editorial matter in an issue of a magazine or a newspaper.

Ad-get feature ➤ An editorial feature commissioned to encourage advertisers to take space along side.

Adjacency ➤ (i) Radio or television programme immediately preceding or following another scheduled program-me on a particular station. (ii) Time duration (usually 2 minutes) that precedes or follows network programmes; also called *commercial break position*. It is offered for sale for local or spot advertisers. Commercial time is sold on the basis of the ratings of adjacencies: the higher the rating, the greater the listening or viewing audience, and hence the greater the advertsng cost. The audience potential of an adjacency is greater than that of a programme commercial as many people keep their television or radio tuned in to the following programme after hearing or viewing the adjacency. Similarly, many who want to see or hear a programme will tune in early and are thus exposed to the commercials in the break position.

Adjacent T-stop ▸ Adjacent T-stop numbers double or halve the amoun tof transmitted light. See *T-stops*.

Ad lib ▸ Speech or action that has not been written or rehearsed i.e. speaking without a script.

ADN ▸ (Advanced digital network) – Usually refers to a 56Kbps leased-line. Also see *BPS*.

Adnorm ▸ It refers to the percentage of readers of a particular publication who remember a specific advertisement in that publication. An adnorm of 10 would mean that 10% of the readers of a particular publication who remember ads of a particular type recalled the ad in question. The research is based on the size of the ad, the use of colour, the type of product, and experience with the publication.

Ad rule ▸ The rule or border separating editorial matter from advertisements on the page of a newspaper or a magazine.

ADSL ▸ See *DSL*

Advance ▸ Story anticipating scheduled event, often as holding story to be replaced by report for later edition.

Advance organizer ▸ A preview of what will be discussed. It can be either text or graphics and may be located on a main page or a "help" page on a computer.

Advanced television (ATV) systems ▸ A generic name for higher definition television configurations.

Adversarial relationship ▸ Press-government interaction in which the press does not act as a cheer/ender or perform public relations for the government.

Advertised price ▸ (i) In broadcast, the established price for an advertiser, based on the frequency of commercials and the total amount of time purchased (volume); the cost to advertise a product. (ii) Cost to the purchaser of a product or service announced or stated in a commercial or an advertisement.

Advertisement feature ▶ The approved term for *advertorial*.

Advertising ▶ Paid-for material advocating goods or services; finances writers, whether they like it or not; can be display or classified.

Advertising agency ▶ An organisation that prepares and designs advertisements for clients and buys advertising space (in newspapers or magazine) and time (on radio or TV or Internet). It contracts with advertisers (firms or individuals attempting to find customers for their products and services) to manage their advertising. Historically, advertising agency services are of a creative nature, but the agency concept has expanded to include research services and media planning and buying. Agencies are typically classified by the type of business they handle (e.g., financial, industrial, or consumer packaged goods) or the range of services they offer (e.g., creative, media, or full service). Compensation for services is derived from three different sources: (1) 15% commissions from the media on the rate charged for media space or time; (2) fees charged for services (usually non-commissionable, such as a market survey); however, situations will occur when the price-value relationship between media placement and creative services is out of balance (e.g., when a client uses the same broadcast commercial for a long period of time, incurring no creative costs, but incurring millions of dollars in broadcast billing), and agencies will be compensated by the substitution of a fee system in place of the 15% commission; and (3) percentage charges on materials and services used in the preparation of advertisements; in this area, clients are charged cost plus 17.65%.

Advertising code ▶ The code of ethics to be followed by the advertisers, the advertising agencies and the advertising media. The code is formulated by the Advertising Council of India.

Advertorial ▶ Word derived from a combination of the words advertisement and editorial. Articles which advertisers have paid for; should not be allowed as independent editorial matter. Its place and date is usually pre-determined.

Advocacy advertising ▶ Advertising that espouses a point of view about controversial public issues. It can be directed at either specific targets, or general targets, such as political activists, the media, consumer groups, government agencies, or competitors, can be sponsored by any type of advertiser (businesses, consumer groups, special interest groups, political parties, or even individuals). An often quoted example occurred in the US in 1960s, when a man bought a two-page advertisement in the New York Times at a cost of $12,0000 to offer his peace plan for ending the war in Vietnam.

Aerial ▶ Device for transmitting or receiving radio waves at the point of transition from their electrical/electromagnetic form.

AFC ▶ Automatic frequency control. It is a circuit that keeps a television receiver tuned to the correct signal.

Affiliate ▶ Independently owned radio or television station that has a contractual agreement with a network to devote a portion of its broadcast time to network programmes. The network offers the programming in exchange for commercial time, which can then be sold to a national advertiser. With a string of affiliates throughout the country, a network can offer advertisers wider audiences and thus attract national corporations with large advertising budgets.

AFP ▶ Agence France Presse, French news agency.

Afternoon drive ▶ In radio broadcasting, the time segment from 3:00 P.M. to 7:00 P.M. Monday through Friday. Afternoon drive time combined with morning drive time (6:00 A.M. to 10:00 A.M.) is considered radio's prime time, because these segments together account for the largest audience.

AFTRA ▶ American Federation of Television and Radio Artists; it is a talent union.

Agate ▶ Old name for 51/2 pt type; classified ads measured in agate lines (US). Fourteen agate lines are 1² deep i.e. there are 14 cigate lines in depth (height) to a column inch (width).

AGC ▶ Automatic gain control; amplifier circuit which compensates for variations in signal level, dynamic compression.

Agencies ▶ Organisation supplying but not publishing/printing a newspaper or producing TV/radio news. Main news agencies (supplying either stories or pictures or both) are Reuters, Agence France Presse, Itar-Tass, Associated Press, APTV, ANI, PTI and UNI. Also, large number of smaller agencies are serving specialist and general fields. Copy (known as wire copy) arrives in newspaper offices from them on computer screens or occasionally on teleprinters. Advertisng agencies are also known as agencies.

Agency copy (wire copy) ➤ Written material received from news agencies, now usually through News room Computer Systems.

Agenda setting ➤ Highlighting certain issues and events in preference to many others, and influencing public perception of the society in a significant manner. The people perceive only those men and matters as important which are given exposure and emphasis in the media and those not covered by the media are considered to be of lesser importance.

Agony aunt ➤ Women who offer advice to people who write in to newspapers and magazines with personal/emotional problems. *Agony uncle*: male equivalent. Not many of these are around but likely to grow in number.

Agony column ➤ A regular newspaper or magazine feature giving advice on personal problems to mainly the young; hence **agony aunt.**

AIFF ➤ One Format of Mac Sound Files.

A-insert ➤ Copy to be inserted (according to marked accompanying proof) into matter already set; separate inserts marked A,B,C, etc, for clarity, and long inserts numbered A1, A2, etc.; always mark the end of an insert.

Air check ➤ An excerpt from a broadcast illustrating how a performer, broadcaster or a programme looks and sounds on the air.

Alignment ➤ Setting the copy text (and headlines) over column. Copy set/aligned left begins on extreme left of column; all lines of copy ranged right are flush to the extreme right of the column and ragged left

Aliterates ➤ People who can read but don't.

Alive/Live ➤ Copy of a story intended for use in a newspaper, magazine, or a news channel. Also, a live story is the one on which the reporter is working and that will be used. See also *kill*.

All in ➤ It is a proof reader's term meaning all copy and proofs are in the reading room.

All in hand ➤ Printer has received and is setting all copy and headings for a particualr story or page.

All out ➤ Printer has dispersed all copy for setting.

All rights reserved ➤ General copyright warning, usually to avoid lifting of exclusive material information.

All up ➤ Refers to all copy in a newspaper or a magazine having been set, but not necessarily read and corrected.

Alphageometric ➤ A system that produces graphics that are more smoothly curved.

Alphamosaic ➤ The graphic creation system originally adopted by the British for their teletext configuration. Alphamosaic graphics are box like in appearance.

Alphanumeric ➤ Describing a code or string of characters that includes both letters and numbers and/or punctuation marks or mathematical symbols. Most match codes, unique codes assigned to computer records as an identifier, are alphanumeric. For example, a match code might include the first, third, and fourth letters of the last name, the PIN code, and the house number. The match code for Abraham George at 761 Africa Avenue in New Delhi would be GOR-110016761. See also *key code*.

Alterations ➤ Changes on proof that differ from original copy (i.e., not simply corrections).

Alternative press ➤ Loose term incorporating wide variety of non-mainstream newspapers and magazines: Economic and Political Weekly, Seminar (India), Asian Times, Socialist Worker (UK), etc. It may include religious, ethnic, municipal and trade union publications.

Alts ➤ Alteration made to newspaper or magazine copy or set matter.

AM station ➤ Any radio station in the amplitude modulation (AM) system, assigned the range of wavelengths from 0.535 to 1.605 MHz (megahertz), or 53 to 160 on the radio dial. Any station within this spectrum is called an AM station.

Ambient light ➤ General uncontrolled light spilling onto a surface. It tends to illuminate shadows and reduce contrast. Especially refers to random light falling on TV picture display, reducing contrast and degrading its image.

Ambush interview ➤ When an interviewee is surprised by suddenly a different line of questioning or by the sudden appearance of journalist(or group of journalists). It has theatrical flavour when done on television. Generally only done when reporters are convinced they are dealing with person who needs to be exposed.

Ampex ➤ Television equipment makers (US).

Amplifier ➤ An electronic device for increasing volume.

Amplitude modulation (AM) ➤ Method of transmitting radio signals by varying the size (amplitude) of the radio wave while the speed (frequency) of the radio wave remains constant. Signals transmitted in this manner cary great distances, particularly at night, but are susceptible to interference; broadcast system using amplitude modulation. See also *frequency modulation* (FM)

Analogue recording ➤ Where sound and/or pictures are recorded directly on to a recording medium (without being digitally encoded).

Analogue signal ➤ A continuously variable and varying signal. The communications devices and systems we are most familiar with such as video cameras and radio stations produce and process analogue signals. Transmission of such signals involves turning the information into a wave, with the peaks and troughs representing various attributes of the message (e.g. for a voice these might be volume and tone).

Analogue technology ➤ A device that physically represents, some other phenomenon, such as a standard thermometer does the body temperature, or reproduces that phenomenon, such as the conversion of TV image into electromagnetic waves and the recoversion of the same by a TV set into a picture on the screen.

Analogue-digital converter (ADC) ➤ An ADC converts analogue information into a digital form. ADCs work with DACs to bridge the gap between analogue and digital equipment and systems.

Anchor ➤ The person who delivers the news, weather, or sports during a TV news programme. In small markets this individual also may be the news director and producer and so on.

And finally ➤ See *tailpiece*.

Anecdotal lead ➤ A newspaper story that uses some interesting incident to start the story.

Angle ➤ An item of information in a news story that a journalist chooses to emphasize. It may be a new angle, giving the latest development in a story, or a local angle, emphasizing the point of relevance of that story to a local audience; 'play up this angle' means give it emphasis. Preferably different from, but not worse than, the angle chosen by someone else. Also called *peg*.

Angle shot ➤ Refers to usually a low or high angle shots can be sloping. Also see *canted shot, camera angles*.

Angle-of-view ➤ A measure of the proportion of the subject and its surroundings which can be included in the image. This depends on both the focal length of the lens and the size of the camcorder chip. A shorter focal length or wider film gives a greater angle-of-view.

ANI ▶ Asian News International; an Indian news agency providing video news services.

Animation ▶ As used in television news usually the technique of adding or changing information on a graphic. Animation makes inanimate objects appear come to life, and is useful in a situation where live action is not possible. In film, it means adding movement to static objects. Because the process of filming requires that each frame be shot individually, animation is very costly.

Animation camera ▶ Camera designed for use when the desired result is animated film. An animation camera shoots drawings or objects one frame at a time as those drawings or objects are moved on a table designed for this purpose (animation stand). Recent advances in technology have created a process of computer imaging where images are done digitally without a camera and transferred directly to film or videotape. The Walt Disney film tron is an example of this new technology. See also *animation*.

Announcer ▶ Various perform-ers who present information, news, commercials, sports, and weather. Narrowly defined, an announcer reads commercials, promotional spots, and station continuity.

Anonymous FTP ▶ A Service available at some Internet sites that gives any user access to data files and applications using FTP. With anonymous FTP, users don't need a special password to retrieve files. They are available to the public. Also see *FTP.*

ANPA ▶ American Newspaper Publishers Association.

Anti-Virus programme ▶ Software that monitors a computer for viruses and eliminates them before damage occurs.

Any to any ▶ Describes a network where any subscriber is able to communicate with any other subscriber or service provider on the network, e.g. *Internet.*

AP ▶ Associated Press, an American news agency.

Aperture ▶ Opening which controls the amount of light transmitted by a lens. Its size can be varied to control the amount of light passing into the camera.

Apology ▶ A newspaper may admit to error and publish correction in apology. Complainant can still claim libel in court and publication of apology provides no defence for newspaper. But if newspaper loses case, the fact that it took prompt and adequate steps to correct error and to express regret provides plea in mitigation of damages tending to reduce the size of damages awarded by the court.

Appraisal ► A formal meeting in which an employee's performance is assessed and discussed.

APTV ► Television arm of Associated Press (AP).

Arabic numerals ► Those we commonly use: 1,2,3, etc. (as distinct from roman numerals: i, ii, iii, iv and I, II, III, etc. The Arabic number system originated in India and reached europe through Arabic translations of Indian books on astronomy written in Sanskrit.

Archie ► A tool (software) for finding files stored on anonymous FTP sites. You need to know the exact file name or a substring of it.

Archive ► File in which previously broadcast material is stored, possibly with clippings and background material.

Arianespace ► A commercial satellite launch agency.

Arm ► Horizontal stroke on T, diagonal lines of Y and K.

ARPANET ► (Advanced Research Projects Agency Network). The precursor to the Internet; developed in the late 60's and early 70's by the US Department of Defense as an experiment in wide-area networking that would survive a nuclear war.

Arrow ► See *pointer*

Art ► Frequently means pictures and other illustrations plus layout and design; its use is changing with increasing role of designer-artist in newspapers and magazines.

Art desk ► Where page layouts are drawn in detail and the pictures edited.

Art editor ► Picture editor, responsible for acquiring photographs and in charge of photographers; or (more recent) design editor.

Art paper ► Coated paper with high finish. Process departments require proofs on art paper to make white-on-black headings, strip type into illustrations, etc.

Artificial intelligence (AI) ► The discipline dedicated, in part, to developing machines that can seemingly think.

ASBU ► Arab States Broadcasting Union.

Ascender ► The part of a letter that rises above its x height or the body of the letter, as in h, k, l and f.

ASCII ► American Standard Code of Information Interchange. Pronounced a 'Askey' and used to mean plain text in digital form without formatting. There are 128 standad ASCII codes. Each of which can be represented by a 7-digit binary number: 0000000 through 1111111.

Asianet ▸ Satellite channel in Malyalam.

ASNE ▸ American Society of Newspaper Editors.

Aspect ratio ▸ The proportionate size of the television screen, three units high and four units wide, with the long side horizontal.

Assemble edit ▸ An edit on videotape where portions of a TV programme are pieced together and the end of one sequence edited to the beginning of another.

Assembly dailies ▸ In film and television production, film *footage* from which the best take of each scene shot on a given day has been selected, cut, and spliced in correct sequence by an editor; also called dailies or rushes. Assembly dailies are used for review on a daily basis to check for technique, concept, and continuity.

Assignment ▸ Reporter's specified task for a day, week, etc.; in office jargon, 'job'.

Assignment editor ▸ The person responsible for sending out news crews to cover the day's events, monitoring the police scanners for breaking stories, and, in general, co-ordinating daily news room activities.

Assignments desk ▸ Department responsible for assigning reporters and camera crews.

Assignments sheet ▸ Written instruction setting out details of an event to be covered .

Assistant news director ▸ (radio/TV) Second in command to the news director. This position is non-existent in most small markets because of budget constraints.

Assistant producer ▸ The person, not usually found in smaller markets; who works under a TV producer and handles many daily newsroom chores related to getting the newscast on the air.

Asterisk ▸ Occasionally used in text to link footnote or to indicate letters of words considered obscene.

Aston ▸ Makers of electronic prompting device which enables performers to read a script while looking directly at the camera.

Atmos ▸ Background noise or music, often achieved by a special microphone placed to get the best natural sound of the event.

Atmosphere ▸ Impression of environment created by use of actuality, sound effects or acoustic.

Attachment/Internship (U.S.) ▸ (i) Time spent by student journalists training (or occassionally just observing) at media organisation. (ii) An encoded file (binary or ASCII text) sent with an e-mail message rather than incorporated in the message itself.

Attenuation ► Expressed in decibels (dB), the extent to which a piece of equipment decreases the signal strength; opposite of amplification.

Attenuator ► Device of known attenuation deliberately inserted in a circuit to reduce the signal level.

Attribution ► Linking information of quote to original source.

Audience ► (i) Group of people assembled in a studio, theatre, or auditorium to witness a presentation or performance. (ii) Personal meeting of a formal nature, e.g. an audience with the President of your country. (iii) Total number of people who may receive an advertising message delivered by a medium or a combination of media. (iv) Total number of readers, viewers, or listeners reached by a medium radio, TV, print or Internet.

Audience accumulation ► Total net audience reached by an advertising campaign, including newspaper, magazine, and outdoor advertising, as well as broadcast commercials. If an advertising campaign for a product runs for a six-week period and uses a combination of media, the audience accumulation would be the total number of people who were exposed to an advertisement or commercial at least once.

Audience composition ► (i) Proportion of various types of people, classified by *Demographic* or *Psychographic* characteristics, reached by an advertising medium or message. (ii) Breakdown by programme of the listening and viewing audience according to gender and age. The number in each category is compared against the total number of listening or viewing audience for that programme. (For example, 20% of a viewing audience for a specific television show might be adult women, while 30% might be adolescents). This information allows the advertiser to position the message in or around a programme that appeals to the people most likely to utilize the product or service. Since different time periods (Dayparts) in programming have different costs, knowledge of audience composition permits the advertiser to select economically those hours during which a specific audience can be reached. See also *audience profile*.

Audience duplication ► Measurement in terms of percentage of the amount of persons in a listening, reading, or viewing audience who are reached more than once by the same commercial or advertisement appearing in different media as reported by the rating and measurement services. Many advertisers feel that their product or service will sell best if they concentrate their efforts on the same people, in which case, a high audience duplication percentage is desirable.

Audience figures ➤ Expressed as a percentage of the potential audience, or in absolute terms, the number of listeners to a single programme or sequence, daily or weekly patronage, or total usage of the station. See *patronage, ratings, reach*.

Audience flow ➤ (i) Gain or loss of the audience during a broadcast programme through turning on or off the television or through changing channels. (ii) Measurement of the traffic behavior of the *Television household audience* or the *radio audience* as reported by the rating and measurement services. Every programme has an audience flow that indicates where the audience came from before the programme and where they are going after it. There are three audience options: (a) the listening or viewing audience who came from a preceding programme on a competing broadcast station, (b) the audience coming from a preceding programme on the same station, and (c) the audience turned on their radios or televisions for a specific programmeme. At the conclusion of a programme these audience options are reversed, becoming. (a) the audience who will turn off their sets, (b) the audience who will remain to watch or listen to the next programme on the same station, and (c) the audience who will switch to another station. Audience flow data are important to the advertiser whose message is positioned in the time period between two shows. The fact that both shows have a high audience rating is not sufficient to assure that the message will be seen or heard. It is also important to know if both programmes share the same audience.

Audience fragmentation ➤ Division of audiences into small groups due to the wide spectrum of media outlets. This is a situation that becomes increasingly baffling to advertisers as the specialization of publications and broadcast opportunities become even more diverse. In addition, the advent of cable television has made a vast number of television stations available to viewing audiences as well as blurring the geographic locations of viewers. For example: New Delhi audiences can now watch programming of Chennai, Mumbai or Kolkata stations, and Chennai receives programming from New Delhi. This leaves a fragmented viewing audience in that consumers in Chennai usually cannot avail themselves of services delivered in New Delhi. Additionally, viewers now have the opportunity to watch two or three times as many television stations as in the past, so that audience size for any one local station is likely to be smaller than in the past. This situation creates an economic problem for advertisers who need to reach large audiences to make their advertising rupees cost effective. In addition, since the number of viewers determines the advertising rates, audience fragmentation will affect the networks' revenues as the audience size diminishes. As audiences become more fragmented, the major networks will need to create new revenue sources.

Audience-holding index ▶ Guide to how well a programme holds its audience, measured on a minute-by-minute or quarter-hour basis

by the research service companies. Many times a large audience will turn on a programme, but will not stay tuned for its entire duration. This is particularly true for sporting events, news broadcasts, and some miniseries. It is important, therefore, for an advertiser to be aware of the audience-holding index of a show before buying commercial time in that show.

Audience measurement ▶ Research into numbers and attitudes of listeners. Methods used include: 'Aided-Recall'-person to person interview; 'Diary'- the keeping of a log of programmes heard; 'Panel'-permanent representative group reporting on programmes heard.

Audience-participation programme ▶ Radio or television show in which members of the audience take part and whose participation is an integral part of the entertainment value of the show — for example, a radio show whose format calls for members of the listening audience to phone in and talk to the host, or a television quiz where the host conducts interviews with members of the studio audience or offers prizes for their ability (or lack of ability) to perform some task.

Audience profile ▶ Socio-economic characteristics of a

readership, viewership, or listener-ship, not to be confused with audience composition, which merely tells the makeup of the audience by age and gender. The profile gives some indication of the spending habits of a particular audience. Factors that determine a profile are income, car and home ownership, leisure time activities, and geographic location. This information is provided by the medium based on its own research or on that of the syndicated research services, and is then supplied to the advertiser or advertising agency. It is important to know the audience profile of the medium to reach the market for a particular product or service.

Audience ratings ▸ The percentage of people watching a programme at a specific time, usually, measures the people who are in the room with the set switched on. Household ratings or set ratings refer to the percentage of households with a set tuned to the programme.

Audience rostra ▸ Specially prefabricated, stepped platforms, fitted with seating and safety rails; collapsible for storage.

Audience share ▸ Portion of the group of people who might receive an advertising message, or who are of interest to the advertiser, and who actually do receive the message. Audience share can be calculated electronically, as with the Nielsen Ratings, or through personal, telephone, or direct mail survey, as is commonly done by magazine publishers. For example, a sample of 2000 share-investors might be sent a survey by a stock magazine publisher asking which magazines they read and the frequency with which they read them. If 1000 respond by saying they read a stock magazine and if 500 of those respondents read the publisher's stock magazine, then the publisher's audience share is 500/1000 (50) or 500/2000(25), depending upon how the audience is defined. See also *share*.

Audio ▸ Literally any sound, but frequently used in radio to mean a recording of speech or sound effects for output. Therefore a voice piece, cut or package are all audio. Technically, the electronic reproduction of audible sound; the sound portion of television and its production.

Audio console ▸ The component that controls microphones CD Players, and other audio equipment.

Audioconference ▸ A form of a teleconference, individuals at two or more sites can speak to and hear each other.

Audio dub ‣ An editing feature which enables the sound track to be re-recorded without affecting the picture. Useful for adding commentary, background music, etc.; the electronic reproduction of audible sound.

Audio frequency ‣ Audible sound wave Accepted range 20 Hz - 20 kHz.

Audimeter ‣ Brand-name electronic device developed in 1936 and used by the A.C. Nielsen company (U.S.) as a means of measuring broadcast audience data. Placed on the television receiver in people's homes, the device records the time the set is turned on, the channel to which it is tuned, and the length of time it is tuned to each channel. (It cannot record whether anyone is sitting in front of the television). This information is then assimilated with other collected data into the *Nielsen Television Index*. Orginally, the audimeter was designed to record radio listening. In early 1950 it was first used for television audience estimates as well. The Nielsen Company discontinued the radio measurement service in 1964.

Audio mixer ‣ Control desk for mixing sound sources such as grams and mike.

Audition ‣ (i) A selection and testing process wherein producers and directors determine which radio, TV, stage or screen performers to hire. (ii) In TV production, a separate audio circuit in the control room that allows the sound engineer to previous sounds origination outside the production studio before mixing them with the production in progress, such as a music clip from an outside source.

Authoring software ‣ Software that can simplify and enhance the creation of a multimedia presentation.

Author's alterations (AA) ‣ Changes made to typeset copy not due to typesetting errors but due to the author's desire to change wording for the better. Printers would change extra money for such alterations. Also see *editorial alteration, printer's error, author's marks*.

Author's marks ‣ Corrections on proof made by author as distinct from those made by proof-reader.

Author's proof ‣ Proof altered, corrected or passed by author.

Authoritarian theory ‣ A political philosophy in which the government controls the flow of information and decides what the people would read, hear or see.

Auto complete ‣ A feature in the Address Bar. When you begin typing a previously used address, this feature completes the address.

Autocue ➤ Makers of electronic prompting device which enables performers to read a script while looking directly at the camera. Other makes include Autoscript, Portaprompt and Teleprompter.

Autofocus (AF) ➤ A system which automatically keeps the image sharp. There are several AF systems. Most camcorders offer manual focus as well.

Auto iris ➤ An automatic aperture or exposure control.

Automatic cartridge recorder (ACR) ➤ Machine for recording video news reports on to cartridge (or carts) for instant replay on air. Carts are stored on a carousel.

Automatic gain control (AGC) ➤ Facility on most sound recorders which automatically maintains a steady level of sound input.

Automatic level control (ALC) ➤ Electronic device to reduce or boost the incoming signal to a tape recorder.

Auto white balance ➤ A camcor-der feature that automatically makes adjustments for different lighting conditions and thus avoiding odd colour casts when moving from one type of lighting to another. Many camcorders have a manual override option.

Auxiliary-out ➤ An audio line output.

Auxiliary output ('Aux') ➤ A secondary output from a mixing desk providing a different mix independent of the main programme output, in order to send to echo, public address, foldback, etc. Also called *auxiliary out*.

AV ➤ Stands for audio/video.

Availability ➤ Broadcast time period available for purchase for a commercial message. When it has been determined by the media planner (who is frequently the media buyer as well) where an advertiser will best profit from commercial placement, he or she will contact the station or the station's sales representative and ask for *avails* (the time periods that are available). The station or its representative will then supply the buyer with a list of these time slots, together with prices and estimated ratings of the shows in or around the available times. The ratings, and thus the prices, are based on the most recent ratings of the shows, as reported by the rating services.

Average audience rating ➤ One of several different kinds of *ratings* used by the A.C. Nielsen company (U.S.) in the Nielsen television index; also known as AA rating. It reflects the average size of the audience on a minute-by-minute basis (average size at minute 1, minute 2, minute 3, and so on) throughout the length of a programme. This rating plays an important role in negotiations between the media buyer and the networks. It is also the number used in computing a programmeme's share of the audience or the cost of reaching 1000 homes (see cost per thousand, abbreviated CPM) with a specific advertising message. See also *cumulative audience rating; share; total audience rating*.

Avid ▸ Manufacturer of non-linear picture editing systems.

AVO script ▸ See *voice over script*.

Azimuth ▸ The extent to which the gap in the recording or playback heads of a tape machine is truly vertical, i.e. at right angles to the direction of tape travel.

Bb

Back announcement (B/A, back anno) ► A final sentence giving extra information to be read by the anchor or presenter at the end of a recorded item or report.

Back bench ► The control centre for a newspaper's production where the night editor and other production executives sit; group of top level journalists who meet to decide the overall shape and emphases in that day's newspaper. Positioning of important pictures, choice of page leads, subject and angle of editorial comments will be among their decisions.

Backbone ► A high-speed line or series of connections that forms a major pathway within a network. The term is relative as a backbone in a small network wil likely be much smaller than many non-backbone lines in a large network. See also *network*.

Back cover ► Outside back of a magazine, called the *fourth cover*. Because this cover is more likely to be seen and read by more readers, it is usually sold at a premium. Often there is a waiting list for advertisements to be placed here. The price of advertising on the fourth cover always includes use of colour whether or not the advertisement will be in colour. The back cover is also usually the most expensive of all the covers.

Back dating ► Starting a magazine subscription with an issue prior to the current issue being seved; also called *back start*. Back dating is used by the publisher as a rate base management tool or to reduce an excessive back issue inventory. Also be done at the request of the subscriber who wants a particular back issue. See also *advance start*.

Background ► (i) A term, abbreviated "B.G.," that refers to anything used to support the message of a radio or TV commercial news or programme or print advertisement. For example, sound effects, music, location or special scenery. (ii) Section of news of feature story carrying information which serves to contextualise main elements. Varies in length and positioning though most news stories will contain only small amount of background detail while length of features often allow them to carry longer background sections. Also, in computer jargon, indicates hyphenation and justification system is operating while copy is being input.

Backgrounder ➤ Feature exploring the background to main story in news. Also see *story types*.

Background light ➤ Artificial light used to give a lighter background behind.

Background music ➤ In film, radio or TV production, live or recorded music played behind the spoken dialogues or announcements to establish the mood or a scene or situation.

Back issue ➤ An earlier copy of a magazine or newspaper.

Back light ➤ Light placed behind and slightly to one side of the principal subject in order to produce highlights which "lift" the figure from its background, eliminate shadows and highlight hair. Also see *Key, Fill*.

Back numbers ➤ Previous issues of a newspaper or magazine.

Back projection ➤ Method of projecting a photographic image onto a translucent screen so that it is viewed from the side opposite to the projector. This is especially useful for effects such as faking a moving background. In TV, this device is used for projecting pictures on to a screen behind the newsreader. See also *front projection*.

Back room, back shop ➤ (US) Mechanical department of a newspaper.

Back set ➤ Section of a newspaper printed and folded separately at the end (back) of the first.

Backspace editing ➤ Occurs when a recorder or camcorder is put in the record/pause mode. The tape is rewound a little to give clean breaks between sequences.

Back timing ➤ The process of predetermining where a performer should be near the end of a segment or programme so, with careful judgement, the programme will come out on time.

Back-to-back commercials ➤ Two commercials in succession, stations (radio or TV) will not broadcast commercials for two competitive products back-to-back. However, a manufacturer may go for back-to-back commercials for its complementary products.

Back up ➤ To back up is to make another copy of computer documents in case the originals are lost or damaged. 'Back-ups' are the copies themselves; fall back supply of equipment, data etc.

Backup space ➤ Advertising space in a magazine that adjoins an insert (such as a coupon or return card bound into the magazine). If advertisers wish to use any of these inserts, they must purchase backup space. magazines never sell inserts without backup space.

Backup tape ➤ Duplicate magnetic tape maintained for security. Some organizations utilize a previous-run tape (also called *father tape* or *grandfather tape*) plus all subsequent transaction tapes so that a duplicate of the current file can be reconstructed if necessary. Backup tapes need to be kept in a secure location separate from the actual file tape.

Bad break ► Ugly or unacceptable hyphenation of a word made to justify line of type. See *justify*.

Bad letter ► Broken type, not printing fully.

Bad spacing ► irregular or overspacing of a line of type; space not distributed correctly for appearance.

Balance ► Relative proportion of 'direct' to 'reflected' sound apparent in a microphone output. Also the relative volume of separate components in a total mix, e.g. voices in a discussion, musical instruments in an orchestra.

Balancing unit ► See *TBU*.

Balloon copy ► In copywriting (see *copywriter*), a visualizing device borrowed from early comic-strip artists, where textual matter representing dialogue is circled and a continuous line is drawn to the speaker's mouth. The name is derived from the balloonlike appearance. These days artists frequently dispense with the balloon, although any copy surrounded by an ellipse is still called balloon copy.

Band ► A wide plastic wrapper or band allowing on extra supplement to be attached (bound on) to an issue.

Bandwidth ► A measurement of how much information can be transmitted at a given time over the Internet or any communication chanel; higher the bandwidth, higher the capacity of the network to transmit information (text, picture, sound or multimedia presentation) from one point to another. The term also refers to semantic or information content. It is expressed in bits per second, bytes per second, or Heartz (cycles per second); measured by the difference between the lowest and the highest frequencies. For transmission of full motion video more bandwith is required than that of just text messages. A full page of English text is about 16,000 bits. A fast modem can move about 15,000 bits in one second. Full-motion full-screen video would require roughly 10,000,000 bits-per-second, depending on compression. See also *bps*, *bit*, *t-1*.

Bank ► (i) Part of a multiple headline; (ii) place where matter in type is assembled (see also *random*)

Banner ► (i) Title of newspaper on front page or above editorials on leader page; (ii) large headline across all or most of top of page. (iii) A combination of text and graphics that appears at the top of many Web pages. It sometimes contains a logo, title, and navigational aids.

Bar code ► A machine-readable serial number placed on a magazine cover.

Barker ► (US) Headline variant in which one line, usually one word, is set in large type over deck of smaller headline.

Barn door ► Adjustable flaps around a studio light used to direct the beam.

Baron ► Media proprietor (e.g. Murdoch, Black, Maxwell, Samir Jain). Other words: mogul, magnate, boss.

Baseline ► A national line along the bottom of a row to type. Discenders fall below the baseline.

Basher ► See *Scoop*.

Bass cut ► Device in microphone or other sound source which electrically removes the lower frequencies.

Bastard measure ► Type set to width different from the basic column width or multiples of it; any type setting of non-standard width.

Basys ► (Broadcast Automation Systems) Makers of computerised newsroom equipment.

Batting down on blacks ► Adjusting video signal to crush the darkest picture tones to black, particularly to obliterate unevenness in areas required to appear as dense black.

Baud ► In common usage the baud rate of a modem is how many bits it can send or receive per second. Technically, baud is the number of times per second that the carrier signal shifts value – for example, a 1200 bit-per-second modem actually runs at 300 baud, but it moves 4 bits per baud (4 x 300 = 1200 bits per second). See also *Bit*, *Modem*.

BBC ► British Broadcasting Corporation.

BBS ► (Bulletin Board System) A computerized meeting and announcement system that allows people to carry on discussions, upload and download files, and make announcements without the people being connected to the computer at the same time. There are many thousands (millions?) of BBS's around the world, most are very small, running on a single IBM clone PC with 1 or 2 phone lines. Some are very large and the line between a BBS and a system like CompuServe gets crossed at some point, but it is not clearly drawn.

Beard ► The space between a letter and the edge of the base upon which it is designed.

Bearers ► Metal devices that reduce the pressure on printing surfaces. One type uses flat surfaces or rings at the end of printing press cylinders to determine the thickness of the packing that applies pressure on the printing surface. Another type consists of metal scraps left around an engraved printing plate to reduce wear on the plate when additional plates are molded from it.

Beat ➤ (i) It refers to a specific field of reporting. You may have crime beat to cover while your female colleague may be in charge of health and family welfare as well as the crimes against women. However, the beat system operates only newsrooms where reporters are allowed time to work their beats and develop their stories. In smaller newsrooms, Sony in Siti Cable, most reporters are general assignment reporters – they do not specialise to-day a reporter can cover a fire and the next day a murder story and yet the third day the press conference by a minister (ii) Exclusive story gained in competition with rivals. See also *scoop*. (iii) Underlying rythmin Music.

Beat calls ➤ Telephone calls made each day by reporters or the assignment editor to see if any news stories are developing on the place, fire, court, and other beats.

Bed ➤ (i) Part of printing press that carries type forme or plate to be printed. (ii) Instrumental backing to which words or singing are added to make a commercial or station ident.

Ben Day ➤ Mechanical tint for producing shadings on blocks.

Betacam ➤ Half-inch (19mm) video format introduced by the Sony Corporation. Colloquially learned "beta".

Betacam SP ➤ Superior performance Betcam.

Betacart ➤ Computerised carousel system for the transmission of Beta video cassettes.

Beta mastering ➤ see *dubbing*.

Beta test (Beta test site) ➤ Second-phase test of a new computer system or programme in a live operating environment. Such a test helps to identify flaws in the system prior to a full-scale introduction. The first test, conducted by the system developer, outside the production environment, is called the *alpha test*; the second is called the *beta test* and requires participation by the user. If results are not good, a third test, the *gamma test*, is conducted.

Bf ➤ Abbreviation for boldface.

Bhasha ➤ An off shoot of the news agency PTI that supplies wire news in Hindi.

Bias ➤ (i) High frequency current combined with audio signal to reduce recording distortion. (ii)

Outlook or point of view in news amounting to prejudice toward or against a particular opinion, on ethical issue in media.

Bi-directional ► A microphone pickup pattern resembling a figure eight that allows two [or more] performers to speak opposite each other while using the same microphone.

Bi-directional mike ► A microphone which will pick up sound in front and behind it.

Big quotes ► Quotation marks larger than the typesize they enclose, i.e., used for display effect.

Big read ► A long feature covering many columns usually an installment of a series.

Bill ► Poster announcing newspaper contents at selected sites; wording is supplied by editorial department but bills are distributed by circulation department. Also called *billboard*.

Bill Board ► (radio/TV) Ten-second announcement at the beginning or end of a broadcast that identifies the sponsor or lists casts of a programme.

Bimap ► A type of file used for pictures.

Bi medial ► Reporters who cover news for TV as well as radio.

Binary digit (Bit) ► A bit is the smallest piece of information in a digital system and has a value of either 0 or 1 that the computer interprets as 'off' and 'on' respectively. Bits are also combined in our communications systems to create codes or represent specific information values. A computer can store data or text or visual only in bignary digits, i.e. 0 or 1 Bandwidth is measured usually in the form of bits per second.

Bind ► To fasten pages together to make a magazine,.

Binhex ► (BINary HEXadecimal) It is a method for converting non-text files (non-ASCII) into ASCII. This is needed because Internet e-mail can only handle *ASCII*. See also, *MIME, UUENCODE*

Bird ► Communications satellite. Named after Early Bird, the first satellite launched **afer** the creation of Intelsat, the organisation set up to establish a global system; hence birding for the process of transmitting material by satellite.

Bite off ► (US) To remove complete paragraphs at the end of a story to fit the space. The noun 'bite-off is what has been removed.

BITNET ► (Because It's Time NETwork or Because It's There NETwork) A network of educational sites separate from the Internet, but e-mail is freely exchanged between BITNET and the Internet. Listservs®, the most popular form of e-mail discussion groups, originated on BITNET. BITNET machines are usually mainframes running the VMS operating system, and the network is probably the only international network that is shrinking.

Black ▸ (i) In days of typewriters this was carbon, back-up copy of top, hard copy typed by reporter. Many contemporary computer systems still call copies of top story black. Also bold face type. (ii) A carbon copy, generally of typed news story.

Blackletter ▸ Old black, angular, spiky typefaces based on handwritten books; basis for modern types in this style.

Black level ▸ The level below which the video system reproduces all signals as black.

Black out ▸ To switch all lights off (or fade to a blank screen) for effect. In a theater, to make a surprise exit or entrance or alter scenery.

Blank ▸ See *Skeleton*.

Blanket ▸ Newspaper page proof , i.e., out of page.

Blanket head ▸ (US) Headline covering all columns occupied by a story or combination of related stories.

Bleach out ▸ A picture overdeveloped to intensify the blacks and remove the tones useful in producing a motif to use as a display label on a story.

Bleed ▸ To print beyond the boundary of the page after trimming. Pictures are said to 'bleed' or be used 'full-bleed.'

Bleep ▸ An electronic interruption in verbal continuity, usually deleting a word or phrase consider legally injurious.

Blind ad ▸ Advertisement in which the identity of the advertiser is not revealed.

Blob par/s ▸ Meaning small black marking (usually a square, outline of a square, a circle or sometimes in the tabloids a star) at the start of paragraph. Bullet in computer jargon.

Blobs ▸ Black circles (properly, fullface, circles), useful for adding colour to a page by itemising or setting out a series of points in a story without numbering (any one can be held out without ruining sequence).

Block ▸ Illustration in metal form, either *half-tone* or *line*, or combination of both.

Blockbuster ▸ (i) Broadcast programme that far exceeds expected or estimated ratings and thus brings in a much larger than expected audience to advertisers whose commercials aired during the programme. (ii) Feature film whose box-office success has been extraordinary. When a blockbuster movie is planned for showing on television, the audience estimates are high and consequently the estimated ratings are also high.

Block heading ▶ Heading enlarged photographically from proof, useful for producing headlines in larger sizes than normally available.

Block programming ▶ Airing radio or television programmes of a similar mood, which also have common demographic appeal, one after the other for a 2-, 3-, or 4-hour time segment. In this manner, it is hoped that the audience will remain the same throughout the block. Usually there is an abrupt change of programming at the beginning and end of a block, which causes a loss of audience for those time periods.

Bloom ▶ (*Burn out*) Area reflecting light beyond the video system's capacity and reproducing as blank white. This is due to overlight tone, specular reflection, overlighting, lighting angle, overexposure. Sometimes it may be used as special effect.

Blooper ▶ A mistake, usually a slip of the front of the tongue, such as "Open tape, roll talent, cue mike," or the famous one, "I present the President of the United states, Hoobert Heever."

Blow up ▶ Enlargement of a picture or type so as to bring out the most interesting part.

Blue pan ▶ See *whip pan*.

Blueprint ▶ (i) Photographic print where lines and solid shapes are developed in white on specially prepared blue paper; also called *blue(s)*. A blueprint of drawings or photographs to be included in a publication serves as a guide for positioning them in a dummy copy of the magazine or other publication. It also assists the printer when making plates for the completed work. (ii) Plan of action.

Blurb ▶ A piece of self advertisement composed of type, and sometimes illustration. Used to draw a reader's attention to the contents of other pages or issues to come.

Board ▶ American term for studio control desk or panal.

Board fade ▶ In recording or broadcast production, using the equipment in the control booth to fade out the sound rather than fading it out directly in the studio.

Bodoni ▶ Type series in common use for headings, etc., distinguished by its clean lines, fine serifs, and vertical stress.

Body ▶ (i) Copy following **intro**. (ii) The space taken up by the strokes of a letter; the density of a letter.

Body copy ▶ Type style of main text, as distinct from display type, which is the style or styles chosen for headlines, captions etc.

Body matter ▶ The reading text of a newspaper as distinct from headings, etc. See *matter*.

Body type ► Typeface in which the main text of a newspaper is set, usually in sizes 43/4, 5,5½,6,7,8,9,10,12pt.

Boil ► Tight editing of a story done to reduce length or to streamline it by deleting minor details; 'boil down a copy' means shortening a copy.

Boiler plate (US) ► Editorial term for timeless raw 'filler' material.

Bold, boldface ► Typeface which varies from the standard (or regular) form by having thicker vertical strokes so that it prints blacker.

Bonus circulation ► Circulation of a periodical above the figure guaranteed by the publisher to the advertisers (who are not charged for the additional readership achieved).

Bookmarks ► A list of favourite world wide web pages stored in a browser programme.

Boolean ► A common system of logic that operators such as AND, OR, NOR, and NOT. Commonly used by search engines.

Boolean searching ► Searching that is based on the logical principles set forth by mathematician George Boole. If you want to find many sources on your topic, you can use two synonyms for your topic combined with OR (e.g., technology OR distance education). If you want to limit the number of sources you find, you should use AND. (Technology AND distance education would result in only those sources that use both terms).

Boom ► Microphone suspended on the end of a movable metal arm attached to a floor stand to facilitate it (the mike) placing over performers, e.g. Orchestra or newsmakers. Also called boom mike.

Boomy ► acoustic Room unduly reverberant in the lower frequencies.

Boost ► A box telling readers what to expect in the next issue.

Border ► A print rule or strip in the computer used to create panels for stories, or for display effects in layout.

BOT ► Type reversed as *black-on-tone* background.

Bounced light ► Light which is not cast directly on the subject but reflected off a white surface such as a wall or ceiling.

Boundary effect mic ► Small microphone mounted on a plate with a gap between it and the plate to give a directional polar diagram. Used on-stage for opera and theatre work. Also called *Pressure Zone* (PZ) effect.

Bowl ► Curved stroke of letter surrounding closed 'white' area or counter as in letters o,b,a.

Box ► Type matter enclosed by rules on all four sides (see *panel*); also the *stop-press column* (see *fudge*).

BPS ➤ (Bits-Per-Second) A measurement of how fast data is moved from one place to another over a telephone or network line. A 28.8 modem can move 28,800 bits per second. See also *bandwidth, bit*.

Brace ➤ Sign (}) linking two or more lines of type; rarely used in newspaper text, occasionally in diagrams or set-out material (e.g. knock-out sports tournament).

Bracket ➤ (i) Curved parenthesis mark: xxxxxx(————————) xxxxxx; (ii) square prenthesis mark: [ ] used for inserting explanatory phrase in a quotation, or for parenthesis within parenthesis.

Bracketed ➤ Serifs are said to be bracketed to the stem when they are joined to it in a continuous curve rather than set at a sharp right-angle. Old face types have bracketed serifs.

Brainstorming ➤ Idea-generating technique often used in advertising by a creative team. The team will gather in a group and throw out spontaneous ideas without evaluation until they hit upon something that may be useful. In this process nothing is too silly or farfetched to be suggested. The process helps to make the leap from the visualization of an idea to the concrete words and pictures

that will actually form the basis of the advertising campaign.

Brand ➤ Identifying mark, symbol, word(s) or combination of these separating one company's product or services from another firm's. Brand is a comprehensive term that includes all brand names and trademarks.

Brand image ➤ Qualities that consumers associate with a specific brand, expressed in terms of human behavior and desires, but that also relate to price, quality, and situational use of the brand. For example, a brand such as Maruti Suzuki will conjure up a strong public image because of its physical characteristics as well as its price. This image is not inherent in the brand name but is created through advertising.

Brand loyalty ➤ Degree to which a consumer will repeatedly purchase a brand. For advertisers to achieve their ultimate goal of brand loyalty, the consumer must perceive that the brand offers the right combination of quality and price. Many factors influence brand loyalty, such as consumer attitudes (see *brand attitude*), family or peer pressure, and friendship with the salesperson. The degree of brand loyalty, i.e. the brand's market share - is known as the *brand franchise*.

Brand name ► That part of a brand, trademark, or service mark that can be spoken, as distinguished from an identifying symbol. A brand name may consist of a word, letter, or group of words or letters.

Break ► (i) Convenient place to break the text with a quote or cross head. But bad break refers to ugly looking hyphenation at end of line of text. (ii) The moment of happening of news. (iii) To stop action, i.e., to take a break. (iv) To move talent and cameras to another set. (v) A commercial break in a news or entertainment programme.

Breakaway ► Prop or scenery designed to shatter easily on impact or to break on cue.

Breaker ► Any device such as a quote or cross head which breaks up the text in the page.

Break-even analysis ► Financial analysis that identifies the point at which expenses equal gross revenue. For example, if a mailing costs Rs 100 and each item generates Rs 5 in revenue, the break-even point is at 20 items sold. A profit will be made on items sold in excess of 20. A loss will result on sales under 20. The breakeven point may be analyzed in terms of units, as above, or rupees.

Breakfast television ► Telecast time of television that coincides with the breakfast time. The service began in India in 1987.such

a programme is usually a mix of news and infotainment i.e. informative as well as entertaining, e.g., Good Morning India (Star News), Subah Aaj Tak (DD1), etc.

Breaking news (Spot story, US) ► Unexpected events that cannot be anticipated, such as fires or crimes; often the event is still continuing when the story deadline is reached, and continues afterwards.

Break line ► Short line of type at the end of paragraph (a single –word break line is called a widow). At the top of a turn, it is called jackline.

Break out ► A secondary story run on a page with a main story, usually on a feature page.

Break-out box ► A simple input/ output unit to give easy pluggable acces to a recording device. e.g. a computer.

Breakthrough ► Unwanted electrical interference or acoustic sound from one source or channel affecting another.

Break up ► Disperse type material from a page, either for melting down and recasting or to type cases. Also see *breakway*.

Brevier ► Old name for 8pt type.

Bridge ► (i) Proof reader's mark showing that words or characters are to be joined together. (ii) See *stand-upper*.

Brief ► (i) Short item of news often of just one par, but occasionally with up to four or five five paras. Other names: snip/nib/ bright/filler; (ii) short advice given to journalist about how to cover a story.

BrightStar ► Dedicated satellite system linking the United States and the United Kingdom.

Bring up ► An editing instruction meaning use certain material earlier in a story.

Broadband ► A term describing high-bandwidth connections that can carry voice, data and video channels simultaneously. Also see *switched broadband network*.

Broadcast ► Refers to one way mode of communication where a party communicates with a large number of other parties, each receiving the same signal, e.g. to radio and television. Also known as point to multipoint or one to many communications device.

Broadcast media ► Electronic instrumentation of radio and television, including local radio and television stations, radio and television networks, and cable television systems. Because of their ability to reach vast numbers of people, broadcast media play a very important role in any advertising campaign that needs to reach a broad market base.

Broadsheet ► Large size (22 × 15 inches) newspaper such as The Hindu (India), The Times (London), New York Times, Guardian, as opposed to *tabloid*.

Broadside ► (i) Full-size newspaper page as printed on a rotary press; (ii) old announcement or newspaper page printed as a single sheet irrespective of how it is to be folded; (iii) fiercely polemical article.

Brochure ► Fancy booklet that differs from an ordinary booklet in that it is constructed of heavier quality paper, uses extensive colour and expensive type, and is generally put together with special care. The name originates from the French verb *brocher*, meaning "to stitch," indicating a booklet bound by stitching, although today other binding methods are also used. Brochures are frequently part of a retail advertising campaign and are sometimes distributed with the Sunday papers. They are also enclosed in direct mail and considered to be the "workhorse" of the direct-mail package.

Broken matter ► Text, headings, etc. that have been taken out of a page and are probably disordered.

Broken word ► Word turned from one line to another, with a linking hyphen at the end of the first line: words should be split to respect sense and etymology; vertical ranks of hyphens should be avoided.

Bromide ▸ Piece of positive film—of either type or illustration—used for sticking on to page in photoset newspapers.

Browse ▸ To navigate the Internet or the contents of your computer.

Browser ▸ Short for Web Browser, it's the tool (programme) that allows you to surf the web. The most popular Web Browsers right now are Netscape Navigator and Internet Explorer. Also called a *Client* programme.

BTW ▸ (By The Way) A shorthand appended to a comment written in an online forum. See also *IMHO*.

Bucket ▸ Rules on either side and below tying in printed matter to a picture.

Budget ▸ (i) A statement of expenditure and income allocated to a departments for a given period. (ii) (US) Day's schedule of news stories and events; in national finance, budget.

Budget forecast ▸ A forecast of expenditure and income for a department in a given period.

Buffalo plan ▸ Computer programme originally developed in Buffalo, New York, that is utilized by wholesalers and newsstand distributors to track magazine sales and return data.

Buffer frames ▸ Extra frames at the start or end of a report to allow for minor delays in screening.

Buffer shot ▸ Shot inserted between two others to disguise a break in continuity, or, occasionally, a shot which itself begins or ends in such a way as to disguise a jump-cut.

Bug ▸ (i) An electronic pick-up used for recording telephone calls. (ii) (US) Fancy typographical device to break up areas of type. See *dingbat*. Also telegrapher's key and union label of the International Typographical union.

Build ▸ The gradual development of interest or tension in a segment to the point of climax.

Bulk ▸ (i) Bench or stone where assembled type is kept ready for use. (ii) Subscription or single-copy orders sold in quantities greater than one per issue to a single buyer; also called bulk order (iii) Measurement of the thickness of paper.

Bulk circulation ▸ Distribution of a publication by bundles as distinguished from distribution by individual pieces. For example: Schools will often subscribe to a local newspaper in bulk to be distributed to students and used as a teaching device in the classroom. Also see *circulation*.

Bulk eraser ▸ A device which generates a powerful magnetic field to erase a spool of tape or other magnetic recording, perhaps several at a time.

Bulldog ➤ (US) (i) First edition of a daily newspaper, including afternoon papers. In case of a morning newspaper its bull dog edition appears the right before the date it bears. Some say it originated in New York City at a time when there were three morning newspapers - the world, the Herald, and the Journal who fought like bulldogs to be the first to get their edition on the street. (ii) Sections of a sunday newspaper printed and distributed prior to sunday.

Bullet ➤ A black dot used for emphasis or in list. Also see *blobs*.

Bulletin ➤ (US) Short message giving new development or latest situation on running story.

Bulletin board system (BBS) ➤ A miniature interactive system established by government agencies, organisations, and private individuals.

Bullet Theory ➤ Also known as hypodermic needle theory; a point of view that considers mass of people as an unidentifiable group of people, straightaway and directly affected by messages received from the mess media without any regard to interpersonal influence.

Bump ➤ Add extra spacing material to type matter to make it fill a given space.

Bumped headlines ➤ See *tomstone*.

Bureau ➤ Newspaper office in a different city or foreign country; team of senior reporters dealing with stories of wider interest as opposed to stories catering to local readers only.

Burn in ➤ A retained image from an excessively bright area remaining on the camera tube long after the shot has changed perhaps permanently. (Not normally with CCD image sensors.)

Burn out ➤ See *bloom*

Burner ➤ Colloquial term for a CD recorder, used because of its heat process.

Bury ➤ When important information or quote is carried within the body of text so its impact is lost.

Bus ➤ One complete channel of a video or audio system. Frequently used of switchers and special effects generators.

Bust ➤ When copy text or headlines run over allotted space.

Buster ➤ Headline whose number of characters exceed the required measure.

Busy ➤ Background so elaborate or detailed that it distracts; design so intricate that it produces a flicker or jiggling effect on the television screen.

Button ➤ Small graphic or icon used for hyperlinks and navigational aids

By-line ► Name of journalist who has written article. Otherwise called credit line. (Subs often calls this the blame line) Known as sign-off when it appears at the end of story.

Bypass system ► A private/leased communications system that bypasses standard commercial and public systems.

Byte ► It refers to a set of *bits* that represent a single character such as letter 'A'. Usually there are 8 bits in a byte, sometimes more, depending on how the measurement is being made. See also *Bit*.

Cc

C & sm c ➤ Caps and small caps, i.e. capital letters with the small capitals (the same height as lower-case letters) belonging to the same size and type. The abbreviation is sometimes rendered c & sc.

C & Lc ➤ Capital letters and lower case of type.

Cabelese, cablese ➤ Set forms of words and abbreviations used in cabled copy to reduce expense of transmission.

Cable News Network International ➤ (CNNI) Atlanta (US) based cable television network. Its 24 hour news service has become the benchmark for others.

Cable TV ➤ A television system in which pictures are sent to a receiving set through coaxial or fiber-optic cable rather than over to air. The central source may transmit programmes either sent by itself or pick up signals from satellites through dish antenna. Reception of such programmes is by subscription. For example, ZEE TV, Star Plus, Sony and Sun TV in India.

Cache ➤ A folder that temporarily stores files on your computer.

Call number ➤ A number found on the spine of a book or collection of documents used by libraries so that specific resources can be easily found.

Calls ➤ Routine telephone calls (but sometimes by face to face visits) by reporters to such bodies as police, ambulance, hospitals, fire brigade to check if any news is breaking. Also called *check calls*.

Camcorder ➤ Combined lightweight video camera and recorder.

Camera angle ➤ Angle from which the camera photographs a subject or scene. There are a variety of camera angles, any of which can add an interesting perspective to that which is being pictured. Sometimes the camera angle can greatly influence the audience interpretation of what is happening on the screen. Major types are normal angle, high camera angle, low camera angle, canted angle (on a slant), reverse angle, subjective camera angle (from the point of view of the subject; the way the subject sees things), and objective camera angle (the way an objective party or outsider sees things). See also *tilt shot*.

Camera lucida ➤ Optical device invented in 1831 that is used in making layouts. Nicknamed lucy, the instrument works on the principles of reflected and deflected light through a prism and enables the artist to enlarge or reduce an image and then to copy it by hand.

Camera-ready ➤ A layout, including artwork and copy, that is ready to be photographed or otherwise reproduced in the printing process. All work must be camera-ready before it goes to the printer.

Camera right ➤ Right hand side of the picture (performer's left side).

Camera shots ➤ Shots obtained by a camera can be categorized by: the distance between the camera and the subject; the angle of the camera; and, the nature or content of the subject. Some basic shots are long shot (wide shot), medium long shot, mid (medium) shot, medium close-up, close-up and extreme close-up. Also see *picture composition, camera angles, two-shot, group-shot, high angle shot*.

Campaign ➤ Series of related advertising or promotional pieces, scheduled for a given period of time. A campaign has common verbal and/or visual themes and objectives. Ideally, each succeeding element in the campaign adds to the cumulative impact. For example, an advertising space sales campaign might include a mailing to prospective advertisers supported by advertisements in trade publications and followed up by a salesperson's call. Each element would centre around a theme featuring the major benefit of advertising in that publication.

Campaigning journalism ➤ Expressly partisan journalism or promoting particular cause; e.g. greener Delhi; save AIIMS hospital; restore Saihin to lead the Indian cricket team. Also called advocacy journalism.

Can ➤ To record on film or tape.

Canadian Broadcasting Corporation (CBC) ➤ Candian radio and television network. The CBC is operated by the Crown in Canada. It has both English- and French-language service and covers all regions throughout the country.

Cancelled matter ➤ Type material removed from stories by corrections, cuts, etc.

Caned ➤ A pre-recorded performance, i.e., one on tape or in a film can.

Canned copy ➤ (US) Publicity material sent to newspaper. See *handout*.

Cannon connector ➤ A high quality secure audio jack also known as an XLR plug.

Cans ➤ Colloquisal term for earphones.

Canted shot ➤ Refers to an off-vertical sloping shot.

Capacitor mike ➤ Battery-operated mike, often of the tie-clip variety.

Caps ➤ Capital letters of type.

Capstan ▶ The drive spindle of a tape recorder.

Caption ▶ Brief descriptive wording for a report; (India) a photograph or an illustration. A caption amounting to a small story is a caption story. Also see *underline.*

Cardioid ▶ Heart-shaped area of pick-up around a microphone.

Cardioid microphone ▶ Microphone which is more responsive to sound sources which are in front of it than to those behind or to the side. The pattern of response is heart-shaped.

Card rate ▶ Cost for advertising in a publication or on a broadcast station or network as published on the rate card (or in standard rate and data service) for that publication, station, or network, See also earned rate.

Caret mark ▶ A mark used in copy mark-up and proof –reading to indicate that some thing must be inserted.

Carrier wave ▶ Frequency wave which is modulated to carry a video or audio signal.

Carry-forward ▶ Instruction to compositor to carry text matter to next page or to turn.

Cartridge (cart) ▶ Loop of tape in a plastic case for recording and playing inserts into bulletins or items (commercials, singles) into programmes. May be audio or video. It is self-cueing.

Case ▶ Tray holding individual type characters or type matrices.

Case rack ▶ Cabinet for holding cases.

Case-room, Case department ▶ Printers workshop, composing room.

Case work ▶ In newspapers, usually composition of headlines and display ads.

Cash-flow ▶ A chart indicating income received and cash spent.

Caslon ▶ A traditional-style serifed type faced used for headlines.

Cassette (radio) ▶ Enclosed reel to reel device of 3mm wide tape particularly used in domestic or miniature recording machines.

Cassette (video) ▶ Recording tape threaded on two reels and self-contained inside a compact closed plastic case. The cassette functions as a recording or playback unit when placed in a cassette recorder or player. Creative personnel (such as artists or photographers), or production companies will often store copies of programmes in which they have participated, or which they have created and produced, on videocassettes. These can be shown to prospective employers or clients with relative ease.

Cast off ▶ To calculate the space occupied by a piece of text; to edit to fixed length; the edited length of a story as estimated.

Cataloging software ➤ Sóftware used to organize a library's holdings.

Catch line ➤ (i) Usually single word identifying story, typed on right hand corner of every page. Sub-editor will tend to use this word to identify story while making the page on layout. US : *slug*. (ii) Syllable taken from a story and used on each folio, or section, along with folio number, to identify it in the typesetting system.

Catharsis ➤ The idea viewing violence reduces violent behaviour, it satisfies a viewer's aggressive drive without his/her resorting to violent behaviour.

CATV (community antenna television) ➤ TV distributed to receivers via cable from a master antenna.

C-band ➤ A satellite communication frequency band and satellite class. Commercial C-band satellites are the older of the contemporary communications satellite fleet.

CBS ➤ Columbia Broadcasting System. A United States radio and television network .

CCD (charge-coupled device) ➤ Also called chip. A small, solid-state imaging device, used in camera pickup tube. Within the device, image sensing elements translate the optical image into a video signal.

CCTV (closed-circuit television) ➤ TV distributed to spe-

cific television receivers but not broadcast to the general public.

CCU (camera control unit) ➤ Remote equipment used in a television room to operate the television camera.

CD (compact disc) ➤ A small, shiny disc that contains information (usually sound signals) in digital form. A CD player reads the encoded digital data via laser beam.

CD-ROMs ➤ (Compact disk-read-only memory) A CD-ROM is a pre-recorded optical disk that stores data. Its applications range from distribution of computer software to electronic publishing. A CD-ROM, which looks like a CD but can store 600 megabytes of data, is preloaded with information and/or programmes. A CD-ROM is also interfaced with a computer via a CD-ROM drive and special driver software. An early CD-ROM release was the electronic text version of Grolier's Academic American Encyclopedia. This disk highlighted the CD-ROM's storage properties: An entire encyclopaedia of some 30,000 articles was recorded on a signal disc with room to spare. It was also integrated in a PC environment, and information from the encyclopedia could be retrieved by word processing pro-gramme. More recent ency-clopaedias have also incorporated sound, graphics and animations. Another interesting earlier disk, which spawned more recent releases was the PC-SIG CD-ROM. The PC-SIG has been a source of public domain and user-supported software (shareware) written for IBM PCs. The programmes have covered everything from computer languages to games and the entire library could fill 1000 or more floppy disks. The library was transferred to a CD-ROM. The application was and remains a valuable one for PC owners, since the CD-ROM is inexpensive when compared to an equivalent floppy disk library. This factor has made the CD-ROM an ideal distribution medium for computer software collections. Other applications include the following: (a) Information pools can be compiled ranging from telephone numbers to street maps; (b) Information is usually distributed as hard copies. Companies have adopted CD-ROMs to complement their print lines; (c) Magazine collections can be compiled. You can browse through hundreds of articles or years of back issues, all on one disk; (d) Spacecraft images have been made available. Through the National Space Science Data Centre (US) and other sources, you can explore Venus and Mars from your armchair by viewing information generated from the Magellan and Viking Orbiter missions.

Ceefax ▸ BBC broadcast teletext system.

Cellular radio ▸ A type of radio where its frequencies are divided into airwave cells and are primarily used for personal communication.

Cellular Telephone ▸ A personal communications tool based on frequency reuse and a monitoring design.

Centred ▸ Type placed equidistant from each side of the column or columns.

Centre spread ▸ Material extending across the two centre-facing pages in a newspaper. Also see *spread*.

Century ▸ Much used modern serifed type with bold strokes.

CERN (Counseil Europien Pour La Recherche Nucléaire) ▸ The European Pasticle Physics Laboratory in Switzerland, where the *WWW* software was devised by Tim Burners-Lee.

Certificate Authority ▸ An issuer of Security Certificates used in SSL connections. See also *security certificate, SSL*.

CGI ▸ (Common gateway interface) This means a set of rules that describe how a *web server* communicates with another piece of *software* on the same machine, and how the other piece of software (the "CGI-programme") talks to the web server. Any piece of software can be a CGI programme if it handless input and output according to the CGI standard. Usually a CGI programme is small and it takes data from a web server and does something with it, like putting the content of a form into an *e-mail* message, or turning the data into a database query. You can often see that a CGI programme is being used by seeing "cgi-bin" in a *URL*, but not always. See also *cgi-bin, web*.

CGI-bin ► The most common name of a directory on a *web server* in which CGI programme are stored. The "bin" part of "cgi-bin" is a shorthand version of *"binary"*, because once upon a time, most programmes were refered to as "binaries". In real life, most programmes found in cgi-bin directories are text files – scripts that are executed by binaries located elsewhere on the same machine. See also *CGI*.

CGO ► (US) Short for 'can go over'. Indicates that the copy may be held over until the following day or days.

Chain ► A company publishing two or more newspapers operated separately in different locations. Also called a group.

Challenger ► The space shuttle that was lost to equipment and systems failure.

Change pages ► Pages that are

to be given new or revised material on an edition, or on which advertising material is being replaced.

Channel ► (i) A communications line. The path or route by which information is relayed. (ii) The complete circuit from a sound source to the point in the control panel where it is maxed with others.

Channel noise ► Any physical or mechanical disturbance in course of the communication process.

Channel width ► Frequency band assigned for transmission, commonly called Band.

Character ► Single letter, number, or other symbol used to represent information. For example, in composition, each metal type slug is a character. The number of character spaces in a fixed field computer record controls the amount of information that can be stored in the file. See also *alphanumeric*.

Character generators ► A machine, called C.G. for short, does the job of superimposing most of the words and numbers on the TV screen. The C.G. puts letters and numbers on the TV picture just as a typewriter types them on a piece of paper.

Characters ► The letters, figures, symbols, etc., in a type range, hence *character count*, the number of characters and spaces that can be accommodated in a given line of type.

Chart-pak rules ▸ Trade name for rules, dotted borders and other designs supplied on transparent sticky tape for use in make up of photoset newspaper.

Chase ▸ Metal frame in which type is assembled to make up a newspaper page; when filled it is called a forme.

Chat ▸ Live communication over the Internet Relay Chat service or an online service. As one person enters text it appears on the other person's screen in "real time", or almost instantly.

Chat areas ▸ Web or other Internet sites where individuals *"chat"* by typing messages to one another. Chat areas are usually focused on a specific topic.

Chat room ▸ A place on the Internet where people go to "chat" with other people in the room. Actually there are thousands of these Chat Rooms. The rooms are usually organized by topic. For example in a Delhi room you would expect that most of the participants in the room are probably from Delhi or a Gay room, where the participants are usually gay. When you're in a Chat Room you can view all of the conversations taking place at once on your screen. You can also get into a private chat room where only you and one or two others may

talk. This can be an inexpensive way to keep up with friends and relatives who are online.

Cheating ▸ An effort by a performer to create the illusion of talking directly to some one [e.g., an interviewee], while positioning the body for a maximum open relationship with the camera. See *Cutaways*.

Check ▸ Confusingly for the layman, printer's readers use a tick (——— which elsewhere denotes that something is correct) to indicate the reed for a check to determine accuracy.

Check calls ▸ Regular newsroom calls to the emergency services and hospitals to find out whether news is breaking

Cheque book journalism ▸ Newspaper s competing to purchase rights to someone's story, e.g. mistress of prime minister. Price can be very high when the person's story is considered of high news value. Some newspapers routinely offer much smaller amounts of money to people in exchange for information.

Chilling effect ▸ Any regulation or threat of regulation that makes the speaker think twice about providing information that might be considered inappropriate by some . In such a situation, the speech is halted before it ever has a chance to be heard.

Chimney ▸ Grouping of pictures or headlines (or advertisements) or both so that they run in a narrow band from top to bottom of the page.

Chinagraph ▸ Soft pencil used to mark radio tape cutting points during editing. It is generally yellow.

Chip ▸ Integrated computer circuit.

Chocolate ▸ A crucial computer term. Chocolate is what you eat when you get frustrated with web functions such as searching for specific items, writing web pages, or just being a *Newbie*.

Choked type ▸ Type filled with ink or dirt, producing blotchy print work.

Chroma key ▸ A special effect; certain colours (usually blue or green) are keyed so that a performer can be inserted in front of computer graphics or a video shot. Under these conditions the performer/ anchor should not wear blue. Also called colour separation overlay (CSO).

Chrome ▸ (i) In photography transparent piece of photographic film with a positive colour image, as a 35mm slide: also called colour transparency. Common chrome sizes are 35mm slides, 1 1/4" x 1 1/4', 4" x 5", and 8" x 10". (ii) In printing apply chromium to a printing plate, to protect the plate from corrosive action and allow the surface to require less ink. If there are a great many pieces to be printed, the application of chromium will give the plate longer printing life.

Chunking ▸ Breaking down information into separate topics, modules, or units.

Cinema verite ▸ A form of the film making which intends to portray candid realism. The term is derived from French, meaning "film truth". The cinema-verite style is distinguished by the filming of the people as they really are with no rehearsal or editing. The intention of the film-maker is to record reality in an unbiased form, often with a hidden camera.

Circled numbers ▸ Instruction to printer to spell out; applies also to abbreviations.

Circle wipe ▸ See *wipe*.

Circular response ▸ The delivery of message from a performer to the audience and the return of the audience's response to the performer.

Circular screen ▸ Circular, rotating halftone screen. In four-colour process printing, each colour must be photographed through a halftone screen placed at precise angles that differ for each colour. A circular screen can rotate to the desired angles. Shooting at angles keeps the various colour dots aligned properly in the printed image.

Circulation ➤ Average number of newspaper magazine copies sold and distributed see per publishing day. Since the cost of advertising based upon the number of readers deemed to be of interest to advertisers, the periodical's circulation is of prime concern. *Consumer magazines* base advertising rates on paid circulation; *trade magazines* base advertising rates on the number of readers with the demographic characteristics of the periodical's target audience. The circulation claims of publishers are audited by the *Audit Bureau of Circulations* (ABC). Total circulation counts sometimes include *pass-along circulation.* Also see *bulk circulation, controlled circulation, effective circulation, frenchise circulation, paid circulation, request circulation, circulation waste.*

Circulation manager ➤ Newspaper executive in charge of paper's distribution to wholesale and retail trade; except for back numbers, newspapers do not sell copies directly to the public.

Circulation waste ➤ The part of advertising going to people whom the advertiser has no interest in reaching.

Citation ➤ The information in a bibliographic entry that allows a reader to locate the same source that the writer used.

City editor ➤ Editor of financial page; in India the name given to the editor in charge of news-gathering in main office.

Civic Journalism ➤ Publishing philosophy that calls for newspapers to become involved in community issues, rather than just covering them as more news topics. Also called *public journalism.*

Clapper board (*clapstick, clapboard* US) ➤ Board with movable arm used to synchronize film with soundtrack. The board is marked with the details of the shot and take. Picture and sound are synchronized by matching the clap of the arm being brought down with the picture.

Clarke belt ➤ Position 22 300 miles (3600 km) above the equator in which orbiting communications satellites appear to be stationary; named after the British science writer Arthur C. Clarke who first advocated the use of satellites for broadcasting.

Class magazine ➤ Consumer magazine intended for a special interest audience, as MIS is a magazine intended for those whose interest is in information or IT management; also called special interest magazine. Sometimes the expression is misused to mean a slick magazine directed at a high-income audience; this is totally incorrect. The word class in this case refers to a specific group (or class) of readers with a common interest. Manufacturers of specialized products will reach a more interested audience when they advertise in a class magazine. The introduction of a new computer, software, for example, will fare much better if it is advertised in MIS and Computers Today than in a more general publication. The information about the software will be read by the select audience most likely to purchase the product. Class magazine advertising offers the advertiser a minimum of waste circulation.

Classic style ► A desktop display option that resembles the Windows 95 desktop.

Classifieds ► Small advertisements gathered into sections.

Clean copy ► Copy that can be read easily and without ambiguity, both for setting and checking for proof.

Clean feed ► Actuality (natural) sound of an event free from commentary.

Clean proof ► Proof of type matter after all alterations and corrections have been made.

Clean tape ► Tape which is either new or has had all previous recordings erased.

Clean up ► Editing instruction to improve tone of copy.

Cliché ► A well-worn, over-used phrase.

Client ► This is a *software* programme used to contact and obtain data from a Server software programme on another computer, often across a great distance. A server is the provider of services, while the *client* is the consumer of services. Each Client programme is designed to work with one or more specific kinds of server programme, and each server requires a specific kind of client. A *web browser* is a specific kind of *Client*. See Also *browser, server*.

Cliffhanger ► A story that still awaits its climax or sequel.

Clip ► This is a name given to any piece of film or tape which is taken out of a sequence and used for another purpose (ii) a piece of news audio usually on cartridge.

Clip art ► Pictures not subject to copyright restrictions, usually obtained in digitised form.

Clipping ► (US) Item clipped (cut) from previous issues or other publications and filed for reference. Also called clip; (radio) when all or part of the first word of a report is cut because the cart or tape is incorrectly cued.

Clipping bureau ► Service whose primary function is to read newspapers and periodicals and to clip articles and other information from these sources to send to customers who pay for this service. Subscribers to a clipping bureau include public relations firms who want to demonstrate and keep track of their ability to get their clients' names in print; advertisers and advertising agencies, who want to keep track of their advertising as well as the competitors; individuals such as political figures, who want to keep track of their publicity; or research groups, who want to be aware of all that is printed about a particular area in which they are working.

Close ► The conclusion of a programme. A closed position is the relationship of a performer's body to a camera that allows the least expression.

Close circuit ► A close circuit feed refers to a programme or information that is NOT for broadcast to begin with, and that is sent by a network's local or regional station to the network's main station or the vice-versa. It may be programme planned for future or an update to be telecast later in the day, etc. Before the TV Satellites came into use in India, close circuit information like any other feed could be sent when regular pro-grammes were not being transmitted by the network for telecast. With satellites, however, this problem is now over. The network can sound its regular program-

ming on the one transponder of a satellite and the close circuit feed on another.

Closed user group ► The term describes a group with access to inform and communication services which are not available to non-members of the group.

Close quotes ► Punctuation marks closing quoted material.

Close up (CU) ► (i) To reduce space between words or lines. (ii) Camera perspective in which the principal subject dominates the picture; a very close shot of a person or an object. There are two types of close-ups, extreme and medium. An extreme close-up, sometimes called a tight shot, is a more extreme version of a close-up, when the camera closes in on the face of a person and then comes in even closer to focus on an eye. A medium close-up emphasizes the principal subject but includes other objects that are nearby. Also see *picture composition*.

Close-up (CU)

Closer ► See *standuppers*.

Closing door wipe ➤ See *wipe*.

Closing pad ➤ At the end of any stand-up, especially after the sign off in a closer, the reporter remains motionless, eyes still at the camera, for five seconds. This is true for live as well as taped stand-uppers. This motionless and voiceless performance by the reporter at the end of a report is called a closing pad, which is necessary to avoid unwanted noise or picture (because of roll-cue error) – Just in care there is a delay in punching up the following item (i.e., the story after the report) and the reporter is seen scratching here head and heard saying: My God! I have a date with my fiancé! This unwanted 'date' on air will certainly spoil the reporter's package. Thus, closing pad is a MUST.

Clustering ➤ Acquisition of newspapers in geographically close areas in order to manage the business efficiently.

Clutter ➤ Mass of *commercials* and *promos* (shot messages about upcoming programmes) broadcast in a time period as short as two minutes, all of which compete for the listener's or viewer's attention and the combination of which lessens the impact of any single commercial message. Any one commercial can get sandwiched in with as many as six or eight other commercials. Advertisers or their agencies will sometimes run clutter tests to measure the ability of their commercials to get the listener's or viewer's attention in this clutter situation. See also *commercial time; competitive separation*.

Coaxial Cable ➤ Shielded cable through which television pictures and sound are transmitted. Most commonly used in Cable TV, and likely to be supplanted by fibre optic cable which is emerging as state-of-the-art in cable transmission.

Cockup ➤ (i) Initial letter rising above the line of smaller type on which it stands. (ii) incompetent confusion at any point of the newspaper-making process.

Codec ➤ A combination of the words coder/decoder. A code converts an analogue signal into a digital format. In a teleconferencing environment, it also compresses the signal so the information can be relayed on lower capacity and less expensive communications channels. A codec at the end of the relay converts the signal back into an analogue form.

Col ➤ short for column.

Cold type ➤ Several methods of composition, in offset lithography and gravure, not utilizing metal, used for a flat plate direct-impression method of printing; also called nonmetallic composition. Examples include photocomposition, varityper, typewriter, photon, linofilm, strike-on composition, monophoto and fotosetter, or preprinted characters arranged by hand. Cold-type composition is less expensive than metallic-type composition but is not as durable for long runs and varies in quality. See also *hot type*.

Collect running ➤ Arranging the presses and folders so that each press unit prints only one of several sections.

Co-location ➤ Usually this refers to having a server that belongs to one person or group physically located on an Internet-connected network that belongs to another person or group. Usually this is done because the server owner wants their machine to be on a high-speed Internet connection and/or they do not want the security risks of having the server on their own network. See also *Internet, server, network*.

Coloration ➤ Effect obtained in a room when one range of frequencies tends to predominate in its acoustic.

Colour ➤ (i) Pleasing or provocative effect of design on black and white printed page, from careful use of illustration, variations of typeface, weight and style, rules, etc. Avoidance of greyness, over-regularity. (ii) Section of newspaper copy focusing on

descriptions, impressions. Thus a colour feature is one which puts emphasis on description and the subjective response of the journalist though the news element might still be prominent.

Colour bars ➤ A test signal in the shape of eight coloured vertical stripes.

Colour burst ➤ A very accurately phased burst of high frequency at the beginning of each scanning line. This determines the colour of the signal.

Colour compensation ➤ See colour correction.

Colour conversion ➤ Use of a control which makes up for slight differences between the colour temperature of the existing light.

Colour correction ➤ Use of a lens filter which makes up for slight differences between the colour temperature of different light sources.

Colour filter ➤ Coloured screen — either blue, red, or green — used in photography to absorb certain colours and enhance others. By photographing an image through colour filters, an image can be produced that reflects only one of the three primary colours that constitute the original image. These are called colour separations and are used in four-colour process printing. The blue filter is used to create the yellow negative, the green filter produces the magenta negative, and the red filter produces the cyan negative.

Colour house ► Where photographs are scanned and united with electronically generated pages and type to produce the film required to make printing plates.

Colourization ► The process by which colour of "colourized" version of black- and - white movies are produced.

Colour overaly ► Transparent sheet of material that can be inked or painted on, used in the printing process when manually separating the colours in full-colour originals for reproduction. The artist will use a separate overlay for each colour, which, when placed one on top of the other, will simulate the original artwork.

Colour plate ► Red, blue, or yellow printing plate used in the reproduction of full-colour original artwork. A printing plate can print only one colour at a time. Therefore, if a piece of artwork is to be reproduced in full colour, the printer must prepare a separate plate for each of the three primary colours, as well as an additional plate for black (which prints the shadows and contrasts). These plates are known as colour plates.

Colour printer ► Different colour printers support the general consumer business markets. They range from ink-jet to thermal-wax units. More expensive and sophisticated printer types are also available.

Colour separation ► The process of separating full-colour originals into three primary colours-red, yellow, blue-for the purpose of duplicating the original. Also see Four Colour process.

Columbia Broadcasting System (CBS) ► One of the major broadcasting networks in the U.S.; began in 1927 as United Independent Broadcasters, Inc., with a group of 16 independent radio stations. CBS was named by William S. Paley, who purchased the radio network in 1928. He instituted a contract relationship with the affiliated stations whereby CBS would provide them with free programming in return for free radio time to sell for advertising. This system is still the basis for radio and television networking today. The CBS Television Network was established in 1948. Currently, CBS, consists of a commercial broadcast television network, with upwards of 200 affiliated stations, and two nationwide radio networks, comprising almost 900 affiliates. CBS also owns television and radio (both AM and FM) stations.

Column ► Standard vertical divisions of a newspaper page, hence column measure; regular article in a magazine or a newspaper.

Columnar space ► Vertical space separating one column of matter from another.

Column-inch ► An area one column wide and one inch deep, used as a unit of measurement of newspaper space, and as a basis for advertising charges.

Columnist ► Journalist or writer providing comment in regular series of articles on political or social developments or personal interests. Usually adopts individual writing style.

Column rule ► Fine rule marking out the columns.

Command ► A keyboarded instruction to a computer.

Commentary booth ► Small booth in which the reporter records the narrative for a news item.

Commercial ► Term for advertising message that is broadcast on television or radio and has been paid for. A broadcast message is structured by time rather than by space (as is a newspaper or magazine advertisement), and so must be creatively designed around words, sound, and music for radio, plus sight and motion for television. Commercials are produced on film or videotape which is then duplicated so that copies may be distributed to the various stations where they will be aired. An advertising message in print is called an advertisement; See also *advertisement; commercial time.*

Commercial audience ► Actual audience that is actively viewing or listening to a particular television or radio commercial.

Commercial break ► Scheduled break in television or radio programming for the insertion of commercials.

Commercial minute ► One minute (60 seconds) of broadcast time that has been set aside by the radio or television station for commercials. See also *commercial time.*

Commercial time ► Allowable amount of time per hour of programming that can be used by a radio or television station or network to broadcast commercials. For example, a network television would generally adhere to the following schedule:

Prime Time (8-11 PM)
Nonprime time
Netword commercials
6 min.   12 min.

Station commercials 1 min.
10 sec.   2 min.
 20 sec.
Other (such as promos or public service) 2 min.
20 sec.
1 min. 40 sec.
Thus during prime time, this

station may show a total of 9 minutes and 30 seconds of commercials per hour of programming; during nonprime time, the station may air 16 minutes of commercial time per hour. Radio commercials are typically 60-second spots, and television commercials, 10- or 30-second spots. Recently, attempts have been made to use 15- and 20-second spots on television. An advertiser may purchase 60 seconds of commercial time and break it up into three 20-second spots, or purchase 30 seconds and break it up into two 15-second spots.

Commission ➤ A contract asking a freelance writer or photographer to produce a piece of work.

Common carrier ➤ An operator carying communication from any source (e.g. *Internet service provider*) rather than the one keeping control over the cotent carried (e.g. broadcaster).

Communication ➤ The process or act of conveying a message, designed to generate a response.

Communication Decency Act (CDA) ➤ This regulation was a part of the U. S. Telecom Act of 1996. It controls the use of obscene as well as indecent material on-line.

Communication gap ➤ A stage in communication process when no meaningful exchange of ideas can take place due to certain physical or mental difference between the parties in the communication act.

Communications ➤ The physical tools—the means and mechanics—through which communication process is carried out.

Communications channel bandwidth ➤ A communications channel's bandwidth, its capacity, dictates the range of frequencies and to all intents and purposes, the categories and volume of information the channel can accommodate in a given time period.

Communications satellite ➤ Man-made device positioned in space as a means of passing television or other signals from one part of the globe to another. See also Intelsat.

Communications Satellite Corporation (Comsat) ➤ A powerful communications satellite that delivers movies and other offerings to subscribers equipped with compact satellite dishes.

Communication system ➤ The means by which information, coded in signal form can be exchanged. The communication system also encompasses the communication tools we use, their applications and the various implications that arise from the production manipulation and potential exchange of information.

Communicator ▸ Source of a message that is transferred to a receiver. The communicator can affect how a message is received by the selection of the communication channel and by variations in tone or context. For example, a written message regarding AIDS is believable when it comes from a perceived authority such as a famous physician. The same message is less believable, however, if it is communicated by the same physician, who appears on television with an unkempt look and a voice lacking confidence.

Comp ▸ (i) Compositor; a printer who composes typeset material or makes up a page. (ii) Short for complimentary; a free subscription to a magazine given by the publisher in a bid to promote sales and subsequently increase advertisement revenue.

Comp list ▸ List of individuals or organizations (usually associates, suppliers, employees, or advertisers) receiving complimentary subscriptions to a periodical or being given other goods or services free of charge. Comp list records on a subscription file usually have no expire date and sometimes receive special editions or promotions directed specifically to them as advertisers or members of the trade.

Compact Disk-Interactive (CD-I) ▸ As introduced, a prerecorded, interactive optical disk system designed for consumers.

Compact disks ▸ A CD is a long-playing, high-fidelity audio storage medium, and its excellent sound reproduction qualities are a reflection of its digital and optical heritage. Interfering noise is reduced, and a disk can store approximately an hour of music. The CD player uses a laser to read the information. A CD player is usually equipped with a microprocessor that allows you to quickly access any of the disk's tracks and to select a pre-defined playback order. These functions, in addition to a disk's small size, durability, and capacity have contributed to its popularity with consumers and radio stations. The CD has however, been faced with competition from digital audio tape (DAT) and other systems. A DAT player can record as well as play back digital tapes and the audio quality is equal to that of a CD.

Compatible picture ▸ A colour picture that is equally effective in monochrome (black and white).

Competitive separation ▸ Amount of space that separates competitive advertisements from each other. A competitive separation is included in the contract for advertising space drawn between the advertiser and the advertising medium. In broadcast, this separation, also a contractual agreement, is known as commercial protection, and is a time interval, usually 10 minutes, between competitive commercials. Even if there were no agreement, the media normally would honoor this separation of competitors as standard industry practice. See also *back-to-back Commercials*.

Complimentary subscription ▸ See *Comp list*.

Compo ▸ Composite artwork made up of type and half-tone.

Composite ▸ Block combining several elements (drawing, photograph, text, etc.), and made as a single block to reduce time and risk of error in making up a page.

Composite shot ▸ Picture displaying separate and distinct components but appearing as one entity - for example, a *split screen* image, where one part of the screen shows one scene and another part of the screen shows another, allowing the viewer to watch both scenes at the same time; or a special effect, where one scene is superimposed over another.

Composition ▸ Arrangement of type and/or art of printing. Composition may be a manual or computerized process. It includes all aspects of letter, word, and line spacing; line justification; indentation; hyphenation; type selection; and arrangement of all image elements on the page. See also *cold type*; *hot type*.

Compression ▸ Compression refers to reducing the amount of space required to store information (for example, digitized video). Compression can also speed up information relays. Different standards include UPEG, MPEG, DVI, MPEG - 2, and Indeo.

Compressor ▸ Device for narrowing the dynamic range of a signal passing through it.

Computer-assisted editing ▸ The process of using a computer to help streamline and enhance the editing process.

Computer conference ▸ A meeting conducted through computers that can support the exchange of information ranging from text to graphics.

Computer forum ▸ An electronic meeting place. A forum can support a special interest group.

Computer graphics ▸ Graphics designed from information put into a computer. There are many variations of computer graphics, based on the technology used, as well as the effects desired. Most of the results achieved by computer can also be drawn by an artist, but if properly programmed, the computer can accomplish more in a shorter period of time. Changes can readily be made and images can be manipulated with relative ease. In addition, computer technology makes possible a multitude of visual effects that can be played with over and over again until the desired result is achieved.

Computer virus ► A programme that "attaches" itself to other programme. It may display a harmless message or cause data to be lost.

Computer vision ► The discipline that duplicates human vision through a computer and video camera system.

Computerised newsroom ► A newsroom that uses computers instead of typewriters to write stories and to accomplish other tasks. The wire services, such as AP and PTI, are sent electronically to the computers rather than being printed out on paper as in the past.

Computerised page makeup ► Computer-aided process that assembles film or type into finished page formats. Some systems can show how the type size and face and line length will look on the printed page, thus enabling the operator to change specifications and view results. Computerized page makeup systems that run on microcomputers have revolutionized publishing by making

fast and inexpensive composition capabilities available to small publishing businesses. See also *hot type; layout*.

Condensed type ► Type narrower than the standard founts; hence *extra condensed* and *medium condensed*.

Condenser mike ► A high fidelity microphone.

Conditional access system (CAS) ► The transmission system encrypts a TV signal so that it cannot be intercepted by unauthorized users or defaulting subscribers; also the subscribers view only the TV channels they want to and pay for any those channels. A *set-top box* decrypts the signal. Also sea *encryption*.

Conference ► Meeting of editorial staff to discuss the previous issue/s and plan the future one.

Conflict of interest ► Gifts, money, stock ownership, political activism or business relationships that might conflict with a media person's ability to do his or her job.

Connectivity ► A measure of the degree to which users are able to connect and communicate with each other using a network, e.g. *Internet*. Any to any network is a high connectivity network. Also a network with higher *bandwidth* will have greater connectivity than that with lower bandwidth.

Connect-time basis ▸ The pricing of electronic media according to the time a reader spends connected to them.

Console ▸ Stationary control panel utilized by the technical staff of recording and sound engineers. The console houses all the switches, levers, and buttons that control the electronic equipment being used in a studio, as well as television screens that display the picture transmitted from each and all cameras being used on a Shoot.

Consultants ▸ Specialists hired by the management to evaluate a station's overall image and the performance of its news department in comparison with competition in the same market. The consultants recommend ways to improve the station's operation and its news ratings.

Consulting editor ▸ See *contributing editor*.

Consumer advertising ▸ Advertising directed at the ultimate user of a product or service in contrast to advertising directed at business and industry. Sometimes consumer advertising is directed toward a purchaser of a product or service who will then pass that product or service on to its ultimate consumer. Most radio, television, newspaper, and magazine commercials and advertisements are consumer advertising.

Consumer-based PC system ▸ A two-way interactive system designed for broader consumer needs.

Consumer goods ▸ Products made to be used by the consumer for personal use; also called consumer products. Such items as food and clothing are considered to be consumer goods. Automobiles are likewise consumer goods, but the brake systems sold to the automobile manufacturer for use in an automobile come under the category of industrial goods. Consumer goods are further classified as nondurables and durables, Soft Goods and Hard Goods, and Packaged Goods.

Consumer magazine ▸ Magazine that cover a broad or narrow interest and is directed to the general public, as distinguished from a trade magazine (professional magazine), which is geared toward the interest of a specific industry or occupation. Such a magazine may be distributed free of charge or sold, according to the marketing goals of the publisher.

Consumerism ▸ Public concern over the rights of consumers, the equality of consumer goods, and the honesty of advertising. The ideology came into full focus in the 1960s after the U.S. President John F. Kennedy introduced the

Consumer Bill of Rights, which stated that the consuming public has a right to be safe, to be informed, to choose, and to be heard. Fuel was added to the fire in 1966 with the publication of Ralph Nader's book 'Unsafe at Any Speed', which attacked segments of the automotive industry. When corruption of government officials in the Watergate scandal of the seventies, and inflation and widespread consumer disenchantment with the quality of many American products were combined with the greater sophistication brought about by consumer advocates, consumerism became a powerful, action-oriented movement. The primary concern of this force is to fulfill and protect the rights of consumers articulated by President Kennedy in early 1960s. The movement is also cutching up in developing countries including India where consumer courts have started getting due attention. Many people erroneously allude consumerism to the irresponsible consumption behaviour of the public to the neglect of their societal responsibilities.

Contact ➤ Journalist's source of information. A journalist is not bound to disclose his/her source even to the editor.

Contact book ➤ A reporter's record of useful personal contacts and their telephone numbers.

Contact sheet ➤ A sheet of photographs made by pressing the negatives directly against the photographic paper. The prints are the same size as the original negatives.

Contempt of court ➤ Illegal interference with the course of justice.

Content ➤ (i) Material in a newspaper. (ii) The actual information or message making up the material on a Website. This could be a written story, a photograph, a voice conversation or video. Content has a equivalent wider meaning beyond Website, e.g. traffic through a telecom network, etc.

Content provider ➤ A business that uses the Internet to supply you with information such as news, weather, business reports and entertainment.

Contents bill ➤ Bill or poster advertising a story or item in a newspaper.

Contiguity ➤ In broadcast, particularly radio, a term describing two programmes next to each other in time and sequence without interruption for commercials or announcements. For example, the ABC Morning Show and the XYZ Noon Show are said to share contiguity, since the morning show leads right into the noon show.

Continuity ► This refers to correspondence between successive shots of the same piece of action or event in terms of such details as dress, glasses, background, lighting, sound level and direction of movement of the subject in focus (see figs.). For example, you are interviewing the Chief Election Commissioner (C.E.C.) in his office. In the meantime his secretary brings to his notice some important documents and he puts on his glasses to read the matter. Your interview is interrupted. When you resume the interview, he continues to wear his glasses. Quite natural. But to the viewers his specs would appear disorienting. They will start thinking from where did the glasses appear all on a sudden? You as a journalist know the circumstances leading to the C.E.C. wearing his glasses, not the audience. So, to avoid this discontinuity you can request the C.E.C. by politely explaining to him your technical compulsions to put off his specs. Quite likely that he would not disappoint you. But if he decides not to put off his specs, you have no choice but to interview him and make do with some cutaway while editing the story. We all live in an imperfect world and one can simply try his or her best to be less imperfect.

Continuous tone ► Image, such as a photograph or painting, comprising all variations of colour or shade from black to white and produced by varying concentrations of pigment. For example, watercolour paint can be applied thickly to produce a dark shade or thinly to produce a light shade.

Contract publishing ► A form of publishing in which professional publishers take a fee to produce magazines on behalf of a commercial organisation.

Contrast range ► *(Subject brightness range)* The ratio of the lightest and darkest tones in a scene that a system can accommodate while still reproducing intermediate tones well (e.g. 30:1). Also used to describe the range of tones present in a scene.

Contrast ratio ▶ The range of brightness between the lightest and darkest objects in a given scene; The relative brightness of any two tones. Given as a luminance ratio (e.g. 2:1).

Contrasty ▶ A picture with extreme tones and few half-tones.

Contributing editor ▶ This a title given to a magazine's highest paid freelances who at times also polish others' work. Also called consulting editor.

Contribution circuit ▶ Network of landlines linking member stations of a network, along which news material is sent and received.

Contributions studio ▶ Small studio for sending reports 'up the line' to the network station.

Control line ▶ A circuit used to communicate engineering or production information between a studio and an outside source. Often also used as cue line. Also see *Music line*.

Control Panel ▶ (i) A group of tools you use to change hardware and software settings in a computer. (ii) See Audio mixer.

Control room ▶ Areas where director, switcher, technical director, and audio technician work during the programme transmission or assembly.

Control track ▶ The track along the length of tape which contains speed control pulses.

Control track head ▶ The stationary head which lays the control track during recording.

Controlled circulation ▶ (i) A form of free distribution in which copies are sent to readers on a mailing list. (ii) Copies of a periodical distributed free of charge to readers of interest to the advertisers; also called *qualified circulation* or *nonpaid circulation*. Generally, the reader must be in a particular industry or profession to qualify. For example, A & M (Advertising & Management) magazine readers must work in related field. Also see *circulation*.

Convergence ▶ The ability of a computer to access, produce and transmit content (text, still and moving images, sound, graphics) through a variety of media (radio, TV, etc.) rather than each medium existing separately. Such computer systems combine several technologies, such as technologies to view TV or listen to radio programmes. An examples would be Web TV and Web radio systems.

Cookie ▶ A "cookie" is an Internet site's way of keeping your track. It's a small programme built into a web page you might visit. Typically you won't know when you are receiving cookies. Ideally a cookie could make your surfing easier, faster, more personal and efficient by tracking sites you visit, topics you search. It can also be used to collect your e-mail address for marketing (*spamming*) purposes. You can set your browser to warn you before you accept cookies or not accept them at all. Some secure sites, such as stock trading sties, won't work if you don't accept their cookies. Cookies do not reach hard drive or send your Internet movements to CBI, but they can be used to gather more information about a user.

Copy ▶ (i) Written material for news. (ii) All material submitted for use in a newspaper.

Copy board ▶ Frame that holds an original image while it is being photographed for reproduction.

Copydesk ▶ (i) Central desk in composing room at which copy arrives from sub-editors or advertising department, and from which it is distributed for setting; (ii) (US) table where copy editors (sub-editors) work and over which all editorial copy passes.

Copy-edit ▶ To sub-edit written material for consistency, accuracy, grammar, spelling and house style.

Copy fit ▶ In newspaper/magazine editing to make an article fit the space available. Sometimes painful but it has come to stay as newspapers are increasingly switching to *modular* style of page make-up. Also called *cover fit*.

Copy fitting ▶ Selecting a typeface and typesize to best accommodate the amount of text that must be printed in a designated page area. Consideration is given not only to the size of the type, but also to the style that best represents the spirit of the copy.

Copy-flow ▶ The movement of journalistic material during the editing and production process.

Copyguard ▶ One of several patent systems to prevent a prerecorded tape being copied.

Copy print ▶ (i) Original artwork or print from which a copy or copies will be made. (ii) Copy made from the original print or artwork.

Copy reproduction ▶ Developing a film negative on the reverse side of the original so that the finished product will be the opposite of the original. Sometimes, after the rough *layout* has been prepared, it can be seen that the copy will read or fit better if the elements face from right to left rather than the reverse. In this case, the printer or photoengraver will be instructed to flop the negative made from the original photograph and then to make the reproduction from the flopped negative.

Copyright ► The legal right of ownership in a creative work invested in its author, composer, publisher or designer. It provides protection in the expression of a concept while a patent protects the underlying concept.

Copy story ► A TV news story with no accompanying audio or visuals.

Copy-taker ► Telephone typists who take down reporters copy on a typewriter of VDU (Visual display unity

Copytaster ► Senior journalist who sifts incoming mail and agency copy to select items that are considered to be worth running.

Copywriter ► Creator of words and concepts for advertisements and commercials. Copywriters are usually employed by advertisers, advertising agencies, production companies, and dot com companies where text is created. Generally, the copywriter work hand in hand with the Creative Director. Together, the two are responsible for the entire creative effort in an advertising campaign.

Corporate advertising ► Advertising whose purpose is to promote the image of a corporation rather than the sale of a product or service; also called institutional advertising.

Corporation for Public Broadcasting (CPB) ► Non-profit, nongovernmental US agency founded in 1968, headquartered in Washington, D.C., and funded by the federal government along with contributions from the private sector. The purpose of CPB is to promote and finance the development of noncommercial broadcasting. The corporation offers grants to local public broadcast stations and works to provide long-range financing for public broadcasting.

Corr ► Short for correspondent. Also see *correspondent*.

Correct ► To put right typesetting errors.

Correction ► Published item putting right errors in a story.

Correspondent ► (i) Usually refers to journalist working in specialist areas, e.g. transport, education, defense. Particularly used with reference to foreign assignments, e.g. London correspondent, US correspondent; also for reporters working in areas far from the headquarter e.g., Delhi based newspaper or TV news organisation can have its Bihar correspondent in Patna, or a Patna based newsroom can have a district correspondent in Muzaffarpur. (ii) Very often, a synonym for a reporter, Much used with such prefix as special, political, economic, etc. and usually considered more prestigious. Also, a person authorised to send report from out of town point and paid on the basis of the length of reports published.

Corrigenda ▸ Corrections to be made; not newspaper term, but occasionally found in hastily printed official reports, etc.

Cough key ▸ Switch, under the speaker's control, which cuts his microphone circuit.

Count ▸ The number of characters in a line of type.

Countdown ▸ Time given in reverse order, usually announced aloud in the control room or given by hand-signal in the studio, to ensure the smooth transition from one source to the next .

Counter ▸ (i) A number on many web pages that will count the number of hits or count the number of times the page has been accessed. Basically, it counts the number of people who have visited that page. (ii) The interior white of a letter, either fully enclosed as in 0 or partially as in E.

Cover ▸ The first page of a magazine.

Cover fit ▸ See *copy fit*.

Coverage ▸ The attendance at, and writing up of news events; also the total number of stories covered.; extent of news organisation's attention to particular events or situations.

Coverline ▸ Words used on the cover to entice readers.

Cover-mount ▸ A free gift attached to the cover.

Cover shot ▸ Picture that shows entire set or entire group of performers.

Cover story ▸ Article in a magazine which is featured on the front cover.

Cps ▸ Centimeters per second (tape speed).

CPU (Central Process Unit) ▸ The computer's brain which carries out the storing, processing and controlling functions of the computer. The CPU consists of the main circuits of the computer and (for a PC) is located in the main box called CPU box. The other parts are main memory and the control unit. The speed of operation of the CPU is essential to the work of the computer system as a whole. A single addition of two numbers may take a computer only a thousandth of a millionth of a second to perform. Also, it can execute large number of operations quickly, automatically and simultaneously. (This is the basic reason why computers are so useful to us.)

CPU time ▸ Length of time the central processing unit (CPU) of a computer is in operation while performing a function. Most functions are performed in segments interspersed by CPU activity related to other functions allowing the computer to process several jobs concurrently. the cost of running a job is usually based on total CPU time instead of wall-clock (actual) time. The difference between wall-clock time and CPU time depends upon the complexity of the job(s) being run, the number of jobs being run, and the speed of the input/output devices being used.

CQ ► (US) Correct. Marked on margin of copy to tell typesetter that what looks wrong is right.

Cracker ► A person who breaks into a site through a computer's security. While basically the same thing as a *"Hacker"*, a Cracker is sometimes considered to be more malicious and destructive.

Crane shot ► Shot during which the camera is raised or lowered vertically.

Crawl ► Graphics or credit copy rotated upward in front of the video image.

Credibility gap ► Distrust about the communicated messages that arises due to the difference between what was promised and what has been actually delivered.

Credit ► Usually the photographer's or artist's name printed with an illustration; hence *credit line.*

Credit line ► A line giving source of copy or illustration.

Credits ► A list of work experiences including all live and media performances. Also, a list of names and titles at the beginning or end of a programme.

Creed ► Teleprinter machine.

Creep ► Forward movement of the print blanket during offset printing; also called blanket creep. Blanket creep is caused by the normal printing process.

Creeping bias ► kind of bias that manifests itself in subtle ways, such as language choices, the placement of stories the choice of photographs, and the captions that go with tham.

Critique ► An evaluation of the strengths and weaknesses of a performer.

Cromalin ► A proprietary proofing system for four colour material from film rather than printing plates.

Crop ► To select the image of a picture for printing by drawing lines to exclude the unwanted area; also to exclude unwanted area on screen.

Crop mark ► Line or lines drawn on a piece of artwork (including photographs), or on a transparent overlay attached to the artwork, which will serve as a guide to cropping the material (see crop). It is best to place crop marks on an overlay, in the event that the artwork is to be used again in some other context where the cropping may not be the same.

Cross ► A movement from one place in the studio to another.

Cross fade ► Transition of two sounds. As one sound increases in volume, another sound decreases. Together, the sounds create a cross fade. This same effect can be achieved with lighting instruments. As one lighting source fades in, a second source fades out. In video, however, the effect created by the simultaneous transition of two images is called dissolve. Also see *fade in*, *fade out*.

Crosshead ► Small heading usually of one or two words within body text of larger typesize than body text, sometimes underlined. Used for design purposes as a relief to eyes and placed between paragraphs. Word is usually drawn from text following but carries no great news value. Written by sub-editor and not reported.

Crossplug ► The temporary transposition of two circuits, normally on a Jackfield. See also *Overplugging*.

Cross ref ► Indication that story continues or begins on another page; symbolized by q.v.

Cross-shot ► A camera viewpoint that is oblique to the action area as opposed to a *frontal* or *head on shot*, in which the camera looks straight onto the scene.

Crosstalk ► Audible interference of one circuit upon another.

CRT ► Cathode-ray tube, used as a light source to create the type image in a photosetter (in cut-and-past make-up).

Cryptography ► The branch of knowledge dealing with the coding (i.e. encryption) and decoding (i.e. decryption) of information exchanged over a public or private communication network. Coding changes the form of data so that it can be read only by someone, usually the intended receiver, with the knowledge of those changes. This knowledge is refereed to as decryption-key. Public-key encryption combines a public key with a private-key for decryption while the secret-key method uses the same key to lock (i.e. encrypt) and unlock (i.e. decrypt) the information. Many of the debates around the state regulation of the Web pertain to the level of coding that should be legal for private individuals and organisations. The basic challenge is transmitting the key to the intended recipient in order to use it. The secret method uses the same key for coding and decoding and it has to be transmitted. In case of the public key method, one key is kept secret and never transmitted and the other is made public. Very often, both the methods are used. It is said that any coding can be decoded given enough computer time to derive all the per mutations.

However, if it takes months to break a code, a financial transaction has little meaning. Also, as computers get faster, the keys get longer to stay ahead of the game that is cracking or *haiking*.

CSO (Colour separation overlay, also known as Chromakey) ‣ An electronic means of merging pictures from separate sources, giving the illusion for example, that a performer in the studio set against a pictorial background.

CTC ‣ Copy to come.

CTG ‣ Copy to go.

CU ‣ Close up shot of any subject.

Cub reporter ‣ Trainee reporter, may or may not get stipend.

Cue ‣ The start point on a recording. ('This tape is cued'-this tape is ready to play.) Also, a start signal to a live speaker. ('I will cue Prannoy at the end of this record...'). An introduction that action is to begin; the written introduction to piece of audio, especially news to select a certain spot in the videotape or film.

Cue card ‣ A large, hand-lettered card that contains copy, usually held next to the camera lens by floor personnel.

Cue light ‣ Light on the top of a camera to tell the presenter that the camera is live. Also used in a commentary box to cue live narration.

Cue programme ‣ The programme which contains a contributor's cue to start.

Cue pulse ‣ Inaudible pulse recorded on tape just before the start of audio or pictures. When the tape recorder finds the pulse, it will stop and the tape will be cued up ready to play.

Cue sheet ‣ List referred to when mixing the master sound track. It is intended to give an indication of timings for particular shots and sections of sound track.

Cultural distortion ‣ Distortion resulting from editing, dubbing, mixing, shortage of time and like while presenting some folk or traditional form by the electronic media, especially television. This also happens because of lack of understanding of the subtle meanings, which are so characteric of these media, by the 'media people-in-hurry.'

Cultural imperialism ‣ The tendency for one powerful country's mass culture to dominate that of another.

Cumulative audience ‣ Audience accumulation for a medium over a specified time period. Individuals or households count only once in this measurement, no matter how many times they may have been exposed to the medium. Sometimes called the cume or reach, cumulative audience for the advertiser represents the unduplicated audience (the number of people who will be reached at least once) for a schedule over a specific time period. Therefore, the higher the cume, the larger the audience. See also *cumulative audience rating*.

Cumulative audience rating ▶ Rating used by A.C. Nielsen Company (U.S.) in the Nielsen Television Index. It is based on the cumulative audience, as compared to the average or total audience, and reflects the unduplicated audience size in 15-minute segments over a four-week period. If a programme has an average cumulative rating of 7 for its first quarter hour over the course of a four-week period, it means that 7% of the total potential audience tuned in to that programme at least once during that quarter hour in the four-week period. See also *average audience rating; rating; total audience rating*.

Current affairs ▶ See *public affairs*.

Current issue ▶ Issue of a periodical currently on sale at newsstands. New issues usually appear at the end of the prior issue period. For example, a monthly magazine's September issue would appear on the newsstands at the end of August.

Current periodicals ▶ The most recent issues of periodicals that are usually found in open stacks. When they are no longer current, they are bound by volume and shelved elsewhere.

Cursive ▶ Any flowing design of type based on handwriting.

Cursor ▶ Electronic light 'pen' on VDU screen, used to manipulate text during writing and editing. It also shows the position of the next input.

Curtain raiser ▶ Story providing background to a forthcoming event. Also known as *scene setter*.

Customer magazines ▶ Magazines published by large organisations to give or sell to their customers.

Cut ▶ (i) A piece of news audio, usually on cartridge; (ii) an edit, immediate change from one scene to another, as distinguished from a *fade* or *dissolve*. (iii) a signal to stop action. (iv) to reduce a story by deleting facts or words.

Cut-away (noun) ▶ The general name given to any shot which can be used to generate parallel action. Parallel action is where two or more activities which may be going on in different places or at the same place at different points of time, are made to look as through they are happening at the same time, e.g. the postman is just coming through the gate, so we need to edit in a cutaway here to see who is waiting for him at the door.

A cut-away shot gets its name from its function. What its function? To help the tape editor cut away from the main action to something else for the express purpose of covering up the jump cuts. For example, in a minister's press conference (see Fig. A), his coughing fit (when he could say nothing worthwhile) could be covered by a cut-away shot of reporters listening to the minister (see Fig. B), or a shot of TV camera trained on him or a shot from behind the minister as he turns

(A)

(B)

his head to the other side, or a close-up shot of reporter' hands while taking down notes – there would be any number of things provided those helped the editor to fill up the jump cut.

Here you can ask, where did the other shots come from because the only camera the newsroom had dispatched was shooting the minister's speech? The cutaway were shot before or after the minister's speech with the sole objective of providing editing tools to the tape editor. During the speech the camera remained trained on the minister in order not to miss away potential newsworthy statement. *The Lesson*: next to the main event itself, cutaways are the most important shots in television news.

There are broadly two types of cutaways: (a) *Reaction Shots*; and (b) *Action Accelerators*.

First, about the reaction shots: these are the shots of reporters listening to a speaker or the subject's remarks. Since a camera cannot be in two places at the same time, reaction cutaways are posed shots. They are also known as reverse angle shots or simply *reverse angles* because the camera has to be moved to the interviewee's point of view (POV) in order to shoot such shots. This camera repositioning is usually a 180 – degree turn (not on the same point from where the interviewee was shot) showing the reverse of the main shot. *Action accelerators*: are used to "compress time" either to eliminate a repetitive action or just to save time to meet the demands of newscast deadlines. Suppose you are writing a story about the 400-metre run held at National Stadium, Delhi. The Videotape shows the participants as they start, running to the far end having covered half the distance, then returning to the near side where the camera captures them on the finish line. Total time 4 minutes. 4 minutes are too long to be devoted to such a story. Now the task is how to show the highlights while reducing the airtime and maintaining the visual flow. You might begin with the runners taking off and running a few seconds, edit in a cutaway of the cheering crowd, return to racers as they reach the other end of the track, edit in another cutaway, perhaps of a watch, then return to the race on the finish line. Total running time: 30 seconds.

Here, you will ask the source of those spectators and coach cutaways. May be there were other cameras as is normal in sports coverage. In case there was only one camera and that was with the reporter-photographer, the cutaways were shot in an another similar heat or after the race if the telecast deadline so permitted. One can say that this is not the representation of reality. True, that is what is called *faithful cheating* in TV news.

Cutaway (verb) ► Editing out of one shot, (to another shot), to another shot which is different in subject matter from the previous one , e.g., cut away from the postman coming through the gate to the dog inside the house, waiting.

Cut-in ► A cut-in is a small duration newscast that a local station presents each day, usually in the evening. For example, the Lucknow Doordarshan cutting away from the regular programming of DD National channel to air its local newscast. It is called a cut-in because the newscast temporarily interrupts or cuts into the network programming of the DD National channel.

Cutline ► One-line copy that describes the illustration, drawing, or photograph next to which it appears. A cutline may also appear as a *caption*.

Cut-off ► A newspaper or a magazine story separated from the text above and below by type rules making it self-contained from the rest of the column; hence *cut-off rule*.

Cut-out ► Half tone picture in which the background has been cut away to leave the image in outline.

Cuts ► Also known as trims or out-takes; pictures excluded from an edited story.

Cut story ► Complete and edited news picture item.

Cutting/clipping ► Item cut or copied from a news paper or other printed source.

Cutting height ► Level at which the human figure is conventionally cut by the frame without giving a displeasing composition.

Cuttings ► Catalogued material from newspapers cut out and stored in a cuttings library for future reference. Also called clippings.

Cuttings job ► A story based on cuttings.

CX ► Correction, to be made in the type. Also called Fix; (US) Correct. This symbol is used on proofs corrected by editorial. Symbols 'Kerect' and 'X-correct'; also used as warning that error is only apparent.

Cyber ► A prefix for anything happening on the *Internet*.

Cybernetics ► Field of Study focusing on the system of feedback in a communication process.

Cyberpunk ► Cyberpunk was originally a cultural sub-genre of science fiction taking place in a not-so-distant over-industrialized society. The term grew out of the work of William Gibson and Bruce Sterling and has evolved into a cultural label encompassing many different kinds of human, machine, and punk attitudes. It includes clothing and lifestyle choices as well. See also *cyberspace*.

Cyberspace ► A term coined by William Gibnson in his science fiction "Neuromancer", in 1984; cyberspace can be described as a computer -generated environment (or world) where you can interact with other people and work and play. It is also used to describe the whole range of information resources, available through computer networks. To a layman it means just the Internet which is a network of computer networks.

Cybersquatting ► The practice of registering trademark-names on the Web with hopes of selling them to companies that actually own them.

Cyclorama ► A huge drape or plaster (hard cyc) wall providing the backdrop for a setting in a studio.

Cypher ► A type character which represents something else, i.e. ampersand & and @ and $ signs.

Dd

D/A converter ➤ Digital-to-analogue converter. Creates an analogue output from a digital input, e.g., CD playback signal is converted in order to feed conventional loudspeakers.

DAB (Digital audio broadcasting) ➤ Radio transmission system offering compact disc quality audio and requiring a special receiver.

Daily ➤ Daily, usually morning newspaper.

Dak edition ➤ (India) Up-country edition containing matter that has already appeared in a previous final edition.

Da-notice ➤ An official instruction to editors that a story is subject to the Official Secrets Act and therefore should not be used.

DAT (Digital audio tape) ➤ Matchbox-sized digital recording medium.

Data bank ➤ Information resources of an organization or business.

Database ➤ Collection of data stored on a computer storage medium in a common pool for access on an as-needed basis. The same pool of information can serve many applications, even those not anticipated at the time the data base was created. This is in contrast to traditional methods of data storage that hold a fixed amount of data retrievable in a predetermined format, often duplicating the storage of information in as many files as there are applications. For example, the name and address of the same customer may be in a marketing file, a billing file, and an addressing file. If any one of these applications changes, and the programmes that access and use the customer record change, then the customer file must change. In data base systems, the customer information is retrievable for each application from a shared file that is not dependent upon the application programmes for its structure.

Data encryption ➤ A process that transforms information into random streams of bits to create a secret code for data security.

Dateline ➤ Place and date of origin of newspaper story; sometimes attached to by-line, sometimes given separately. With the Internet and other communication devices making the news delivery possible without much loss of time, some newspapers have stopped mentioning the date of news in its dateline.

Date-tied ▸ Only relevant if published at a specific time.

DAVP (India) ▸ Directorate of Audio Visual Publicity. It is the central agency of the Government engaged in undertaking advertising and visual publicity campaigns on behalf of various Government, semi-Government and autonomous bodies in the print and the electronic media on concessional rates. Its main functions are: (i) planning, production and release of display and classified advertisements; (ii) production and displaying of outdoor publicity material and (iii) regulating accreditation of advertising agencies in India.

Day in the life of ▸ Profile feature focusing on particular day in the of a subject. Not to be confused with "Life in the day of" profile which covers the subject's life but in the context of talking about currently typical day.

Day-for-night ▸ Technique of under-exposing footage shot in daylight to give an impression of night time.

Daypart ▸ Refers to time segment in a broadcast day. Broadcast stations (Radio/TV) have divided the day into time segments to reflect broadcast programming patterns and audience composition throughout the day. Commercial time may be purchased by the daypart (rather than by the programme), and its cost is based upon the average size of the audience for a specific daypart. Prime time is an example of a television daypart where the programming is usually of a general nature with family appeal for a wide demographic range of viewers, and is usually the daypart with the largest viewing audience. Dayparts are set by the individual stations, but they typically follow a standard pattern. Radio is typically divided into five dayparts as follows:

6:00 A.M. - 10:00 A.M.
Morning drive*
10:00 A.M - 3:00 P.M.
Daytime
3:00 P.M. - 7:00 P.M.
Afternoon Drive*
7:00 P.M. - 12:00 A.M.
Nighttime
12:00 A.M. - 6:00 A.M.
All night
(*The combination of drive times accounts for radio's prime time.)
Typical television dayparts may be as follows:
7:00 A.M. - 9:00 A.M.
M-F
Morning
9:00 A.M. - 4:30 P.M.
M-F
Daytime
4:30 P.M. - 7:30 P.M.

M-F
Early fringe
7:30 P.M. - 8:00 P.M.
Sun-Sat   Access
8:00 P.M. - 11:00 P.M.   M-Sat
Prime time (7:00 P.M. - 11:00
P.M. Sun)
11:00 P.M. - 11:30 P.M.   M-F
Late news
11:30 P.M. - 1:00 A.M.   M-F
Late fringe
1:00 A.M. -
Sun-Sat   Late night

DBS/DTH ► (Direct Broadcasting by Satellite) System of transmitting broadcast signals to individual households using high powered satellites. Also known as Direct-to-home.

Dc ► Double-column.

DCC ► (Digital compact Cassette) Rival medium to DAT, using standard-sized compact cassette.

Dead ► Props, scenery no longer required either having been used or found unnecessary. *Also* when suspended scenery is raised/lowered, its required final position is its 'dead'.

Dead acoustic ► Environment with very low reverberations, in which sound is absorbed and "deadened" by surfaces such as carpets.

Dead air ► Silence during a broadcast because of some technical error.

Deadline ► Time by which copy must be delivered to appear in a particular edition; varies from page to page for each edition. And also according to whose deadline it is (on the same story there will be progressively different deadlines for copy to subs, copy to printer, set matter to page, and page to press.)

Deaf aid ► Close-fitting earpiece through which a performer in the studio or in the field can be given instructions directly by editorial/production staff.

Decibel (*dB*) ► A logarithmic unit which expresses ratios of powers, voltages, and currents. The scale is logarithmic. It is commonly used for signal-to-noise ratio for the evaluation of sound volume.

Deck ► One unit of a multiple headline, or one line of a two-or-more-line heading.

Decoder ► A device for turning transmitted material into usable form, i.e. pictures or text; the device that strips the teletext information from the *VBI* and displays the information.

Dedicated information retrieval operations (DIRO) ► A two-way interactive system that support specialized information pools and narrow subscriber groups.

Dedicated line ► Telephone or computer line that is reserved for one function or user, such as incoming customer phone calls.

Deep Throat ► Derived from the title of infamous porno film starring Linda Lovelace, the term means a secret whistle-blower on some major scandal. First given to the secret source for Woodward and Bernstein in Watergate Scandal involving the U.S President Nixan.

Default ➤ A predefined setting. For example, the double-click option is the default setting in Microsoft Windows 98.

Default-setting ➤ Standard typesetting in a given computer program unless overridden by a keyboard command.

Defendant ➤ A person or organisation subject to a legal action.

Deferred relay ➤ The broadcasting of a recorded programme previously heard 'live' by an audience.

Define ➤ to specify on a computer screen the material a command is intended to cover.

Definition ➤ The degree or amount of detail clearly visible in a television picture.

Defragmentation ➤ The process of rewriting a file to adjacent sections of a hard disk. Over time, part of the same file can become fragmented - that is, spread over different areas on a hard disk. Fragmentation causes slower disk speed. Windows 98 includes the disk defragmenter, which may help improve disk performance. See also *file allocation table (FAT)*.

DEG (digital effects generator). ➤ A computer-controlled special effects generator that provides many special video effects.

Delay (also profanity D). ➤ A device which inserts a time delay between studio and transmitter output, usually of seven seconds. Once in operation, a delay is not obvious to the listener. But the broadcaster can prevent the last seven seconds of studio output from reaching the transmitter by dropping back to 'real time'. this enables censoring of undesirable material on programmes such as public phone-ins.

Delayed drop ➤ An intro which reserves the point of a story till later.

Delayed lead ➤ Keeping the most important information in the latter part of the story to achieve added interest and mystery.

Delete ➤ Take out; proof reader's mark.

Democratization of information ➤ New equipment (for example, PCs and desktop publishing video systems) contribute to the free flow of information in society. The implication: more people can now be come information producers and it may be harder to institute cenorship on a broad scale.

Demographic editions ➤ slightly different versions of the same edition of a magazine that are circulated in different regions for subscribers with different occupations and other economic characteristics.

Demographics ► The breakdown of viewers by age and gender for any particular programme. This information is ascertained during the ratings process.

Demo tape ► A recording of a broadcaster (or would-be broadcaster) sent with a job application. Two or three minutes is usually plenty, and cassettes are customary.

Density ► Measure of the relative blackening of photographic images consisting of silver particles spread in varying densities into a surface. The particles create images of light, dark and shadow.

Depth ► Vertical length of a column in a newspaper, or magazine measured in inches or agate lines. See also *column inch*.

Depth of field ► Variable range of distances from the camera within which a subject appears to be sharply focused. The depth increases with focused distance, with smaller f-stops, and as focal length of the lens is reduced (i.e. lens angle widened). Often wrongly called 'depth of focus'.

Depth of focus ► The distance between the TV lens and the subject on camera.

Descender ► (i) That part of a lowercase letter that extends below the main body of the letter. The letters g, j, p, q, and y all have descenders. (ii) Any lowercase letter with such a descending stroke. See also *ascender*.

Descriptors ► Keywords from the text of an article used when storing information in a database or when retrieving information.

Design ► (i) Selection of typefaces, illustrations, rules, determination of spacing and general visual style of a newspaper; (ii) layout of individual pages or articles.

Desks ► Departments of newspapers are often in terms of desks; thus picture desk; news desk; features desk; etc.

Desktop ► Your workspace on the compute screen See also *active desktop*.

Desktop publishing ► Software which enables pages to be typed and displayed electronically. A term that describes both the field and process whereby near-typeset quality documents can be produced with a PC, a laser printer, and software. DTP also implies that you have access to enhanced layout and printing options.

Desktop video ► Advancements in video technology have made it possible to assemble cost effective yet powerful video production configurations. PCs typically play a major role in this environment.

Development ➤ Refers to the body of a news story.

Development news ➤ Type of news relating to some development aspect/aspects of a situation, event or incident.

Developmental journalism ➤ Mobilising media in the national effort for the socio-economic development of a country, generally in the underdeveloped countries.

DFP (India) ➤ Directorate of Field Publicity. The directorate aims at reaching the people at grassroot level through its country wide network to inform then about the policies, programmes and achievements of the government and to motivate them for participation in the nation's development programmes. The directorate uses films, exhibitions, slides, seminars, symposia, paintings etc., for the purpose, the organisation serves as a two-way channel of communication as it assimilates as well as disseminates information to the people concerned.

Diagonal wipe ➤ See *wipe*.

Dialogue box ➤ A window in which you provide information to a programme.

Dial-up networking ➤ A feature that allows you to use a phone line and modem to connect to another computer.

Diary ➤ Daily list of jobs to be covered by the newsroom.

Diary column ➤ (i) A gossip column; (ii) a day to day personal account.

Diary piece ➤ Article delivered from routine sources (press conferences, press releases, council, meetings, Parliament) listed in diary (originally in written form, now increasingly on computer screen) which helps news desk organise their news gathering activities. Off diary stories are those which come from reporter's initiative (not prompted by desk) and from non-routine sources.

Diary story ➤ News event covered by pre-arrangement. See *diary piece*.

Didone ➤ British Standards Institution classification of types that are popularly called modern Romans- such as Bodoni, Didot and Walbaum.

Didot point ➤ Unit of type measurement in Europe, except Britain and Belgium. It is larger than the American-English point, being 0.01483 in.

Difuser ➤ (i) In TV production, screen used as a filter and placed over a light to soften the light and eliminate harsh tones or shadows. (ii) Screen used over a camera lens to give the image a kind of fuzzy effect, as in a dream.

Diffusion filter ➤ Filter placed over the lens to give a soft-focus effect.

Dig ➤ To do deep research.

Digerati ➤ The digital version of literati, it is a reference to people considered to be knowledgeable, or otherwise in-the-know in regards to the digital revolution.

Digital ➤ A way of representing light or sound values as a series of electronic pulses that is, in Is and Os, which then become computer readable. Any carrier wave, as a result, has only an 'off' and 'on' setting. Transmission through this method greatly reduces signal degradation and allows perfect replication of any stored information.

Digital age ➤ Term used to refer to the information age or age of technology as opposed to the age of print or the age of books.

Digital audio broadcasting (DAB) ➤ A CD-quality audio signal that could be delivered to subscribers by satellite or terrestrial means.

Digital audio tape (DAT) ➤ A recordable digital tape system that can match a CD's audio quality. DATs have also been used for computer data backups.

Digital audio workstation ➤ A set of digital equipment complete in itself for editing and manipulating audio material, mixing, dubing, adding voice, making packages, etc.

Digital broadcasting ➤ Transmission of text or images to a group of people via personal computers. This gives viewers the option to access information or services at their convenience and allows interaction with a remote data base from home or office. Digital broadcasting has been used to book airline reservations, to provide stock quotations or sports results, and to sell real estate. See also Electronic catalog; Teletext; Videotex.

Digital counter ➤ Accessory on most VCRs and sound recorders which "clocks up" the length of tape that has been played. If it is always set to Zero at the start of a tape, the numbers can be used as reference points.

Digital effects unit ➤ Electronic equipment capable of affecting sound quality in a variety of ways, e.g., by changing frequency response, adding coloration or reverberation. Capable of creating synthetic or 'unreal' sounds.

Digital effects VCR ➤ A video recorder that uses computer memory chips to create special effects.

Digital imaging camera ➤ Camera that electronically relays, reads, or enters information by first converting it from hard copy to digital signals. This technology allows a direct marketer to relay orders received in various locations to a central location for key entry of the orders to the fulfillment system. Some digital imaging cameras also perform a scan entry function, entering data directly to the fulfillment system. Digital imaging equipment is costly and would be economical only for large-volume operations.

Digital mode ➤ The encoding of a signal as on/off pulses which represent its amplitude and frequency.

Digital radio ➤ Radio device that sends and receives signals as a series of electronic pulses (Is and Os) rather than analogue waves.

Digital recording ➤ Recordings that convert sound or visual information into a numbered code for perfect re-recording without any deterioration through use. DAT is digital audio tape.

Digital signal ➤ An electrical signal that represents its original accoustic or view information as a series of pulses in binary code, i.e. bits or 1s and 0s. A digital signal is non-continuous and assumes a finite number of discrete values.

Digital television (DTV) ➤ A generic designation for television systems based on digital signalling device. Also see *digital signal*.

Digital tracking ➤ A system which automatically adjusts the tape tracking for optimum picture quality.

Digital Versatile Disk (DVD) ➤ A new, high capacity CD developed in the 1990's. Designed for commercial and consumer applications, it could replace the home VCR.

Digital-to-analogue converter (DAC) ➤ A DAC converts digital information into an analogue form.

Digitize ➤ To turn a picture or a printed page into a computer format that flows the data to be transformed. After editing on a non-linear machine the picture is transformed into video format for telecast. This process is called *upgrading*.

Digitized photographs ➤ Photographs that have been put on disk and that can be resized or edited.

Dingbat (US) ➤ Any typographic decoration; also *bug*.

Dinky dash ➤ (US) Shortest horizontal line used to separate sub-divisions of a story. Also called *jim dash*.

Diopter lens ➤ Magnifying lens used in close - up work. It is placed in front of the main lens and the power is rated in diopters.

Dipping ➤ Lightly dyeing white or very light toned fabrics(e.g. coffee or blue tints) to reduce reflectance and avoid 'blooming'/'crushing out' on camera. White shirts, blouses, sheets, coats, dust covers, or lace curtains are frequently dipped before use.

Direct access storage device (DASD) ➤ Computer input/output device that stores information magnetically. Direct access means that the Central Processing Unit of a computer can directly access the information it requires without searching sequentially through the information stored. It is similar to playing a song on an album without playing all preceding songs first.

Direct contact ➤ Eye-to-eye contact with a live audience and/or by means of looking directly into a camera lens.

Direct input ➤ Process by which text goes straight from editorial screen into computer for typesetting thus cutting out process in which printers used to type out copy.

Direct media ➤ Various communication channels (e.g. direct mail or telephone) utilized in direct marketing to bring the promotion message to the individual prospect, as opposed to communication media that cannot be directed to a specific individual (e.g. television or radio.)

Direct quote ➤ A speaker's or interviewee's exact words enclosed in quotation marks as

part of the story; sometimes polished to correct grammar or improve syntax. See also, *indirect quote, partial quote* and *paraphrase*.

Directional ➤ The dominant pickup pattern of a microphone, i.e., uni-,bi-,omni directional or cardioid.

Directional lighting ➤ Illumination from a clearly defined direction, usually casting sharp shadows.

Directly pattern (pickup) ➤ Area over which a microphone will pick up sound.

Director ➤ Not to be confused with the news director who heads a newsroom, the director is responsible for giving the newscast the most professional look possible. In some stations, the directors also perform all the electronic switching needed to put the anchors on the air, run videotape, and other things essential to the newscast.

Director's cut ➤ Version of a film the director delivers to the studio representing his creative vision, often disregarding commercial aspects.

Directory ➤ (i) Groups of files stored together. Similar to folders and subfolders macintosh and Windows environments. (ii) Search engine in which *Web sites* are arranged. (ii) A list of stories of a given classification held in a computer and available those with access.

Dirty copy ► Copy so heavily marked and corrected that it cannot be read easily or is ambiguous.

Dirty proof ► (i) Proof so marked that changes cannot be easily followed; (ii) proof containing so many literal and other errors that it cannot be worked on until matter is corrected.

Dirty tape ► Tape which has not been fully erased. If a dirty cartridge is used for another recording, the previous signal will still be heard in the background.

Disaster caps ► Large heavy, sanserif type, used on a major (usually disaster) page one story.

Disc Jockey (DJ) ► Radio show host whose programme consists of the playing of recorded music interspersed with light conversation and commercials or announcements. Disc jockeys usually feature a particular type of music, such as jazz, rock and roll, or easy listening, and throughout the years, different DJs have built up definite radio personalities specific to their particular brand of music. With the advent of the discotheque and the video disk, the term has been widened to include anyone who plays popular recorded music for a group of listeners. In India FM stations have thrown up many DIs.

Disclaimer ► A printed item explaining that a story printed previously has nothing to do with persons or an organization with the same or similar name as used in the story.

Dish ► Dish shaped antenna for transmitting or receiving satellite signals.

Disk ► Electronic storage system for storing computer information. Also called disc. see *disk drive*.

Disk drive ► Computer hardware on which you can store information. Disk drives are assigned a letter. For example, most users store their files on their hard disk, which is typically labeled, 'C'.

Display ► (i) Headline and illustrations for feature; ii) display ads department.

Display ads ► Large advertisements usually containing illustrations (cf. Classified ads) and appearing on editorial pages. Advertising department will organise the distribution of ads throughout the newspaper which is usually indicated on a dummy handed to the sub editors before layout of paper begins. Such ads are usually designed in ad agencies and supplied to newspapers.

Dissolve ► Visual effect, used most frequently in television production in which one scene *fades out* to black as another scene *fades in* from black.

The scenes appear to dissolve one into the other. A dissolve is used primarily to make a smooth transition between scenes in order to show the passage of time in a given situation, or to show simultaneous action in two different scenes. In audio, this simultaneous fading in and out is called a *cross fade*.

District man ▶ Reporter, usually on regional paper, responsible for coverage of town or area outside publishing centre.

Divided word ▶ See *broken word*.

DOA ▶ Dead on arrival. Emergency services jargon for a victim who has died either before help could arrive or before the ambulance could reach the hospital.

Document ▶ (i) A file you create when you save your work in a programme. Examples of documents include word-processing files, spreadsheets and bitmaps. (ii) Another name for a Web page. It is a single.htm file.

Documentary film ▶ A form of film-making where real life, without any fictional element, is presented for educational or persuasive purpose.

Documentary ▶ Usually, one long report — perhaps a half hour or an hour — on a single topic. Similar to a series. See *story types*.

DOG ▶ Digitally originated graphics.

Dog ▶ A non-story, one that fails to live up to its promise.

Dog watch ▶ Late shift in a morninger or early shift in a morninger.

Dolby ▶ System for reducing audio noise and improving high frequency response.

Dolly ▶ (i) Tripod or pedestal that supports the camera and enables it to be moved in all directions; (ii) to move the camera toward or away from an object.

Domain ▶ A group of computers through which individuals access the Internet.

Domain name ▶ It denotes the name of a specific Internet area controlled by a company, School, or Organization. This is uniaque name that identifies an Internet site. Domain names always have 2 or more part, separated by dots. The part on the left is the most specific, and the part on the right is the most general. A given machine may have more than one domain name but a given domain name points to only one machine. For example, the domain names:— Netlinkis.com, Mail.netlinkis.com, Sales.netlinkis. com — can all refer to the same machine, but each domain name can refer to no more than one machine. Usually, all of the machines on a given *Network* will have the same thing as the right-hand portion of their domain names netlinkis.com in the examples above. It is also possible for a domain name to exist but not be connected to an actual machine. This is often done so that a group or business can have an Internet e-mail address without having to establish a real Internet site. In these cases, some real Internet machine must handle the mail on behalf of the listed domain name. See also: *IP number.*

Domain suffix ► The domain is the place where your Internet service originates. The suffix is the end portion of an Internet address that indicates the nature of your site. For example, edu indicates an educational site, whereas gov indicates a unit of government.

Domestic cut off ► By domestic cut off is meant an area which is lost when the picture is transmitted and appears on a domestic television set. Also see *TV cut off.*

Doorstepping ► Journalists pursuing sources by standing outside their front doors. Now journalists increasingly wait in cars.

Dope sheet (camera report) ► (i) Camera operator's written record of each camera take. Also, an accurate record of all persons and locations of which a reporter has the footage (the videotape shots). This is very important because you cannot trust your memory alone, especially when you have to deal with a number of things the day. And, there is no day when you are not required to piece together a story or two of chaos – from the newsroom to the field whose every reporter from competing channels tries to out compete the other. So depesheet is a MUST, not only to, deliver our story before the deadline but also to get the maximum of what you have shot and noted down in the field.

Dot,dot,dot ► Properly ellipsis (..) used to denote omission from quotation or, at the end of sentence, idea that does not need to be stated.

Dot leaders ► Dotted lines (e.g. those relating one column of figures to another.)

Dotted rule ► Rule composed entirely of dots.

Double ► (i) The same story, whether in identical or different form, appearing twice in the same edition; (ii) repetition of words in different headlines on the same page.

Double action ► A cut in which part of an action is erroneously overlapped from another angle.

Double chaining ► Where two telecine (film chain) machines are used alternately to screen a report.

Double column ► Any newspaper item: text/heading/graphics over two columns. Double page spread is a feature occupying two facing pages, it includes the space between two columns.

Double-ender ► Short length of audio cable with a Jack plug on each end used to connect pieces of equipment or jacks on a Jackfield or break-out box.

Double headed ► Style of radio presentation using two presenters.

Double-page spread (DPS) ► Two pages opposite one another, whether used for a single editorial item or a single advertisement.

Double system (sepmag) ► Where film and sound are recorded separately to be synchronized later. See also *single system.*

Down ► Instruction on copy or proof: make capital a lowercase letter.

Down link ► Transmission path from a satellite to a ground station; sometimes used to describe the ground station capable of receiving a satellite signal.

Download ► The transfer of information from the Internet to your computer. Every time you instruct your computer system to retrieve your mail, you are downloading your mail to your computer. You may also download programmes to your computer. However, be careful about downloading files or programme from a site in which you are not familiar. You could download a virus and never know it until it's too late.

Downstage ► In a *theater*, it refers to the part of the stage area near the audience or proscenium arch. In *TV*, usually indicates a position *nearer the camera* irrespective of the camera position. Hence 'come downstage a little' mans 'Move slightly nearer the camera'.

Downstyle ► Style with minimum of capital letters. For example, non-distinguishing nouns in names, as in Man Singh hotel, are not capitalized. Also see *upstyle.*

Downtable ► Subs other than chief and deputy subs are known as downtable subs. The term is a hold-over from the past when chiefs subs used to sit at the top table of the subs' room.

DPR, NPR ► Telegraph symbols for day press rate and night press rate.

Dress ► Redress or revision of a story; also rejig.

Drive ► See *disk drive.*

Drive time ► The period during radio listening when a substantial part of the audience is travelling in cars early morning, lunchtime, early evening.

Driver ► Software that the operating system uses to control a specific piece of hardware.

Drop cap ► A large letter at the beginning of a paragraph, hanging below the top line and usually at least as deep as two lines of body text.

Drop in ► (i) Put type metal into page; (ii) insert, e.g. local TV commercial aired during the broadcast of a nationally sponsored network show.

Drop-in ads ► Ads that are added to regular ads of a different nature.

Drop letter ► (i) A large initial letter usually extending up or/ and down to more than two beginning lines of scripts. (ii) An outside initial capital letter on the intro of a story; also drop figure.

Dropout ► (i) A fault in camerawork or plate making meaning light areas of a picture lose all detail; (ii) a subsidiary headline; (iii) momentary losses of the sound in a recording caused by dust or imperfections in the tape.

Dry ► A non-newsy or lean period.

Dry run ► Rehearsal without the camera, mixe, musical effects not necessarily in the studio. Also called run through

DSL ► (Digital subscriber line) A method for moving data over regular phone lines. A DSL circuit is much faster than a regular phone connection, and the wires coming into the subscriber's premises are the same (copper) wires used for regular phone service. A DSL circuit must be configured to connect two specific locations, similar to a *leased line*.

A commonly discussed configuration of DSL allows downloads at speeds of upto 1.544 megabits (not megabytes) per second, and uploads at speeds of 128 kilobits per second. This arrangement is called *ADSL*: "Asymmetric" Digital Subscriber line. Another common configuration is symmetrical: 384 Kilobits per second in both directions. In theory ADSL allows download speeds of up to 9 megabits per second and upload speeds of upto 640 kilobits per second. DSL is now a popular alternative to leased lines and *ISDN*, being faster than ISDN and less costly than traditional leased lines. See also *bit, bps, ISDN, leased line*.

DTH (Direct to home) television ► TV networks which allow direct broadcast of programme signals from a geostationary satellite to individual homes through local satelite dishes or antennas. Also see *cable TV, terrestrial*.

Dub ► To add or re record sound to edited pictures .The duplication of an electronic recording. Dubs can be made from tape to tape, or from record or disc to tape and vice versa.

Dubbing ▸ It refers to (i) combining several sound tracks together; (ii) transfer of one tape to another. In TV, *picture loss* occurs not only in shot size, but also in quality i.e. sharpness or clarity, during each stage of transmission. Add to this the quality loss due to dubbing. The original tape on which the actions were shot is called the *first generation*. The tape onto which the edited version is built is called the *second generation*, which is apparently not any different from the first generation tape. However, if a second generation tape is used as the raw material for a re-edited version, the *third generation* tape would show a considerable loss in quality. The pictures would look dull and the colours less clear – one colour merging with another. Can you recall such a programme afflicted with picture loss? If you watch Doordarshan and Siti Cable regularly, you would not be disappointed in finding out a current affairs programme having intolerable level of picture loss. *From High-8 to Beta Mastering*: in Doordarshan, apparently because of accessibility problems, some of the private producers used to shoot their commissioned programmes partly or fully on Semi-professional (Hi-8) or no professional (VHS) tapes. Then they transferred these onto U-matic taper for editing purposes. Thus the second generation tape becomes a raw material for making the final copy, which in fact, is now the third generation. A good number of producers were in the habit of keeping this third generation final copy with themselves as the producer's copy and submit its dubbed version that is the Telecast Copy with Doordarshan. You must be by now scratching your head and pressed your memory buttons into action to calculate the latest generation! Well, it was the fourth generation that was shown to you!

This *fourth-generation – telecast-syndrome* is not limited to the U-matic format alone. If the agreement with Doordarshan binds the producer to submit the telecast copy in Betacam format, he or she would simply submit a dubbed version of the third generation producer's copy onto a Betacam tape. Thus, what changes here is not the generation the shot material and consequently the picture quality, but just the format of the telecast copy. This fourth generation tape gives a picture of truly marginal quality, which is equivalent to radio's UFB (Unfit for Broadcast).

Thus it is: always good to

make the telecast copy from the first generation tapes.

Ducking unit ▸ Automatic device providing 'voice-over' facility. See Voice-over.

Dummy ▸ Small version of editorial pages used for planning overall contents of newspaper and usually containing details of display advertising. It can be an electronic dummy on screen. Dummy is often considered at early news conference where decisions on newspaper size and advertisement, distribution are made; mock up of newspaper for launching, design experiments, etc. Also see *dummy run*.

Dummy run ▸ Producing a new newspaper or section up to any stage short of actual publication. It is a general practice to bring out dummy runs before the formal launch of any newspaper or magazine. Also see *dummy*.

Duotone ▸ A black and white picture reproduced by printing in black and one other colour.

Dupe ▸ Duplicate See *black*.

Duplex ▸ Line-casting matrix which carries two characters; also (US) a make of newspaper press.

Duplicate ▸ (i) In general, copy or reproduction of a magnetic tape, printing plate, film, or photographic negative; also called DUB if a film or video duplicate. (ii) In computers, two or more records on a file that can be combined into one record according to the matching logic being used; also called dupe.

Duplicated audience ▸ Listeners, viewers, or readers reached more than once by the same commercial or advertisement appearing in different media. See also audience duplication.

Duplicate readership ▸ Readers reading more than one newspaper or magazine available in a market.

Duplicate subscribership ▸ Persons subscribing to more than one newspaper available in a market.

Duration ▸ Exact time/length of a programme or item within it.

Dutch wrap ▸ (US) Running text type from one column to another without covering column 2 (or 3,4, etc.) with a headline.

DVD ▸ A high-capacity compact disc. This disc can store enough data for a full length movie. You must have a DVD disc drive or player to use DVD discs.

DVE ▸ Digital video equipment.

Dynamic fonts ▸ Also called embedded fonts, dynamic *fonts* allow a web author to use any font he wishes to on his web pages and have them embedded in the web document so that the *Net* surfers can view the document as well without having installed those fonts before. What this basically means is that the fonts are downloaded from the server to the user's computer when the page downloads much like an image file with a word document.

Behind dynamic fonts is a technology from Bitstream called Bitstream WebFont technology. When built into authoring tools and web browsers, Bitstream WebFont technology provides an easy and secure way to transfer font data from a web author's server to a user's browser. If a web author includes Times New Roman in the headline of an *HTML* document, that's what users see in their browsers.

This technology has two main components: a recorder and a player. Authoring tool developers include the recorder in their products. The recorder records characters from the fonts that web authors use in their documents and stores them in a highly compact data structure called a Portable Font Resource (PFR). The player is built into the *browser*.

How dynamic fonts work for web authors: dynamic fonts let you, the *web* author, use your installed fonts in a web document. The authoring tool captures characters from the fonts you use, and stores them in a PFR (Portable Font Resource, a highly compact data file). Then you post the PFR and the HTML document on your web site. *How dynamic fonts work in web browsers*:

To view dynamic fonts, you need Netscape Communicator 4.x for any platform, or Internet Explorer 4 (or higher) for Windows and the Microsoft Font Smoother for Windows 95 only. Dynamic fonts are downloaded with an HTML page, the same way as GIF and JPEG images are. A browser that can display dynamic font files, such as Netscape Communicator or Internet Explorer, renders the fonts on the screen (or on a printer). Browsers that cannot display dynamic fonts use alternate (default) fonts on the user's system.

Benefits of dynamic fonts are that they rely on standard HTML tags; allow web authors to format text without resorting to bitmap graphics (GIFs, JPEGs); reduce *download* time; allow you to copy and paste the text you have preserved; allow search engines to include in their databases the text you have preserved; and, dynamically display text based on the user's display.

But there are drawbacks. Not all fonts can be used as dynamic fonts as only serif, sans-serif, cursive, monospace , and fantasy are standard fonts while the rest fall in the category of default fonts. Other drawbacks include: increase in the page size; fonts can be large, and will increase the download time; there are two methods to embed fonts, but one only works in Internet Explorer and the other doesn't work on Netscape 6 or IE for the Mac. Also see *browser*, *download*, *font*, *HTML* and *web*.

Dynamic range ▸ Measured in dB, the difference between the loudest and the quietest sounds.

Early fringe ➤ Delineation of time made by the television broadcast media for the purposes of selling commercial time on the basis of audience size and demographics. Early fringe is the time period from 4.30 P.M. to 7:30 P.M. The name derives from the fact that the time period precedes prime time and is therefore on the early side (or fringe) of prime time. The cost of advertising in early fringe is less than in prime time, and the audience composition is similar (all-family). Thus, advertisers will purchase time in this segment in the hope of catching the prime-time viewer for less money than the cost of prime time. See also *daypart*.

Ear panels ➤ Boxed ads, which appear as a regular feature on the two top corners of front page of a newspaper. Such type of ads are also popularly known as ears. Also called *earpieces*.

Earpiece ➤ Device used by presenter to listen to instructions from the studio control room.

Earpieces ➤ Advertisements on either side of the mastheads, or centred title piece of a newspaper's page one. Also called *earpanels*

Ears ➤ (i) Curved projections of letters such as r,g. Also see *ear panels*.

Earth station ➤ The earth station comprises a dish and transmitter that can relay a high-frequency microwave signal. Some Earth stations, also called ground stations, can transmit and receive signals, while others can only receive signals.

Eastman colour ➤ Colour film rolls used for various filming acts, named after its inventor, Eastman.

E-book ➤ Both the software and the hardware of books that exist as digital computer files; also known as electronic book.

EBU ➤ European Broadcasting Union.

Echo ➤ Strictly a single or multiple repeat of an original sound. Generally refers to reverberation.

Echo plate or spring ➤ Device for artificially adding reverberation.

E-commerce ➤ Electronic commerce describes direct sale of goods and services through automatic processing of transactions by the use of information technologies, e.g. Internet.

Edit ➤ (i) To cut, check, rewrite and otherwise improve an article; (ii) To be an editor either of a whole magazine or of a section; (iii) Prepare copy for the press.

Edit controller ► The heart of a computerized tape editing system which is programmed to control the precise location of each edit.

Edit decision list (EDL) ► Essentially a list of editing instructions used by a high-end editing system to assemble the final tape from the original source material.

Edit switch ► A control which helps to improve the picture quality of dubbed material.

Editing (film) ► This is the name given to the complete process of putting an entire film together.

Editing (radio) ► Changing a radio recording after it has been made, usually by removing part of it. Editing can be achieved by splicing the tape, or else by dubbing selected portions.

Editing (video) ► It is a process of putting together the best of the shots of a story coverage. It is done electronically or digitally as the case may be. If the shooting has been done on a digital camera or videotape shots have been transferred onto a hard disc, the resulting editing will be non-linear and done digitally, not electronically. Only videotape shots (Beta or U-matic) are edited electronically. The purpose of edit-

ing shots and sounds is to give the resulting news item or similar output the look of a coherent hole.

Everything that goes on air must be edited. Only in exceptional circumstances when there is a late newsbreak and the bulletin is on the air with no time to edit the tape, it is better to air the unedited raw tape than no tape at all. But this mostly applies to hard stories involving no controversies – fire, accidents, flash floods, fall of a government, etc.

In a normal situation, a newswriter would quickly rewind the tape to spot the shots which are good – both journalistically and visually. A shot is visually good if it is steady, and not shaky because of camera movements caused by the cameraman changing his position for different shots.

In small newsrooms or stations, a reporter or Cameraman may be expected to do the editing job. But in big new programme production companies like TV Today, NDTV, and in networks like Doordarshan and Zee, news départments have editors whose sole job is to edit stories.

Editing block radio ► Specially shaped metal guide which holds tape in position during the cutting and splicing process.

Editing house ▸ Business specializing in the postproduction of film and videotape. After the actual shooting, an editing house will join the selected scenes together with *titles*, *opticals*, and *sound track*, as directed by the production company, to produce the finished product. Some editing houses that specialize in editing commercials will also duplicate the master copy and send the dubs to the various stations and networks on which the commercial is to appear.

Edition ▸ An issue of the paper prepared for a specific area; hence editionize, to prepare such a newspaper.

Editor ▸ The journalistic head of a newspaper, magazine, journal radio or TV newscast, etc., who is responsible for its news and editorial activity. This class of journalists are usually classified into Managing Editors, Executive Editors and Resident Editors. The Editor (Editor-in-Chief in case of one or more sister publications) has many a functionary to assist him, such as a News Editor, Assistant Editors, magazine Editor etc. The structure of functionaries, however, differs from paper to paper, depending upon their status or category.

Editorial ▸ A write-up, (also known as leader) usually done by the Editor, his deputy or assistant editor/editors. Unlike a news-story, it contains comments, usually on a current situation or development. The editorials usually reflect the policy of a particular newspaper or magazine; all non-advertising copy; department dealing with news.

Editorial alteration (EA) ▸ Change made to an accurately typeset copy at the request of the editorial staff. See also *printer's error, author, alteration.*

Editorial authority ▸ Medium generally considered to be very credible by its audience because of its high journalistic standards and continuing efforts to report honestly, accurately, and objectively. Sometimes, advertisers will compose advertisements in an editorial format (*advertorials*) for placement in media of this nature, in order to receive the same respect for their copy (and thus their product) as that enjoyed by the publication.

Editorial classification ▸ Arrangement of various departments of a magazine or newspaper according to editorial content, such as the news department, feature department, sports department, or business department.

Editorial copy ▸ All the reading matter in a publication that is not advertising. Editorial copy is written by the staff or contributing staff of the publication, whereas advertising copy is prepared by the advertiser or advertising company.

Editorial environment ► Philosophical environment in which the editorial content of a medium is created. This environment encompasses the philosophy of the medium's management and ownership as well as the talents and attitudes of the creative and editorial staff. many advertisers believe that the editorial environment of a medium will affect their advertising. Therefore, advertisers will carefully research the media to be sure of the appropriate vehicle for their product or service.

Editorialise ► Insert the reporter's opinion in what is meant to be an informative copy; Most newspapers and broadcast stations allow opinion in news analysis stories, columns and editorials.

Editorial judgement ► The professional philosophy which leads to decisions on programme content and treatment.

Editorial mention ►Promotional copy about a product that is inserted free of charge into a magazine because the editor feels it has some value to the reader relevant to the subject matter of the magazine. Editorial mentions are usually in-

cluded as part of a magazine "shopping section." Editorial mentions are written by the seller and submitted to various publications in the hope of being accepted.

Educational Broadcasting Corporation (EBC) ► Non-profit, nonpartisan organisation chartered by the New York Board of Regents (U.S.) and licensed by the Federal Communications Commission to operate WNET/Channel 13 in the public interest. In addition, EBC produces Programmes distributed by the Public Broadcasting Service (PBS) to noncommercial television stations in the U.S., Guam, and Puerto Rico. EBC depends on viewers, corporations, government, and its own revenues to achieve its mission of "producing and presenting quality television that educates, enlightens, and entertains." In 1972, the EBC absorbed the National Educational Television organization.

Educational channel ► Noncommerical television station that specializes in educational programmes for classroom or home use.

Educational television ► See *School television.*

Effective circulation ► Readership of a publication that is part of the advertiser's target market. Also see *circulation.*

Effects track ► Recording of sounds, used to simulate special conditions - for example, thunder, fire, screaming, sirens, and the like-in broadcast situations. See also *sound effects* (SFX).

EFP (electronic field production) ► See *ENG*.

Egyptian ► Type family distinguished by thick slab serifs and heavy main strokes; also known as '*antique*'.

Eight millimeter (8mm) ► One of several sizes of motion picture film. (The other sizes are 16mm and 35mm) Film size is determined by measuring the width of the film in millimeters. Eight-millimeter film is used primarily by amateur moviemakers for home movies. Some smaller station and production studios use super 8mm as a low-cost alternative to 16mm. Although super 8 is exactly the same as that used by amateurs, the equipment used is more sophisticated, thus producing satisfactory result for broadcast. However, because of its size, 8mm film has less production flexibility in terms of splicing and editing.

Electromagnetic pulse (EMP) ► A by-product of a nuclear explosion; a brief but intense burst of electromagnetic energy that can disrupt and destroy integrated circuits and related components.

Electromagnetic spectrum ► The entire collection of frequencies of elctromagnetic radiation that can be used for transmitting radio waves with electricity.

Electronic communications ► Any transfer of signs, signals, writings, images, sounds, or data transmitted via wire, radio, electromagnetic, photoelectronic or photo-optical systems.

Electronic Communications Privacy Act (ECPA) ► This act was passed (US) in 1986 to close some regulatory loopholes that existed in the Omnibus Crime Control and Safe Streets Act. This protects the acquisition of the contents of any wire, electronic, or oral communication via an electronic or mechanical devices.

Electronic mail (e-mail) ► Electronic messages or mail that can be relayed short distances (for example, over a LAN) or around the world. It can be sent from one person to another using a computer network (Internet or Internet). It can also be sent automatically to a large number of addresses.

Electronic media ► Mass media, which carry out transmission through electromagnetic waves, such as radio, television.

Electronic newspaper ► Recent invention which contains the facility of screening newspapers on television as and when required.

Electronic newsroom ▶ Newsrooms broadcast in many modern newspaper and broadcast officers where electronic devices like video display terminals and computers are used for reporting and writing news stories.

Electronic publishing ▶ Process of publishing material through electronic means, substituting the conventional means of publishing. The information is stored electronically on computers and the publication is carried out on video display units.

Electronic sources ▶ Sources that are in non-print media: radio, TV, Internet.

Electronic University ▶ An institution that offers courses via computer.

Elife stage of media development ▶ A phase in the evolution of media in which only the richest and the best educated members of the public make use of a particular medium, as with the first books, Internet connection or new brands of TV sets.

Ellipsis ▶ Omission of letters, words or sentences needed for complete sense. Normal practice to use dash(—) to denote omission of letters; line of dots (........) for omission of words; and line of stars (***********)

when whole sentences or verse are to be omitted.

Elrod ▶ Machine which casts rules, borders, spacing.

Em ▶ Unit of linear measurement, the square of any type size but usually the 12 pt. Em (zix to 1 in) also called a '*mutton*'.

E-mail ▶ See *electronic mail*.

Em dash ▶ Dash one em long.

Em quad ▶ Spacing unit; below type height, one em wide.

Embargo ▶ Time (often found on press releases) before which information should not be published. It is a request and is not mandatory. The system based on trust between source and media outlet. Some newspapers, however, have the habit of breaking embargoes and attracting considerable publicity (good and bad) in the process.

Emoticons ▶ Punctuation symbols used to show humor or emotions using ASCII characters.

Emotional appeal ▶ Type of advertising in which the copy is designed to stimulate one's emotions, rather than one's sense of the practical or impractical. They attempt to appeal to the consumer's psychological, social, or emotional needs. The copy is written to arouse fear, love, hate, greed, sexual desire, or humor, or otherwise create psychological tension that can best be resolved by purchase of the product or service. See also *fantasy commercial; fear appeal.*

En ► Half an em. Also see *em.*

Encoding ► Electronic circuitry which combines three colour signals into one composite video signal.

ENG (Electronic news gathering) ► A system using a light-weight camera or cameras which can feed pictures directly into TV transmission. Also known as Electronic Journalism.

English ► Old name for 14pt type. Double English is old name for 28pt.

Engraving ► Printing plate produced by engraver.

Enlightened self-interest ► The idea that if one does what is right for himself it will probably be right for the society at large in the long run.

Entertainment and Information Utility (US) ► A company that will deliver entertainment programming and information services. A precursor of such a system was Qube, a cable system in Columbus, Ohio.

Entrance ► A performer's movement into view or recognition on microphone.

EPD ► Electronic picture desk.

Equalization ('EQ') ► Changing the frequency response of a device (that is, which types of sound it responds to most) usually a microphone. A voice may be improved (made deeper or crisper) by equalization, but EQ controls should only be adjusted by the experienced.

Erasable optical disks ► A class of optical disk where data can be stored and erased.

Erase head ► The first head of a tape recorder which cleans the tape of any existing recording by exciting it with a high frequency signal. Consequently, the magnetic pattern on the tape is realigned.

Ergonomic design ► The philosophy of developing equipment and systems around people, making equipment conform to an operator's needs, and not the other way round.

Erratum ► Error discovered after printing: errata is plural of erratum.

ESS (electronic still store) ► A process whereby a single image or graphic can be stored on a video disc for newscasts.

Establishing shot ► A long shot or wide shot to orient viewer to the setting or situation. The shot usually comprises the main actors or newsmakers with easily identifiable background or location.

Etaoin shrdlu ► Letters on the first two vertical rows of linecasting machine. When deliberately set are a sign by operator that this is a line he intends to discard.

Ethernet ► A very common method of networking computers in a LAN. Ethernet will handle about 10,000,000 bits-per-second and can be used with almost any kind of computer. See also *bandwidth, LAN*.

Ethnic press ► Newspapers or magazines aiming at particular cultural groups, such as Hindus in the U.S.A.

ETV ► Eenadu TV, Satellite channel in Telugu; also educational television. See *school television*.

Eudora ► E-mail program available in Macintosh or IBM –compatible versions.

Euronews ► French-based international news provider.

Eurovision ► European international network for the exchange of television programmes.

Eurovision News Exchange (EVN) ► System for the daily exchange of news pictures through Eurovision links.

EUTELSAT ► European Telecommunications Satellite Organisation .

Excelsior ► (i) Old name for 3pt type. (ii) A newspaper published from Jammu (India).

Exclusive ► Story supposedly uniquely carried by newspaper. Vast number of stories in every newspaper would qualify for this description so should really be limited to few major stories. Description becomes devalued when attached to stories too frequently or when the same story is carried in other newspapers on the same day (as often happens) (see *scoop*).

Execute ► Computer command meaning to put into effect.

Executive producer ► The person who supervises newscast producers in a news department and ultimately is responsible for how each newscast looks on the air. This position is not found in smaller markets.

Exit ► A performer's movement out of view or microphone pickup.

Exp ► Expanded (of type).

Expert systems and Neural networks ► An expert system manipulates knowledge and can serve as an in-house expert in a specific field. It combines "book information" with the knowledge and experience of human experts. A neural network, for its part, simulates the way the brain processes information through its network of interconnecting neurons.

Explorer bar ► A pane that opens on the left side of windows, such as when you click the search button or Favorites button.

Exposure ► The process of exposing a camera chip to light. The degree of exposure is a product of the time for which each frame is exposed and the aperture setting of the lens. In video the time element is determined by the scan rate, which is controlled electronically (see Electronic shutter).

Extended, expanded ▸ typeface with width greater than normal.

External link ▸ A connection between a location in one document and a document within the same or another Web site.

External microphone ▸ A microphone which plugs into a socket on the side of a camcorder. External mics usually give better sound quality than built - in microphones.

External publication ▸ An organisational publication meant for its public outside the institution, as distinguished from a House journal or Internal publication.

Extra ▸ Extra or special supplement or edition; special item in a TV news programme, i.e. Star News extra.

Extra-condensed ▸ Exceptionally narrow typeface.

Extreme close-up (ECU) ▸ See *picture composition*.

Extreme long shot (ELS) ▸ See *picture composition*.

Eyebrow ▸ (US) Short line in smaller type, often underlined, above main deck of headline—other US terms: *teaser, highline, overline*; (UK) *strap*.

Eye camera ▸ Device used by researchers to measure and observe eye movements of respondents reading advertising copy.

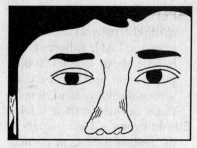

Extreme Close-Up (ECU)

Extreme Long Shot (ELS)

Eye cameras are used in copy testing to discern what parts of the copy attract attention. The eye camera also indicates the holding power of the sales message. This information helps the copywriter in placing headlines, and in making decisions about copy length and layout.

Eye light ▸ Lamp arranged to produce an attractive glitter in the subject's eyes.

Eye line ▸ The direction in which a subject is looking relative to the camera. It involves consideration not only of left-to-right orientation but also of height.

Eye witness reporting ▶Presence of reporter at news event can provide unique opportunities for writing descriptive, colourful copy.

Face ► (i) Engraved image which carries the ink to be impressed on the paper. (ii) Style of type used for printing - that is the typeface. See also **bold face,** *gothic, italic, sansserif, serif.* See *typeface.*

Facing matter ► An advertisement that is facing matter is one that is placed opposite editorial.

Facsimile ► Exact reproduction of the original. Also method of transmit`ting news pages by wire or radio waves for printing in second centre. Also called *fax.*

Fact file ► Listing of facts (often boxed) relating to story. Useful way of creating visual and copy variety on page.

Fact sheet ► An outline and/or list of titles or topics to be discussed on a programme. A background sheet or biography of a guest. Sometimes called a run down.

Fade ► A descrease in soune volume (fade down or out)

Fade in ► (i) Camera, editing or laboratory effect in which the image slowly disappears into darkness. (ii) An increase in sound volume (fade up).

Fade out ► (i) Where a picture fades out, usually to black or to white. (ii) Gradually bringing down the volume of an audio signal until it disappears.

Fader ► Volume control of a sound source used for setting its level, fading it up or down or mixing it with other sources. Also *'Pot'.*

Fair comment ► A defence to certain libel action based on permissible opinion or criticism.

Fair dealing ► The permitted use of copyright material.

Fair use ► Law that allows the copying of a work (e.g. book) for a noncommercial use. This is valid as long as the copying does not impinge on the business of that work.

Faithful   cheating ► See *Cutaways.*

Fake ► Falsified story.

Fake-colour process ► Manual colour-reproduction process that creates colour prints from a black-and-white photograph or drawing. Colour separations are created manually by an artist, who decides which colours should be used in each area of the original image. Fake-colour is less costly than true Four-Colour Process printing.

Faking ► Patching several photographs together for special effect.

Fall off ► The rate at which brightness diminishes over a surface. Gradual shading has a 'slow fall off' : coarse shading a 'fast fall off'.

Family ➤ All the type of any one design.

Fantasy commercial ➤ A type of commercial that uses special effects to create the idea of fantasy about the product, the technique of a fantasy commercial principally appeals to the emotions to rouse interest in the product. Here, the focus is the message itself, whereas in a testimonial commercial, the focus is the source of the message.

FAQ ➤ (frequently asked questions) FAQs are exactly what they sound like. They are documents that list and answer the most common questions on a particular subject. There are hundreds of FAQs on subjects as diverse as pet grooming and cryptography. FAQs are usually written by people who have tired of answering the same question over and again.

Fast shutter ➤ Also known as a high speed or electronic shutter. Camcorders normally record 50 pictures per second - equivalent to a shutter speed of 1/50 sec. Fast shutters electronically increase the shutter speed (sometimes up to 1/10,000 sec) to allow fast moving objects to be recorded without blur. However, the benefits of fast shutter can only be seen on video recorders equipped with good slow motion or frame advance facilities.

Favourite ➤ A link to a favourite Web page.

Fax ➤ Facsimile machine, capable of sending/receiving documents, scripts and news copy via a telephone line.

Fc ➤ Follow copy

FCC (Federal Communications Commission) ➤ One of the U.S. government's administrative agencies, charged with regulating interstate and foreign communications (broadcasting) in or from the United states.

FDDI (fiber distributed data interface) ➤ A standard for transmitting data on optical fiber cables at a rate of around 100,000,000 bits-per-second (10 times as fast as ethernet, about twice as fast as T-3). See also *bandwidth, ethernet, T-1, T-3.*

Fear appeal ➤ Advertising that attempts to create anxiety in the consumer on the basis of fear, so that the consumer is encouraged to resolve this fear by purchasing the product or service. For example, an advertisement may use people's fear of offending or of rejection to influence them to purchase personal products such as mouthwash or deodorant. Another example of fear appeal is an advertisement for life insurance that pictures a family devastated in a bus fire. See also *emotional appeal.*

Feature ➤ As distinct from news story it tends to be longer, carrying more background information, colour, wider range of sources and journalist's opinion can be prominent, e.g. column on politics or economy. As verb, to display prominently or emphasize. Also see *story types*.

Feature film ▸ A feature film usually portrays non-real life situations with entertainment as its chief motive, as distinguished from the documentaries, which document real life event, person, places or situations.

Feature opener ▸ Informally written introduction to a soft news story designed more to arouse curiosity and to entertain than to inform.

Feature syndicates ▸ News organisations which offer articles, features, etc. on contemporary and current affairs including entertainment to the media.

Features files ▸ Collection of information about items for possible future news coverage.

Featurize ▸ To play up an interesting or unusual angle of a story rather than rely on the usual straight news approach that deals with five W's.

Feed ▸ A feed is a transmission of a story or even a raw tape to a station from its own reporter, another station or any other source via a special telephone live, microwave hook up or a satellite. In India such feeds are normally through the govern-ment telecom network or through OB Vans (out Broadcasting Vans using microwaves to transmit their signals to the nearest TV station). For example, Delhi Doordarshan Kendra can receive the feed from its O.B. Van stationed near Parliament to air a live telecast of the confidence motion put up by the government. Even if there is no live telecast, the use of OB Vans to receive the feed of a required videotape saves a lot of time that would have been spent in physically reaching the tape to the nearest station.

Feedback ▸ (i) In video, effect created when the camera is focused on its own monitor. This will produce a series of random patterns on the television screen. (ii) In audio, sound effect created whenever a microphone is held too close to its monitor speakers. At low levels, the sending of the audio signal back on itself in this way will produce an echo effect, which is sometimes used by recording artists to add another dimension to a recording. At higher levels or when uncontrolled, feedback will produce a loud noise or howl. (iii) Response (from colleagues/public) to a journalist's copy. Also see *howl-round*.

Feeder ▸ Mechanism that automatically feeds paper to the printing press. Feeders may handle individual sheets of paper or continuous forms.

Feedspool ➤ Tape recorder spool which supplies the tape to the recording head (As opposed to 'take-up' spool).

Fibre-optic ➤ Cable system composed of hollow fibres which carry light. Pulses of light are converted into information. Fibre-optic cables are used to carry telephone calls, computer data and TV signals.

Fiber-optic line (FO) ➤ A hair-thin glass fiber that can handle information ranging from voice to video. An FO line has a wide channel capacity and a superior transmission capability.

Fidelity ➤ Accuracy with which an electronic recording device can reproduce the original sound or image. The primary value of all recording equipment lies in the exactness of its ability to reproduce the original sounds and / or images (in comparison, of course, to its price).

Field ➤ Half of a complete TV picture. Two field and when interlaced combine to make one frame.

Field producer ➤ Editorial supervisor of off-base assignment. See also *Fixer*.

Fifth colour ➤ An extra colour, often day-glo or metallic, used to create a striking effect beyond the means of the normal four-colour process. Often used on covers.

Figure of eight ➤ See *bi-directional*.

File ➤ (i) Send a report, (ii) document stored electronically on computer. (iii) A programme or document stored on a disk. Also see *document*.

File allocation table (FAT) ➤ A method used by operating systems to keep track of where files are stored on a hard disk. See also *defragmentation; file sytem*.

File bridge ➤ Editorial / camera team assigned at short notice to cover news breaks, usually abroad.

File footage ➤ This is an archival footage from the news department's own library or borrowed from some one else's library (see Fig.). It might have been first used a day, a month or even years before. A file footage is used to illustrate a news dealing with some background information. It is mandatory to inform the viewers about the use of file footage so that they do not mistake it for current footage. This is done by supering

File Footage

the newstory with 'Library', 'File Pictures', 'News File', 'Archives', etc. Another way to simple label the date or month: 'July 15, 1997', June 27, 1997', 'Last Autumn', 'Last Sunday', and so on.

Files ► Back issues; library clippings/cuttings are also 'on file'.

File system ► The overall structure in which files are named, stored, and organized by the operating system. For example, MS - DOS and earlier version of Windows use the FAT 16 file system. Windows 98 can use the FAT 16 or FAT 32 file system.

Filename ► the name given to a computer document.

Files transfer protocol (FTP) ► The process that allows a user to transfer files to and from remote sites or the internet.

Fill ► To rewrite a piece of type, whether a heading, standfirst, caption or body text, to fit a given space.

Filler ► A short story, usually of one or two parts. Filling in space when a longer story runs short(also known as brief); second-string items used as make weights to bring a bulletin or programme up to length.

Fill light ► A light originating from the opposite side of the key light; it removes some of the shadows produced by the key light.

Film ► (i) Material produced by image setting machines and color separation equipment and used to make printing plates. (ii) Strip of plastic or celluloid with a silver emulsion high-sensitive coating, available in a wide variety of formats and used for the production of photographs, motion pictures, or television *video* (vedio film). In television production, a difference of opinion exists among producers and directors as to whether film is better than videotape. Those who favour film feel it offers greater creative capabilities, with a softer, more glamorous quality to the image. In addition, although film requires processing time, filming equipment is quite compact, as well as durable and highly reliable. (iii) Use film to record an event, performance, entertainment, or the like. (iv) Colloquially, used for movie.

Film clip ► Short *footage* that has been clipped from a longer reel of film and then inserted into another film, or shown by itself to a live audience or used as part of another programme or performance. For example, a documentary about the World War II that uses film clips of the actual detention camps is more authentic and should have greater impact than one that simulates these scenes. Film clips are commonly used in instructional or educational programmes and in news or documentary productions where the location or the activity cannot be duplicated or re-created in the studio or where such re-creation would lessen the effect or reality of the production. Also called *film sequence*.

Film I.D. ▸ Notation ("Film") marked on a container or on a broadcast schedule that identifies a filmed programme or commercial, as distinguished from taped or live programmeming.

Film library ▸ (i) Collection of films. Often, a film studio's film library is a valuable asset to the studio because the films in the collection can be marketed individually or in packages to television stations or networks for a considerable profit. Film libraries are generally maintained by production companies, film owners or advertising agencies. (ii) Place where a collection of films is housed. These films are used for viewing (and sometimes production, as in stock footage - see *stock shot*), but they are not for sale.

Film pick-up ▸ Transmission of film over the airwaves as compared to transmission of a live performance or situation. For example, a programme may be a film pickup. Both types of

transmission may appear in televised news programmes.

Film print ▸ Reproduction of a film used for distribution to movie theaters, television stations, or the like.

Film sequence ▸ Segment of a programme or performance that appears on film. *See also film clip.*

Filmset type ▸ Photoset type (as used in paste-up pages).

Film speed ▸ Indication of the amount of light needed to maximize the reproduction capability of film. Fast film is very sensitive to light and therefore can be used in situations where there is not a high level of illumination. Slow film, on the other hand, has a lower sensitivity to light and therefore needs a high level of illumination to produce an image. While fast film offers greater flexibility to the photographer, the resulting image will have a grainy quality, whereas slower film will produce a higher - quality picture. Film speed is expressed as an ISO number, which refers to an internationally standardized exposure index that utilizes a numerical scale as a method of rating film; the higher the ISO number, the faster the film.

Film strip ▸ Film that looks like motion picture film but is actually a series of *slides* spliced together and shown sequentially in still projectors designed exclusively for this purpose. Typically, filmstrips are used as speech supports in speaker presentations or as visual aids in company training Programmes.

Film transfer ► Transfer of *videotape* to *film* using equipment designed for this purpose. Film transfers must be done for television stations lacking facilities for videotape broadcasting. The process of transferring film to tape is called a *tape transfer*.

Filter ► (i) Disk of coloured glass or gelatine which fits over the lens. It is used to cut down particular wavelengths in the light entering the camera or to create special effects. (ii) Device used to reduce or alter sound, such as one that makes ordinary speech sound as if it were being spoken into - stadium or *filer microphone*.(iii) Electrical circuitry for removing unwanted frequencies from a sound source, e.g. mains hum, or surface noise from an old or worn recording. Also in drama for simulating telephone or two-way radio quality, etc.

Final print ► "Ready-for-air" product, that is the final stage in the film production process. The final print is the competed work after client approval and detail corrections (such as *colour correction* or *synchronization*) have been achieve. It is

from this print that duplicates are made

Finger ► An Internet software tool for locating people on other Internet sites. Finger is also sometimes used to give access to non-personal information, but the most common use is to see if a person has an account at a particular Internet site. Many sites do not allow incoming Finger requests.

Fingernails ► (US) Slang for brackets.

Finish ► Surface texture of paper. There are many types of finishes, including coated or uncoated, dull glossy, and smooth or textured. Smoothness is important for the high-quality *halftone* print for which glossy coated paper is most often used; generally, the smaller the halftone dots, the smoother the finish required. Textured paper with a ribbed, leather like or textile like surface is popular for stationery and book covers. Uncoated or rough-finish paper is usually used for offset lithography printing.

Fire ► To start a piece of audio, especially on cartridge.

Fireman ► Person sent out from newspaper's headquarters to cover major story (either at home or abroad).

Firewall ► A barrier (a computer programme) typically placed between your computer network (LAN) and the outside world to prevent unauthorised entry.

First generation copy ► A copy taken from the original recording. A copy of this copy would be a second generation copy.

First proof ► First pull of a setting after line-casting which is read from copy. It is then corrected and reproofed as 'clean'.

First rights ► The rights to publish an article once in Britain. This is the standard commission, unless the writer agrees otherwise.

Fisheye lens ► Extreme wide - angle lens, giving a circular image.

Fishpole ► Hand-held sound boom. See *boom mike*.

Fit ► When text or picture does not overrun (bust) its allotted space

Fit-up ► Artwork involving several elements jointed together.

Five W's and one H ► The basic questions that a news report must address to: what, when, who, where, why and how.

Fixed direct costs ► Costs incurred in production but not proportionate to the volume of production.

Fixer ► Co-ordinator accompanying the production unit in the field. Often acts as the main point of contact between home / base and team on location.

Flag ► (i) Notation placed on a hard-copy or computer file record that marks it for special handling or indicates that some action has occurred, such as selection of the record for a mailing test panel. (ii) Title or logotype of a publication printed on the cover page, such as "A&M" for "the magazine of advertising and management professionals". (iii) Graphic device used on package labels and other promotional pieces to highlight a brief message such as "30 off regular price." Also called *pointer*. (iv) Sheet of metal placed in front of a lamp to block light off a specific area. (v) A piece of paper or *slug* inserted in galley of type to remind printers that a correction, or insert, is required at that point.

Flagship ► Typically the first or the largest or the most prestigious paper in a newspaper group or *chain*.

Flame ► Originally, flame meant to carry forth in a passionate manner in the spirit of honorable debate. Flames most often involved the use of flowery language and flaming well was an art form. More recently flame has come to refer to any kind of derogatory comment no matter how witless or crude. See also *flame war*.

Flame war ► This refers to a situation when an online discussion degenerates into a series of personal attacks against the debators, rather than discussion of their positions. A heated exchange. See also *flame*.

Flannel panel ► The magazine's master head, including its address, telephone numbers, staff box and copyright notice.

Flare ► Light deflected from any bright highlight into a darker area of the frame. It may be caused by mechanical or optical defects, but usually it is generated by the sun shining onto the front element of the lens.

Flash ► (i) Urgent, brief message on wire service announcing big story, e.g. FLASH, PAKISTANI INTRUDERS TO WITHDRAW, (ii) A design device in computer to draw attention; used mostly in designing a web page.

Flash card ► Solid-state recording medium

Flash exposure ► (i) Photograph taken with the aid of a sudden bright light, produced by a flash bulb, that better illuminates the object to be shot. (ii) Second exposure to light of a *halftone* photographic *negative* to darken the dots in shadow areas. Flash exposures are frequently necessary to achieve the desired.

Flashback ► (i) A story or picture taken from a past issue. (ii) Theatrical technique used in dramatic presentations where the chronological sequence of events is interrupted by a scene recalling an event or occurrence from an earlier time; also called *cutback*. Flashback technique is

often used effectively in television advertisements, for example in a commercial for a refrigerator where a housewife flashes back to a time when she had to cook twice a day and was always short of time for movies, etc.

Flatbed press ► Small, mostly old-time, press that prints from a flat surface, i.e. not rotary.

Flat plan ► A single-sheet plan (on paper or screen) showing all newspaper pages with advertisement position. It is an essential tool for planning.

Flat proof ► In *letterpress* printing, a *proof* pulled before the *print plate* has been processed to print evenly (makeready processes). The flat proof is proofread to check the accuracy of the copy and the overall look of the printed piece. the copy will be spotty in some areas and heavy in other, making the proof a poor 0-qualty reproduction. However, it is necessary to pull a flat proof, because the makeready process is time- consuming and costly, and, therefore, all elements of the copy must be checked for accuracy and appearance before continuing the printing process.

Flats ► Boards used as a backdrop to the set.

Fleet Street ► (UK) National Newspapers as a collective group are known by this name though most newspapers have dispersed from this street in east London between the Strand and St Paul's cathedral.

Fletcher-Munson effect ▶ The apparent decrease in the proportion of higher and lower frequencies, with respect to the middle range, as the loudspeaker listening level is decreased. Significant in correct setting of monitoring level, particularly in music balance.

Flier ▶ Advertising medium that is usually a single, standard-size (8.5" X 11") page printed on one or both sides with a advertising message; also, *flyer*. Fliers are most often used in direct-mail advertising and as *handbills* given to customers by local retailers. Fliers offer market coverage at low cost with little waste and good flexibility; have a high throwaway rate.

Flimsy ▶ Thin-paper carbon copy of a story.

Flip wipe ▶ See *wipe*.

Float ▶ Addressing procedure that "right justifies" (aligns along the right edge) each line of *copy* for a neat look. See also *justify*.

Flood ▶ General term for soft light source. Also adjustment of a spotlight to provide a wide light beam (hence 'fully flooded').

Floor monitor (TV Monitor) ▶ High quality *picture monitor*, used in studio to check shots, display film and videotape, show studio output, etc. It has no sound channel.

Floor plan ▶ A plan of the studio floor and set showing the walls, the main doors and the location of the control room.

Floor stand ▶ (i) In adverting freestanding rack, frame, or mount used by retailers for merchandise in a point -of- purchase advertising display. (ii) In TV production, device used for mounting lights that stand on the studio floor and Easel used for holding title cards or graphics to be displayed on camera.

Floppy disk ▶ Flexible disk used for storage of information on computers

Flowchart ▶ Diagrammatic representation of a system or process utilizing various symbols connected by arrows showing the step-by-step sequence. Flowcharts are universally used in the design of computer systems and programmes and may also be used to describe manual processes. For example, a very simplified diagrame of the conversion of hard-copy information to magnetic tape is as follows:

Document → Process → Tape

A more sophisticated flowchart would describe the "process" with a series of symbols that fully represent every step in the process.

Fluff ➤ An error in speaking, usually in pronunciation on TV/Radio. (ii) Accumulation of dust on the stylus of gramophone pic-up.

Flush ➤ To set type even with the column rule or margin, on either left or right. A 'flush left' head has all the lines ranging evenly on the left.

Flush (left or right) ➤ Copy in which each line is *"left justified"* or *"right justified,"* so that the characters are aligned evenly along the left or right edge. Virtually all copy is set flush left and with either left-side *identations* to mark the beginning of a paragraph (paragraph ident), or additional spacing between paragraphs. See also *ragged left or right*.

Flush cover ➤ Cover of a catalogue or book that is the same size as the pages, forming an even edge. Most softcover books, brouchures, magazines, and catalogues are inexpensively covered with a flush cover made from a slightly heavier paper stock than that used for the pages. Very wide hardcover books are given flush covers because it keeps them from sagging when they are set upright on a shelf.

Flush paragraph ➤ Copy that is set completely flush left, even at the start of each paragraph, without any indentations. Extra space must be left between paragraphs so that the beginning and end of each paragraph is clearly defined. See also *flush Left or flush right*.

Flutter ➤ A fault in recorded sound producing a gurgling effect on speech, usually caused by unsteadiness in the sound recorder or reproducer.

Flying paster ➤ Printing press mechanism that automatically pastes a new roll (*web*) of paper to the end of an almost exhausted rol while the press continues to run; also called automatic paster. The paster speeds up the printing process and reduces paper waste.

Fly-on-the-wall (Verite) ➤ Documentary style unmediated by reporter or narrator. The camera watches the action unnoticed, like a fly on the wall.

FM ➤ (Frequency modulation) Converting of signals into high frequency bands to wipe off usual disturbances. Thus FM is chracterised by a more faithful reproduction of sound.

F-number/f-stop ➤ Term denoting lens aperture.

Focal length ➤ The distance between the lens and the camcorder chip when a very distant object is brought into focus. Different lenses are usually described by their focal lengths; a greater focal length will give a larger image while shot lenses have a wide 'angle of view.

Focus ➤ (i) Point where light rays coverage to produce an image that is clear and sharp in definition. (ii) See a clear and distinct image. (iii) Subject or issue that is the centre of attention, as in a focus group. (iv) Concentration on the identity of a magazine.

Focus feature ➤ A label sometimes used for ad-get features.

Focus group ➤ (i) A small group of readers and potential readers assembled for research purposes; (ii) key editorial staff in some magazine or newspaper houses.

Focus in ➤ Bring a scene into focus by beginning with the camera totally out of focus, so that the picture appears as little more than a blur, and slowly coming in on the scene until the image becomes clear. See also *focus out*.

Focusing ➤ Altering the distance between the lens and the chip until a sharp image is obtained.

Focus out ➤ Refer to slowly defocusing the camera so that the pictures goes from a clear, sharply defined image to little more than a blur. To focus out will produce a dreamy quality that can be used effectively to show changes in time or place or to suggest an altered perception such as an hallucination. See also *focus in*.

Focus zone ➤ Camcorder auto focus systems usually focus on whatever is at the centre of the picture. This is the focus zone. Some models have two zone systems for greater accuracy and to minimise "hunting " in awkward situations.

Fog ➤ Photographic defect caused by a deposit of silver on the image areas creating a cloudy area. It is caused by incorrect exposure of the film or by a poorly balanced chemical developing solution. Photographs with fog are usually discarded, except when needed for special effect.

Fog filter ➤ Special effect filter which diffuses the image while retaining sharpness.

Fold ➤ (n). Point at which the newspaper is folded horizontally during printing. Commonly 'below the fold' means, in a broad sheet 22 inches deep, any point below 11 inches. *Folder* is a device which does this job.

Foldback ➤ Means of allowing artists in the studio to hear programme elements via a loudspeaker even while studio microphones are live.

Folder ➤ (i) Heavy printed sheet folded usually into four to ten folds. The folder or the brochure is prepared usually on a single topic. (ii) Metaphor for an area on a computer where individual files (and other folders) are stored.

Folio ► (i) A magazine for people in the magazine industry, published monthly by Hansen Publishing. It covers all aspects of magazine publishing from editorial to fulfillment. Folio also holds or sponsors several conferences and seminars each year. (ii) Page numbers of a book or catalogue, often placed at the outside top of a page. Right-handed pages are usually odd-numbered; left-handed pages are even-numbered. A drop folio is a page number printed at the bottom of a page; brouchure, magazine, or catalog comprised of signatures and consisting of four pages printed onto one sheet of paper that is folded once, forming two leaves with four surfaces or pages. (iii) Sheet of 17" x 22" paper. (iv) (Colloquial) book with exceptionally large pages.

Folio line ► Technically, line at top of page carrying page number, but generally now means inside page line carrying page number, name of newspaper, and date.

Follow ► (US) Story that follows up a first day story to report new developments. See *story types*.

Follow copy ► Instruction to printer to set copy exactly as written despite apparent errors.

Following focus ► The technique of keeping a moving subject constantly in focus.

Follow up ► To seek new information on an earlier story; a story that takes an earlier story further. Also see *story types*.

Folo ► Abbreviation for follow. Usual use is to mark related news story 'folos President' meaning it should be added to end of the President story.

Foner/Phoner ► Tape recorded telephone interviews are called Foners/phoners. Phoners are done with the express permission of the interviewee. This is done especially when there is a late night news break. For example, the BBC World doing the phoner of a New Delhi based journalist Pran Chopra on bomb explosion in a train on a remote station in Assam. If the newsroom has the picture of the interviewee in its library, it can show him in split frame (half of TV screen) while the other half showing the electronically generated version (super or tittle) of the interview to make its content more clear to the audience, just in case the phoner is having some noise.

Font ► Typographer's name for the complete selection of type of one size and face. A font will include all 26 letters in the alphabet (including uppercase and lowercase as well as small caps), the numbers from 0 through 9, punctuation marks, and some commonly used symbols, such as the ampersand (&) and dollar sign ($).

Footage ▸ (i) In newsroom, this means nothing more than a videotaped news or event or location. Suppose you missed the President's speech, and now you phone your friend in a different network and ask: "Hey Vijay, have you got the footage of the President's speech?" This term is hold over from FILM which was increased in feet. (ii) The raw material with which the editor works. It is a general name given to the processed images, either on video tape that has a recording on it, or on exposed and chemically developed film. It is packaged in different ways.

Foot candle ▸ A unit of illumination, the amount of light produced by one candle one foot away from a portion of an object.

Footer ▸ A line, often including the magazine's name, that appears at the bottom of every page.

Footprint ▸ The area of the earth over which a given satellite signal can be received.

Forgetting rate ▸ In media research, measurement of the rate at which memory of advertising is lost from one advertising period to another without continued reinforcement. This rate can be very important in planning advertising strategies. In one experiment, two randomly chosen groups of women were mailed thirteen different magazine advertisements for an ingredient food. One group received one advertisement a week for thirteen weeks; the other group received the same thirteen advertisements at intervals of four weeks throughout the year. The retention in the first group decreased steadily, and by the last week, there was almost no recall, reflecting a high forgetting rate. The second group, on the other hand, showed strong retention of the advertising over the year, and although memory rate fell between mailings, it never fell below the level of awareness of the preceding mailing. Overall, it reflected almost no forgetting rate.

Form ▸ (i) In direct mail, order document, letter, invoice, or renewal notice that constitutes a mailing package component. They are usually computer-printed continuous forms. (ii) In merchandising, physical state of a product such as solid, liquid, or aerosol. (iii) In printing, set of type or film elements enclosed in a metal chase (frame) and ready for printing.

Format ▸ (i) Style or content of the material aired by a radio station, such as all news, country-western music, or rock-and-roll music; also called *personality*. Other common formats include classical music, easy-listening music, talk shows, general interest programmes, or special interest broadcasts, such as religious or Hindi-language programmes. The programme format is part of the context in which an advertising message is received and effects how the message is perceived. See also *Communication*. (ii) Style or content of a television programme, such as variety show, talk show, game show, situation comedy, police drama, and so forth. (iii) General design of an original or printed image or of a completed print product, such as the arrangement of elements on a page or the size and shape of a newspaper or magazine or book. (See also *composition*, *graphic design*, *layout*); page size expressed in terms of the number of pages per signature, usually in multiples of four. (iv) Videotape size or recording pattern. (v) Any preset instruction programmed into a computer.

Formating ▶ (i) Conversion of computer file elements to a different format for processing on a different system, such as the rearrangement of fields in each record or the conversion of a magnetic tape file to labels for mailing. (ii) Preparation of a floppy disk as required for the software with which it will be used. See also *format*.

Forme ▶ Combination of type, blocks, etc., locked up in a *chase* and ready to go to press or to the foundry for duplicating.

Formula broadcasting ▶ Adopting of peculiar, stereotype or typical type of broadcasting programmes with run-of-the-mill stuff to attract and keep a large number of viewers or listeners captive. The formula is also known as excessive generality.

Fotog ▶ Slang for Photographer.

Fototype ▶ (Trademark) brand of specific fonts imprinted on individual pads of white cardboard, with characters that can be peeled off separately and mounted as original copy to be reproduced by any printing process. Fototype is used when there is not a lot of type matter in the copy as a way of economizing, because it eliminates the need for a compositor. However, when the body copy is extensive, this becomes a false economy, because the individual fototype characters must be hand set, which can become a tedious and time-consuming process.

Foul copy ▶ Copy so heavily corrected and marketed it is difficult to follow.

Foul proof ▶ Proof set aside by the compositor (usually spiked) after he has made the corrections marked on it; proof containing errors, so not to be used for sending corrections to printer.

Foundry ► Printing plant that produces printing plates called electrotypes or stereotypes and utilizes them for the printing of books and magazines in a duplication process called the electrolytic process. A foundry also produces metal type character (called foundry type), which can be sold to compositors and printers, and are set by hand. With the advancement of technology, foundry has become obsolete since there now exist faster and more economical methods for duplication.

Foundry proof ► Proof pulled from original type matter and engravings before the electrolytic process of duplication (which can only be done in a foundry). Foundry proof is kept in the files as a record of the original copy. The foundry proof is characterized by heavy black borders made by the foundry rule, a piece of metal placed around the page to keep it in place during the process of making the electrotype. With technological advances in printing this entire process has become obsolete.

Fount ► (i) All the characters of any one typeface in any one size needed for a piece of printing; pronounced 'font'. Also see *font*. (ii) Pronounced 'font' and sometimes written that way, mean typeface. See *font*.

Fountain solution ► (i) Dampening solution used in *lithography* to keep the nonimage areas of the plate from holding ink. Since *offset* lithographic plates have a smooth surface, in contrast to *printing plates* with a raised (relief) or recessed surface, the nonadherence of ink to the nonimage areas of lithographic plates must be chemically controlled. The fountain solution is applied at intervals throughout the printing process as it depletes. The solution is stored in a device called an ink fountain, which automatically applies solution to the plate. (ii) Ink stored in an ink fountain on the printing press for automatic application to the image carrier i.e. plate.

Four-colour process ► Halftone printing process utilizing four ink colours (Black, Magenta, Cyan, Yellow) to produce a printed image that matches the colouring of the original image. Four-colour process printing is more expensive than two-colour printing but has a greater impact on the viewer. It is accomplished by creating a *colour separation* for each of the three primary colours perceived by the human eye; blue, red, and green. The image is photographed through blue, red, and green colour filters, producing a negative for each colour that effectively blocks out that colour. The red filter produces a cyan positive; the green filter, a magenta positive; the blue filter, a yellow positive. The three positives are combined to produce a preliminary print that requires the addition of black and variations in the primary colour proportions to achieve the desired effect. Four-colour process is used in gravure, letterpress, offset, and screen printing. See also *colour correction; duplicating film; progressive proofs; two-colour process.*

Fourth Estate ► A term supposedly coined by the English orator and Parliamentarian Edmund Burke (1729-1797) and mentioned by Thomas Carlyle (1795-1881), English prose-writer and philosopher in his 'Heroes and Hero-Worship" (1841). During debate in Parliament, Burke (according to Carlyle) referred to the Press Gallery and said, ":Younder sits the Fourth Estate, more important than all." The other three Estates at that time were the Lords Spiritual (the Church), Lords Temporal (the Nobility) and the Commons. The term is a measure of the importance and influence of the press in modern society.

Fourth-generation-telecast syndrome ► See *dubbing*.

Fragmentation ► Refers to rapid increase in the number of titles, channels or services in any given medium, such as newspapers, radio or television.

Frame ► (v) In Internet, a smaller window (or pane) within the browser window containing a separate *HTML* document. Frames can have separate backgrounds, sizes, or locations, and can scroll.

Frame advance ► A feature which enables a sequence to be analysed frame by frame. Useful for editing.

Frame (film) ► (i) When you physically examine a piece of exposed and processed movie film it is fundamentally the same as the film which has been processed after exposure in a normal still camera. It has the image either in positive or negative, square sprocket holes down one or both sides and numbers which identify each individual exposed picture image or frame. In film 24 frames are produced per second.

Frame (video) ► (ii) In video it is a complete TV picture made up of two fields interlaced except that you cannot see the frames, or the numbers down the edge, and there are no sprocket holes. In video reproduction, 30 frames are produced per second.

Frame (video/film) ► (iii) Outline of a TV or motion picture sireen used by the director to dertermine which elements to include or exclude when settling a scene - "to frame a shot."

Frame (newspaper) ➤ (iv) The adjustable easel at which paste-up pages are made up from photoset and photographic elements.

Frame/picture/stills store ➤ Electronic method of storing and displaying still pictures.

Franchise ➤ (i) License granted by a company (the franchisor) to an individual or firm (the franchisee) to operate a retail, food, or drug outlet where the franchisee agrees to use the franchisor's name; products; services; promotions; selling, distribution, and display methods; and other company support. NIIT, McDonald's, Midas, and Lee are all examples of franchise operations. (ii) Right to market a company's goods or services in a specific territory, which right has been granted by the company to an individual, group of individuals, marketing group, retailer, or wholesaler. (iii) Specific territory or outlet involved in such a right. (iv) Right of an advertiser to exercise an option to sponsor a television or radio show, as well as the granting of such a right by the broadcast medium (as "to exercise a franchise" or "to grant a franchise"). (v) Right granted by a local or state government to a cable television operator to offer cable television service in a community.

Free circulation ➤ Readership of a periodical obtained by sending copies free of charge to the customers of a business organization. Also see *circulation*.

Free line-fall ➤ (US) Ragged right setting of text type; also called unjustified setting.

Free perspective ➤ Design in which normal perspective has been exaggerated in order to enhance the impression of depth in a shot.

Free puff ➤ News item which publicises an event or product.

Free sheets ➤ Newspapers that rely solely on advertising income and are given free to readers.

Freebie ➤ Range of services and entertainment (e.g. drinks, meals, trips abroad funded by government/ tourist organization, tickets to concerts) provided free to journalists. Some journalists believe acceptance of freebies compromises "objectivity" and refuse to accept them.

Freelance ➤ Journalist contributing to several media outlets and not on permanent staff of any one organization (increasingly a euphemism for unemployed). Freelancer in US/India.

Freelancer ➤ American term for *freelance*.

Freestanding insert ► Advertising material in a variety of formats, including broadsides or multiple-page booklets, enclosed in a newspaper (particularly the Sunday edition); also called freestanding stuffer. The advertisement is called freestanding because it is not printed by nor is it a part of the newspaper. The newspaper distributor will generally charge a fee for including the inserts.

Free-to-air ► Television or radio broadcasting services funded entirely by the state exchequer TV licence fee or advertising, with no additional fees paid by the audiences.

Freeze-frame ► Effect produced on videotape where the action on the screen appears to stop. The freeze-frame is achieved by continually repeating the same video frame. On film this effect is called a stop motion.

French flag ► Opaque panel which is used to deflect direct light from the camera lens or to shade part of the action,

French fold ► Method of folding a sheet of paper that is printed on one side only, so that the printed side shows and the unprinted side does not. The result is a four-page folder. French folds are most often used for printed invitations or announcements.

Frequency ► (i) Wavelength allocations made by a competent authority (Federal Communications Commission in the U.S,; Prasar Bharti in India) for broadcasting, including radio stations, television chaannels, amateur radio (ham) operators, citizens' band radios, police radios, and the like. See also *meghahertz*. (ii) In general, number of times something occurs within a specified period of time. Frequency may refer to the issues of a periodical, the purchases made by a customer over time, or the number of times a commercial is aired.

Frequency channel ► Describes area on the *electromagnetic spectrum* used for broadcast transmission. Digital transmission allow a single frequency to carry several programmes while analogue allows only one programme per frequency channel.

Frequency distortion ► Distortion caused by inadequate frequency response.

Frequency radio ► Expressed in cycles per second or hertz, the rate at which a sound or radio wave is repeated. The note 'middle A' has a frequency of 440 Hz. A long-wave transmitter with a wavelength of 1500 metres has a frequency of 200 kHz (200000 cycles per second). Frequency and wavelength are always associated in the formula $F \times W = speed$. Speed is the speed of the wave, i.e. sound or radio, and, in each case, remains constant.

Frequency Rate ➤ At which a sound or light wave or an electronic impulse passes a given point over a specific time. See Hertz.

Frequency response ➤ The ability of a piece of equipment to treat all frequencies within a given range in the same way, e.g. an amplifier with a poor frequency response treats frequencies passing through it unequally and so its output does not faithfully reproduce its input.

Fringe area ➤ Listening or viewing area on the periphery of broadcast reception for a particular radio or television station. For example, the outlying regions of Rohtak in Haryana may be a fringe area for the New Delhi television stations.

From High-8 to Beta Mastering: in Doordarshan, apparently because of accessibility problems, some of the private producers used to shoot their commissioned programmes partly or fully on Semi-professional (Hi-8) or no professional (VHS) tapes. Then they transferred these onto U-matic taper for editing purposes. Thus the second generation tape becomes a raw material for making the final copy, which in fact, is now the third generation. A good number of producers were in the habit of keeping this third generation final copy with themselves as the producer's copy and submit its dubbed version that is the Telecast Copy with Doordarshan. You must be by now scratching your head and pressed your memory buttons into action to calculate the latest generation! Well, it was the fourth generation that was shown to you!

From the top ➤ An expression meaning to start at the beginning.

Front cover ➤ Front outside cover of a magazine that states the name of the magazine and the date of issue, and sometimes indicates editorial content; also called *first cover*. In Indian consumer magazines, this cover is usually not sold for advertising space.

Front of book ➤ Section of a magazine ("book") that comes before the main editorial content of the magazine. Although advertising space rates are usually the same throughout the book, most advertisers prefer to have their advertisements placed in the front of the book. Therefore, many magazines charge a premium to guarantee a front-of-book position.

Front projection ➤ Where pictures are projected from in front of the newsreader on to a screen alongside.

FST (Flatter Squarer Tube) ► A TV screen that gives a flatter display than conventional TV picture tubes.

F-stop ► Short for fixed stops; the calibration of the lens, indicating the aperture, or diaphragm opening (and therefore the amount of light transmitted through the lens). The larger the F-stop number, the smaller the aperture; the smaller the F-stop number, the larger the aperture. Film speed ans shulter speed also impact the exposure of the film.

FTP ► An acronym for File Transfer Protocol. It's the tool you would use to transfer files through the Internet from one computer to another. For example, you would use an FTP to upload your web page from where you built it (like your computer at home) to a web site so that all of your friends and neighbors can look at it.

Fudge ► Part of the front or back page of a newspaper where late news is printed from a separate cylinder 'on the run', sometimes called the 'stop press', i.e. the presses are stopped so that the late news can be fudged in.

Full-cover display ► This refers to an agreement between magazine publishers and retail newsstand dealers that their magazines will receive preferential and prominent display position on the news-stand in return for a retail display allowance (RDA) of say 7% to 11%. The adherence to this agreement is almost impossible to enforce. In many cases, there is an unspoken agreement that the RDA is really being paid to provide an incentive to the dealer for allocating space to that magazine. This incentive has become necessary as the cost of retail space increases and the profit margin on magazines (particularly for newsstand dealers at airports and railway stations) declines.

Fullface ► Old term for boldface. Contraction: ff.

Full line ► Line set 'flush' both to left and right.

Full measure ► Type composed to the full width of the column (or page).

Full motion video ► Describes just a video image moving at normal speed, e.g. TV or Cinema. With increase in *bandwidth* of network, now full motion video can be played on computers as well.

Full out ► Type composed in the full normal measure of page or column. Full left is type full out to the *left*, but ranging freely on the right; full right is type full out to the *right*, but ranging freely on the left.

Full point ► Printer's term for full stop.

Full run ▸ Order for advertisements to be placed in all editions of a newspaper that are put out on any one day. Some regional daily newspapers published different editions for each of the regions of a country in which they are distributed. Each of these editions has its own rate card for advertising, but the publisher also sets a special rate for advertisers who wish to advertise in all the editions i.e. to advertise on a full run.

Full shot (FS) ▸ (i) Camera shot that shows in full length the person or object featured in the scene/frame (see Fig.). (ii) Sometimes called a *long shot*, that encompasses an entire scene, equivalent to one the audience would see if the produc-

Full Shot (FS)

tion were a live presentation in legitimate theater, in contrast to a *close-up* shot, which excludes all elements from view except the principal subject.

Full text letter ▸ Personalized computer letter that is printed in one step in its entirety with the exception of the letterhead and/or signature, in contrast to a fill-in letter that has personalized elements printed within the blanks on a preprinted form letter; also called full-out letter. The visual merging of personalized text with standard text can be achieved more effectively with a full-text letter. Full-text letters can be more expensive than fill-in letters because computer printing tends to be more expensive than press printing and because full-text letters require more computer time to print.

Full-track ▸ Recording made across the full width of the tape. Other common types are half-track, quarter-track and multi-track. Tapes recorded on one type of machine will not give satisfactory reproduction if played back on another.

Furniture ▸ (i) Design elements common to every page of a magazine; (ii) regular features and fixed items in the magazine as a whole.

Future ▸ Note in 'futures book' or 'futures file' of story to be followed up later.

Future book ▸ See *future*.

Futures file ▸ File in which stories and news events which are known to be happening on a certain data are placed, so that coverage may be planned in advance.

Fuzz ► Fibers or pieces of lint that stick out along the surface of paper. Paper with smooth finishes, such as *coated paper*, has very little fuzz. Fuzz interferes with fine Halftone printing that requires small dots; therefore, this type of printing is usually done on coated paper.

FX ► Shorthand for sound effects

FYI ► For your information, wire service abbreviation. Used in computer education also.

Gaffer ► In movie and television production, the chief lighting electrician on the set.

Gaffoon ► In broadcast, especially television production, the person responsible for sound effects is informally called a gaffoon.

Gag orders ► Judicial command against speaking and writing about or publishing/broadcasting the trial proceedings.

Gag writer ► Writer (usually for television) specializing in comical lines of situations.

Gain ► The degree of amplification of an electrical signal.

Gallagher report ► Weekly newsletter published by The Gallagher Report, Inc., in New York City. Its target readers are: executives in advertising, management, marketing, and media. The report offers news and analysis on corporate acquisitions and mergers, advertising programmes, marketing trends, executive decisions, media patterns, and advertising-budget allocations. It also issues a monthly supplement, the Gallagher President's Report, which is written by specialist, physicians and contains information concerning executive health problems, new medical technology, and the latest trends in health maintenance.

Galley ► (i) Shallow, three-sided metal tray in which type is assembled and proofed; also, about twenty column-inches of text matter. See also *gallery proof*. (ii) Computer-printed hard-copy listing of selected records from a file. See also *format*.

Galley boy ► Apprentice who pulls proof and stores galleys.

Galley press ► Press which produces printed image on proofing paper of type in galley.

Galley proof ► Impression taken on a strip of paper by inking a gallery of type, and 'pulling' a proof so that the type can be checked with the original copy for errors; also called *galley*. See also author's alteration, editorial alteration, proof reader's symbol.

Galley slug ► Slug with catch word, phrase, or number placed on galley of type to identify it, e.g. News 10.

Game show ► Radio or television programme with a contest format in which the participants selected are celebrities or members of the listening or viewing audience, or a combination of both, who compete against each other or against the house, according to a prescribed set of rules, for some kind of reward. See also *give-away*.

Gang ► See *gang run*.

Gang run ► Concurrent printing of two or more printing jobs in the same press run for purposes of saving labor and time. Since more than one job is printed at the same time, there will also be a cost savings for each job, which can then be passed on to the customer. The sheet printed in a gang run is called a *gang*.

Garalde ► British Standards Institution term for classifying what is popularly called old face roman type, such as Bembo, Garamond, Caslon.

Gate-fold ► Wider or deeper page in magazine or book which has to be folded to fit the format. To be read properly it has to be swung open like a gate. Usually the inside front cover which folds out to accommodate a large advertisement. Gatefolds carry a premium, and arrangements for their inclusion must be made well in advance of the closing date for an issue.

Gatekeepers ► Individuals or groups who decide what messages will be delivered to media consumers: newspaper readers, radio listeners, TV viewers or Net surfers. They also decide how those messages will be constructed and when will they be delivered. Sponsors, editors, producers,

reporters, sub-editors and other executives would have done the power to influence mass media messages. For example, on any normal door, the input editor in a TV news room will select and reject news items out of a host of such items available at their disposal. Sociologist's name for copy taster.

Gateway ► The technical meaning is a *hardware* or *software* set-up that translates between two dissimilar *protocols*, for example Prodigy has a gateway that translates between its internal, proprietary e-mail format and Internet e-mail format. Another, sloppier meaning of gateway is to describe any mechanism for providing access to another computer system, e.g. VSNL might be called a gateway to the *Internet*.

Gatherers ► Journalists who gather and write material for a newspaper-a sociological term.

Gel (Jelly) ► Colored Gelatin or plastic sheeting placed over lamps to produce coloured light. See jelly.

General assignment reporters ► In the news media, those who can identify and write stories in any area. See *beat*.

General desk ► See *universal desk*.

General view (GV) ► Camera shot showing an entire scene to establish a location.

Generation ▸ Term referring to the number of times a film, audiotape, or videotape has been reproduced since the original master. First generation refers to a film or tape that has been duplicated directly from the master; second generation refers to a film or tape that has been reproduced from the first generation; and so on. The technical quality diminishes as the number of generations increases. Generic term for the various postal codes used throughout the world such as the ZIP Code or the Postal Index Number. Also see *dubbing*.

Genlock ▸ The locking or enslaving of one or more recording systems to the sync of a master recorder or Special Effects Generator.

Genre ▸ A distinctive group or type of story, movie, or television programme that follows a recognisable pattern and can be categorised by style and purpose. Examples include the horror film, the police drama, and the television comedy.

Geo-stationary orbit ▸ A desirable orbital position/slot for a communications satellite. The satellite's motion is synchronized with the Earth's rotation and appears, to ground observers, to be stationary. This has technical advantages for maintaining a communications links.

Geostationary ▸ A satellite with the identical speed of rotation as the earth. it appears, as a result, to remain stationary over the earth. Also termed synchronous.

Get in ▸ Instruction to printer to make adjustments to spacing, etc., to accommodate extra letters, or words.

Ghost ▸ (i) Ghost writer is the author of stories that bear someone else's name. Sports pages especially used to be haunted. (ii) To soften or lighten obtrusive background in a photograph, without removing entirely. (iii) Old record maintained on a computer file after a change has been made to create a new record from the old. It is kept as a pointer to the new record in case a transaction must be made involving both records. (iv) Television or printed image that is a poor duplication of the primary image. A ghost on a television screen is a reflection of the image transmission. A printed ghost may be caused by mechanical or chemical printing errors.

GIF ▸ (Graphic Interchange Format) A common format for image files, especially suitable for images containing large areas of the same colour. GIF format files of simple images are often smaller than the same file would be if stored in JPEG format, but GIF format does not store photographic images as well as JPEG. Preferred format for graphics (as opposed to a photo). See also *JPEG*.

Gigabite ➤ 1000 or 1024 megabites, depending on who is measuring. See also *byte, megabyte*.

Giveaway ➤ A kind of radio or TV *game show* in which a prize or reward is given away to contestants or viewing audience.

Give it some air ➤ Instruction to printer to add white space.

Glass shot ➤ Scene in which part of the set is created by a picture carried on a sheet of glass. The glass is placed between the camera and the rest of the set.

Global village ➤ Media thinker Marshal McLuhen's theory that modern communications technologics will make information about people of different cultures, in different countries thousands of miles away, meaningful to electronic media audiences/readers/consumers as things happening in their neighbourhoods. This way people throughout the world are said to experience similar thoughts at the same time.

Globalisation ➤ A concept referring to the process of penetration of national markets by systems of capital that remain unattached to nation states and technologies which are claimed to be easily and rapidly redeployable in new locations. The process of globalisation is said to be evening out the differences in consumption patterns while the prevalent models of consumptions seemingly encourage violent cultural and social fragmentation.

Glossy ➤ A shiny-finished photograph usually preferred for making half-tone engravings; a magazine printed on glossy paper.

Gobbledygook ➤ Jargon-laden and often garbled officialese intended to confuse rather than communicate.

Gobo ➤ A sound absorbing screen used to isolate performers and instruments.

Gone to bed, gone to press ➤ Page or edition forme has left the composing room and is being, or about to be, printed.

Good and no good ➤ Because there may be a lot of takes there must be a simple system of noting which ones are usable in the next stage of production and which are not. The words good and no good are used, and abbreviated as G and NG. Some times an NG is referred as an out take.

Good catch ➤ Detection of a bad error in proof or copy.

Good matter ➤ Matter in type which can be used again.

Goodnight ➤ Signal from wire agency or news department that it is closing down.

Gopher ▶ (i) A menu-driven system that simplifies connecting to other sites and retrieving files on the Internet. Gopher is a client and server style programme, which requires that the user have a Gopher *Client* programme. Though largely supplanted by *Hypertext* or *www* (World Wide Web), there are still thousands of Gopher *Servers* on the Internet.

Gopher (anorak) ▶ (ii) Radio enthusiast, usually on work experience, who fetches, carries and generally 'goes for' on a radio station.

Gothic (US) ▶ Type family of monotone letter forms without serifs and with vertical emphasis. Europeans prefer to call these types grots (grotesques).

Grab ▶ See *sound bite*

Graduated filter ▶ This has a tinted half, which diffuses into clear glass.

Graduated tint ▶ A tint which changes in density or hue from top to bottom or side to side.

Graf ▶ (US) Abbreviation for paragraph.

Grafthead ▶ (US) Heading to a paragraph.

Gramophone, gramdeck or grams ▶ Turntable and associated equipment for the reproduction of records.

Graphical user interface (GUI) ▶ A visual, rather than text-based, interface.

Graphics ▶ (i) Usually any drawn illustrative material used in page design. Graphics; (ii) General name for TV artwork or artwork department; all visuals prepared for a production, including cameracards, slides, titles, lettering, illustrations, diagrams, electronically generated symbols and letters, and all pictures, maps, charts and graphs.

Graphics generator ▶ The component that is used to create computer graphics. The graphics can be produced either with special, dedicated stations or properly configured PCs.

Graphics programmes ▶ The generic classification for computer graphics software. These range from paint to CAD software, and they excel at certain applications, Paint programmes, for example, are used to create/manipulate bitmapped images. CAD programme are tailor made for architectural/technical drawings.

Great primer ▶ Old name' for 18pt type.

Green proof ▶ Uncorrected proof.

Grid ▶ Basic divisions and subdivisions of a page which the designer uses as a skeleton for his layout. Also clear sheet of plastic used in making up photoset papers. It is a bit larger than page size and is graduated in lines: a blank sheet of paper is attached to the grid and bromides are assembled on it in the same way that type is put into chase. Now usually exist only in computer form.

Grip ► In film and television production, a person who functions as a handyman on the set. The grip will assist wherever necessary and will help with moving scenery and lighting instruments or *prop* storage.

Gross audience ► Total number of individuals (or households) in a listening, viewing, or reading audience without regard to duplication of audience members. For example, in television, a person is counted twice if that person appears in the audience of two of the programmes in the broadcast schedule being counted. When gross audience is expressed in terms of percentage, it is often referred to as homes per rating point or *gross rating points*; when expressed in terms of numbers of individuals (or households), it is referred to as *gross impression*.

Gross impression ► See *gross audience.*

Gross rating point (GRP) ►
(i) Sum of all rating points over a specific time period or over the course of a media plan; sometimes called homes per rating point. The rating of a show represents the percentage of people watching television program-me as compared to the number of television sets in the

particular television universe (geographical location). Each rating point is equal to 1%. If a show has a rating of 11, that means that 11% of all persons (or households) who have a television were tuned in to that show (whether the other televisions were turned on or not). If there are two shows on a particular station during a particular time period, and the first show has a rating of 8 and the other a rating of 10, then the GRPs for that time period equal 18. GRPs are calculated by multiplying the total reach (the unduplicated audience) of the schedule by the frequency (average amount of exposures) of the insertion in the proposed schedule. The gross rating points then will represent the product of reach and frequency and will express the "gross" duplicated percentage of audience that will be reached by the proposed plan. (It is important to note that GRPs are a percentage. Therefore, if a given market has 1000 television households, each GRP represents 10 viewing households, whereas in a market of 10,000 television households, each GRP represents 100 viewing households. Thus, the largest amount of GRPs does not necessarily mean the largest audience.) Media Planners use gross rating points as a method of designing a media schedule in an attempt to deliver a given number of GRPs at minimum cost. (ii) Percentage of the population that passes an outdoor advertising structure on a daily basis; GRPs are the same as showings.

Grot ► Abbreviation for grotesque, type family of monotone letter forms without serifs. Modern types based on early nineteenth century forms and, despite name, have subtle appeal which makes them best of sans serifs for newspaper display. See ·gothics.

Group shot ► A shot showing a number of people. Also see *two-shot*, *three-shot*, *picture composition*.

GTS ► Greenwich Time Signal ('the pips').

Guard bands ► The gaps between video tracks on a tape which prevent "cross - talk".

Gum Arabic ► In offset lithography, a substance used to coat nonprinting areas of a *printing plate* to make them nonreceptive to ink.

Gumming ► Applying gum arabic to the nonprinting areas of lithographic printing plates to make them nonreceptive to ink.

Gun mike ► See *rifle mike*.

Gutter ► Space between pages in centre spread. Sometimes used on computer layout screen to describe space between columns. Also a river of white caused by wide spacing or spacing in an awkward pattern.

Gutter press ► Sometimes applied to tabloid press.

Hack ► Insult and jocular word for a journalist which journalists are happy to use to describe themselves. Also hackette.

Hacker ► Also known as a "*cracker*", a person who breaks into a site through a computer's security.

Hair line ► Thinnest stroke in letter form; thinnest rule used in newspapers. Also unwanted wisps of metal which sometimes adhere between letters on a slug and so impair printing.

Hair space ► Thinnest spaces in line-casting, six to an em or thinner.

Half-lead (pronounced leed) ► The second most important story on a page.

Half-tone ► The reproduction process, consisting of dots of varying density, by which the tones of a photograph are reproduced on a page.

Half-track ► Recording over half the width of tape. See also Full-tack, Quarter-track.

Hammer ► One- or two-word heading set flush left over main heading of about half the size.

Hammocking ► Scheduling term referring to the need to support a low audience or specialist programme by placing more popular material before and after it in order to maintain a strong average listening figure.

Hamper ► Story displayed horizontally usually at the top of a page.

Handbill ► Single sheet of paper, usually 8 1/2" x 11", in any colour stock, imprinted with an advertising message or announcement of a sale or special event, and distributed by a local retailer. Distributed by hand on the street or left on parked cars, the handbill offers a quickly produced and inexpensive form of advertising. Handbills are also called throwaways. See also *flier*.

Hand carried ► Equipment or material transported personally rather than sent as freight or by electronic means. See *Pigeon*.

Hand held ► Camera or other equipment used without a tripod or other steadying device.

Handling noise ► Unwanted clicks and sounds picked up by a microphone as a result of handling and moving it.

Handouts ► Story sent to media outlets by press relations office or organization of PR company.

Hand-over ► Form of words used as a cue for another performer (e.g. Now, with the sports news ..)

Hand-set ► Type set by hand; newspapers try to avoid much hand-setting, though Ludlow headline matrices are assembled by hand before casting.

Handsetting ▶ Setting type by hand rather than by machine. Originally, all type was handset. Even today, the resultant copy of hand set type has a distinguished, high-quality appearance. However, handsetting is both time-consuming and costly and is done only when there is not a large amount of text in the copy.

Hand signals ▶ A silent method of sending instruction to performers while they are on air. This method of communication is used through the glass window between a studio and its control area, or in a studio with a 'live' mite. Also see *wind-up*.

Hanging indent ▶ Style for text and headline composition in which first line is set full measure and all succeeding lines are indented an equal amount at the left. This entry is set with a hanging indent.

Hanging par ▶ One paragraph set with a hanging indent.

Hard copy ▶ Copy typed on sheets of paper (usually A4 size) as opposed to copy into a computer. Each page is known as a folio; printed paper version of computer-generated material.

Hard dot ▶ In a Halftone image, a dot with a sharp, clean edge. A soft dot has a Halation or fringe around it. Hard dots cre-

ate a better image. Wear on some printing plates eventually produces a soft-dot image. There are plastic plates in use that do not wear as much as metal plates.

Hard news ▶ A news story about an event having significant current impact usually on many people. It often deals with disaster, economic and political events. It is straight serious news containing little description, comment or analysis. Also see *soft news* and *story types*.

Hard news formula ▶ A hard news story will cover most of the basic facts by asking the questions, who? what? where? when? and how?

Hard proof page ▶ Proof in hardcopy form as distinguished from proof displayed on a computer screen. Hard proofs are the traditional means of reviewing typeset material before final printing, so that errors can be identified and corrected. However computer-generated proofs are a relatively new technology that makes corrections quicker and easier to implement.

Hardware ▶ Mechanical and electronic parts that constitute a computer system, as distinguished from the computer programmes (software) that drive the system. The main hardware elements are the Central Processing Unit, Disk or Magnetic Tape (data storage devices), Cathoderay Tube Display terminals, Keyboards, and Printers. Also see *CPU, software, keyboard & printer*.

Harmonic distortion ➤ The generation of spurious upper frequencies

Hdg, head ➤ Abbreviation for headline.

HDTV (High Definition TV) ➤ A new generation of TV broadcast systems for greatly improved picture quality. HDTV will probably be the in thing in the next century. It is a system of thousand lines offering superior quality pictures.

Head amplifier ➤ Small amplifier within a microphone, especially capacitor type.

Header ➤ The part of a *VDU* screen in which menus and basic instructions are entered, and in which the computer communicates with the user.

Head gap ➤ Narrow vertical slot at the front of tape recorder erase, record and replay heads.

Headline ➤ Short summary of a news story given at the start or end of a bulletin or grouped with other headlines in lieu of a longer bulletin. Also known as *highlights* or *summaries*. See also *Teasers*.

Headline schedule ➤ Sheet or booklet displaying all headline types used by a newspapers. Displays are grouped in column widths, or scored with pica rulings: unit count per column may be given.

Headline sentence ➤ See *Intro*.

Head margin ➤ Empty space above the first line on printed page. The size of the head margin is determined by the individual responsible for graphic design but is usually equal to three to five lines of type and may include a running head.

Head shot ➤ A close-up of the face.

Head sked ➤ (US) Headline schedule.

Head to come ➤ Notice to composing room that headline will be sent after the story.

Head up ➤ Headline that has been written for casting.

Headhunter ➤ Independent employment service (or individual) that seeks out personnel for high-level executive positions; formally known as an executive search company (or consultant). Headhunters are generally used by companies that are looking outside their present staff to fill executive vacancies.

Heavies ➤ Quality or serious press, as opposed to the tabloid press. The Times of India , Financial Express, The Hindu, The Times, Washington Post etc. are heavies.

Helical scan ➤ Systems which scan videotape in slanting tracks .

Helper app ► Add -on applications that support sound, image, and other formats that your browser can't support by itself.

Hertz (Hz) ► Frequency of sound measured in cycles per second, for example 800 hertz is 800 cycles per second. 1000 hertz is a kilohertz (kHz).

Hicky, James Augustus ► An employee of the East India company, who resigned from his job (i.e. of printer) and started Bengal Gazette or Calcutta General Advertiser on January 29, 1788 to expose the corrupt practices and the private lives of the top executives of the company, including the Governor-General, Warren Hastings.

J.A. Hicky introduced him in the first issue of the Gazette as the 'first and late printer to the honourable company' and described the journal as "A weekly political and commercial paper open to all Parties but influenced by None". Hicky's Gazette, the first newspaper of India, was probably a major milestone in the Indian social reform movement which gave birth to the Indian struggle for Indepence from the British rule Hicky had to suffer a lot for the freedom he excercised through his paper. He was once even imprisoned became poor and was in distress.

Hidden camera commercial ► Television commercial showing unrehearsed genuine users of a product talking about or using the product while their actions are being recorded by a concealed camera.

Hidden camera technique ► Technique of filming or videotaping action to be in a *hidden camera commercial*.

Hide ► Construction used to camouflage the camera operator while filming wildlife.

Hi-fi ► High fidelity. Unlike stereo, a hi-fi signal is encoded onto a deep layer of video track, reducing hiss.

High – 8 ► See *Video – 8*.

High angle shot ► Shot from a camera placed above the subject and pointing down. Also see *camera angles, canted shot, angle shot*.

High-band (or Hi-Band) ► A video recording system with very high - frequency response and consequently excellent quality. Now being overtaken by still higher quality Beta systems.

High Definition TV ► See HDTV.

High key ► Lighting in which the overall level is bright. This kind of Hollywood "look" is also conventionally associated with glamorous back lighting.

High key scene ► Predominantly light to mid-tones. No deep shadows.

Highlight ► See *Headline*.

Hiss ► Unwanted background noise in the frequency range 5 – 10 kHz, e.g. tape hiss.

Hit ▸ (i) A match between a search term and a word in one of the titles or texts that are in the database. (ii) As used in reference to the world wide web, "hit" means a single request from a web browser for a single item from a web server; thus in order for a web browser to display a page that contain 3 graphics, 4 "hits" would occur at the server: 1 for the HTML page, and one for each of the 3 graphics. "hits" are often used as a very rough measure of load on a server, e.g. "Our server has been getting 3 lakh hits per month." Because each "hit" can represent anything from a request for a tiny document (or even a request for a missing document) all the way to a request that requires some significant extra processing (such as a complex search request), the actual load on a machine from 1 hit is almost impossible to define.

Hitchhike ▸ (i) Brief mention of a commercial at the tail end or immediately following the sponsor's final commercial in a broadcast programme. The hitch-hike advertises a product manufactured by the sponsor but heretofore unmentioned during the time period presented by the sponsor. It is so named because it "hitches a ride" with a commercial for another of the manufacturer's products. (ii) Ten- to twenty-second period for commercials or announcements immediately following a programme and immediately pre ceding station identification.

Hoax ▸ Deliberate deception of the media consumers or public to increase circulation or ratings.

Hold ▸ To stop all movement, action or speech, usually for laughter or applause.

Holding copy ▸ The first version of a story left by a reporter to be run in his/her absence while he/she is out of the newsroom getting further information on that story.

Holding ▸ Delaying sending a page or edition to press while waiting for a late story.

Hold instruction ▸ (usually known as set and hold) Ensuring that copy is prepared for publication but not printed. For instance an obituary of some eminent figure or advance copies of speeches supplied by handout.

Hold over ▸ Instruction to keep, rather than discard, the type of all or part of a story which has not been published. A held-over story is one which is intended to be publish at the next opportunity. Also see *overmatter*.

Hole ▸ Gap in page chase or dummy where type and illustrations are insufficient to fill; see also *news hole*.

Hologram ➤ A record of the optical information that composes a scene. It can be used for applications ranging from advertising to security.

Holographic interferometry ➤ A holographic industrial application (for example) for material testing.

Holographic optical element (HOE) ➤ An application where a hologram functions as a lens or other optical element.

Home page (or Homepage) ➤ There are several meanings to home-page. Originally, the starting 'page' or the first screen in a set of kleb pages. The more common meaning refers to the main web page for a business, organization, person or simply the main page out of a collection of web pages, e.g. "Check out so-and-so's new home page." The home page typically contains links to other page in the web site. Another informal use of the term refers to practically any web pages as a "homepage," e.g. "That web site has 65 home-pages and none of them are interesting." See also *browser, web*.

Home service book ➤ Name for a magazine, such as Better Homes and Gardens, that is directed at an audience whose interests lie in the areas of home and dometsticity; also called a *shelter magazine*.

Hood ➤ Rules arranged around three sides of a headline, top, left and right.

Hook ➤ A term used in some computer system for a queue or desk to which stories can be sent after tasting to await possible use.

Horizontal make-up ➤ Style in which multi-column headlines are arranged across the page with text type running underneath in short legs.

Horizontal resolution ➤ The number of vertical lines that can be distinguished by camera or receiver in a horizontal direction on a test chart.

Horizontal sync ➤ The sync pulses that control the line - by - line scanning of the target.

Horizontal wipe ➤ see *wipe*.

Host ➤ A computer on which a *web site* is physically located. It refers to any computer on a network that is a repository for services available to other computers on the network. It is quite common to have one host machine and provide several services, such as *WWW* and *USENET*. See also *node, network*.

Hot ➤ Any overbright area. It may appear to pale off or reproduce as a blank white patch ('bloom').

Hot links ➤ words and graphics on a page of computer text that can be clicked to take the reader to a different page.

Hotlist ➤ A list of favourite world wide web pages held in a browser programme.

Hot metal ▸ The now disused printing system in which type was cast from molten metal into 'slugs' for assembly into pages. Now the metal type has been replaced by film-set type which is pasted up as bromides. See *Hot type*.

Hot spot ▸ Overbright localized patch of light, usually due to specular reflection. Also in *rear projection* uneven illumination causes the centre of the screen image to be brighter than its edges.

Hot type ▸ Automated composition technique that utilizes a machine to create properly spaced metal type in one complete line at a time. This solves some of the problems of manual composition, such as the storage, retrieval, and composition of individual type slugs. Hot type is melted down after use rather than returned to storage. It is used for newspapers, print advertisements, business forms, and all types of promotions. Hot type is not as versatile as computerized composition because word-breaks at the end of each line must be operator controlled. There are two types of hot-type composition. Monotype systems create individual slugs of metal type for each character of space. Linecasting machines create a solid line of metal type. See Also

letters pacing; nonmetallic composition.

House ▸ A media organization. Thus in-house (meaning within a particular media organization). House organ is company's own newspaper or magazine. See also *style*.

House ad. ▸ An advertisement placed in a magazine by its own publisher.

Households using television (HUT) ▸ A.C. Nielsen Company (U.S.) term representing the percentage of households in a specific area and in a particular time period that have their television sets turned on as compared to the total number of television households in that area. If, for example, there are 1000 television households in a particular survey area and 500 of those TV sets are turned on in a given time period, the HUT level for that area in that time period is 50. The HUT level can be figured as an overall number for the entire United States (a figure used for network programmes) or for a local market, as in the case of local pogramming.

A programme's share of the audience is calculated on the basis of the HUT level. If a programme carried a 20 share, that means that 20% of all households using television watching that programme.

House journal ▶ A magazine produced by a company whose editorial content is relative to that company's business. There are two types of house journals, internal and external. The internal bubli cation is designed for company personnel and its editorial content consists of company activities which are of interest to employees. The external house journal is intended primasily for customers, potential customers, dealers, or such others who may have some interest in the company's affairs, The external publications features articles and information concerning company's growth, technological advances, produnt development and any other information that will help sell the company's image and products.

House lights ▶ Powerful ceiling lights used to illuminate the studio for general working purposes (e.g. during rigging, setting, etc.). Switched off when specific production lighting is in use.

House rules ▶ Style notes and procedures laid down by individual offices, Also see *house style*.

House style ▶ A set of rules about disputed spellings, matters of punctuation, capitalisation, use of numerals, etc.

Housewife time ▶ Broadcast media research indicating that part of the broadcast day when women over 16 make up the bulk of the listening or viewing audience. In both radio and television, housewife time is the daytime hours, generally between 10:00 A.M. and 3:00 or 4:30 P.M. Even though a large portion of women are in the working force, research shows that women still make up the largest share of the audience in these daytime hours.

Howl-round ▶ Acoustic or electrical positive feedback generally apparent as a continuous sound of a single frequency. Often associated with public address systems. Avoided by decreasing the gain in the amplifying circuit, cutting the loudspeaker or in contribution working through the use of a clean feed circuit.

HTC, HTK ▶ Head to come.

HTML ▶ (HyperText markup language) The coding language for creating *Hypertext* documents for use on the *world wide web*. Not only a programming language, *HTML* looks a lot like old-fashioned typesetting code, where you surround a block of text with codes that indicate how it should appear, additionally, in *HTML* you can specify that a block of text, or a word, is linked to another file on the Internet. *HTML* files are meant to be viewed using a *world wide web client programme* such as *netscape* or *Mosaic*. If you are comfortable with macros for spread sheets and have access to a word processing programme wit an ASCII option you can create web publications.

HTTP ▶ (HyperText transfer protocol) The protocol that tells computers on the Internet how to communicate with each other. Requires a HTPP *client* programme on one end, and an HTTP *server* program on the other end. HTTP is the most important protocol used in the *world wide web(www)* and used for moving hypertext files across the Internet. Most web page locations begin with "http://" See also *client*, *server*, *www*.

Hue ▶ Colour. Red, blue, and green are the primary hues that, in varying propertions, produce all the colours we see. Variations on these primary colours plus black are the basis for Four-Colour process printing that is able to duplicate all the colours of an image with only three colours of ink.

Hum ▶ Low frequency electrical interference derived from mains power supply.

Human-computer interface ▶ The tools we use to work with computers. They range from keyboards to touch screens.

Human interest story ▶ Soft news item. Of interest to the audience, but of no great significance or importance. Typically showbiz, animals, lottery winners, etc. Such stories focus on success, failures, tragedies, emotional/ sexual histories of people and eliminate or marginalise deeper cultural, economic and political factors, giving importance to the aspects which may transcend regional or linguistic limits.

Hype ▶ In broadcast, special promotional activities by a station or network in order to attract a large audience and therefore generate higher audience ratings for a particular time period; also called *hypo*. For example: Traditionally, broadcast rating measurements are made for local stations in February, May, and November. Accordingly, local stations have been known to hype their audiences during these time periods.

Hyper card ▶ The first widely released hypertext programme designed for Macintoshes.

Hypercardioid ▶ A cardioid microphone having a particularly narrow angle or acceptance at its front which decreases rapidly towards the sides.

Hyperfocal distance ▶ The distance between the camera and the nearest point of the subject which is sharp, when the lens is focused on infinity at any given aperture.

Hyperlink ► Connection between two locations. It may be text or a graphic. When you click a hyperlink, you can go to another location on the *web* page, another location on the Web site, or an external Web page. Also see *link*.

Hypermedia ► Media (such as pictures, videos, and audio), on a web page that links the user to another web page by clicking on the media.

Hypertext ► A nonlinear system for information storage, management and retrieval on the world wide web. Links between associative information can be created and activated. Hypertext or links will usually be a different colour than the other text on the page and is usually underlined. This concept has been extended to pictures and sounds.

Hyphenation ► The insertion of a hyphen into a word as it breaks at the end of a line. Controlled by dictionaries put into desktop publishing programs but subject to manual override.

Hypo ► (i) See hype. (ii) In photography, short for sodium hyposulfite; a chemical fixative used in photography; also called sodium thiosulfate, ammonium thiosulfite. Hypo makes the nonimage areas of a photograph insensitive to further exposure to light.

IANS ► Originally India Abroad News Service, an Indian news agency feeding overseas news to local newspapers and Indian local news to non-resident Indian in west asia, and north America; now renamed Indo-Asian News Service.

Icon ► A small abstract graphic representation of an object or idea; a picture representing a programme, disk drive, file, folder, or other item.

I.D. ► Station identification or ident. Eight- to ten-second station-break announcement that accompanies the broadcast station identification and is just long enough to identify a product. Also see *ident*.

Ident ► (i) An identification mark on the head of a videotape. (ii) Piece of recorded music played to introduce or identify a particular programme, feature or presenter. Also known as *stab, jingle, sounder*. See also *I.D.*

Identification ► See *ident*.

Idiot card ► Large cards with lines of dialogue or cues that are hand held in easy view of the performer.

Idiot tape ► Magnetic tape that provides input to computerized phototypesetting is called idiot tape. The tape contains in an unformatted (unjustified and unhyphenated) mode all of the data to be typeset. The computerized typesetting Programme formats the contents as required.

IFPI ► International Federation of Phonographic Indiustries. International organisation of record manufacturers to control performance and usage rights.

IFWJ ► Indian Federation of Working Journalists.

Igranic jack radio ► Jack plug providing two connections.

IIMC ► Indian Institute of Mass Communication, New Delhi (India). The institute of international repute that runs post-graduate diploma courses in Print Journalism, Broadcast Journalism and Public Relations and Advertising. It also trains the Indian Information Service (group A and gorup B) officers. IIMC has been conducting post-graduate diploma course in Development Journalism for the media professionals from developing countries.

Internet (lower case i) ► This means two or more inter-connected networks.

Illustration ► Visual element in an advertisement. The illustration is an efficient way to represent an idea and works in tune with the headline to attract the reader. It is the ilustration that helps to make the copy believable.

Image ► (i) Visual counterpart or likeness of an object, a person, or a scene produced by an optical device such as a mirror; a positive impression developed from a negative after having been shot by a still or film camera. (ii) Illusory conception created by advertising and projected by the media, that embodies emotions, perceptions, attitudes, and intellectual orientation group toward an entity.

Image area ► The part of a page which is normally inked.

Image enhancer ► An accessory for sharpening the video image.

Image map ► A graphic image that's used on a Web site as a navigational tool *i.e.* as link to other pages or sites. It's made up of two elements: the graphic that you see on the page through your browser, and a text file that contains the link information.

Image processing ► The field and technique in which an image (for example, created by a video camera) is digitized and manipulated. Typical operation include image enhancement and correction.

IMHO ► (In My Humble Opinion) A shorthand appended to a comment written in an online forum, IMHO indicates that the writer is aware that they are expressing a debatable view, probably on a subject already under discussion. One of many such shorthands in common use online, especially in discussion forums. See also *BTW*.

Imposing stone ► Full title of the composing room 'stone'.

Impression cylinder ► Cylindrical device on a printing press that pressures the paper against the printing plate (direct printing), or against the blanket (offset printing)

Imprint ► Name and address of printer and publisher required by law; often at the foot of the back page; in a magazine within first few pages.

Incremental radio ► In the UK, an additional Independent radio station (usually fairly small) in an area which already has at least one commercial service.

In-cue and out-cue ► These are written instructions to say when a report begins and ends. The in-cue is the first few words of that report, and the out cue the last few words. The in-cue is a useful check that the right report is being relayed, and the out-cue tells presenters, directors and technical operators when the report is finishing. However, an in cue can also be a reporter's final words leading up to a sound bite. For example, if a reporter is going live and does not have time to give the producer a detailed script on phone, the reporter can tell the producer the last few words that he will be speaking before the start of the sound bite of some expert on the subject of his story. These last few words of the reporter going on air would serve as the incue of for the sound bite. This way the producer can inform the newscast director in advance when to switch to the tape with the sound bite. Otherwise, you will see the reporter staring into the camera or at the TV monitor to wait for the sound bite tape to roll (start). Notably, the producer would have also told the newscast director the outcue of the soundbite in order to know when to switch back to the reporter going live. In fact, many such instructions are passed on-line when there is live coverage. For example, a reporter is on live with Ms. Mayawati of the Bahujan Samaj Party who goes on repeating the same thing in different words. In such a case the producer would ask the newscast director to switch over to the anchor who might start like this: *"Thank you MayawatiJee for being with us and thank you Deepak (reporter). We shall come back to you later"*.

Indecent material ► Non-obscene language that is sexually explicit or includes profanity.

In Delhi ► A cable channel in Delhi doing local programme. Sister concerns being In Bombay, In Hyderabad, etc.

Indent ► Abbreviation for inden-

tation. A shorter line than usual, leaving a white space at the beginning or end. Used to mark paragraphs.

Independent Radio News (IRN) ► Company which supplies hourly bulletins of national and international news to most independent radio stations in the UK.

Independent station (US/UK) ► A TV station that is not affiliated with one of the major networks such as ABC, CBS, or NBC. These stations have to program their entire day, whereas a network affiliate runs programming supplied by the network during most of the day and evening.

Independent television market ► (i) Home market for an independent television station (See *independent station*). (ii) Television market area where the viewing audience is inconsistent with the typical Network audience, because the local television stations pull the largest share of the audience. Generally, if there is network programming at the same time as local one, the network programmes will draw the largest audience. In an independent television market, this is not the case.

In-depth reporting ► Coverage of issues/events in considerable detail and after good research.

Index ► Front page listing of stories which are in the rest of paper. To ease reading and "sell" / "flag" the contents in prominent place.

Indian Newspaper Society (INS) ► The Indian Newspaper Society (INS) earlier known as The Indian and Eastern Newspaper Society was set up in 1939 as the central body of newspapers in the country. At a time when the Press was growing at random without organisational support or any protection from the numerous pressure groups, the foundation of the Society at the beginning of World War II was the first in giving direction and cohesion to the newspaper industry. INS has played a significant role in protecting and promoting the freedom of Press in India, the largest thriving democracy in the world.

By December 2003 the membership of the Society rose to 707 including large, medium and small newspapers, periodicals, and other publications besides 767 advertising agencies. INS is member of various international agencies such as World Association for Newspapers (WAN), Commonwealth Press Union (CPU) and International Federation of the Periodical Press (FIPP).

Indirect quote ► Refers to the use of an edited or paraphrased version of a speakers words and hence not enclosed in quotation marks. Such a quote represents what a news-maker said but in the words of a reporter. See also *direct quote*, *peraphrase* and *partial quote*.

INFA ► Indian News features Agency. A syndicate which supplies news and features etc. to different newspapers on payment, written by prominent journalists on its staff.

Inferior letters/figs ► Small letters or figures cast on the lower part of typeface as in H_2O.

In-flight publication ► Magazine distributed exclusively through the airlines and given free of charge to passengers. There are several different in-flight publications, published by private individuals or companies. The editorial content of such a magazine, say Swagat distributed in Air India flights, may be of interest to business people and frequent flyers.

Infomercial ► A contraction of "information" and "commercial." An infomercial is usually 30 minutes in length and thinly hides its commercial message in a programme format.

Information ► A collection of symbols that when combined, communicates a message or intelligence.

Information economy ► Financial system with thrust on not what people grow or build but the information they produce, store and sell.

Information meter ▸ A small fee charged for accessing specific information and other functions (on the Web). An information meter would keep track of these transactions.

Information overload ▸ A certain stage in which the available quantity of information far exceeds the receiver's capacity to use it in a meaningful way.

Information provider (IP) ▸ An organisation that provides information carried by an interactive service.

Information resources ▸ Computer-accessible books, journals, pictures, audio files, etc., that can be retrieved via the Internet.

Information society ▸ The notion of a post-industrial society driven by the production, manipulation and exchange of information. Information can be viewed as a social, economic and political force.

Information technology (IT) ▸ Refers to the use of computers and other associated devices (e.g. tele-cummunications) for the collection, storage and manipulation of data to produce, present and communicate information. Data can be thought. IT is a tool for efficient production of information to carry out a huge variety of tasks. The starting point of information technology is data. Data can be thought of as raw facts and figures which must be collected and put into a form which the computer system can deal with. The data may be of several types: numeric data (sales figures of Maruti 800 car, 2001-2003); textual data (description of the figures); graphical data (bar diagram showing the sales figures). Much of the data are mixed, a mixture of these types, as put together they turn into a package of intelligent information showing trends which help in decision making i.e. peak sales figures, their duration and time, and the reasons for the same.

Informative entertainer ▸ Radio or televisions programmes which tend to educate as well as entertain the audience simultaneously. Hence the term infotainment Discovery Channel & National Geographic are entertainment channels.

INFRA-red photography ▸ Spatial, forensic or medical photography which enables us to see what cannot otherwise be seen normally.

In hand ▸ Copy is being set or a block is being made.

In-home ▸ It refers to the media that is seen, heard, or read in the home, as compared to "out-of-home" media such as billboards which can only be viewed out of the home. Radio, television, newspapers, and magazines are all considered in-home media. See also *out-of-home*.

Initial letter ▸ Large letters used at the start of a story, rapidly going out of use in newspapers, see *drop cup*.

Inject ▸ Live contribution to a news programme from a distant source.

Injunction ▸ A court order.

Ink fly ▸ A fine spray can hand in the air in rotary printing operations.

Ink fountain ▸ Printing press device that stores and supplies ink to the plate or other image carrier. A system of rollers transfers ink from the fountain to the plate. Some presses intended to be used for a single purpose, such as newspaper presses, are able to directly access ink storage tanks, but presses used for a variety of purposes must obtain ink from ink fountains that are manually filled with the correct ink for each print job. The amount of ink used to make each impression depends on the type of plate, the type of paper, and the quality of the ink. See also fountain solution.

Inline ▸ Typography style characterized by a thin white line through the center of the letters, surrounded by a black border.

In metal ▸ Copy has been set into type now out of use.

In-point ▸ Frame selected during editing to be the beginning of a shot.

Input ▸ (i) To type copy into computer; information fed into a computer from another source. (ii) Individual's ideas on a given subject, as in "we need Mr. Singh's input on this problem."

INS ▸ Indian Newspapers Society.

INSAT System ▸ The series of Indian satellites started in shape of INSAT-IA on April 10, 1982, to provide an impetus to the domestic long distance communications, besides conducting meteorological surveys and direct network transmission of the TV stations in India, which are inter –linked with the help of a terrestrial microwave connection, are networked through this satellite system.

Insert (print) ▸ Copy or type to be inserted in the body of a story to interrupt the sequence already set or being set. Inserts are marked A, B, C, etc., and their placing is indicated on galley proof.

Inserts (video) ▸ An insert is the replacement in part of one video image by another. It is usually a close-up or a extreme close-up inserted into a sequence of shots to show in detail an object or process being described either by the reporter himself or by a newsmaker or an interviewee. Suppose you are interviewing the mother of a school student shot dead by terrorists.

She says: *"Look there! My son's swimming medals, the certificate of merit by the education department. ...He ...he ...he always goaded us into laughter. How could be a danger to anyone?"*

The shot of the victim's mother is in close-up. It does not show the swimming meals, the certificate of merit, a framed photograph of the victim, etc.

But a reporter with an eye for a visually rich report would note down these details while listening to the interviewee and shoot these objects after the interview. The edited version can start with the sound bite (related portion of the interview) of the lady and the tape editor can then insert the video pictures of the medals, certificate and photograph to match the words of the interviewee. This makes not only for the better visuals than mere the taking head of the victim's mother, it also allows the reporter to park more details into his story; failing which he might have to devote additional sentences in his script to a separate description of the medals, certificates, etc.

In fact, inserts are very valuable shots and journalists must train themselves into spotting the objects of such shots. In particular, they should be on the look out for documents such as (a) government reports; (b) still photographs of accident or murder victims; and (c) any small objects referred to by the speaker which, in the journalists' opinion, might be used in the story anyway. Since these objects – documents, still photographs, etc. are small enough, they should be photographed in close-up or extreme close-up. Also see *picture composition*.

Inset ► Visual representation of news item , usually placed over a presenter's shoulder during a newscast .

Inside columns ► Columns on any page which are not either at extreme left or extreme right.

Inside front cover ► Preferred advertising position in a magazine; also known as second cover.

Inside page ► Any page except the front or back.

Inside story ► Reporters investigation on their experience and research within organizations at the centre of controversy and/ or on quotes from insiders within organization.

Intaglio ► Printing process from sunken images; see *offset gravure*.

Intake / input ► Department responsible for news gathering. See Assignments desk.

Integrated services digital network (ISDN) ► A digital communications platform that could seamlessly handle different types of information (for example, computer data and voice).

Intellectual property ► The rights of artists, authors, and designers of creative works; the products of the creative intellect.

Intelligent agent ► Software searching the Internet for specific kinds of information. Such agents are intelligent in so far as they keep track of what they have found, refine search methods in view of previous successes and failures, and extrapolate new demands on information by the user.

Intelsat ► (International Telecommunications Satellite Organisation) An international satellite consortium credited to be the originator of the global system by which television signals and telephony are beamed from one country to others. Also see *Communications satellite.*

Interactive forums ► Discussion or chat software accessible through websites. Messages are stored for easy reading and responding.

Interactive system ► An information system you can interact with to request and subsequently retrieve specific information.

Interactive television ► Television service that enables consumers to shop, vote, bank, play games, and so forth, via a television/telephone/computer combination. For shopping, merchandise is displayed on the television screen and may be ordered by hitting keys on a special keypad or on a touch-tone telephone dial that is linked electronically to the seller. See also *digital broadcasting; electronic catalogue; teletext; videotex.*

Interactivity ► (i) The ability of two parties to both send and receive information, doesn't imply that the two parties enjoy equal opportunity to send and receive messages. (ii) The term also pertains a computer application/programme in which cach command or data entry to the computer system invokes a response from the system; may mean a continuous dialogue between the system and the user. For example, search engines such as Google, Yahoo! or Altavista. (iii) The ability of a communication network to carry two way transmission, e.g. telephone.

Intercom ► Local voice communication system.

Intercutting ► Technique used in film editing to provide a particular emotional effect. The same scene is filmed from all possible angles, and then the best frames of each are chosen by the editor, who splices them together in rapid, succession to produce the desired effect.

Interface ► Also called user interface, describes the space and the ways in which a computer and its users communicate. A command-driven interface requires the users to type in instructions for the computer to perform certain tasks (i.e. opening a blank word document) while a graphical user interface (GUI) offers commands in the form of icons, dialogue boxes, monus and window's.

Interim injunction ➤ A court order banning publication in advance of a court hearing

Interlaced GIF ➤ A GIF that is written so that when it is downloaded, it looks like it is out of focus ad then gradually comes into focus.

Interlibrary loan ➤ The process of ordering a library item from another library when your local library does not own it.

Interlock ➤ A phase in the film editing process during which the opticals and sound track are synchronized with the work print.

Intern ➤ Most often a college student working in a newsroom to learn what the television business is really like. The intern usually receives college credit plus the advantage of practical on-the-job training. Also see *attachment*.

Internal link ➤ A connection between two locations within the same document

International Federation of Journalists ➤ The organisation comprises mainly journalists from the western countries. It aims at setting up a new world information order, independent of any kind of pressure groups.

International Maritime Satellite Organization (Inmarsat) ➤ An international organisation that extended satellite communication to ships at sea and other remote sites.

Internet ➤ It refers to global network of computers linked by modems; set up in the 1960s as a bomb-proof information exchange by the US Defense Department. It has mushroomed into a new and personalized media, allowing individual access, via a modem, to uncensored pictures, sound and text from around the world. Technically, it refers to a vast collection of inter-connected networks that all use TCP/IP protocols.

Internet service provider (ISP) ➤ A company or organization that provides Internet access, usually for a fee, satyam, mantraonline, etc.; are ISPs. Generally, you use your modem to connect to your ISP. In India, VSNL, MTNL.

Interpersonal communication ➤ Communication between two individuals as distinguished from mass communication.

Interrogation marks ➤ Question marks, or queries.

Intertype ➤ Trade name of keyboarded line-casting machine.

Interval recording ► A camcorder feature which records shots at timed' intervals, e.g., every 60 seconds.

Interviewer bias ► Opinion of an interviewer, which is displayed during the interview process and thus affects the outcome of the interview. In research interviews, it is necessary for the interviewer to conduct the interview with total objectivity, so that respondents are not influenced by him in their responses. For this reason, interviews should be conducted by well-trained and qualified interviewers.

In the page ► Type already transferred from galley to chase.

Intranet ► A private network inside a company or organization that uses the same kinds of software that you would find on the public Internet, but that is only for internal use.

As the Internet has become more popular many of the tools used on the Internet are being used in private networks, for example, many companies have *web servers* that are available only to employees. Notably, an Intranet may not actually be an internet – it may simply be a network. See also *internet, Internet, network*.

Intro (introduction) ► (i) The first, audience winning, and most important paragraph of a news story, giving the main angle of the story and the central facts. (ii) The introduction (cue or lead) to a report or recorded item. Also known as the headline sentence, *lead-in*, *link* or *nose* (US).

In type ► Warning to printer to indicate that what appears as copy to be set is already available in type from earlier setting.

Invasion of privacy ► Breaching an individual's right to be left alone.

Inverted pyramid ► Traditional representation of news stories, with main point (who, what, where, when, why and how) at the start and information declining in news value thereafter and ending with short background. Tends to oversimplify structure of news story. Better to imagine series of inverted pyramid within an overall large pyramid.

Investigative journalism ► A form of reporting in which a news situation is examined in 'depth by a team of reporters under a projects leader, i.e. as an investigation of all aspects.

Investigative reporter ► One who works on special stories involving more extensive research into a subject or individual than normally would be found on a typical news story.

Investigative reporting ► In one respect all journalism involves investigation. But investigative reporting tends to reveal something of social/political significance which someone powerful or famous wants to hide. US: Investigative reporters are known as *muckrakers*.

In-vision ▸ Instruction on script to indicate anchor or reporter should be on-camera at this point.

In vision / on camera (story) ▸ Item or part item read by performer in the studio without further illustration.

IP number ▸ (Internet protocol number) – Sometimes called a dotted quad. A unique number consisting of 4 parts separated by dots, e.g. 166.114.244.2. Every machine that is on the *Internet* has a unique IP number which is, in away, its Internet address, and is unique. If a machine does not have an IP number, it is not really on the Internet. Most machines also have one or more domain names. IP number and domain name both signify the address of a machine on the Internet, the difference being that IP address is difficult to remember because it is in four sets of digits, while the domain name is easy to remember as it is alphanumeric. See also *domain name, Internet, TCP/ZP.*

IPS ▸ Inches Per Second. Tape-recording term, refers to speed of tape travel past the recording and replay heads.

Ips ▸ Inches per second. Unit measuring the speed at which magnetic tape runs.

IRC ▸ An acronym for Internet relay chat. Worldwide real-time conferencing on the Internet. There are hundreds, may be thousands of IRC channels, also called *chat rooms*. These *chat rooms* typically focus on specific topics, issue or commonality.

Iris ▸ (i) Component of a camera lense, the iris is an expandable circular opening through which light passes, thus allowing the varying levels of illumination. When the iris is open as far as it will go, a maximum amount of light is transmitted through the lens to the camera. Conversely, a minimum of light is transmitted to the camera when the iris is closed. The size of the iris opening is measured in F-stops, ranging from f/1.4 to f/22, with f/1.4 being the widest opening. (ii) Elliptical masking device that blocks out a portion of the picture appearing on the motion picture or television screen. A scene may begin while the iris is completely closed and, as the iris is slowly expanded to an open position, the scene will seem to "grow" in an expanding circle from the center of the screen. When a scene closes from its boundaries in a slowly shrinking circle, the iris is being contracted from an open to a closed position. These moves are respectively called *iris-in and iris-out.*

ISDN ► (Integrated services digital network) Basically a way to move more data over existing regular phone lines. This digital telephony scheme allows two simultaneous connections over the same wire, can include audio and data. It can provide speeds of roughly 128,000 bits-per-second over regular phone lines. In countries with meagre connectiivty infrastructure most people will be limited to 56,000 or 64,000 bits-per-second.

Island ► (US) Style of planning newspaper advertising so that it is completely surrounded by editorial.

ISP ► (Internet Service Provider) An institution that provides access to the Internet in some form, usually for money. In India, VSNL, MTNL, Satyam online, etc are ISPs. *See also Internet.*

Issue ► One of a series of regularly published periodicals, such as a magazine, newspaper, or newsletter, defined by the date of publication or the content. For example, a magazine published in January is the January issue. The last magazine published each year may be a special "an-

nual" issue. India Today has a "annual" issue published each year summarising the year's events. Similarly, an isue also refers to all copies of one day's newspaper and an may consist of several *editions.*

Issues-to-go ► number of issues remaining to be served on a magazine or newsletter subscription prior to expire. Renewal promotion campaigns begin at a point determined by the issues-to-go. Most begin when there are six or seven issues remaining in the subscription term.

Italic ► Type face tilting to right. Not commonly used in body text. Sometimes in headlines. Some French newspapers put all direct quotes in italics but this style not adopted Britain or US.

Ital(s) ► Abbreviation for italic.

ITC ► (Independent Television Commission) Regulatory body for independent television in U.K.

ITN (Independent Television News) ► Company responsible for providing national television news to Channels 3 and 4 in the United Kingdom , and for services to other broadcasters.

ITU ► International Typographical Union.

Jack ➤ Socket connected to an audio circuit. Can incorporate a switch activated by insertion of Jack plugs-a 'break'Jack.

Jackfield or patch panel ➤ Rows of Jacks connected to audio sources or destinations. Provides availability of all circuits for interconnection or testing.

Jack line ➤ A short line left at the top of a column (usually avoided in page make up). Also a *widow*.

Jack plug or post office Jack ➤ Plug type used for insertion in Jack socket comprising three connections a circuit pair plus earth, known as 'ring tip and sleeve'. See also *Double ender*.

Jamming ➤ The practice of disturbing the clear transmission of radio/TV programmes through some other electronic means.

Java ➤ Java is a network-oriented programming language invented by Sun Microsystems that is specifically designed for writing programmes that can be safely downloaded to your computer through the *Internet* and immediately run without fear of *viruses* or other harm to your computer or files. Using small Java programmes (called "Applets"), web pages can include functions such as animations, calculators, and other fancy tricks.

A huge variety of features can be added to the *web* using Java, since you can write a Java program to do almost anything a regular computer programme can do, and then include that Java program in a web page. See also *Applet*.

JavaScript ➤ JavaScript is a programming language that is mostly used in *web pages*, usually to add features that makes the web pages more interactive. When JavaScript is included in an *HTML* file it relies upon the *browser* to interpret the JavaScript. When JavaScript is combined with Cascading Styles Sheets (CSS), and later versions of HTML (4.0 and later) the result is often called *DHTML*. JavaScript was invented by Netscape and was going to be called "LiveScript", but the name was changed to JavaScript to cash in on the popularity of Java. JavaScript and Java are two different programming languages. See also: *HTML, Java*.

Jazz journalism (US) ➤ A style of news presentation in the US newspapers of the 1920s, which emphasized action and scandal. It reminded the days of yellow press (see *yellow journalism*) but used a tabloid-style format with extensive photography.

JDK ▸ (Java Development Kit) A software development package from Sun Microsystems that implements the basic set of tools needed to write, test and debug Java applications and applets. See also *Applet, Java*.

Jelly ▸ Colour medium Used to indicate 'diffuser', see gel.

Jim das ▸ See *dinky dash*.

Jingle ▸ Catchy repetitious sounds or words used in rhyming fashion and usually set to music to form a simple musical verse, which is featured in a commercial and used in conjunction with other advertising for a product. Also see *ident*.

Jingle package ▸ The set of jingles used by a station to establish its audio logo. Also see *ident*.

Job ▸ A journalistic assignment.

Jock ▸ See *Disc jockey*.

Jog mode ▸ In hard disk, non-linear editing, reproduces samples of the sound in direct relation to the movement of the cursor over the defined region being listened to or edited.

Jog shutter dial ▸ An editing control that varies the tape speed from frame by frame advance (jog) to high speed picture search (shuttle).

Joining tape ▸ Adhesive tape used in tape editing.

Joint operating agreements (US) ▸ Arrangement between two competing newspapers to share business staffs and printing facilities without violating anti-trust laws.

Journalese ▸ Offensive term for shoddy, cliché ridden language.

Journalism ▸ The profession of reporting or writing news for the public by various means, e.g. *newspaper, magazine, TV, radio* and *Internet*.

Journalism reviews ▸ Publications that study and analyse the *press*.

Journalist ▸ Person whose profession is to report and write news stories that are disseminated through various media: *radio, TV, newspaper, magazine* or *Internet*.

Journals ▸ Articles collected together on Internet sites. Sometimes these journals are "referred" (sent out to reviewers in the field before acceptance), web journals are typically done in hypertext format.

Journo ▸ Slang for journalist.

JPEG ▸ (Joint Photographic Experts Group) A file format using a compression technique to reduce the size of a graphics file by as much as 96 percent. JPEG is most commonly mentioned as a format for image files. JPEG format is preferred to the GIF format for photographic images as opposed to line art or simple logo art. See also *GIF*.

Jump ➤ (US) (i) To continue a story from one page to another. (ii) To move from one Web page to another.

Jump cuts ➤ A jump cut is an aberration that makes the subject appear to jump from one position to another in two camera shots. Jump cuts may cause viewer disorientation and are sometimes used deliberately to create that effect. However, they are usually accidents that happen as a result of such factors as an extreme change in subject, size, camera angle, screen position, or a camera shift form a moving action to a stationary shot. For example, suppose you have videotaped the Indian prime minister's speech. He says: *India will not be provoked into an arms race by the testing of Ghouri missiles by Pakistan* (smiles, then coughs up). *Oh!... sorry* (clears his throat, turns his head to the other side)... *But I want to assure the nation that we will answer the challenge appropriately if the situation warrants.*

In radio, here would be no problem. The sound editor will simply skip off the coughing fit by cutting after "... missiles by Pakistan" and then again pick up from "I want to assure..."

But editing a videotape picture is quite different. If you silence the picture, that would look odd because the prime minister's facial expressions and lip movements would will be visible. In the meantime he has also turned his head to the other side, say right. That creates additional editing problems. Supposing that just before the coughing fit, his head was towards the left and with his last sentence he turned to right. Now, if we cut out the visuals of the coughing fit, and edit with the visuals where he turns to right and starts speaking," But I want to assure...", it would appear as if the P.M. has broken his neck because the viewer would see him suddenly jerking his head to right. That is because the visuals proceeding his turning to right have been edited out to cut the coughing fit.

It will be apparent that something has been cut out and that would send the viewers pondering over the jerk and disorient them from the main news story. This distraction resulting from the lack of visual continuity in editing is called a jump cut. However, it can be also be used as a technique for compressing time. You can get over the jump cut by inserting a cutaway shot. See also *Cut aways*.

Jump head ➤ (US) Headline on continued part of story.

Jumpline ➤ (US) 'Continued from page I...'. In stories appearing on more than one page, a jumpline is used to indicate the page on which the next portion of the story is printed or 'jumped'.

Jump story ▶ (US) See *Run on*.

Junior page ▶ Space designation for magazine advertisements, so named because the space is the standard size of a page in a small magazine (4 3/8" x 6 1/2"); also called *junior unit*.

Junk mail ▶ Derogatory term used colloquially for promotional mail; also, unsolicited mail.

Justification ▶ (i) Adjustment of the spacing between words and characters .'Justified' type is set so that lines are full out at both ends. (ii) Proving the truth of an allegation when defending a libel action.

Justify ▶ Line of text set to fit a given measure.

Kk

K (kilobyte) ▶ A thousand bytes, actually 124 (2) bytes; it is a measurement of computer memory.

Keep down ▶ Instruction to printer to set in lower-case.

Keep in ▶ Instruction to compositor to use thinnest spacing possible to keep all words in a line or section.

Keep up ▶ Instruction to printer to set in capitals.

Kelvin ▶ Measurement of the color quality of light; its colour temperature. Lower colour temperature sources have warm yellowish red quality (candles, dimmed tungsten). High Kelvin Typical interior lighting 3200 3400 K: day light 5600K.

Kern ▶ Any part of the face of a letter which extends over the edge of the body, as in italic or script type. A kern is supported on the shoulder of an adjacent letter. It provides the illusion of even spacing and reduces the amount of white space between letters.

Key ▶ Switch or button on a computer keyboard.

Keyboard ▶ (i) The panel out line of type to fit a nominated width. (ii) Computer input/output device that resambles a typewriter and is used for data entry into a computer.

Key entry ▶ Type of computer data entry accomplished by manually typing the information on a computer *keyboard*. Key entry is much less efficient than other types of entry, such as Scan entry or tape entry, because it is slower and more prone to human error. However, the computer equipment required to key enter data is easily affordable by most business organizations. Scan entry equipment can be quite costly, and tape entry applies only to situations where orders are received from intermediaries, such as telephone agents, and not directly from consumers who submit their orders in hard-copy format or over the telephone.

Keying ▶ The matteing of one video image over another.

Keying colour ▶ Colour chosen to activate CSO/ chromakey.

Key light ▶ Chief source of artificial light for a camera scene.

Keyline ▶ Outline drawing used as a guide over finished artwork to show the position, shape, and size of the other elements that will appear in the layout. The keyline is sometimes referred to as the type mechanical.

Key map ▶ A locator map of news departments that send reporters to the scene.

Key shot ► See *master shot*.

Keywords ► (i) Words related to a given topic used to locate information on that topic in a database. For example, searching the Web for the keyword "Terms" might help you find a site containing Internet terms. (ii) One or two words which sum up the most important point of a news story.

Kicker ► (i) Small headline, usually underscored, placed above and to left of main headline. Also *eyebrow, teaser, overline*. (ii) An amusing story at the end of a newscast. Also see *tailpiece*, and *story types*. (iii) Lighting instrument, located behind the subject and casting light the subject (backlight) Its purpose is to add highlights to the head and hair, typically used for glamour effect.

Kill ► (i) Instruction not to use (or drop) story/ feature. Newspapers are supposed to pay "kill fee' when they break an agreement to use freelance copy. (ii) To cut, remove or get rid of sound, action, lines, stories, shots or production element in radio, TV and film. (iii) Break down a presingint plate after a rug or when the plate is no longer required. A publisher will issue a kill order when the plate is no longer required.

Kilo ► Thousand, Kilohertz-frequency in thousands of cycles per second. Kilowatt – electrical power, a thousand watts.

Kilohertz ► See Hertz.

Kiss impression ► Clean print image created while applying the least amount of pressure possible (approximately .004 inches of pressure) against the paper with the plate, or against the plate with the blanket. A harder impression might produce smudged ink around the edges of the printed areas. A lighter amount of pressure would not adequately transfer the image.

KISS rule ► Abbreviation for "Keep It Short and Simple," the principle used for drafting news items for the newspapers, radio, TV etc.

Knock down ► To disprove story usually in rival newspaper.

Knowledge workers ► This term refers to employees such as journalists, software developers, library professionals or business analysts who use the Internet for research as part of their job.

Ku-band ► A newer satellite communication band and class. Ku-band satellites also support more powerful downlinks and have news (media) applications.

Label ➤ Headline merely categorizing the news: e.g. "Interview with President" Or intro: "A report on child abuse". Such headlines are dull with no force or life.

Lag ➤ *(Trailing)* Camera tube limitation causing persistence or smearing after image following a moving object; particularly evident with light-toned subjects in very dark scenes.

LAN ➤ See *local area network*.

Landline ➤ A special cable link which can carry sound and or video at full bandwidth, so giving 'studio quality' (unlike a telephone line, which restricts the frequency).

Landscape ➤ A picture with horizontal emphasis.

Lap dissolve ➤ A special visual effect in which a second image gradually replaces the first image by increasing its amplitude or brightness.

Laptop ➤ A computer small enough to be placed on your lap. The laptop computer's small size allows you to take it almost anywhere and access the *Internet*. It is very helpful for those who a lot and don't want to go too long without e-mail or knowledge of what is happening in their remote offices.

Laser diode (LD) ➤ One of the mover versatile communications tools. As an FO system's light source, LDs have supported high-speed and long-distance relays.

Laser printer ➤ One of the primary components of a DTP system, laser printer is a computer-driven device that utilizes a laser beam to print forms, letters, and labels. Laser is an acronym for Light Amplification by Stimulated Emission of Radiation. Laser printers are high-speed, high-quality printers with unique flexibility as to combinations of type fonts and orientation of characters on the page. They can create personalized computer letters with a combination of type fonts, such as boldface or italics, to highlight words or passages. With a laser printer, by rotating the printed image 90° or 180°, more forms can be printed on any given quantity of paper. The laser printer is fast because it creates an image in its entirety at once, in contrast to a line printer that prints one line at a time. This eliminates the need for line charges usually levied by printer for long letters.

Late fringe ➤ Segment of every broadcast day from 11:00 P.M. to 1:00 A.M. (on some stations until *sign-off*), which has been designated by the television broadcast media for the purpose of selling commercial time on the basis of audience size, composition, and demographics. Late-firing time is charged at a lower rate than prime time or other dayparts.

Late man ▸ Deskman who stays behind to fudge or replate for late news when last edition has gone to press.

Launch ▸ Term used to start an application such as Telnet of FTP.

Launch Vehicles ▸ Expandable (ELV) and piloted vehicles used to launch satellites and space probes. ns NASA and Ariane space are prominent organisations in this field. Other countries are developing their own capabilities. India is one country which has recently acquired this capability.

Lavalier ▸ Chord used to hang a throat mike around a performer (lavalier mike) who can be a newsreader or an interviewer ; also a microphone worn or hung around the neck.

Lawyer's alts ▸ Alterations made according to lawyer's advice (usually to avoid libel).

Layering ▸ Technique of beginning with general information, then providing links to more detail and supplementary information

Layout ▸ Design of page, originally by sub editor using pencil and sent to compositor for guidance but increasingly done totally on screen. There are three types of layouts, depending upon the extent which they represent a finished product accurately and completely: a rough layout, a finished layout and a comprohensive layout.

Lazy arm ▸ Small boom-type microphone stand suitable for suspending a microphone over a 'talks' table.

Lead ▸ (i) Prounced 'leed'. Opening item of a newscast (ii) Opening sentence of a broadcast news item. The main story in a newspaper's front page; also the main item in other pages; thus the phrase page lead. Also see *intro.* (iii) In stage, screen or television production (especially fiction primary player or players around when the story develops; the principal role; in a vocal group, see main singer, who usually sings the melody.

Lead all ▸ A lead (leed) or intro containing a general summary of a long news story. Also called a *news lead.*

Lead out ▸ (i) The concluding words of the author to a news story. (ii) Programme immediately following another programme on the same station.

Lead sheet ▸ Basic musical score indicating instrumentation of melody. Used for microphone control during music balance.

Lead story ▶ Story supporting the main display headlines on a page.

Lead time ▶ Period between writing an article and seeing it in print.

Lead to come ▶ Signal to printer that the opening paragraphs-lead or intro-will come later.

Leader ▶ (i) (UK) Leading article or editorial carrying newspaper's opinion. Leader page carries the leader and other opinion; also see *editorial*. (ii) Tape or film which leads up to the start of an item. On audio tape, the leader is transparent or coloured, on film it is usually numbered with countdown sequence.

Leaders ▶ Dots to lead the eye across the page.

Lead-in ▶ (i) Opening or introducing sentences of a story called lead-in. This would be a copy preceding a sound bite or a reporter's package. Same as in radio but with a difference. Here it is not necessary to identify the person who speaks the lead-in in the newscopy itself because this identification can be visually done by a super or an electronic title., Anchors like Prannoy Roy (NDTV) and Riz Khan (CNN), introduce the stories of their respective newscasts by first speaking out the lead-ins. In fact, their main job is to deliver the lead-ins of their newscasts. The rest of the narration is normally done by reporters (packages) and other persons.(iii) In a dramatic presentation, opening monologue.

Leading ▶ pronounced 'ledding' The vertical space between lines of type. Measured in points.

Lead-out ▶ (i) In broadcast, programme immediately following another programme on the same station; said to lead the audience out of the advertiser's programme on the same station. See also *audience flow; lead in*. (ii) Concluding lines of a news item in a broadcast.

Lead (pronounced led) ▶ (iv) Space between lines of type (derived from former hot metal printing system when metal, or leads, were used for this purpose). Leaded out copy has its lines paced out to fit allotted space.

Leak ▶ (i) Information by an anonymous source, often a member of a public body, which was intended to be secret (to leak); information obtained in this way (a leak). (ii) The system where the Government virtually manipulates the media.

Lean period ▶ Period when there is a general scarcity of news items to be reported for a mass media organisation.

Leased line ▶ Refers to a phone line that is rented for exclusive 24-hour, 7-days-a-week use from your location to another location. The highest speed data connections require a leased line. See also *T-1, T-3, DSL.*

LED ➤ Light emitting diode. Low powered light used for electronic displays (on/off indicators, level meters, etc.).

Leg art ➤ (US) Any sexy illustration.

Leg ➤ Vertical sub-division of text type arranged in several columns. Thus in horizontal layout there are three legs of type under a three-column headline.

Leg up ➤ To raise the height of scenic unit by adding supports at floor level.

Legal (vb) ➤ To send copy to lawyer to be checked for libel, contempt etc.

Legend ➤ (i) See *caption.*(ii) Explanatory list of symbols on a charter map, including the mileage scale on a map. (iii) Lettering in an inscription, as on a coin or medal.

Legman ➤ Reporter who collects facts but does not write the story.

Lens ➤ One or more pieces of precisely curved glass arranged in a tube to direct light rays from the subject into camera . The rays are bent by the lens so that they converge on the chip, forming a focused, inverted image.

Lens angle ➤ The camera lens sees a 4 x 3 shaped wedge of the scene. The *horizontal* cover-age angle of a lens is simply termed the 'lens angle'. In a zoom lens this can be varied from 'narrow (telephoto)' (e.g. 10°) to wide (i.e. 50°). The lens angle can be drawn on scale plans to show what a camera will see from any given position. The *vertical* lens angle is three quarters of it corresponding horizontal angle and can be used on scale elevations. HDTV systems use a 16:9 aspect ratio, so that their horizontal and vertical coverage angles are in those proportions.

Lens aperture ➤ (f-stop; iris) Adjustable diameter diaphragm within the lens housing. Altering its size simultaneously affects the image brightness ('exposure') and the 'depth of field.

Lettering ➤ Drawing or inscribing copy by hand, as compared to the mechanical setting of metal type. Also called hand lettering, it is done by an artist when the desired effect requires a quality that is not obtainable with type. It is also done to accommodate the space available when the required space prevents the use of type or as an economy measure to save on the cost of typesetting. Lettering is considered an art form and is also used for inscriptions on gold, silver, or other metal pieces.

Letterpress ➤ Process of printing from an inked raised surface.

The raised type and block, which are inked, come in diract contact with paper in this process. Letterpress is the oldest printing method and is used primarily for jobs consisting mainly of reading matter (without illustrations), such as price list, parts lists, timetables, rate schedules, and directories. Now almost out of use. See also *lithography*.

Letterset ▸ Dry offset printing technique that uses a relief plate and an intermediate printing Blanket; also called *dry offset; indirect relief printing*. Letterset does not require a dampening system. It derives from a combination of letterpress and offset printing techniques.

Letterspacing ▸ A composition techniane used in modifying the distance between the letter within a word. It helps to create lines of equal width on a page or to shorten or lengthen text. It is effectively used for copy or headlines in capital letters, but with lowercase or italic letters nonuniform spacing between the letters in body text is aesthetically unappealing and makes reading difficult. Uniform line lengths can also be created by spacing-in or spacing-out—that is, modifying the distance between words in a line; also called *wordspacing*. See also *justify*.

Level ▸ The volume of a voice as registered on a volume unit's meter on an audio console. *"Give me a level"* is an engineer's request for the performer to keep talking until audio equipment is adjusted properly.

Libel ▸ Any expression (printed, broadcast, etc.) that damages your reputation within the community, causes others to disassociate themselves from you, or attacks your character or professional ability.

Liberal bias ▸ A point of view that is generally pro-big government, pro-progressive values, pro-ethnic diversity and anti-big business and anti-republican party (USA).

Libertarian theory ▸ A political system in which there is free flow of information without any restrictions.

Library ▸ Collection of clippings, newspaper files, reference books and photographs.

Library material/tape ▸ See file footage

Library shots ▸ *(Stock shot)* A library of filmed or video taped shots of particular action, subject, location, etc. (e.g. view of Mount Everest) that can be inserted into any program requiring this illustration.

Licence ▸ An agreement to use copyright material within negotiated restrictions.

Lift ► To use whole or section of story from one edition to the next; to pinch story from other media outlet changing and adding only a little. When only barest minimum is changed it is known as "straight lift".

Ligature ► Two or more letters joined together and forming one character or type, as in ffi.

Light box ► Back-lighted work surface for viewing transparencies, negatives, and for marketing on back of photo prints.

Light face ► Type with lighter appearance, compared with bold.

Light level ► Intensity of illumination falling on or reflected from a scene. It is measured with a light meter in *lux* (formerly 'foot- candles')

Light pencil ► An instrument used for erasing undesirable portions or material from the copy or the TV screen.

Light setting ► The process of directing lamps, adjusting their precise angle, coverage, light quality, colour, and intensity to suit their individual purposes.

Light table ► Back-lighted work surface used in photo-composed newspapers. The compositor places the page on it to assemble the elements of the page.

Lighting balance ► The relative intensities of lamps that together produce a specific effect.

Lighting grid ► Construction suspended from the ceiling of a studio to support the lights.

Lighting ratio ► Ratio of the power of the key light to that of the filler light.

Limbo ► (i) In filming, any shot whose background has no identifying characteristics (e.g., showing time or place), therefore giving the illusion that time and space are endless. (ii) Lighting technique in which the scene is lighted so that the subject or object is displayed in the foreground and the background appears either gray or black.

Limited-time station ►Broadcast station that is assigned a frequency or channel for broadcasting only during a specified time period. At other times, the frequency or channel is shared by other stations. Many local television stations operate on a limited-time basis.

Limiter ► Device to prevent the signal level exceeding a pre-set value.

Line ► (i) An imaginary line used as a reference for positioning the camera when taking different shots of the same scene . It may be the subject's eye line or direction of movement or some other line of interest . Filming from the same side of the line preserves continuity. (ii) Single line of headline or test type.

Lineage, linage ► Measure of printed material based on the number of lines printed. Freelance copy is lineage copy because it is normally paid so much a line. In US, term more commonly used for amount of advertising printed in specific period.

Line-and-tone ➤ Process-engaged printing block combining both screen and line-etching techniques.

Linear sound ➤ A sound track which is recorded by a fixed audio head. Linear sound track takes the form of a thin strip running along the tape edge. Sound quality is poorer than hi-fi stereo recordings.

Line beating ➤ (*Strobing*) A localized rapid flickering effect, as a fine pattern in the scene coincides with TV scanning lines in the picture, particularly visible on engravings, close horizontal lines, close mesh etc.

Line block ➤ An engraved plate, as in the hot metal printing system, which reproduced the lines of a drawing in continuous black, as opposed to the half-tone block which rendered tones by means of dots of varying density.

Line-casters ➤ Typesetting machines such as Linotype and Intertype which cast test type in lines. Also operator who uses keyboard of a line-casting machine.

Line crossing ➤ Moving the camera from one side of the ac-tion to other . This may be for creative motive , but more often it makes the spatial narrative incoherent to the audience.

Line cut ➤ (US) *Line block.*

Line drawing ➤ Brush or pen drawing consisting of black-and-white elements as in a cartoon

Line equalisation ➤ The process which compensates for frequency distortion at the receiving end of a landline.

Line input ➤ A socket which accepts a video signal . Found on all VCRs but on few camcorders.

Line producer ➤ Person dealing with the day-to-day work of making a TV programme or a film within budget and on time. Also know as production manager.

Lines ➤ The dialogue a performer must deliver.

Line up ➤ (i) In broadcast, period immediately before a recording or programme transmission during which the final technical checks are carried out. (ii) Randown of shows (TV) to be broadcast in a specific season or items of a newscast. (iii) Broadcast stations that will be carrying a particular broadcast. (iv) To arrange the type set evenly flush left or right.

Lining ➤ Type in which the faces of the characters align along a base line. Lining figures, in contrast to old-style figures, are of uniform size and height.

Link ▸ (i) Narrative linking or bridging interviews in a TV report, summarizing or giving additional information. See also *package*. (ii) A link will transport you from one *Internet* site to another with just a click of your mouse. Links can be text or graphic and are recognizable once you know what to look for. Text links usually will be underlined and often a different colour than the rest of the text on your screen. A graphic link usually has a frame around it. For example, at the bottom or top of a search engine page the mailbox is a link as well as the text (i.e., astrology, news, fashion). The mouse pointer usually changes to a hand when positioned over a link.

Links vehicle ▸ Mobile vehicle used as a platform for a microwave transmitter. See also Microwave.

Lino ▸ Abbreviation for Linotype.

Linofilm ▸ Trade name of photosetting machine.

Linotron ▸ Trade name for photosetting machine using cathode ray tube.

Linotype ▸ Trade name for keyboarded line-casting machine.

Lip mic ▸ Noise-excluding ribbon microphone designed for close working, e.g. OB commentary.

Lip sync ▸ The precise synchronisation of lip movements and speech sounds.

Lip synchronization ▸ In television and film production making the recording of the spoken dialogue (or singing) simultaneous with the visualization of the spoken dialogue (or signing); synchronizing the voice track with the video track. The term derives from the fact that the movement of the lips is synchronized with the sound of the words, its short form is *lip sync*.

Listener diary ▸ Journal of radio/television programmes heard/viewed that is kept by a participant in a market research study that measures audience share. See also *media reach; Nielsen rating*.

Listings ▸ Lists usually of entertainment events giving basic information : data, times, venue, phone numbers etc.

Listserv® ▸ The most common kind of maillist, "Listserv" is a registered trademark of L-Soft international, Inc. Listservs originated on BITNET but they are now common on the Internet. See also *BITNET, e-mail, maillist*.

List server ▸ Computer used to administer and organize mailing list. Two popular mailing list programs that run on list servers are *listproc* and *listserv*.

Literals ▸ Typographical errors in composition.

Lithography ▸ Printing process in which the printing surface is neither raised (see *Letterpress*) nor etched into the plate (i.e. Gravure), but in which the printing and nonprinting areas exist on the same plane, and printing is effected by means of a chemical process that allows ink to adhere to only the parts of the surface to be reproduced. The process, which was developed in the late eighteenth century, depends on the fact that water and grease repel each other. Originally, the image to be reproduced was drawn on a slab of stone with a grease crayon. The stone was then dampened with water, but the grease from the crayon would repel the water so that, when a grease-base ink was rolled across the stone, the ink would adhere only to the drawing, and the stone would be ready for the application of paper to reproduce the drawing. Lithography ("writing on stone") is accomplished according to the same principle today, but the stone has been replaced by a metal plate and the technology of preparing the plate has become more sophisticated. Lithography is less expensive than either letterpress or gravure printing and is a reasonable alternative, particularly when an order calls for a short run.

Little magazines ▸ Literary magazines with small circulation.

Live ▸ (i) A performance in which the talent is working in the presence of an audience. Also, direct transmission of a studio programme at the time it is originated or performed. (ii) Turned on, such as a live mike. (iii) Type that will be used in the edition going to press. (iv) Copy of a story that is intended to be used; a line story is the one on which the report is still working. Also see *kill*.

Live acoustic ▸ A resonant recording environment.

Live copy ▸ Copy yet to be set into type.

Live matter ▸ (i) Area of a printing plate that carries the image to be printed. (ii) Printing materials, such as type compositions or plates, that have been prepared for use and are not to be broken down after that use because they are likely to be used again.

Live on tape ▸ A recording system in which a programme is transferred to tape without breaks or edits , to be shown later as if it were being transmitted live.

Live real audio ▸ Internet radio system, making it possible to download radio programmes onto a computer via a modem.

Live shot ▸ A live report from the scene of a news story that is in progress or has already occurred.

Live tag ▸ In broadcast, live ending that has been added to a prerecorded message.

Live time ▸ Time on a broadcast schedule that has been set aside for a live broadcast.

Live title ▸ Title of a programme filmed or videotaped directly from a source appearing on the set at the time of shooting, as distinguished from a title inserted during the editing process.

Live van ▸ The vehicle holding the remote live reporting equipment such as the transmitter and antenna. The van transmits the signal in a straight line or "line-of-sight" path back to the studio, free from such obstacles as buildings or tall trees.

LO (local origination) programme ▸ Programmes produced by a local cable company to be telecast over its system.

Load ▸ It is a short for download and upload. If someone asks how long did the page take to load? He/She is referring to the time it takes a page to appear on your screen. If a web page is loading slow it means that it's taking a long time to fully appear on your screen. You can often scroll through a page and look at the parts that have loaded while the rest of the page continues to load. Also, you can usually click a link on the page

you are loading and link to another page without waiting for the current page to fully load.

Lobby (UK) ▸ Specialist group of corespondent reporting House of Commons.

Lobbying ▸ Attempts to influence the top devision makers (e.g. legislators), the term derived from the practice of PR executives intercepting the lawmakers in lobbies outside their hearing rooms.

Lobster trick, shift ▸ (US) Early-morning news workers or printers on a daily; night-shift of an afternoon paper.

Local angle ▸ see *Angle*.

List server ▸ Computer used to administer and organize mailing list. Two popular mailing list programs that run on list servers are *listproc* and *listserv*.

Local corr ▸ A district correspondent.

Localise ▸ To stress local appeal or angle in story.

Local loop ▸ The segment (local) of a telecommunications network connecting the user to the local or the nearest exchange.

Local media ▸ Media vehicles, such as newspapers, radio stations, television stations, and cable stations, that function primarily to serve the communications needs of the communities or metropolitan areas in which they are located.

Local programme ▸ Radio or TV programme that originates

from a local broadcast station, in contrast to a network programme.

Location ➤ (i) Geographical position of an event. (ii) This refers to an *Internet* address. While you are in your browser you will see a section at the top of the page that is titled "location". For example, *home page* of the Times of India has its location: http:/ www.timesof india.com. If you type in the address of someone's web page and hit enter, your *browser* will take you to that page. However, the address you type in the location bar must be an exact match.

Location box ➤ Place in the Netscape or Internet Explorer screen that displays the address of the Internet site currently being viewed.

Locking-off ➤ A special effect technique whereby the camera is locked in position half way through a shot. After a period of time the camera is restarted for a trick effect.

Lock up (a page) ➤ The process of placing the type and illustrations in a chase, and adjusting the *furniture* and *quoins* so that the type is firmly held and the forme can be sent to foundry or presses.

Log ➤ (i) Generally, all the shots are written down while shooting. This list is called a log. From this log another list can be made up of the actual shots needed in the scene, this second list is called the edit list or EL. Sometimes the log is called a shot list and sometimes a time code log. (ii) The schedule of broadcasting, the assignment book under the control of the Editor and the record of matter having been sent to the printer.

Login ➤ Used as both noun and a verb.
Noun: the account name used to gain access to a computer system. Not a secret (contrast with password).
Verb: the act of entering into a computer system, e.g. login to the WELL and then go to the GBN conference. See also *password*.

Login name ➤ The set of letters and / or numbers used to identify yourself to the computer. This name is often used as part of you e-mail address.

Log in or log on ➤ When you log in to a computer you identify yourself to the computer so that it can check to see if you are an authorized user. Typically, you need both a login name and a password to identify yourself with a computer.

Login prompt ➤ Typically, the word "login": appears on the screen of a computer that requires an access code, as a way of "prompting" or reminding you of what you need to do next. In this case, a login prompt indicates that you need to enter your login name and press <enter>.

Logo ▸ Abbreviation for *logotype*.

Logotype ▸ Nameplate for a newspaper or identification of a section, Business, Family, etc., cast on one block of type.

LOL ▸ An acronym for 'Laugh Out Loud'. Look for it in your *e-mail*, or *chat rooms*.

Long form ▸ Longer than the usual length for a news feature; a longer 60-minute plus news documentary or a documentary in-depth series.

Long measure ▸ Width of line longer than usual for the size of type. An 8pt line of 24 picas, say, would be long measure.

Long primer ▸ Old name for 10 pt type.

Long run ▸ When a printing press is not interrupted for a long time by a new edition, or when a page similarly remains unchanged; or greater-than-usual space given to a single story or feature.

Long shot (LS) ▸ Shot taken from a distance to include the overall scene. (Also called *wide shot*). Also see *picture composition*.

Long stop ▸ Late man.

Loop ▸ A large circle of film or tape used in dubbing sessions. If you want to re-voice an actor's reading, you "loop it." The actor stands in a recording studio watching the projected film loop on the screen, which keeps repeating until the actor has matched his or her voice to the movement of the lips on the screen.

Loose ▸ Too much letter-or word-spacing in composition.

Low angle shot ▸ Shot taken from a distance to the ground and pointing upwards.

Low-band ▸ A low frequency colour recording technique commonly used on ½ inch machines.

Lower third ▸ Caption or super in the lower third of the picture.

Lower-case ▸ Letters which are not capitals, thus c, d, e. Also the name given to the composing case which holds these letters.

Low key ▸ Low level but possibly ·high contrast lighting which emphasises dark tones and shadows, creating a dramatic or sinister atmosphere.

LP (Long play) ▸ A feature which runs the tape at a slow speed to increase playing time. ·Some times called half speed.

LS ▸ Long shot. See *picture composition*.

Ludlow ▸ Trade name for machine which casts larger sizes of headline on a slug from hand-assembled matrices.

Luminance ▸ The true measured brightness of a surface. Doubling the illumination produces double the luminance, unlike the impression received by the eye. Snow has a high luminance and black velvet extremely low luminance.

Lunch ▸ Time-tested technique for gathering information, cultivating contacts and producing ideas. Not liked by accountants as they have to pass the bills for the seemingly a productive job.

Lurking ▸ Reading online messages or chat room conversations without taking part in the discussion. Users are encouraged to lurk in the Newsgroups or chat rooms until they have some idea what the discussion is about and the style is like.

Mm

MAC ► Multiplexed analogue components . A television system based on digital sound and FM analogue picture transmission . It is designed to be compatible with future developments such as wide screen and high definition, Variations include D-MAC and D2-MAC.

Machine border ► Border cast on such machines as Elrod, Linotype, Intertype, Monotype.

Machine minder ► Operator in charge of a press.

Machine room ► The room or hall containing the presses used to print a newspaper or magazine.

Machine-set ► Type which can be set mechanically on a keyboarded line-casting machine, as distinct from hand-assembled type or matrices. Now with the coming of computers, most of the newspapers have done away with this system.

Macro ► The technique of filming in extreme close up to give a highly magnified image.

Macro lens ► A close -up lens capable of very high magnification .

Magazine ► (i) Publication issued periodically, containing a variety of editorial items: articles, detailed reports, short stories, interviews, photographic essays, etc. of either a specific or general nature, e.g. Down to Earth. (specific-environment) and India today (general interest). Superior in production quality magazines are sold by subscription and at newstands. Often newspapers, particularly sunday editions, will feature a separate magazinesation. (ii) Container which holds matrices on a line-casting machine; lightproof compartment in or on a camera or projector for film.

Magazine programme ► TV or radio programme which is a mix of hard news and feature items .

Mail address ► The unique set of letters followed by a computer's location name that is provided to you so that you can send and receive messages across the Internet.

Mailers ► (US) Staff who count and pack papers for delivery: equivalent to UK publishers or packers. Also a *folding wrapper* for protecting posted materials.

Mail server ► A computer that holds email messages for clients on a network.

Maillist (or Mailing list) ► A (usually automated) system that allows people to send e-mail to one address, where upon their message is copied and sent to all of the other subscribers to the maillist. In this way, people who have many different kinds of e-mail access can participate in discussions together.

Mailto ▸ A command that provides a link to your e-mail address from the Web page. The browser automatically opens an e-mail program.

Main head ▸ Main headline; primary or most important headline in a piece of editorial matter. It is the main head that catches the reader's eye and invites further reading of the copy that follows.

Main menu ▸ The opening list of selection tat appears on the opening screen of a program or on a subsection of a program.

Mainframe ▸ Main computer or Central Processing Unit in what is typically a full-size computer system. Computers have made it possible to handle large amounts of data quickly and accurately. The major drawbacks to the large mainframes are that they generally require climate-controlled rooms and a technically adept staff to run, maintain, and programme them.

Mainstreaming ▸ Refers to a situation in which heavy television viewing produces a common view of the world and common values.

Majuscules ▸ The capital letters of the alphabet.

Make ▸ In newspaper it means 'space' required for a story. '*How much will it make*?' means 'How much space will the copy occupy?'

Make even ▸ Instruction to typesetter to make a section of type matter even with the end of the line, so that another type-setter, working on the next take, can *start even*.

Make over ▸ Process of rearranging a page of type or series of pages to accommodate later news, improve appearance or make corrections.

Make-ready ▸ The process of preparing a page forme or stereo plate for the presses. Sheets of paper are trimmed and laid beneath areas, especially blocks, to assure an even impression on every part of the printing area.

Make-up ▸ To take type from a galley and arrange in pages with illustrations; the physical appearance of the paper; the dummy page plan or design for the disposition of stories and pictures.

Make-up editor ▸ (US) Journalist who supervises the make-up of the paper in the composing room. See *stone sub*.

Managing editor ▸ Senior editorial executive. In US, frequently man in charge of news department while 'editor' controls the editorial page. In UK-usually subordinate to the editor and with administrative as well as editorial duties. In India, the coming of this designation has meant loss of editorial freedom and power to the newspaper management. Here he is the senior most executive of the newspaper, Editor/Executive Editor being subordinate him.

Manual ➤ A book containing useful instructions in a complied form.

Manufacturing automation protocol (MAP) ➤ An industrial-based network that has linked equipment and had automated various tasks.

Marching box ➤ Sound effects device comprising small box partially filled with gravel used to simulate marching feet.

Margins ➤ The unprinted surround of the area occupied by reading matter

Marker ➤ (US) Story from one edition clipped from the paper and pasted on copy paper to be marked for changes for the next edition—adds, inserts, corrections, cuts. Or a page proof or page from one edition marked with cuts and new stories. Also called a *mark* or *markup*.

Marketing ➤ Division of newspaper which deals with sales strategy, including sales promotion and circulation.

Market penetration ➤ See *reach, cumulative audience, penetration*.

Marking up ➤ Marking a story with important details, such as

who wrote it and when, and the catchline.

Marks ➤ (*Floor marks*) Small L-shaped marks crayoned or taped on the floor to indicate the position of furniture, scenery, props, actors, (toe marks), etc., to ensure accuracy in repeated positioning.

Mark up ➤ To prepare typewritten proofed copy for typesetting.

Masking ➤ (i) Any surface positioned to prevent the camera from seeing a particular area. (ii) Technique of obscuring part of a photograph (e.g. by paper overlay) to indicate the section not to be printed.

Mask out ➤ In printing, block out a portion of a drawing, illustration, photograph, or layout so that it will not appear on the reproduction.

Mass communications ➤ The mechanical means through which messages are transmitted to large, different and unknown individuals in various places. Often used as a synonym for mass media.

Mass magazine ➤ Magazine that is not targeted to appeal to a specific audience, but that has editorial content of a general nature, so that it appeals to a diversified readership—for example, the Reader's Digest, Frontline, India Today.

Mass media ➤ Forms, means or avenues of communication

through which it is possible to transmit identical information to a large number of people at different places. These are generally, press TV, radio, film, etc.

Master ➤ (i) The basic type shape inside a photosetter from which printed type is generated for cut-and paste production. (ii) Primary and most complete copy of a film, audio recording, file, document, tape, or other item that involves a significant effort to create or re-create, and from which all duplicates are made. To be used should the duplicate be damaged, lost, or stolen.

Master proofs ➤ Set of proofs, galley or page, incorporating all writer's and editor's corrections.

Master shot ➤ Main shot of a scene, filmed continuously from one camera. Other shots of the scene may be cut in to the master shot during editing. Also called *establishing shot*.

Master tape ➤ See *rough cut*.

Masthead ➤ The title of the newspaper and statement of its ownership and policy, usually carried on the front page. It also appears on the upper left-hand corner of the editorial page.

Mat ➤ Abbreviation for matrix.

Matrix, matrics (pl.) ➤ A die or mould from which type is cast. Also, the papier-mache mould from which a stereo plate is made.

Matte ➤ (*mask*) Grafics or electronically generated shape used to obscure part of one picture in order that a corresponding area of another shot can be inserted there.

Matt finish ➤ Dull finish to photograph or printing paper; contrast *glossy*.

Matter ➤ Any type or blocks. It may be body matter (the text setting); standing matter (not intended for immediate use); straight matter (simple setting); solid matter (without leads); open matter (leaded); live matters; dead matter; and so on.

MC ➤ Master of ceremonies, the compere. Also master copy/print.

MCPS ➤ Mechanical Copyright Protection Society. Organization which controls the copying or dubbing of copyright material.

MD (Mini Disc) ➤ Digital recording medium using miniature compact disc.

Mean-line ➤ The line indicated by the top of the lower-case x.

Measure ➤ (i) A working interaction between the message and the audience. (ii) The width of a line, column, or page of type, usually expressed in pica ems. Also, a graduated ruler showing the point size of type.

Mechanical ➤ Camera-ready paste-up of artwork and copy on a sheet of white carboard or posterboard, which includes all the elements to be reproduced, such as set type, photographs, illustrations, drawings, and line art. The term refers to a mechanical process that involves only the cutting, trimming, and pasting of previously prepared copy and artwork.

Media ➤ The means, the avenues, the vehicles, the instruments, the channels, the forms of communication-through which messages (news, entertainment, information, advertisement, etc.) are transmitted. (Plural form of medium). Media serve as the vital link between the communicator and the audience e.g. advertiser of a product and its potential consumer or political party and its supporters.

Media association ➤ Organization whose membership consists of persons affiliated with a particular form of media, such as a daily newspaper, and whose purpose is to build acceptance for that medium. Media association include National Union of Journalists, Indian Newspaper Society (INS), etc.

Media buy ➤ Purchase of time or space in an advertising medium, such as radio, television, or print space. The media-buy decision is based upon the amount of money available, the number of exposures desired, the target market the advertiser wants to reach, the frequency of exposure desired, the number of people each medium will reach, and the impact each medium will have on the message — for example, the impact of a soap advertisement in a fashion magazine versus one in a general magazine. Since there is no one right way to spend advertising dollars, it is the *media buyer's* job to choose a reasonable optimum. See also *media class; media option; media weight; multimedia.*

Media buyer ➤ Individual responsible for the purchase of time and space for the delivery of advertising messages in the media. A media buyer may be an employee of an advertising agency who specializes in such purchase, but, technically, a media buyer is any advertiser, advertising manager, or individual who buys the commercial time or the advertising space. In some large agencies, the purchase of advertising media has become quite specialized, and there are those who purchase only broadcast time (time buyers), others who purchase only print space (space buyers), and stil others who purchase only outdoor space (outdoor space buyers). In any case, the overall nomenclature is that of media buyer.

Media circus ➤ The congestion and chaos resulting from journalists reaching the scene of news.

Media class ➤ Type of media, as compared to a particular vehicle. For example, magazines are a media class, whereas Inside Outside (home decor magazine) is a vehicle.

Media imperialism ➤ Dominance by the Western Media over the underdeveloped countries in the area of mass communication.

Media option ➤ Specific description of the characteristics of an advertisement or commercial excluding the copy and artwork. The media option will detail the size (full page, half page, etc.), colour (black-and-white, or four-colour), and location (inside front cover, interior, etc.) of a print advertisement, or the length (60, 30, 10 seconds, etc.) and placement (morning drive, prime time, etc.) of a broadcast commercial. Media options are generally listed in a media plan.

Media pack ➤ Details of a magazine's circulation, readership and technical specifications. Used to attract advertisers.

Media planner ➤ Advertising agency employee in the media department who is responsible for the planning of media to be used in an advertising campaign. The primary function of the job is to match the *target audience* in each *campaign* with the appropriate media. The media planner will identify the desired target audience (from the advertiser's or account executive's input) and then make media selections based on the profiles of the various available media while also evaluating the media in terms of cost. The planner will make client recommendations as to the medium or combination of media that will best reach the target audience and meet the media objectives. In a smaller agency, the media planner is also the *media buyer*, but larger agencies will have a staff of buyers usually grouped according to *media class*.

Media reach ➤ Size of audience exposed to an advertisement through a particular medium. For example, the media reach of a television commercial could be millions of viewers, but the potential media reach of a local newspaper advertisement could be only hundreds of people. Also see *exposure*.

Media relations ➤ The practice of developing and maintaining contact with reporters, editors, and other media persons influencing news selection. Also called *press relations*.

Media survey ➤ Study conducted about the media, among the general public to determine the depth of penetration of the communications media and to what extent the media reaches a particular market or audience.

Media weight ► Volume of audience delivered by an advertising campaign in terms of the number of commercials and advertisements, amount of insertions, time parameters, and budget; the total audience delivery.

Medium ► (i) A weight of type between light and bold, or heavy. (ii) Singular of media. Also see *media*.

Medium close-up (MCU) ► Relative average framing for a shot; often framed from the waist up. Also see *picture composition*.

Medium shot (MS) ► In photography, film, or videotape production, shot where the subject and background share equal dominance in the picture (See Fig.). A medium shot of an individual will take in the body often from the knees or waist up. Also called *mid shot*. See *picture composition*.

Medium Shot (MS)

Megabyte ► A million or 10 lakh bytes. Actually, technically, 1024 kilobytes. See also *byte, bit, kilobyte*.

Megahertz ► In radio transmission, frequency unit equal to one million hertz, which is a unit of frequency equal to one cycle per second; abbreviated MHZ.

Memory ► The part of a computer that retains information fed into it; where written and edited stories are stored.

Menu ► (i) Collection of teasers at the start of a programme giving forthcoming attractions. (ii) A list of selections that appears on the opening screen of a programme or on a subsection of a programme.

Merchandizing ► Information about price and place of purchase in consumer journalism features.

Merge/Purge ► Process of combining two or more lists or files, simultaneously identifying and/or combining duplicates and eliminating unwanted records such as deadbeats and nixies. The purpose of the merge/purge is to provide a mailer with the best possible list of names to which to mail a promotion.

Message ► Primary element of the communication process, consisting of the information passed from the communicator to the receiver, such as the message of a television commercial or magazine advertisement. For example, the message of a body soap commercial is usually that the product will add more glow to user's skin than other products.

Metacrawler ➤ See *meta search engine*.

Meta search engine ➤ A type of software or a search engine that searches other search engines at the same time and combines the results from them. Also called metacrawler.

Metro area ➤ Metropolitan area that is the core of a market. A metro area would generally include a city of 5 lakh or more as the central core (from whence all broadcast originates), the county in which it is located, and the surrounding areas that share a high degree of economic and social integration with the central core city. Metro areas are used by the various rating services in the computation of *ratings* and *shares*.

Metro rating ➤ *Television households in a metro area* tuned in to a particular station or Programme, computed as a percentage of all the television households in the metro area.

MF ➤ Abbreviation for more to follow.

MFL ➤ More to follow later.

Mic/mike ➤ Microphone Device which converts sound air-waves into mechanical , then electrical energy.

Microcomputer ➤ Small- to medium-capacity computer that utilizes microchip technology to perform some of the functions of a large computer at a lower cost, uses a high-level Programming language that is easy to learn, and is encased in a relatively small cabinet that does not require special temperature or antistatic controls; also called personal computer or PC. The scope and range of microcomputer capabilities broadens every day as software becomes more sophisticated, but are largely dependent upon the data-storage capacity of each computer. Microcomputers can also serve as remote terminals providing access to a large computer. See also mainframe; minicomputer.

Microfiche ➤ Hard-copy print-out of a microfilm galley. Microfiche must be read with a special magnifying screen. It is frequently used to store customer file data and/or to duplicate customer files so that copies can be distributed to customer-service clerks.

Microform ➤ A type of film or paper that contains information in a miniatureized form, such as microfiche or microfilm, that requires a special machine to read it.

Microphonic ➤ Faulty piece of electronic equipment sensitive to mechanical vibration-acting like a microphone.

Microwave ▸ Usually refers to the transmitter used in live vans or satellite trucks to send the live report (signal) back to the studio (or to a satellite) where it can be recorded or broadcast live.

Microwave and Laser ▸ Two wireless, line-of-sight communications systems.

Middle leads ▸ 2pt leads (leds), called middle because they come between thin and thick leads.

Middle managers ▸ Those responsible for the co-ordination of activities designed to help the organization achieve its overall goals and targets.

Middle market ▸ Newspaper's such as Blitz and Evening News lie(in terms of overall style and appearance) between heavies and pops.

Middle of the road (MOR) ▸ Popular, mainstream music with general appeal, Non-extreme.

Middle space ▸ A space of four ems.

MIDI ▸ Musical Instrument Digital Interface. A standard that lets electronic musical devices communicate with each other. Music stored in MIDI format contains instructions for playing the music, rather than the digitized audio signal itself.

Mid shot ▸ See *medium shot.*

Milled rule ▸ A simplex rule or

border with a serrated edge as on the edge of a coin.

Milline rate, millinch rate ▸ Unit for measuring the advertising cost of a newspaper in terms of its circulation. The '*line*' rate is the cost of reaching the readers of one thousand copies of the paper with one line of classified advertising. The millinch rate is the cost of reaching one thousand with one inch of space.

MIME ▸ (Multipurpose Internet Mail Extensions) MIME types are extensions to files that tell your computer what kind of programmes to use to view the file. Technically, it refers to a standard for attaching non-text files to standard Internet mail messages. Non-text files include graphics, spreadsheets, formatted word-processor documents, sound files, etc. An email program is said to be MIME compliant if it can both send and receive files using the MIME standard. When non-text files are sent using the MIME standard they are converted (encoded) into text, although the resulting text is not really readable. Generally speaking, the MIME standard is a way of specifying both the type of files being sent and the method that should be used to turn it back into its original form. Besides email software, the MIME standard is also universally used by Web *Servers* to identify the files they are sending to Web Clients, in this way new file formats can be accommodated simply by updating the Borwsers' list of pairs of MIME-Types and appropriate software for handling each type. See also *browser, client, server, binhex, uuencode.*

Mimeograph ▶ Image duplication technique utilizing a porous image carrier through which ink is forced. Mimeograph machines were typically used for low-valume offset duplication and have been almost completely replaced by photocopy machines. Special 20 lb. paper measuring 17" x 22" was used.

Miniature ▶ Small realistic scene (often called 'model').

Minicam ▶ (also microcam) Lightweight, often self-contained, portable video camera for shooting news events, and with live capability.

Minidisc (MD) ▶ Digital recording and playback system using 64 mm disc in portable recorders and studio decks.

Minidoc ▶ A short news feature or documentary.

Minion ▶ Old name for 7pt type.

Minionette ▶ Old name for 6½ pt type.

Miniseries ▶ Television drama serialized for at least 2 episodes but for less than the standard 13-week season. One of the more famous mini-series was the dramatization of Alex Haley's book Roots, which drew a very large audience share.

Mini wrap ▶ Brief package, often used in the news.

Minuscules ▶ Lower-case letters of the alphabet.

Mirror ▶ (*Print & TV*) To reverse a graphic, setting, composition, etc., left to right as if seen in a mirror.

Mirror (Internet) ▶ "To mirror" is to maintain an exact copy of something. Probably the most common use of the term on the Internet refers to "mirror sites" which are web sites, or FTP sites that maintain exact copies of material originated at another location, usually in order to provide more widespread access to the resource. Another common use of the term "mirror" refers to an arrangement where information is written to more than one hard disk simultaneously, so that if one disk fails, the computer keeps on working without losing anything. See also *FTP, Web.*

Mirror shot ▶ Refers to a shot that is taken while the object is looking into a mirror which: (a) changes the object-polarity; (b) increases the distance and the depth of the shot, and, (c) provides greater angles. Also see *picture composition.*

Misprint ▶ Inaccurate setting, a typo-graphical error, a literal.

Mistracking ▶ Incorrect tape to head contact or tape path contact causing picture distortion as bursts of noise on replay.

Mitre ▶ Corner-piece of rule or border cut at angle of 45 degrees to form a perfect joint; to bevel a rule or border so that there is neat fit at the right-angle.

Mix ▶ (i) A combination of different sound elements, such as music, direct voice, sound effects, announcer voice, or singing voice, into a sound track for radio and television commercials or programmes or audio recordings. Here separate sound tracks are combined through a mixing console. (ii) In television broadcast, combination of programmes in a television contract for a series. For example, a contract for a 13-week series may call for 13 original performances, or it may call for 9 original and 4 rerun performances, or any combination of originals and reruns.

Mixdown ▶ The point, usually in post-production, when all the separate audio tracks are combined into a complete final version.

Mixer ▶ A device for combining several audio or video inputs.

Mobile unit ▶ (i) Television filming and recording facilities capable of moving or of being moved from location to location with relative ease and speed, used most frequently by the news departments of television stations; usually a car, van or truck equipped to produce programme material. (ii) Research facilities, libraries, blood banks, and the like, built into trailers that can be pulled by truck or driven under their own power from place to place as the demand arises.

Model release form ▶ A form to be signed by a photographic model, indemnifying the magazine against various legal claims.

Modem ▶ (Modulator, DEModulator) A device that translates computer signals to analogue signals suitable for sending across phone lines. Thus, a modem allows the computer to talk to other computers through the phone system. A modem is used at each end, i.e. computers at both ends have a modem. Basically, modems do for computers what a telephone does for humans.

Modern ▶ Term for typefaces having abrupt contrast between thin and thick strokes: the axis of the curves is vertical; and there are often no brackets on the serifs.

Modern media ▶ Avenues or means (media) of communication which came into existence as a result of scientific inventions, like Radio, TV, Press, Film, etc.

Modulation ► The process adding video and audio signals to a pre -determined carrier frequency for relay purposes.

Mofussil ► (India) Newspaper term for local or regional news; also mofussil desk, reporter, etc.

Mole ► A secret source for investigative journalist buried deep in heart of organization whose activities they are prepared to reveal.

Monitor ► Screen for displaying television pictures or computer-generated data. Also a television set used in the studio for checking what is being picked up by a camera or what is being broadcast; check the technical quality of a transmission.

Mono ► (i) Black and white (film). (ii) Non-stereophonic sound.

Monopod ► Single extendible pole fitted to the base of a camera to keep it steady.

Monotype ► Composing machine which casts each character on a separate type body.

Montage ► (i) In radio, series of sounds blended together in sequence and used in the same manner as a television montage.

Montage (print media) ► (ii) Arrangement or mounting in one composition of pictorial elements from several sources.

Montage (video) ► (iii) A rapidly cut sequence which produces a generalised visual effect even though it may be made up of dissolves or superimposition.

MOO ► (Mud, Object Oriented) One of several kinds of multi-user role-playing environments, so far only text-based. See also *MUD, MUSE.*

Mood music ► Background music put into play in an effort to synchronise it with the requirements of the scene.

Mood picture (or shot) ► A picture in which atmosphere is more important than content.

Moonlighter ► Journalist who works during the evening for media organization while holding another full time post during day. Such people are normally not respected by the media community.

MOR ► Middle Of the Road music.

More ► Written at the foot of each page of hard copy except last when "end" is written. "More follows" (mf) "more follows later"(mfl) used when reporter ends sequence of pages (or "take") temporarily (in order to give the news desk copy at the earliest opportunity) but later returns to story.

More later ► Written as tool of copy or proof to show that more copy will follow but not immediately; printer can use the interval to correct this matter and go on to other setting.

Morgue ▶ (i) A reference file of stories, photographs, films, and tapes. (ii) Old name for library; or file of prepared obituaries.

Mortise ▶ To cut an opening, usually rectangular, in an engraving so that type or another picture can be slotted in. An external mortise or notch is such an opening cut out of the corner of an engraving. An internal mortise is a hole surrounded by engraving; a bay is an opening with engraving on three sides.

MOS ▶ Mit-Out Sound; i.e. silent, or mute shooting.

Mosaic ▶ The first WWW *browser* that was available for the Macintosh, Windows, and UNIX all with the same interface. Masaic really started the popularity of the *web*. The source-code to Mosaic has been licensed by several companies and there are several other pieces of software as good or better than Mosaic, most notably, Netscape. See also *browser, client, WWW*.

Motif ▶ An illustration used to symbolize a subject, or to identify a feature or story.

Motion picture film ▶ Film used exclusively for the production of motion pictures. Generally, 35-millimeter film is used for feature films, but, in the case of wide-screen presentations, 70-millimeter film is used. See also *eight millimeter; film; sixteen millimeter; thirtyfive millimeter.*

Motion video capture cards ▶ PC cards that can capture and save video(for example from a VCR). The quality can vary depending on the card and computer.

Motion videoconference ▶ A motion video conference can duplicate a face-to-face meeting. In a two-way motion configuration, for example, the participants can see and hear each other.

Mot-up ▶ A story that puts together information already used in separate ways, or on separate occasions.

Mouse pointer ▶ An icon, typically an arrow, that appear on your screen and is controlled by the movement of the mouse. You use the mouse pointer to work with menus, icons, links and other screen objects.

Move ▶ A planned rearrangement of props or scenery at a given moment. *Also* any repositioning by a performer (e.g. making a move from the door to a chair).

Movielight ▶ Small quartz light mounted on top of the camera.

Moving shot ▶ In motion picture or television production, technique used to give the audience a feeling of motion by moving the camera along with the action, as a scene depicting a moving automobile, shot by a camera attached to the automobile and moving along with it. A familiar example of this technique is chase scene in a movie in which the audience members actually feel as if they were in the chase because the scene is filmed through a camera inside the fast-moving car.

MPX filter ➤ Electronic filter used to cut out interference when recording from FM radio.

M signal ➤ The combination of left and right stereo signals, i.e. the mono signal.

MS, MSS (pl.) ➤ Manuscript typed or (properly) handwritten copy of book or article; displaced in newspapers by *copy*, but survives in book production.

MTC ➤ Abbreviation for 'more to come'.

MUD ➤ (Multi-user dungeon or dimension) A (usually text-based) multi-user simulation environment. Some are purely for fun and flirting, others are used for serious software development, or education purposes and all that lies in between. A significant feature of most MUDs is that users can create things that stay after they leave and which other users can interact with in their absence, thus allowing a world to be built gradually and collectively. See also *MOO, MUSE*.

Mug shot ➤ Photo showing just face (and sometimes shoulders). Also known as head and shoulder shot.

Multi-angled story ➤ One which carries a number of different angles. See also *umbrella story*.

Multilateral ➤ Shared communications satellite booking by three or more users.

Multimedia ➤ (i) Bringing together words, images, sounds and moving pictures to be accessed on a computer. (ii) Pertaining to a cross section of media: radio, TV, print, Internet, film, etc.

Multiple rules ➤ Three or more type rules of the same or differing point sizes cast on a single body and running parallel.

Multiplexer ➤ Vision and sound link which allows several video sources in succession to be routed at high speed on to one line for transmission.

Multiplexing ➤ The process whereby multiple signals are accommodated on a single communications channel.

Multi-track ➤ Professional recording system in which eight or even sixteen separate sound tracks may be recorded simultaneously; They are then mixed to produce a balance between the components of the sound or to add special effects.

Multi-user system ➤ A computer that can accommodate multiple users, typically through terminals. The computer provides central processing and data storage capabilities.

MUSE ▸ (Multi-user simulated environment) One kind of MUD- usually with little or no violence. See also *MOO, MUD.*·

Musical instrument digital interface (MIDI) ▸ A MIDI interface makes it possible to link a variety of electronic musical instruments and computers. The MIDI standard also enables musicians to tap a computer's processing capabilities.

Music line ▸ High quality landline or satellite circuit suitable for all types of programme, not only music, Compare with *Control line.*

Music track ▸ Sound track of back ground music played under the action in a film or videotape.

Musical bridge ▸ A musical transition used to link various scenes or segments of a single programme on television.

Must ▸ An instruction, from a senior newspaper executive, that the copy or proof on which it is written must be followed and published without fail.

Mutton ▸ Printer's old name for an em space.

Mutton quad ▸ An em quad-a metal body one em square and less than type high which is used for spacing.

My computer ▸ A feature you can use to manage files stored on your computer or network drives. You can also gain access to system tools from my computer. The My Computer icon appear on your *desktop.*

NAB (US) ➤ National Association of Broadcasters; organisation which helps set standards of procedure and equipment, e.g. NAB spool, a professional tape reel type.

Nab center (radio) ➤ A circular device clipped into the centre of a tape spool, and fitted over the spindle of a tape recorder.

Nagra (trade name) ➤ High-quality portable tape recorder; now out of use.

NANA ➤ North American Newspaper Alliance, an editorial syndication service.

Narrow angle lens ➤ A camera lens with a narrow coverage (e.g. <10°). The shot appears to bring subjects nearer, compressing distance, and reducing and thickness.

Narrowcasting ➤ Producing and disseminating programmes for a specialised audience, ignoring, or, at the cost of general interest.

NASA (National Aeronautics and Space Administration) ➤ The U.S. space agency empowered to oversee the civilian space and aeronautical programmes. Also participates in programmes of international cooperation in areas of space and aeronautical activities meant for peaceful purposes.

National advertising ➤ Advertisements placed in media with a national circulation; an advertising campaign on a national scale.

National dailies ➤ Daily newspapers whose coverage and treatment of news on various issues are from a national angle.

National Documentation Centre on Mass Communication (NDCMC) (India) ➤ Set up in 1976, the Centre is involved in collecting, interpreting and disseminating information relating to events and trends in the fields of mass media and traditional media. It documents and indexes all news items, articles and other material covering all aspects of mass communication.

Nationals ➤ Newspapers available for sale at the same time in all parts of a country.

Natural language processing ➤ Natural language processing focuses on simplifying the human-computer interface. Rather than using special keywords to initiate computer functions, you use conventional word sequences.

Natural sound ➤ Sound recorded on to tape at the same time as the pictures are taken.

Natural sound on film (NAT SOF) ➤ Location sound recorded on the tape as the footage is recorded.

Navigation ▸ The pattern through which users move around a web site. Types of navigation are global (for the entire site), local (within subject or area), hierarchical, and sequential.

Navigational aids ▸ Tools to help you navigate through a document on the web. They range from color coding of links to the use of icons to quickly move to a specific page.

Navigation software ▸ A software that allows you to to easily select a service of your choice. *Web browsers* like netscape are a type of navigation software helping you reach a site you want to. Also see *navigational tools*.

NBC ▸ National Broadcasting Company, U.S.A.

NCTBJ ▸ National Council for the Training of Broadcast Journalists, U.K.

Near-video-on-demand (NVOD) ▸ Refers to a broadcast system where the same programme is shown with a time delay across several channels. This way, for example, a consumer finds that a movie is always available written 10 to 15 minutes. NVOD environment simulates *Video-on-demand (VOD)*.

NEA (US) ▸ National Editorial Association, a group of editors of weekly and small daily papers. Also, Newspaper Enterprise Association, a syndicated feature service.

Nebitype ▸ Trade name for Italian machine now mostly out of use which casts metal slugs from hand-assembled matrices.

Neck ▸ Link connecting the two bowls of alphabet *g*; sometimes loosely used to specify the *beard*.

Neck / Personal mike ▸ Small lightweight microphone which clips on to clothing or suspended from a cord round the neck and thus leaves the hands free.

Negative ▸ An image in reverse from the original print.

Negative lead ▸ A lead sentence that contains the word 'not', to be avoided.

Negative-working ▸ Process used in production of photoset web offset newspapers. Most pictures are inserted as negatives. On the paste-up an opaque patch is placed where a picture is to go. When the page is photographed, the patch, being reversed, becomes a window and shows clear on the page negative. The screen negative of the illustration is then placed in the window.

Nemo ▸ Distant television or radio broadcast signal origination point. When television or radio programmes are aired, their signal points may originate outside the studio, for example, live telecast of a cricket match.

Net ► Short for Internet.

Net circulation ► (i) Total number of persons viewing a billboard, painted display, or any other form of outdoor advertising, within a given period of time. An outdoor advertiser's goal is to have a sign with maximum net circulation, given certain budgetary constraints. Net paid circulation refers to circulation sales figure adjusted to account for discounted sales. (ii) See *circulation*.

Net coverage ► Measure used to quantify *audience reach*, representing the entire area or number of persons reached by a communications medium. High net coverage is desirable when introducing a new product, or when an advertising message does not require many repetitions.

Netiquette ► Slang for the unwritten etiquette on the Internet, i.e. rules of the Internet courtesy. See also *Internet*

Netizen ► Derived from the term citizen, referring to a citizen of the Internet, or someone who uses networked resources. The term connotes civic responsibility and participation. See also *Internet*.

Netscape ► A WWW browser and the name of a company. It is a graphical browser that integrates newsgroups, mail, FTP, Gotper and web access into a common programme. The Netscape™ browser was originally based on the *Mosaic* programme developed at the National Center for Supercomputing Applications (NCSA). Also known as Netscape Navigator.

Netscape has grown in features rapidly and is widely recognized as one of the best and most popular web browsers. Netscape corporation also produces web server software.

Netscape provided major improvements in speed and interface over other browsers, and has also engendered debate by creating new elements for the *HTML* language used by Web pages –but the Netscape extensions to HTML are not universally supported. The main author of Netscape, Mark Andreessen, was hired away from the NCSA by Jim Clark, and they founded a company called Mosaic Communications and soon changed the name to Netscape Communications Corporation. See also *browser, mosaic, server, WWW*.

Network ► (i) National broadcasting system. (ii) In the US and other developed markets, group of affiliated radio or TV stations interconnected for the simultaneous broadcast of the same programmes. A network usually consists of a programme-producing central administering organization, owned and operated stations, and independently owned and affiliated stations. The network produces or buys a programme that is economically unfeasible for a single station to produce and sells it to national advertisers for an amount equal to programme production costs plus the affiliates' air-time charge. With the network system, advertisers reach larger audiences at a lower cost per person than with a single station, and local stations get quality programming to attract sponsors. National networks offer complete national coverage of an advertising message. Regional networks concentrate on a specific geographic area, providing a means to cater to regional preferences. Tailormade networks are a group of station joining together on a temporary basis for a special programme. Cable networks deal with satellite-delivered Programming. After the programme is aired, the network is dissolved, although it may be reformed at a later time. (iii) Any time you connect 2 or more computers together so that they can shares resources (such as documents, programmes and pictures), you have a computer network. Connect 2 or more networks together and you have an internet. See also *internet, Internet, Intranet, workgroup.*

Network buy ► It refers to purchase of commercial broadcast time made directly from the network, so that time on all the affiliated stations is bought at once. A network buy is similar to "one-stop shopping" in that many geographic areas can be bought at the same time in the same order. Advertisers who wish to advertise throughout the country wil purchase commercial time in this manner. The air dates for commercials in a network buy can be scheduled to run concurrently throughout the country or staggered according to the needs of the advertiser.

Network card ► Hardware that is inserted in computer to connect the computer to a network.

Networking ► Television or radio stations and programmes banded together for *network* broadcasting. Stations agree in affiliation contracts to broadcast the programmes furnished by the network. Stations are provided with a varied programme schedule, and advertisers are given the chance to tie their commercials to network programming. See also *spot.*

Newbie ► Link Someone new to the *Internet*.

New journalism ► Literally, subjective form of reportage pioneered in US in 1960s and 1970s by Norman Mailer, Tom Wolfe ,Joan Didion and Truman Capote. (See: *The New Journalism*: edited by Tom Wolfe and E.W.Jonhson; Pan Books, London; 1977)

New lead ► Pronounced new *leed*. A new intro paragraph or several paragraphs making a new *news lead* to replace the existing intro or news lead when this is poorly written or overtaken by later developments.

New media ► It is a general term for products or services that combine elements of computing technology, telecommunications, and content (text, audio, video, still pictures, graphics, etc.) to permit interactive use by consumers (net surfers, researchers, students, teachers, etc.) and business users. Examples-streaming video, online communities and virtual reality environments, new media include multimedia and hyper-media.

New Wave ► An experimental style of film-making, popularised first in France in the 1950's without any elaborate plot, chronological continuity and generally, free from theatricalities but, nevertheless, marked by freshness of vision and originality of treatment. In India, the pioneers of this trend were directors like Mrinal Sen, Shyam Benegal, Adoor Gopalakrishnan and Arun Kaul.

New World Information and Communication Order ► A concept promoted by UNESCO in 1970s and 1980s to counter the dominance of international news flows by five major news agencies. Western countries particularly US and UK, saw it as a threat to "free flow of information".

News ► Information about events and occurrences which includes elements of timeliness, usefulness, education, proximity (local or specific interest), controversy and impact (significance).

News agency ► An organization that collects, edits and distributes news to subscribing newspapers, magazines, radio and TV newsrooms, etc. For example, PTI, UNI, AP, Reuters, AFP, ANI.

News components ► Five W's (what, when, where, why and who) and one H (How) are regarded as the components of news.

News desk ► The newsroom, where the collection of news is organised, and where reporters are based (in US, city desk).

Newsbooth ► Small studio where bulletins are presented on air.

Newscaster ➤ See *anchor, newsreader, presenter*.

Newsclip (cut, insert) ➤ Short extract of an interview to illustrate a story.

News director (US) ➤ The individual in charge of a news department who is responsible for its overall news effort. In small markets this person also may be the news anchor and producer.

News editor ➤ (UK) Editorial executive who assigns reporters and cameraman their tasks; (US) executive who lays out the stories in the paper and is sometimes called make-up editor.

Newsflash (*bulletin* US) ➤ Interruption of normal programming to give brief details of an urgent breaking story.

Newsgroups ➤ Also called *usenets*, they are groups that often have nothing to do with news. Newsgroups are ongoing discussion groups among people on the Internet who share a mutual interest. Also refers to an area on the *Internet* reserved for discussion of a certain topic. Messages are posted in the newsgroups and replies are encouraged.

News hole (US) ➤ Space left for carrying news, features, editorials etc., after adjusting advertisements on its various pages.

News – interest newspaper ➤ Publication devoted primarily to current events, public affairs, politics and international news.

News judgement ➤ Ability to recognize the importance of various news stories.

News lead ➤ First few paragraphs summarising key points of a long or complex story.

Newsletter ➤ A publication usually of the size of a letter having a definite periodicity.

Newsmaker ➤ (i) Refers to a person who is the subject of news as opposed to the one who reports the news event. (ii) Computerised newsroom system.

Newsman ➤ A person who gathers, processes, writes, or edits the news irrespective of its medium (print, radio, TV, net) of delivery.

Newsmix ➤ A news summary comprising a mixture of local and national news.

Newspaper ➤ A publication devoted chiefly to presenting and commenting on the news. Newspapers provide an excellent means of keeping well informed on current events. They also play a vital role in shaping public opinion. Newspapers have certain advantages over other major news media– TV, radio and magazines as they can cover more news and in much greater detail than TV and radio newscasts do. Newspapers are printed on coarce paper called newsprint.

There are two major sizes of newspapers–standard and tabloid. A standard sized newspaper has pages that about 15 by 23 inches (38 × 58 centimetres). The pages of a tabloid are about half that size. The three main kinds of newspapers based on periodicity and nature of news, are: a) are daily newspapers, b) weekly newspapers and c) *special interest newspapers*.

Newspaper insert ► Printed promotional enclosure in a newspaper; also called *preprint*. Newspaper inserts vary from a response card to multiple-page inserts. Sunday newspapers are the primary carriers of inserts, particularly cents-off coupons. Newspaper inserts enable advertisers to target their advertisements to specific geographic markets.

Newspaper (big) ► A paper which has a circulation of more than 75,000 copies per publishing day.

Newspaper (small) ► A newspaper having circulation up to 25,000 copies per publishing day.

News peg ► The current event or central aspect about which a news story is written.

News release ► Publicity handout from an organization or public relations company informing the newsroom about a possible news item. See also *WPB*.

News server ► A remote computer that controls access to a newsgroup in a group of interconnected computers.

News values ► Elements that constitute news; consequence, prominence, proximity, timeliness, action, novelty, human interest, sex, humour.

News writer ► Newsroom based journalist responsible for assembling and writing items for broadcast .

Newsprint ► Generic term to describe the pulp paper widely used for newspaper production.

Newsreel ► Cinema, television or radio programmes which tend to provide news material containing segments of different events arranged in a serialised form.

Newsroom conference ► Discussion between producers and the news editor about what stories to run in the news and how they should be covered.

Newsroom diary (prospects) ► A diary or sheet in which is listed all the known stories and news events that are taking place that day and require coverage.

Newsstand ► Retail outlet for single-copy magazine and newspaper sales; abbreviated N/S. In addition to the typical street corner and lobby newsstand, other outlets include bookstores, pharmacies, supermarkets, and convenience stores. Newsstand dealers buy publications from wholesalers or distributors, usually on a returnable basis, whereby unsold copies may be returned for a refund. The newsstands in some locations, such as airports, must pay a fee to the owner of the space occupied equal to a percentage of their gross revenue. This has discouraged some newsstands from selling magazines, because magazines offer a smaller profit margin than other items they could sell. Newsstand space at railway platforms, airports may be allocated on the basis of who will pay the highest percentage of revenues to the concerned authorities. The usual profit margin before deduction of the rental fee is 20% to the newsstand retailer and 40% to the wholesaler. The newsstand dealer may also get 6% to 10% more in the form of a *retail display allowance*. See Also *full-cover display; newsstand draw; newsstand returns; newsstand sales*.

Newsstand circulation ▶ Percentage of a publication's circulation that is accounted for by retail sales. Unsold publications are returned to the distributor on a weekly or monthly basis so that the number of is-

sues sold can be calculated and measured against the subscription circulation. Newsstand circulation is an important percentage of a publication's total circulation, particularly in terms of advertising revenue, since the total circulation figures provide the basis for advertising rates.

Newsstand draw ▶ Magazine copies taken by newsstand dealers in advance of sales; also referred to as N/S draw. Most magazine wholesaler begin distributing copies 5 to 10 days prior to the on-sale date. See also *newstand returns*.

Newsstand Price ▶ Retail single-copy selling price of a periodical; usually printed on the cover. The newsstand price is the nondiscounted basic rate.

Newsstand returns ▶ Unsold copies usually reported back to the wholesaler or distributor for refund to the newstand dealer; also referred to as N/S returns. Returns are reported either by a return of the front cover of each unsold copy or simply with a document stating the number of copies sold and remaining.

Newsstand sales ▶ Periodical copies sold through newsstand outlets. The newsstand sales represent the difference between *newstand draw* and *newstand returns*. There is a great variance in the degree to which any one periodical depends for its revenue upon newsstand copy sales versus subscription copy sales (and advertising space revenue). Certain publications such as National Geographic may derive more revenue from subscription sales, because the magazine are targeted to special interests and contain information of a nature that people like to receive regularly or save for reference or display in complete sets. Newsstand publications sold primarily, or entirely, on newsstands, such as Woman's Era are purchased by many consumers on an irregular basis, depending upon the buyer's interest in an article or item featured on the cover. Publishers maintain statics on newsstand sales rates by cover subject and experiment with various covers to increase sales. Different covers are sometimes used on newsstand copies from those used on subscription copies to test reaction to them or because the cover subject will generate higher newsstand sales but is not as appealing to subscribers.

Newstar ▸ Computerised newsroom system. Also Basys, News Centre, News Wire, News Maker, etc.

Next week/month box ▸ A box or panel indicating what the magazine's next issue will contain.

NF ▸ (UK) Printers' abbreviation for 'no fly'-slang meaning that an instruction is cancelled.

N.G. take ▸ Shot rejected during editing ("No good")

NIBS ▸ News In Brief Section, usually in a column.

NIC ▸ (i) (Networked Information Centre) Generally, any office that handless information for a network. The most famous of these on the Internet is the InterNIC, which is where new domain names are registered. (ii) NIC also refers to Network Interface Card which plugs into a computer and adapts the network interface to the appropriate standard. ISA, PCI, and PCMCIA cards are all examples of NICs.

Ni-Cad ▸ Nickel cadmium rechargeable batteries.

Nicam ▸ (Near instantaneously companted audio multiplex). A digital stereo TV sound system

Nielsen rating ▸ Refers to the number of people watching a particular television programme (as calculated by the A.C. NIELSEN COMPANY). The Nielsen rating is actually used to calculate the *total audience rating* of a programme, rather than the *abverage audience rating*, and refers to households whose television sets are tuned to a particular programme for a minimum of six minutes.

Night editor ▶ (UK) Senior executive in charge of a morning paper, especially presentation, though sometimes subordinate to a deputy editor (night). (US) *news editor*, of a morning paper.

Night side ▶ Night shift on a newspaper.

Nine light ▶ Set small quartz lights which provides powerful studio illumination

NNTP ▶ (Network news transport protocol) The protocol used by client and server software to carry USENET postings back and forth over a TCP/IP network. If you are using any of the more common software such as Netscape, Nuntius, Internet Explorer, etc. to participate in newsgroups then you are benefits from an NNTP connection. See also : n*ewsgroup, TCP/IP, USENET*.

Noddies ▶ Shots of the reporter nodding or listening carefully, which are recorded separately and usually after an interview and will be used when doing the final edits.

Node ▶ Any single computer connected to a network. See Also *network, Internet, internet*.

Noise ▶ Any interference to video or audio signals electrical as well as acoustic .

Noise gate ▶ Device which allows a signal to pass through it only when the input level exceeds a pre-set value.

Noise reduction ▶ The electronic reduction of interference induced by the transmission system.

Non-aligned News Agencies Pool (NANAP) ▶ An arrangement for exchange of news among the news agencies of non-aligned countries, and extablished in 1976 with India as its first Chairman (1976-79). Set-up with the purpose of correcting the imbalances and biases in the flow of news against the developing countries, NANAP is a world-wide operation embracing four continents, viz., Asia, Europe, Africa and Latin America, and works in four languages–English, French, Spanish and Arabic.

A coordinating committee, an elected body, coordinates the Pool activities with chairman as its head whose term is coterminus with the tenure of the committee and goes by rotation. The mambers of the committee are elected on the basis of regional representation, continuity, active participation and rotation. It meets once a year and the meetings are open to all member agencies.   Till now (2001), six general conferences, 17 regular meetings and one special meeting (Belgrade, September 2000) have been held since the inception of the Pool in 1976. The last general conference was held in Tehran in 1992.

India has played a leading role in the creation and expansion of the Pool, with India News Desk Operated by the *PTI* (Press Trust of India). PTI receives news copy from Pool partners and contributes Indian news in turn on a daily basis.

As part of the news pool operation, the Indian Institute of Mass Communication (*IIMC*), New Delhi, a premier institute imparting training in journalism and conducting communication researchs, has been offering a regular course in News Agency Journalism (now changed to Development Journalism) to journalists from non-aligned countries.

Nondaily ▶ A newspaper published less than five times a week.

No-news lead ▶ A lead with no basic information, e.g. a lead beginning "The cabinet met today". The cabinet met but what for and what did it come out with?

Non-linear editing ▶ Editing video sequences in random access fashion, i.e. out of sequence editing, afforded by digital storage of studio and video data. Segments of sound or pictures can be cut and pasted like words in a word processor. This offers greater flexibility than linear editing, where sounds or pictures have to be assembled in order.

Nonmetalic composition ▶ Method of *composition* using film or photographic paper image carrier rather than a metallic carrier such as *hot type*. Nonmetalic composition is used primarily in *lithography* and *gravure*. It is inexpensive compared to metallic composition and suitable for print product, such as newspapers, for which fast make ready and printing is more important than print quality. In contrast to to metallic composition, in which the image surface is raised above or engraved into the plate surface, nonmetallic composition uses a flat image surface, in which the image areas are distinguished chemically, or via black or transparent areas on film, form the nonimage area. A more technologically advanced type of composition that does not use a metallic image carrier is *computerized composition*.

Nonmotion videoconference ▶ A non-motion videoconference supports the relay and exchange of still pictures.

Nonp ▶ Abbreviation for *nonpareil*. Commonly used to indicate spacing-'add a nonp' means add half a pica (12 pt) em of spacing, or about one-twelfth of an inch.

Nonpareil ▶ Pronounced nonprul. Old name for 6pt.

Nose ► The intro or start to a story; hence to *re-nose*.

Notch ► Opening cut out of corner of engraving to accommodate type: an external *mortise*, q.v.

Notification date ► Specific date that radio or television programme sponsors must let a Network know about their decision to cancel or renew their contract. Sponsors making firm commitments into the future are likely to get more favorable rates than are those who refuse to make such a commitment. On the other hand, advertisers willing to take unsold time on a flexible, last-minute, leftover basis, too, will have a favorable negotiating position for lower rates.

NPA ► (UK) Newspaper Proprietors' Association. Association of owners of national newspapers; British equivalent of the Indian INS, which includes provincial newspapers also.

NPR ► Telegraph symbol for night press rate.

Nrm ► 'Next to reading matter'; request by advertisers for the placing of their ad, and written in newspaper dummy.

NS ► (UK) Newspaper Society, association of provincial newspaper proprietors.

NTSC ► National Television Standards Committee which gave its name to the US system of colour television.

Nuggets ► Small items of news; separate sections of a story.

NUJ ► (UK) National Union of Journalists, trade union. There is a another union in India by the same name.

Nut and nut ► Type indented one en at each end of line.

Nut quad ► An en quad-a metal body one *en* square and less than type high, used for spacing.

Nutted ► Type indented one *en*.

NVQ (UK) ► National Vocational Qualification: an industry-wide in-service training scheme.

O/P side ▸ (*opposite prompt*) The left side of the stage seen from the audience or camera position. *Stage right*.

OB ▸ Outside broadcast

OB Van ▸ Outside broadcast van.

Obit ▸ Abbreviation of obituary, an account and appreciation of life. Usually prepared in anticipation of death of famous people.

Objective expectation privacy ▸ Society agrees with an employee that he/she has a reasonable expectation of privacy in workplace items.

Objectivity ▸ The journalistic standard or ideal of making efforts to report news stories without taking a specific stance. A journalists is expected to describe a thing or event according to its characteristics rather than his feelings.

Oblique ▸ A form of *italic*, q.v. It slopes to the right but has the same form as its roman counterpart and does not have the hand-written appearance of italic.

Oblique stroke ▸ One sloping to left or right, diverging from vertical or horizontal.

Obscene speech ▸ Language that appeals to indecent interest is patently offensive and lacks serious literary, artistic, political or scientific value.

Obscenity button (profanity button) ▸ Switch used for taking a programme instantly out of delay to prevent an obscene caller from being heard on the air. See also *delay*.

OC ▸ On camera. See *in-vision*.

Octopus cable ▸ A multi-plug cable with a number of tacks at one or both ends for interfacing video equipment.

Odd folio ▸ First, third, and all unevenly numbered pages. The odd folio is always a right-hand page.

Off beat ▸ Usually story with a humorous twist. Can be used on front page to provide light relief from all other major hard news stories.

Off its feet ▸ Type which is not standing straight, causing the characters to register inexactly.

Off line ▸ (i) An electronic medium that does not require a connection to a remote computer. (ii) Computer system that does not allow the user direct access to the mainframe or stored files. Information is typically stored on magnetic tape and must be loaded onto the mainframe before information can be retrieved. New data entered to the system accumulates in temporary storage until a file update can be run that merges the new data into the existing file. The update applies all of these transactions to the old file, thus creating a new file. From this updated file, output such as mailing labels, invoices, or List Rental selections can be generated. Off-line systems use *central processing unit* time more efficiently than On-line systems and are therefore more economical, but they do not offer the advantage of instant input and retrieval of information. (iii) Refers to a situation when your computer is not connected to a network or the Internet. See also *online*.

Off mike or mic ► In broadcast, refers to sounds made or voices spoken in the background, away from the microphone, to give the illusion of noises in the distance, called distant effect. It has greater proportion of reflected to direct sound. In normal broadcast journalism, it can sound wrong.

Off stage ► A position outside the acting area. To move 'off stage' is to move away from the centre of the acting area.

Off the record ► An agreement by writer and interviewee that the information about to be given cannot be used. Non attributable means that the information can be given, but without naming the source.

Off-camera announcer ► See *off camera*.

Off-diary ► Story that does not come from predictable event, like court appearance or meeting.

Office style ► House style; standard system of spellings and punctuation laid down for news organisation so that continuity is recognizable, depending on style.

Official newspaper ► A newspaper designated by a government agency as being the official carrier of public and legal notices released by the the government.

Offline favorite ► A link that opens a favorite Web page without connecting to the Internet one can schedule offline favorites to be updated regularly with new content.

Offline reading ► To view a Web page without being connected to the Internet one can download the page to his hard disk, disconnect from a network or the Internet, and read the material later.

Offprint ► Reprint of an article or illustration specially run off after publication in a newspaper or magazine.

Offset blanket ► Blanket made of rubber which takes designs from the lithographic plate and impresses them on the paper.

Offset gravure ► Fine printing process giving wide range of tonal expression. Printing is by plates and impression rollers as in offset, but here the image is in intaglio or beneath the surface of the plates.

Offset ▶ One of most misused terms in the history of newspaper production. It is not a description of setting, but of printing. Papers set by photographic methods are often printed offset, but papers set in metal can also be printed offset, which means printed by the planographic printing process in which the image is transferred from a lithographic plate to a rubber roller, then set off this on to paper. Offset has become a synonym for lithography.

Offset paper ▶ Absorptive, non-curling paper suitable for offset printing process; or the newspaper produced by off-set printing.

Offset press ▶ Press which prints, by the indirect method of *lithography*. Also see *offset*.

Off-stone ▶ When a page is ready to be made into a printing plate—a hot-metal term that has lingered on in some offices.

OK ▶ Proof-reader's sign to indicate that there is no error on the proof.

Old English ▶ A style of black script type.

Old face ▶ Style of typeface in which the axis of the curves is to the left; there is a gradual transition from thick to thin; and the serifs are bracketed, e.g. Garamond, Caslon. British Standards preferred term is Garalde. US, *Old style*.

Old-style figures ▶ Numerals that follow the old forms with ascending and descending strokes e.g. 3,4,9.

Ombudsman ▶ An independent arbiter, employed by a newspaper to look into the complaints of its readers.

Omni-directional ▶ A type of pickup pattern in which the microphone can pick up sounds equally well from all directions.

On ▶ To be on the air, camera or microphone.

On spec ▶ Uncommissioned article submitted voluntarily to news organisation.

On stage ▶ A position inside the acting area. To move 'on stage' means moving towards the centered of the acting area.

On the hook ▶ Edited copy awaiting setting in the composing room.

On the record ▶ When there are no restrictions on reporting what is said by an interviewee or any newsmaker.

On-air ▶ programme being broadcast or recorded.

On-camera story ▶ See *in-vision story*.

On-line ▶ (i) Description of a computer- based service that permits many local computer (*clients*) interact with a larger distant computer (*host*) on a real time basis by using a telecom network. Typical used to refer to commercial operations and the Internet, rather than intra-office applications. For example, subscribers accessing a Web newspaper's data banks to receive information through a telephone modem linked to their personal computer; simply put, description of being connected to the Internet. (ii) A term describing equipment, or devices, that are in direct communication with the central processing unit (CPU) of a computer.

On-line communities ▸ Group of people who communicate with one another through electronic means, such as *chat groups, news groups* and *listservs*.

On-line data base ▸ A database specializing in a topic, such as media or stock market information, and is available from a network to authorized subscribers who may or may not have paid for the same depending upon the nature of their relationship with the owners of the database.

On-line help feature ▸ On-screen definitions of command and suggestions for how to use the commands to access a computer system or network.

One shot ▸ Single performance not scheduled to be rebroadcast.

One way ▸ Describes a mode of communication where sending parties 'don't have or are not provided with the facility to get information back from receiv-

ing parties, e.g., traditional radio and TV.

One-man band ▸ A reporter in a smaller market who doubles as a photographer. Also may be a photographer doubling as a reporter.

Onion bag ▸ String bag used for carrying videotape cassettes, so called for its resemblance to the bags in which onion are sold .

Op ed ▸ Abbreviation for opposite editorial, being page opposite one on which newspaper's editorial /leader comment appears. Usually contains important features and commentary by prestigious columnists.

Opacity ▸ Characteristic of paper that can be printed on one side without the image showing through on the other side. The thicker the paper stock, the greater the opacity.

Open ▸ The beginning of a programme. Also, the relationship of the body of a performer to a camera that allows fullest expression, an open position. A live or open microphone. To open up means to be freer in movement and interpretation.

Open-end ▸ (i) In broadcast, ending to a network programme or commercial that is left blank for local advertising. Leaving an open end gives local advertisers the opportunity to sponsor a national programme, or to add their address and location to a national advertiser's product.

Commercial spots may also be left blank for local advertisements at a programme's start or in its middle. (ii) Radio or television programme with no specific scheduled completion time. For example, a radio talk show may be scheduled to go on until the subject matter is exhausted, rather than rigidly adhere to the usual time schedule. (iii) Unscheduled termination of a television or radio programme. A sudden cessation of programming may be due to a special news alert or may be caused by technical difficulties.

Open-ended ➤ A programme without a pre-determined finishing time.

Open format ➤ Style of newspaper page with white space dividing columns.

Open matter ➤ Text which is either well leaded or has lots of short lines. Also see *matter*.

Open quotes ➤ Begin with quotation marks ("); the beginning of a quotation set off by quotation marks.

Open source ➤ Computer programmes whose source code is in the public domain and is freely available. Anyone can modify or repurpose such programmes. The system software LINUX is an example of open source programme.

Open spacing ➤ Wide spacing of text, whether by white between letters, words, or lines.

Open video system (OVS) ➤ As an alternative to traditional cable system, the OVS model allows telcos to deliver video without incutting certain regulations.

Operating system ➤ Software, such as Windows 98, that runs a computer. An operating system controls programmes and *hardware*.

Operators ➤ Terms used to describe *and*, *or* and *not* when used to separate keywords in a search. Each of these terms directs the way the search "operates". Also called Boolean operator. See *boolean searching*.

Opinion leader ➤ Individual who influences the opinion of others; whose ideas and behavior serve as a model to others. Opinion leaders communicate messages to a primary group, influencing the attitudes and behavior change of their followers. Therefore, in certain marketing instances, it maybe advantageous to direct the communications to the opinion leader alone to speed the acceptance of an advertising message.

Opinion piece ➤ Article in which journalist expresses overt opinion, usually a column.

Oppenners ➤ See *standuppers*.

Optical character recognition (OCR) ➤ Either a stand-alone unit or a software option for a scanner that makes it possible to directly input alphanumeric information from a printed page to a computer. After a document is scanned, an OCR system can recognize the text.

Optical disks ➤ The umbrella term for optical storage systems. These are high-capacity storage media. This is partly a reflection of a laser's capability to distinguish between tightly recorded information tracks. Like floppy and hard disks, optical disks are random access devices. They provide almost immediate access to the stored information.

Optimod ➤ Audio compressor to maximise the modulation of a transmitter in order to obtain optimum signal strength.

Optimum format ➤ (US) Page format where the optimum line length for easy reading-around 15 picas in 9pt-determines the column width.

Opt-in and opt-out ➤ The process of switching between local and network transmissions. Opting in occurs when a local station goes over to a live network programme and opting out takes places when it returns to its own programmes. 2. Opt-out is an early point at which a report may be brought to an end.

Orbital spacing ➤ Buffer zones that physically separate the satellites to help eliminate interference.

Organizational papers ➤ Newspapers published by business or non-profit groups such as companies, labour unions and voluntary agencies as part of their organizational communication.

Orphan ➤ One or two words at the bottom of a column considered ugly and best avoided.

Orthochromatic ➤ Film that is insensitive to red light, reproducing only blue or green tones. See also Panchromatic.

Out-point ➤ Frame selected during editing to end a particular shot.

Out of phase ➤ The condition in which two loudspeakers are wrongly connected to the amplifier so that their cones vibrate in opposite polarity . The stereo effect will be lost if the speeders are out of phase in this way.

Out of sorts ➤ Shortage of some characters in a fount of type.

Outcue ➤ The last few words on a sound bite, VO-bite, or package. It's necessary that the newscast director have this information in order to know when to cut away from the videotape and go back to the anchor on the set. A standard outcue is the regular ending to a voice report, such as *Vishnu Som, Kargil, Star News.*

Outdoor advertising ➤ One of the oldest and most enduring forms of advertising, outdoor advertising can be broadly identified as any sign that publicly displays advertising or identifies something, such as a sign for a restaurant or other place of business. More specifically, though, the term has come to represent the advertising medium we casually call *billboard advertising*, which is a large standardized segment of the Out-of-Home advertising media industry.

The structures are scientifically located in places of heavy traffic volume along highways, alongside railroad lines, on rooftops, or on the outer walls of buildings so as to deliver an advertising message to the entire market in the community.

Outdoor advertising displays are most commonly used in an advertising campaign to supplement other media.

Outline ➤ A type which, on the British Standard definition, has a continuous line of more or less consistent width outlining the shape of the character.

Out-of-focus dissolve ➤ Camera transition from one scene to the next effected by fading one shot out of focus while simultaneously fading the following one into focus. Out-of-focus *dissolves* are commonly used for special effects or for transition (such as just before commercial breaks in news and dream sequences in films).

Out-of-home ➤ Advertising media that must be viewed outside the household and is not available in the home, such as bus-shelter advertising, shopping-cart displays, billboards, painted displays, transit advertising, and skywriting. See also *in-home*.

Output ➤ (i) News department responsible for the selection, processing and presentation of news materials for broadcast. Counterpart of intake / input. It also denotes the programme-making operation of a newsroom; typeset version of a story that is printed out of the computer. (ii) Products of a computer system, such as printouts, labels, reports, or list rental selections. Output can be printed on paper, displayed on a cathode-ray tube screen, punched onto keypunch cards, written onto magnetic tape or disks, and so forth. The intended use of the output and the capabilities of the system generating it determine the format.

Outro ➤ See *tag*.

Outs ➤ Photographs submitted for a layout but not used.

Outsert ➤ (i) Separate piece of printed matter attached to the outside of a Package. An outsert is frequently used when the advertiser cannot risk inserting the message in an envelope that may or may not be opened. (ii) Separate cover used on the outside of a magazine or catalogue. An outsert is frequently used in magazine marketing to inform advertisers of upcoming features, rate changes, advertising opportunities in special issues, and so on. In addition, it is used by catalogue marketers to feature such things as special discount offers, product announcements or changes, or premiums.

Outside source ► Programme originating point remote from the studio, or the circuit connection from it.

Outtake ► Shot rejected during editing.

Over ► (i) Too much text for the allocated space, also called over matter or leftover matter. (ii) Printing placed over a first impression, a superimposition.

Over (exposed) ► The positive image which comes out thick dark after having been exposed in excess to light.

Over exposure ► Allowing too much light onto each frame giving a pale washed out effect.

Over measure ► Type set too wide for space allocated.

Overall metering ► Built in camera system which measures the light received by the whole frame area.

Overbanner ► Banner headline running higheer than the nameplate of the newspaper. Also

called sky-line (r) and *over-the-roof* in US, where it is more common.

Overheads ► Costs not directly related to the production of magazine, newspaper, newscast, etc.

Overlay ► (i) Editing technique for matching a recorded sound track with relevant pictures. Also known as *underlay*. (ii) To place a transparent covering over an illustration, or a filmset page over a filmset page, to indicate colour separation or alterations or corrections. (iii) Acetate sheet used in television animation when producing commercials. The sheet is used to draw motions that come after those in the original drawing.

Overline ► Display type over a picture, also sometimes called a *title*. Also a line of smaller type over the main headline, which, in turn, may be called (UK) a *strap* or (US) an *eyebrow*.

Overload distortion radio ► The distortion suffered by a programme signal when its electrical level is higher than the equipment can handle. When this happens non-continuously it is referred to as 'peak distortion'. Also referred to as 'squaring off'.

Overmatter, over-set ► Type set for an edition but squeezed out by shortage of space.

Overnight pages ► Pages scheduled to go to press early, late p.m. or early a.m., before work begins on the pages of the day's newspaper.

Overnight set ▸ Practice of erecting scenery at night in readiness for early daytime camera rehearsals.

Overplay ▸ To overemphasize dialogue or movement.

Overplugging (radio) ▸ The substitution of one circuit for another by the insertion of Jack plug in a break Jack.

Overprinting ▸ (i) Printing over already-printed images without obscuring the underlying image. This technique may be used to highlight elements of copy, to add new copy, or to include some copy in only part of a print run. (ii) Placing a Lacquer coating over a printed image to enhance the colour of the underlying image.

Overrun ▸ (i) To reset type to insert matter omitted, or have better word-breaks, or to run round a block more neatly. (ii) Excess production. Printed material such as magazines, catalogues, and newspapers are frequently printed in quantities greater than the expected distribution in order to cover unexpected contingencies, such as damaged or lost copies, requests for *back issues*, or distribution of copies as samples to prospective advertisers or buyers. See also *overset matter*.

Overs ▸ See *outs*.

Over-the-roof (US) ▸ See *overbanner*.

Over-the-shoulder shot (OSS) ▸ This shot is taken from behind in which the main object is seen along with the back of the other person's head and shoulders in the foreground (see Fig.).

Over-the-shoulder long shot (OSS & LS)

Oxford rule ▸ Heavy and light rules running close together in parallel, not to be confused with simple parallel or double rules; also (UK) house rules of the Oxford University Press, as published.

Ozalid ▸ Process whereby a photograph, artwork, or other material can be duplicated from the original copy, in the same size as the original, without first making a negative. Ozalid prints lack the sharp quality of the original but will be sufficient to check the accuracy of the copy before continuing the printing process; a type of proof.

Pp

P ➤ Abbreviation for page, hence p_1; p_2, etc. Its plural is pp.

PA ➤ (i) Press Association, a British domestic news agency; (ii) production assistant; (iii) programme assistant.

PAB (Programme As Broadcast) ➤ Details of programme content for record and payment purpose.

Pace ➤ The overall rate or flow of continuity in a production.

Pack ➤ Collection of journalists (sometimes known as "rat pack")

Package (radio) ➤ A broadcast report consisting of journalist's voice plus at least one insert of actuality.

Package (TV) ➤ This is story completely done by a reporter and is the mainstay of a newscast. It usually consists of video on the story subject and interviews with those involved and a stand-up by the reporter who also narrates the story. This stand-up may be either as an Opener, Bridge or a Closer. The most common stand-up is the bridge that links the two story elements of the story. The other common stand-up is the closer that gives a perspective to the story.

In package, the news anchor just introduces the story and informs the viewers something like: Our reporter Vijay Vidrohi has more on this from Jaipur . ." At this point the edited story appears on the screen with the reporter's narration and the anchor will appear only after the taped portion of the story concludes . The reporter may give an opener, a bridge or a closer in the package depending upon the structure he finds most suitable for his story and agreeable to the newsroom policy or conventions.

Packets ➤ A block of data that can be transmitted from one computer to another on a network like the Internet. A packet contains data to be transmitted, data to guide the packet, and data that corrects errors along the way; and, the data are coded at transmission and decoded at the destination.

Packet switching ➤ The method used to move data around on the *Internet*. In packet switching, all the data coming out of a machine is broken up into chunks, each chunk has the address of where it came from and where it is going. This enables chunks of data from many different sources to co-mingle on the same lines, and be sorted and directed to different routes by special machines along the way. This way many people can use the same lines at the same time.

Pad (video) ➤ This is a kind of breathing space at the end of a tape. The tape editor allows the tape to run about five seconds more than the desired time (outcue), thus killing any unwanted sound if the tape ends with a sound bite. This additional soundbite which is not meant to be seen or heard on the air, is called PAD. A pad of about two seconds worth is also used at the start of a reporter's package to bridge any error in the roll cue.

Padding ➤ Portions of copy not necessary for the narrative; to pad out is to make a story or headline longer than what is required. Padding is required when broadcast ends before its allocated time. For example, if a 5-minute radio bulletin ends in 4 minutes 40 seconds, a disc jockey may pad the bulletin by playing a 10-second comment about the weather. Also see *fillers*.

Page facsimile transmission ➤ Method by which completed pages are digitized and reduced to an electronic signal for transmission by wire or satellite to another printing centre for simultaneous production.

Page rate ➤ (i) The price of a page of advertising; (ii) The sum an editor can spend on a page of editorial.

Page time ➤ It is the total time or duration of a story no matter how many script pages the story runs. The page time is entered on the first page only. If a story assigned page-5 runs longer than a single script page, successive script pages of the story are numbered 5-A, 5-B, and so on. During a newscast the technical staff refers to a story by its page only – that denoting the position of the story in the newscast. Stories are updated, added, or replaced by using page number as identification of their position in the complete order of news items scheduled for a newscast.

Page traffic ➤ Measurement of how well a given page is read.

Pagination ➤ The numbering of pages; the number of pages of a publication.

Paid circulation ➤ total copies sold of a periodical consisting of net paid subscription copies and single copy sales. Paid circulation is usually calculated on an issue-by-issue basis or as an average over a six-month audit period. See also *ABC; average paid circulation & circulations*.

Paintbox ➤ A brand of electronic graphic machine.

PAL (Phase Alternation (by) Line) ➤ A colour television system.

Panel ➤ (i) Text larger than body text with lines top and bottom. Serves to break up grey block of copy. Written by subs, see *box*. (ii) Studio mixing desk, control board or console.

Panning handle ➤ Handle used to turn the head of a camera.

Pan-pot (radio) ➤ Panoramic potentiometer, control on studio mixing desk which places a source to the left or right in a stereo image.

Pans ➤ A pan shot is obtained when the camera itself moves horizontally on a fixed or movable axis instead of just the lens. The camera moves side ways either to the left or to the right – as in pan left or pan right. The purpose of rotating the camera up and down or from left to right is to televise a panoromic scene or a moving subject. Also see *tilts*.

Pantone ➤ A proprietary color-matching system. Fifth colours are sometimes called 'Pantone colours' because this is the system used to define them.

Paparazzi ➤ Plural of paparazzo (Italian). Horde of freelance photographers usually following an unwilling news maker, e.g. the most talked about case of princess Diana's death in a car crash resulting allegedly from such a chase by paparazzi in Paris in 1997.

Paperless society ➤ A society in which information is increas-ingly created, stored and exchanged in an electronic form, i.e. computers.

Par/para ➤ Abbreviation for 'paragraph'.

Parabolic reflector ➤ Microphone attachment which focuses sound waves thereby increasing directional sensitivity. Used for nature recordings, etc.

Paragraph indent ➤ Beginning the first line of a paragraph with a white space, usually one pica em quad.

Paragraph mark ➤ Signal to a line-caster to begin the line with an indention.

Parallel action ➤ Sequence intercut with the master shot , it is usually a simultaneously and related scene which does not occur in the same place as the main action . It may also be a flashback or an imagined future event .

Parallel rule ➤ Rule with two lines in parallel and of equal weight.

Parallel strip ➤ An inert row of jacks mounted on a Jackfield not connected to any other equipment but connected in parallel to each other. Used for joining programme sources together, connecting equipment, or multiplying outputs from a single feed. Also available on its own in the form of a 'Junction Box'.

Paraphrase ➤ This puts a quotation into different words, usually those of the reporter; to give a clearer or more interesting meaning; quotation marks are not used.

Parentheses ► See *brackets*.

Partial quote ► Use of actual words of a speaker but less than a complete sentence. For optimum impact, partial quotes should be complete phrases rather than one or two words and put into context. see also *paraphrase*, *direct quote* and *indirect quote*.

P As R ► Programme As Recorded.

Pass along circulation ► (i) Refers to those readers who have not received a copy by purchase or request. Such readers may receive the publication's cop8ies from a family member or a public library. (ii) Readership beyond the original subscriber of a newspaper or magazine. Also see *circulation*.

Passive satellite ► A satellite that does not relay its own signals back to earth.

Password ► It is a secret way or code to identify yourself to a computer on which you have an account. On the other hand, the login name is the public way of identifying yourself to the computer. Good passwords contain letters and non-letters and are not simple combinations such as virtue7. A good password might be: Cold$2-7. See also *login*.

Paste-on ► Cold type pasted on to page plan for the platemaker.

Paste up ► To create pages from bromides of type and halftones, ready to go before the camera. Effectively replaced by desktop publishing programmes.

Patch panel ► See *Jackfield*.

Path ► The means of navigating to a specific location on a computer or network. A path can include a computer name, disk drive label, folder names and a file name. The location of files is frequently referred to by giving its "path" or place in a directory structure. For example, a file named "book.txt" is stored in a subdirectory of a directory called "pub" its path would be /pub/ book.txt. Longer paths indicate deeper directory and subdirectory structures.

Patronage ► See *reach*

Pay off ► Last para with twist or flourish.

Pay-per-view TV ► A system where a specific audience is supposed to pay the bills for some individual programmes. Also *cable TV*.

Pay TV ► Describes a broadcast environment in which the consumer must pay for the television services (programmes, channels, etc.) in order to avail of them.

PBS ► (Public broadcast service). A system of public TV stations that broadcast non-commercial and educational programmes.

PC ➤ Personal computer.

PCM ➤ See *pulse code modulation*.

PDF ➤ Portable Document Format. A standard used by Adobe Acrobat to display any sort of document on any computer. The adobe Acrobat Reader can be downloaded as freeware.

Peak distortion ➤ See *overload distortion*.

Peak programme meter (PPM) ➤ Meter for measuring peak signal level. Its specially damped action prevents flickering and produces a steady reading. See also *VU meter*.

Pearl ➤ Old name for 5pt type.

Peg ➤ The event to which a story or feature has to be tied to make it topical: 'The peg for this is the delay in salary revision.' See *angle*.

PEN ➤ Short for International Association of Poets, Playwrights, Editors, Essayists and Novelists.

Penetration ➤ Measure of the degree to which a product or promotion has reached the individuals in a geographic area or market. For example, an ethnic food product such as prawn pickle would have a high penetration in Kerala and a low penetration in New Delhi. However, if it is a popular brand of prawn pickle, it could have a high penetration in the consumers of Malayali food within New Delhi. Similarly, a Bhojpuri radio programme would have a higher penetration in the Bhojpuri speaking pockets within New Delhi.

Penny press (US) ➤ Inexpensive advertiser supported newspapers of 1830s during which period the New York Sun lowered the cost of a newspaper from six cents to one (in 1833). This was done to appeal to the public's growing thirst for news.

Perfect bound ➤ A method of binding, using glue, that creates a magazine with a hard, square spine.

Perfecting press ➤ Printing press that prints both sides of the paper, in one colour, in one pass through the press; also called perfector. Perfecting presses save printing time and reduce paper usage. They are commonly used in offset *lithography* and in laser printers.

Perforator ➤ Machine which punches holes in tape to a pattern which, when fed into a line-casting machine, produces lines of types. Also the operator of a perforator or tape-punching machine.

Performer ➤ Anyone who appears on camera and/or microphone, especially those who are paid to do so (i.e. media professionals) and those who do so because of their expertise in area out side media (community experts) Narrowly defined, a person paid to appear on television or radio.

Period ➤ Another name for full point, full stop.

Periodical ➤ The time gap between issues of a newspaper (daily, weekly, fortnightly, monthly, etc) Also, the term refers to a journal, magazine, or a newspaper. Somtimes the term is used to mean a serial.

Periodical article ➤ An article published in a journal, magazine, or newspaper

Periodical index ➤ A listing of all articles published in journals, magazines, or newspapers. There are different types of periodical indexes, each specializing in a broad category, such as magazine articles.

Personal column ➤ Regular column signed by writer (i.e. with his by-line), e.g. "With Malice Towards One and All" in The Hindustan Times by Khushwant Singh.

Personal Communications Services (PCSs) ➤ A family of mobile services designed to meet the communication requirements of people on the move. Computer-to-computer and voice relays can be supported.

Personal computer (PC) ➤ A computer typically designed to serve one user.

Personal home page ➤ Web page that an individual creates to display his personal or professional information. For example, portfolio and resume.

Personal mike ➤ A chest microphone worn by a speaker which leaves the hands free.

Personal publishing ➤ Desktop publishing systems make it possible for individuals to produce and potential market their own work.

Personal satellite communications ➤ A new generation of satellites that can deliver personal communications services—you are not restricted by location. In one configuration, satellites are placed in low earth orbits.

Personal videoconferencing ➤ Personal video-conferencing is a general term that describes desktop videoconferencing systems.

Personality ➤ The innate charm or essence of an individual. Also, a performer, whose personal characteristics dominate whatever role he or she portrays, is refereed to as a personality.

Perspective ➤ (i) Sense of depth in a two dimensional image created by the relative size, position and shape of the objects that appear. (ii) Effect of space created by audio-matching the distance of a sound source. To achieve the desired perspective, sound technicians place audio sources and mikes at different distances.

PGP (Pretty good privacy) ➤ A security system employing public key cryptography. Based on the notion that users should be able to choose who they can trust, the security system is mainly used for e-mail. Also see *cryptography*.

Phantom power ➤ Method of providing a working voltage to a piece of equipment, e.g. a microphone, using the programme circuit and earth (ground).

Phase distortion ➤ The effect on the sound quality caused by the imprecise combination of two similar signals not exactly in phase with each other.

Phone-in ➤ See *phoner/foner*.

Phoner ➤ See *foner*.

Phono ➤ Report or interview made by telephone. Also a type of lead or cable used to connect one piece of equipment to another.

Phot-Lathe ➤ Trade name for mechanical engraving machine.

Photo CD ➤ An optical disk that can store pictures. Professional and consumer applications have been supported

Photo Division (India) ➤ It is the largest photographic unit of its kind under the Ministry of Information and Broadcasting. It also stores invaluable negatives of archival value and those relating to the socio-economic development of the country.

Photo-chase ➤ Film bromides pasted on to thin strips of polystyrene for easier movement. Often used to collate columns of classified advertising.

Photocomposition ➤ Non-Metallic composition technique using photographically created characters such as film or photographic paper rather than metal type slugs; also called *cold type*. See also *hot type* and *photomechanical*.

Photo-engraving ➤ See *process engraving*.

Photoflood ➤ Lightbulb with standard screw fitting but very high power output and color temperature of either $3,200°K$ or $3,400°K$.

Photograph and image manipulation ➤ The manipulation of photographs as in electronic retouching (used in advertising). A potential problem is the alteration of news images.

Photographer ➤ In TV news, One who photographs the day's news events with a videotape camera. In newspaper, he would do the same with a still camera.

Photogravure ➤ Fine printing method. The paper sheet passes between a rubber-covered impression cylinder and an intaglio plate, photographically prepared, and in so doing takes the ink from the finely etched recesses in the plate.

Photojournalism ➤ The use of photography to record events and occurrences as news (rather than for artistic purposes).

Photomechanical ➤ Print image carrier produced by photographically exposing a surface coated with light-sensitive material. Photomechanicals are used to reproduce Continuous Tone images such as photographs. The photomechanical process makes it possible to combine both type and picture images on the same image carrier. See also *photocomposition*.

Photo-montage ➤ A photograph assembled out of several originals or extensively retouched; (usually blown up).

Photon ➤ Trade name for phototype-setting machine.

Photorealistic ➤ A video display card/monitor that can produce realistic or lifelike images.

Photoset ➤ Abbreviation for photo-composition. The reproduction photographically on film or paper of lines of type characters. Photoset newspapers are called cold type papers in contrast to hot metal papers composed from lines of metal type.

Photostat ➤ Misused as general term for photo-copy. It is a trade name for the machine and the photo-copies it produces.

Phototypeseting ➤ See *nonmetallic composition*.

Pic ➤ Abbreviation of picture meaning photograph . Plural : pix.

Pica ➤ Printer's unit of measurement, one pica equals 12 points. Also old name for 12pt type.

Pick up ➤ (i) Journalist attending function might pick up or take away photograph supplied by the organisers. This is known as a pick up job. (ii) Journalist following up an event after it has happened (speaking to participants and establishing views and outcome) is "picking up" meeting. (iii) Proof instruction from editorial to pick up the type already set, and incorporate with new material. (iv) The range with which a microphone can get a sound signal. A pickup pattern refers to the shape of the sensitive area surrounding a microphone. (v) To accelerate the pace of a programme largely by means of responding more quickly to cues, to begin where the action last stopped. (vi) Gramophone record reproducing components which convert the mechanical variations into electrical energy these include pu-arm, pu-head, and pu-shell, pu-stylus.

PICT ➤ The default graphics format on Macintoshes.

Picture by-line ➤ A by-line incorporating a photograph of the author.

Picture composition ➤ In TV news, as in feature films, there are five basic shots describing the distance between the camera *lens* and the *subject*: Extreme long shot — ELS; Long shot (also called wide shot)—LS; Medium shot—MS; Close up-CU; Extreme close up — ECU.

ELS: an ELS is the widest, most comprehensive view possible of an event, location or a person (see Fig. on *Extreme Long Shot*). This is what a feature film director might use to show a lone herdsman singing a song of melancholy in the vast expanse of the valley of Kashmir, or to show the flocks of birds in the background of a sunset, etc. Such scenes can be effective on the large screens of a theatre, not the small screen of TV. Naturally, such shots are rare in TV news. Here the herdsman or the marching soldiers *would appear like ants*.

LS: an LS is a wide and comprehensive shot but not so wide that you cannot identify the subject even on the small screen (see Fig. on *Long Shot*). Long shots are used briefly but frequently in TV news, because they serve the purpose of establishing the location of an event – shots of Parliament, stadium or an election booth. In fact, in TV news, such shots are customarily used at the beginning to establish the location of an action and then again to show a radical change of the location — from Parliament to Stadium.

However, such shots are brief because it is difficult to make out details from them on the small screen of TV sets.

MS: this is the shot that best captures an action and frequently used in TV news (see Fig. on *Medium Shot*). This is close enough to the subject to show what the subject is doing in relation to its environment on location. For example, your mid shot when you are picking up the items of your daily need in a supermarket. When you go to the counter to pay the bill, a mid shot also shows the cashier giving you a receipt of the payment.

CU: the head-and-shoulders shot of a news anchor is a close-up shot (see Fig. on *Close-up*). Close-ups are the second most frequently used shots in TV news and mostly used in interviews.

ECU: the extreme close-up shot, as the name suggests, moves the camera even more close to the subject. For example, it shows only the face of a person who is in a state of dilemma or deep emotion (see Fig. on *Extreme Close-up*). Here is a danger: if a cameraperson preoccupies himself or herself with close-ups of the interviewee, the details of his face – eyebrows, lips, nose, etc., may distract the viewer's attention from the main action of the news. ECUs also show documents and small objects closely enough to read any printed matter. Such shots are called *inserts*, because they are inserted at specific points where the script refers to the objects being shown.

Picture desk ► Where collecting and checking of pictures is organized; hence *picture editor*.

Picture element (Pixel) ► A pixel is a segment of a scan line.

Picture loss ► See *TV cutoff and Dubbing*.

Picture search ► The rapid scanning in vision only of a recorded tape.

Pictures store ► Device for electronically storing wire pictures.

Piece ► (i) Describes an article. (ii) Usual journalese for a story.

Piece-to-camera (PTC) ► Report spoken directly to the camera in the field (see Fig.). Also see *standuppers*.

Piece-to-camera (PTC)

Piezo system ► This is a focusing system that reduces hunt-ing where the lens moves back and forth searching for the focal point .

Pigeon rider ► Person entrusted with the delivery of videotape from camera unit to base.

Piggyback commercial ► Two or more broadcast commercials aired one after the other, featuring different products of the same sponsor. Sponsors use piggyback commercials to get two or more unrelated advertising messages into the time allocated for one, without increasing commercial time.

Pilot ► Sample radio or TV programme produced to introduce networks or prospective sponsors to the potential of an entire new series. The pilot affords advertisers the opportunity to become acquainted with the specific format, talent, and quality of the production, which in turn will help facilitate their sponsorship decision. The creation of pilots is an expensive proposition. Producers must invest many hours in script editing, shooting, and hiring talent.

Pinch roller ► Rubber wheel which holds tape against tape recorder drive capstan.

PIP (Picture in picture) ► A digital special effect which puts a small picture in the corner of the main TV display.

Pitch ► The range of vocal sound a performer can produce from deep tones with relaxed vocal folds through falsetto.

Pix ➤ Informal term for pictures, usually still photographs.

Pixel ➤ The smallest sensitised unit of a video screen picture or *CCD*.

Pixillate ➤ To treat a picture electronically so that the subject is unrecognisable. Used to protect anonymity in stories where this is legally necessary, and in imitation of television practice.

PL ➤ The phone line or intercommunications systems among control - room staff and studio personnel.

Plagiarism ➤ The use of any part of another's writing without attributing it; passing it off as your own work.

Plain rule ➤ Rule with plain, straight lines, in variety of sizes, but without decoration.

Plaintiff ➤ A person or organisation bringing a legal action.

Planning ➤ Planting or fixing publicity material with the media.

Planning board ➤ Large board used in some newsrooms to show the stories that are being covered and which reporters have been assigned to them.

Planning meeting ➤ A meeting dedicated to future issues of newspaper or newscasts. .

Plate ➤ Semi-cylindrical metal printing sheet cast from a *flong*

for attachment to rotary press; or photographically engraved metal.

Platen ➤ Surface which holds the paper in typewriter or printing press and presses it against an inked surface.

Play ➤ Editorial term indicating emphasis to be given to a story. Points or angle in a story can be played up or down or played lightly; if the story itself is played up it is given a big display.

Playback ➤ The replay of a recording on audio or vedio tape immediately after it has been made. This is done to determine if the recording is of high standard. After playback, problems are rectified.

Playback deck ➤ A deck used for playing prerecorded video insets into in to a programme. Also the source deck in an editing set up .

Playback head ➤ Tape head which plays back previously recorded material by translating the magnetic pattern on the tape into electrical current.

Plug ➤ (i) To push the popularity of a show, book, or song by publicity; free advertisement. (ii) A wedge of wood used in some printing and engraving.

Plug-in ➤ A usually small piece of software that adds features to a larger piece of software. It allows a web browser to display multimedia online. Common examples are plug-ins for the *Netscape® browser* and *web server*. Adobe Photoshop® also uses plug-ins. The idea behind plug-in's is that a small piece of software is loaded into memory by the larger programme, adding a new feature, and that users need only install the few plug-ins that they need, out of a much larger pool of possibilities. Plug-ins are usually created by people other than the publishers of the software the plug-in works with.

PM ▸ (US) An afternoon paper.

Point ▸ Abbreviated to pt. The fundamental unit of typographical measurement. There are 72 pts to the inch and 28.35 to the centimeter.

Pointer ▸ See *flag, mouse pointer.*

Point size ▸ The measurement of a type from the front of the base to the back. Also called the body size.

Points ▸ Punctuation marks. A full point is what follows the last letter of this sentence.

Point system ▸ System of casting type and measuring areas in multiples of the point.

Point to point ▸ A mode of communication where there are two parties to any exchange, e.g. telephone.

Polar diagram ▸ Graph showing the area of a microphone's greatest sensitivity. Also applies to aerials, transmitters and loudspeakers. Directivity pattern.

Police blotter ▸ (US) Register of day's events kept in a police station and hopefully open to the press.

Policy story ▸ (US) News item or feature which supports an editorial opinion of the newspaper.

Political advertising ▸ Advertising whose central focus is the marketing of ideas, attitudes, and concerns about public issues, including political concepts and political candidates. The essential task of political advertising is to gain the confidence of the people for their acceptance of ideas and, in the case of political campaign advertising, to influence their vote. Political advertising differs from commercial advertising in that the product is either a person or a philosophy rather than goods and services, and, in addition, the advertising objectives must be met within a specific time frame. Also, political advertising carries a moral implication, because the results have potentially far-reaching effects on the population at large. Political advertising raises many controversial social questions concerning the funding of political campaigns, the truth or reality of political claims, and the likelihood of slanderous or libelous claims made by political candidates.

Politics of accommodation ➤ A sort of compromise in which professional standards and public interest are negotiated at various levels, such as between professionals and the management, between the corporation and the Government, etc.

Poll (opinion) ➤ A survey of opinion, attitudes, viewpoints etc., of a specific group of people towards a certain thing.

Pony service ➤ (US) Abbreviated teleprinter news service delivered by commercial telegraph or telephone.

Pool ➤ Privileged, small group of journalists with special access to event or source. Their reports and findings are then distributed to those news organizations outside this group.

Pool cameras ➤ One camera crew shared by several TV news organizations.

POP ➤ (i) (Point of Presence) A point of presence usually means a city or location where a network can be connected to, often with dial up phone lines. So if an *Internet* company says they will soon have a POP in Bangalore, it means that they will soon have a local phone number in Bangalore and/or a place where leased lines can connect to their network. (ii) Post Office Protocol refers to the way *e-mail* software such as Eudora gets mail from a mail *server*. When you obtain a SLIP, PPP, or shell account, you almost always get a POP account with it, and it is this POP account that you tell your e-mail software to use to get your mail. See also *SLIP, PPP*.

Pop-in ➤ Short paid announcement by a radio or television advertiser that may be of special interest to the viewer or listener. For example, during the holiday season a common pop-in by advertisers may be, "MTNL wishes you and your family a happy new year." In this example, there is no mention of the company's product, but the viewer or listener is informed that MTNL is the sponsor of the message also called *image liner*.

Pop-off ➤ In television programme, it refers to quick and instantaneous movement of objects or information from on camera to off camera; also called *bump out*. In a popoff, new optical picture information, such as titles to a frame, are removed from the field of the camera.

Pop-on ➤ Quick addition of new optical picture information in the field of a television camera; also called bump in. When objects or information such as titles to a frame are popped on, they appear suddenly on a television pro-gramme's camera, as opposed to being *popped off*, or removed from the field of the camera.

Popping ► Descriptive term applied to 'mic-blasting', the effect of vocal breathiness close to microphone.

Pops (UK) ► Abbreviation for *popular press (q.v.)*. Also called *populars*.

Popular Press (UK) ► Papers of high circulation and mass appeal, i.e. the *Daily Mirror* rather than *The Times*, which is classified as 'heavy' or 'quality' newspaper. Also see *heavies* and *quality press*.

Populars ► Mass circulation newspapers of popular appeal.

Pork-chop ► (US) Tiny half-column engraving of someone's face; also called *thumbnail*.

Port ► It has three meanings. First, a place where information goes into or out of a computer, or both. e.g., the serial port on a personal computer is where a modem would be connected. On the Internet, port often refers to a number that is part of a *URL*, appearing after a colon (:) right after the *domain name*. Every service on an Internet server listens on a particular port number on that server. Most services have standard port numbers, e.g. Web servers normally listen on port 80. Services can also listen on non-standard ports, in which case the port number must be specified in a URL when accessing the server, so you might see a URL of the form:
Gopher://peg.cwis.uci.edu: 7000/.
It shows a gopher server running on a non-standard port (the standard gopher port is 70). Finally, port also refers to translating a piece of software to bring it from one type of computer system to another, e.g. to translate a Windows programme so that is will run on a Macintosh. See also *domain name, server, URL*.

Portal ► Usually used as a marketing term to describe a Web site that is or is intended to be the first place people see when using the Web i.e. the site acts as a gate way to the rest of the Internet. Typically a "portal site" has a catalogue of web sites, a search engine, or both. A portal site may also offer email and other service to entice people to use that site as their main "point of entry" (hence "portal") to the Web. Home pages of Internet service providers (ISPs), search engines (Google, Altavista), browsers (netsope, Internet explorers) are portals. Also see *vortal*.

Portaprompt ► See *autocue*.

Portfolio ➤ (i) Group of magazines owned by a single company. (ii) A folder or videotape of samples of your work, showing your strengths and experience.

Portrait ➤ A picture with vertical emphasis.

Position ➤ (i) In General, place on page where an advertisement or insert appears, in relation to its placement on the page and/or the front, middle, or back of the publication. Because of a reader's viewing habits, the position of an advertisement plays an important role in determining its effectiveness. For example, certain positions, such as the back cover of a magazine or page 3 of a newspaper, frequently are desirable and command premium rates because studies have shown that they are almost always read. A publication's advertisement may be positioned on a right - or left-hand page, at the top of or below an editorial column, near or completely surrounded by editorial copy, adjacent to the *gutter*, or close to or enclosing around other advertisements. Most advertisers place print advertising on a run of paper (ROP) basis; that is, the position of the advertisement is determined by the publisher, and the advertisement may appear anywhere within the run of the publication. However, some advertisers feel that a Preferred Position warrants the added expense and may request such a position on their insertion order. For example, sporting goods manufacturers may pay a preferred position rate to have their advertisements run in the sports section of a newspaper. On the other hand, some advertisers may elect to go with an ROP rate but will indicate a preference for a certain position on their insertion order (e.g., front forward, right-hand page, top of column, outside the column, adjacency to editorial matter) and will hope that the publication honours their request. (ii) Programmes or time spots that advertisers perceive to be particularly desirable in terms of ratings. In both radio and television, position is determined by time periods, with those spots watched and listened to by large audiences commanding high rates. For example, station-break spot announcements following programmes with high rating are sought after by advertisers and are offered at a premium price. See also *adjacency*.

Positioning ➤ See *position*.

Positive ➤ Photographic image that looks like the original, as distinguished from a negative, which reverses the black and white (or high density and low density) areas of the original. Some printing is done from positives.

Post ► To send a message on e-mail to a mailing list or to a newsgroup

Post-echo ► The immediate repeating at low level of sounds replayed from a tape recording. See pring-through.

Poster make-up ► Format which uses the front page as poster-headlines and pictures, with little or no text, designed to attract the reader inside.

Poster type ► Big sizes of type, upwards of 72pt.

Posting ► A single message entered into a network communications system, e.g. a single message posted to a newsgroup or message board. See also *newsgroup.*

Post-mortem ► A meeting to discuss a previous issue or issues.

Post office jack ► See *jack plug.*

Post-production ► The third and the final stage in the film and TV production process, when the recorded material is edited, sometimes re-recorded and mixed.

Post-script ► A device-independent page description language that is a popular and flexible DTP standard.

Pot cut ► The cutting off of a radio recording during replay before it has finished by closing its fader-generally to save time. 'Instant editing'.

Pot ► Holds the molten type metal in a line-caster.

Pot point ► A suitable moment, such as the end of a sentence, at which a piece of audio can be stopped early if required. (E.g.: This piece is 2 minutes, but there is a pot at 1'12".)

PP ► Pages.

PPM ► Abbreviation of peak programme meter. A device with scale and needle measuring sound levels. (More technically, the measurement of peak values of broadcast output.) See also *VU meter.*

PPP ► Point-to-Point Protocol. A communications protocol that lets users connect their computers directly to the Internet through phone lines. Put differently, this is a protocol that allows to make TCP / IP connections using telephone line and Real Audio modem. Also see *IP number, modem, TCP.*

PR ► Public or press relations.

Prasar Bharati ► (India) The autonomous organisation established under an ordinance (1997) and later an Act of Parliament to regulate and develop the public broadcasters All India Radio and Doordarshan. The organisation which is answerable only to Parliament, was established to free the AIR

& Doordarshan from Government control. Also called Broadcast Corporation of India.

Precede ➤ A new lead or story which takes precedence over an earlier story. Also a preliminary paragraph or two set up in different type to introduce, summarise or explain a succeeding story. Also see *blurb*, *standfirst*.

Precedent ➤ An established rule of law set by a previous court deciding a case involving similar facts and legal issues.

Precision journalism ➤ Use of quantitative methods of collection information, facts or opinion, for writing reports and analyses. For example, report based on an opinion poll of a carefully selected sample.

Pre-date ➤ (US) Newspaper printed before the date of publication on the front page. In the US, a number of city newspapers put out as late night edition with the next day's date on it.

Pre-empt ➤ Acquiring television time for high-priority programme by a network by excluding regularly scheduled programmes; local broadcast time subject to change to accommodate network broadcasting.

Pre-fade ➤ Listening to an item without playing it on air. Used to check levels, cue records and check the network signal before

opting – in (connecting) to the network news.

Preferred position ➤ Advertiser's request for position on a newspaper of magazine page; usually for a higher rate. For example, a women's dress manufacturer may request a women's page, or a sporting goods manufacturer may request the sports page, yet, some advertisers may prefer space surrounded by editorial matter.

Pre-plan ➤ A meeting to discuss future features.

Pre-press ➤ Print planning, film assembly, plate-making and other activities required before printing,

Preprint ➤ Most recently the advertising manager's delight and the production manager's worry; advertising, usually colour, printed on reels, rewound, and fed into newspaper presses to be folded in with the other pages of the newspaper; also any material printed before normal production and fed into the newspaper.

Pre-production ➤ (i) The first stage in the production process, during which the creative, technical and business planning takes place. (ii) The initial or the planning phase of movie or TV programme making that includes scheduling, budgeting, casting, script development, set and constume design, location scouting, and special effects design.

Pre-record ➤ To videotape a section of a show *before* the main recording session. This may be replayed during the main taping session and re-recorded on the master tape or inserted later during *post production* editing.

Pre-roll ➤ The process of the running of two tapes in sync in preparation for an electronic edit.

Presence ➤ A sense of 'realistic closeness' often on a singer's voice. Can be aided by bosting the frequencies in the range 2.8 kHz to 5.6 kHz. Optimum clarity of sounds. Also, the psychological status of beeing in the same room, i.e. being present.

Presenter ➤ Any performer appearing live or in recorded programme, usually as a news or information specialist.

Press ➤ (i) Informal term for the news media, i.e. journalists at a news conference. (ii) Manual or automatic machine that uses an inked surface to print words and images on paper or any other comparable surface. The platen press, *flatbed cylinder press*, *rotary press*, and *web press* are examples of printing presses frequently used by printers. The platen press can print colour or monotone on all types of thicknesses and is generally used for Lettershop print-

ing jobs requiring heavy pressure. The flatbed cylinder press contains a "flat-bed" support that holds the printing surface and is used both in letterpress and lithographic (see *lithography*) printing. The rotary press features two Cylinders as its primary mechanism and is used for letterpress and Gravure printing (direct rotary) or lithographic printing (indirect rotary). The web press uses curved plates to print on a continuous roll of paper at unusually high speeds and is used in newspaper printing by letterpress and in rotogravure work. All presses contain a feeding device, which feeds each sheet to the printing unit; an inking mechanism, which sets forth ink to the cylinder; and a delivery system, which removes the sheets from the press and assembles them on top of each other. (iii) Informal term for publicity received for a product, service, accomplishment, or any activity surrounding corporate/marketing activities; also called press coverage. A company could receive favorable press coverage in a publication about the merits of a new product. On the other hand, a negative commentary could be written in publication about the hazardous effects of a company's product. (iv) A generic word for all forms of journalism. (v) A meeting called to inform the media about a news event and to provide them an opportunity to ask question about the said news development. Such a meeting is also called by a person, a party, an organisation, an institution or some department to brief them about their activities, achievements, accomplishments, etc.; sometimes also called in response to allegations carried out by the opposition camps or due to some communication gap.

Press(es) ▸ The printing machine(s) house in the pressroom and tended by pressmen. Derivation of 'press' to identify newspapers and reporters or newspersons. Also see *press*.

Press Council of India (PCI) ▸ Set-up on July 4, 1966 under the Indian Press Council Act, 1965, with the express objective of preserving the freedom of the press and of maintaining and improving the standards of newspapers and news agencies in India. The council is an autonomous quasi-judicial body and is reconstituted every three years. It has 28 members (20-from newspapers; 5-members of parliament, three from the Lok Sabha and two from the Rajya Sabha; 3-one each nominated by the Sahitya Akademy, the Bar council of India and the University Grants Commission) with its Chairman, by convention, being a retired judge of the Supreme Court of India.

PCI was abolished during internal emergency or a result of repealing the press council Act, 1965, with effect from January 1, 1976. It was reconstituted on March 1, 1979 under a new Act which was enacted in 1978. The Council had moved a proposal in 1998 to replace itself with Media Council to include in its ambit both the Print and the electronic media. The proposal was accepted by the Ministry of Information and Broadcasting, though the media council is yet to be established.

PCI functions primarily through adjudications on complaint cases received by it either against the press for violations of journalistic ethics or by the press for interference with its freedom. The decisions of the council are final and cannot be questioned in any court of low.

Press Information Bureau (PIB) ▸ It is the main channel of communication between the Government and the media. As the central agency of the Government of India for informing the people about its policies and programmes, PIB functions upon the basic premise that a democratic Government must ensure that its polices, programmes and activities are properly presented and interpreted to the public on whose goodwill support it holds office. The bureau provides professional advice to the Government of India and also extends temporary accreditation facility to foreign correspondents and cameramen coming to India on short visits. The Bureau is the implementing agency for exchange of visits of journalists between India and foreign countries under cultural exchange programmes and protocol.

Press Institute of India (PII) ► Founded in 1963, the Press Institute of India is supported by the leading newspapers of the country and the international agencies dealing with mass media. For many years it was the nodal agency for sending journalists — reporters, sub- editors and even photographers — for training to the Thomson Foundation, UK. Now PII's training workshops for journalists are conducted in-house or in cities and rural areas of India. There is a strong focus on rural reporting, development writing and writing on women's empowerment through the panchayats (i.e. locally elected/nominated body to decide on the issues relating to a village or group of villages). Over the years, the PII has trained over 4,000 professionals – editorial and management – from India, Pakistan, Sri Lanka, Bangladesh and other parts of Asia.

PII publications include: 'Grassroots', a tabloid-size monthly journal in English that carries selected field reports depicting the human conditions even in the remote parts of the land. To encourage journalists to report on grassroots' issues, a prize of RS 5,000, is awarded to the best story published in Grassroots every month. 'Vidura' is a professional quarterly magazine in English, with a section in Hindi, that reports and comments on trends and developments in the media: The quarterlies, 'People' and 'Hum Log', have been started as part of the media advocacy project.

Press proof ► Prints made just before print production begins for a final quality check before the print run begins. Although it is advisable for the print buyer to review the press proof. See also *pre-press proof.*

Press relations ► See *media relations, public relations.*

Press release ► Information put out by an organisation in order to receive coverage especially in media.

Public Service Broadcasting Trust (PSBT) ▶ Founded in late 1990s as a non-profit NGO by a group of eminent broadcast and communication professionals like Kiran Karnik and Rajiv Mehrotra, PSBT was set up to strengthen and help sustain an independent, participatory and pluralistic space in the non-print media. It is working towards setting standards in TV, radio and film production that promote value of community and citizenship; in-depth insights with accuracy and impartiality; and, reach out to audiences that do not interest advertisers.

In partnership with Prasar Bharti, India's public broadcaster, PSBT is commissioning public service documentaries produced by independent filmmakers. It has completed a series of 30 documentary films on *Ideas That Work,* to promote and inspire innovation, imagination and commitment in problem solving, both at local and national levels in India. It is also engaged in producing a series of instructional, "how to" videos, that will introduce potential and young filmmakers to techniques of the discipline. The Trust is publishing a book 'The Story of Indian Broadcasting' that draws upon, among other sources, the expe-riences and views of a large cross-section of common people, and covers a wide range of topics such as programmes, personalities, important events, and policy.

Primary ▶ (i) Targeted group for the editorial content of a publication. For example, the primary audience for an article on financial strategies would be investors. A publication will first identify its primary audience and then gear its editorial toward the wants and needs of this target group. (ii) Total number of a publication's primary readers. For example, if one hundred individuals either subscribed to, read, or purchased a publication, this figure would represent its primary audience. (iii) Individuals to whom, or places where, a publication is delivered or sold. For example, if one hundred copies of a publication are delivered among residences, newsstands, and libraries, this figure would be its primary audience.

Primary letters ▶ Lower-case letters without either ascender or descender, i.e. x.o.a.etc.

Prime lens ▶ Lens with a fixed focal length.

Primer ▶ Old name for 18pt type; long primer (LP) is old name for 10pt.

Prime time ▶ In radio or TV, that

part of the day when the listening or viewing audience is the largest, as compared to other parts of the day. Programming during prime time is usually of a general nature designed to appeal to a wide demographic range. In radio, prime time is actually divided between two segments: *morning drive time*, 6:00 A.M. to 10:00 A.M., and *afternoon drive time*, 3:00 P.M. to 7:00 A.M., Monday through Friday. Television prime time is 8:00 P.M. to 11:00 P.M. Monday through Saturday, and 7:00 P.M. to 11:00 P.M. on Sunday. See also *daypart*.

Print ▸ (i) Total number of newspapers printed of one issue. (ii) A picture or bromide printed from a photographic negative.

Printer ▸ (i) Sometimes means *the* printer, the man in charge of the composing room. Strictly, a craftsman who makes up formes or operates the presses; (ii) but loosely used to describe compositors line-casters, proof readers, and all those engaged in the making of print, (iii) abbreviation for teleprinter. (iv) A device that produces a hard copy of the computer's information.

Print line ▸ Matter published usually at the bottom of the back page of a newspaper and on the front pages of magazines which comprises names of the editor,

printer, publisher and the publishing house.

Print media ▸ Printed, as distinguished from broadcast or electronically transmitted communications. The print media include al newspapers, newsletters, booklets, pamphlets, magazines, and other printed publications, especially those that sell advertising space as a means of raising revenue. Most print media, with the exception of magazines, are local, although there are some national newspapers (The Hindu, The Times of India, The Hindustan Time) and trade publications (A&M, Computers Today, Screen) that have become quite successful. Magazines, on the other hand, have always been national, although there is a trend today toward localization and specialization. Also include in print media category are directories, school newspapers and yearbooks.

Print order ▸ (i) The number of copies of an issue ordered to be printed. (ii) Request given to a commercial printer describing the type of material to be printed and all necessary specification, such as ink colours, paper weights and finishes, and quantity. A magazine print order would also have separate instructions for any special editions to be printed. Most print orders include a small print overrun to allow for unexpected contingencies and waste.

Print run ► The total number of issues printed.

Print tape ► Magnetic tape containing information to be printed, along with print format instructions such as line spacing and margins. The print tape is used to control a computer printer.

Printer's devil ► Apprentice in the printing trade.

Printer's error (PE) ► Errors on a proof that are the fault of the printer, either through typographical error or imperfections caused by the machinery. Since these errors are the mistake of the printer, they wil not be charged to the client. See also *author's alteration; editorial alteration.*

Printing ► (i) Variety of type 18 points or larger in size. Display type is heavier and sometimes larger than textual type and is sued in copy for emphasis, or for headlines in advertising, or for chapter tables, sub-heads, and the like in books or journals. (ii) Instruction to printer to set section of copy on a line apart from the rest of the copy.

Printing plate ► The plate, metal or polymer, from which he page is printed.

Print-out ► A copy of material in a computer printed out for reference in advance of page make-up or printing. Print-outs sometimes show the type as it will look when set.

Print-through ► The reproduction at low level of recorded programme through the magnetic interaction of layers of tape due to their close proximity while wound on a spool. The cause of post-and pre-echo. Often the result of tight winding through spooling at high speed, and storage of recorded tape at too high a temperature.

Prior restraint ► Legal action preventing publication.

Prism shot ► Photographic shot taken with a prism lense, used primarily for multiple-image effects. A prism lens arrests the image briefly and refracts light into a rainbow spectrum, reproducing the desired image again and again. For example, a prism shot is used in motion pictures to create a dreamlike image of a person's face. In this example, the prism lens is focused on the person's head, and the face repeats and rotates to give the feeling of disorientation.

Privilege ► A defence to some libel actions.

Problem-solution advertisement ► Advertisement that focuses on a consumer problem and offers a solution to the problem. For example, a problem-solution advertisement for a sunburn relief product will remind consumers of the problem of sunburn pain and promote its product as offering a fast, safe, and soothing solution to this pain. Product-solution advertisements are most effectively used when the consumer can readily identify with a problem, and when the solution to this problem is easily solved by purchasing the product.

Process engraving ➤ General term for producing an image on a sensitised metal plate.

Process plate ➤ Two or more colour plates used together in *four-colour process* printing to produce other colours and shades. Process plates are *halftone* engravings made from colour separation negatives involving the application of the primary pigments of yellow, red (magenta), blue (cyan), and black to reproduce an original full-colour design. A colour separation is first prepared for an original's yellow, red, and blue values, and a final negative and plate is then made for the design's black value. A design using two colours, on one colour and black, is called a *"two-colour process"*; one using three colours is called a *"three-colour process."* If a reproduction uses four colours, it is called

"four-colour process" or full colour. Colour photographs and coloured drawings are created using process plates.

Processor ➤ The part of a typesetter that produces the bromide print of the type for paste-up; or equipment that produces the print from a photographic negative for paste-up.

Producer ➤ Person responsible for (i) entire news programme; (ii) items within it. He is responsible for the proper assembling of the elements of a newscast so that it will have a polished and professional look.

Producer copy ➤ See *dubbing*.

Production ➤ (i) Preparation of television or radio programme, motion picture, or play for its showing. Production involves determining the show's format, staffing, supervising script editing and rehearsing, coordinating camera men, securing a proper studio, and assuring that the entire programme runs smoothly. See also *producer*. (ii) The material that is produced, i.e. a newscast. (iii) In manufacturing process of physically creating an offering for a target market. For example, the production of helmets produced for target market Mumbai.

Production assistant ➤ Something confused with the assistant producer, the production assistant usually handles the more basic chores in the newsroom, working under a producer or assistant producer.

Production control room ➤ A room next to or above studio from where production and technical operations are controlled during transmission of programmes.

Production director ➤ Individual responsible for the production activities of an agency, publisher, or broadcast station. A production director supervises the production department and staff, and has ultimate responsibility for the scheduling and quality of all advertising publication or programme.

Production manager ➤ See *line producer*.

Profanity button ➤ See *obscenity button* and *delay*.

Professional journals ➤ Publications that professionals such as journalists, doctors or lawyers rely on for the latest inform and research in their respective fields, e.g. Columbia Journalism Review, International journal of Advertising, Communicator and MIS.

Profile ➤ (i) Picture in words. The term is used to mean a story intended to reveal the personality or character of a person or organisation. Cars, horses,

weapons, buildings, etc. can also be profiled. (ii) A collection of Windows settings for a specific user. Profile information includes user setting such as color schemes, screen savers, and desktop backgrounds, so that multiple users can retain their own preferences.

Programme ➤ A group of instructions a computer uses to perform specific tasks. For example, Microsoft word is a word -processing programme. Programmes are also called applications.

Programme analyzer ➤ Voting-type machine used to analyze and continuously record the reactions of listeners or viewers to an entire broadcast programme or a commercial. Programme analyzers are used in test situations where research participants (chosen on the basis of sex, age, education, and geography) are gathered together to view or listen to a programme. The participants are instructed to push the programme analyzer's green button if they like what is being seen or heard and the machine's red button if they are not pleased with a portion of the programme. If the participants are indifferent, they are told to push nothing. At the end of the Programme, a second-by-second analysis of the participants' reactions to the Programme is produced by the programme analyzer in the form of a rising and falling curve. The programme analyzer is generally used to test a show before it is broadcast, but it can be used to earmark weaknesses in current programmes.

Programming language ➤ A computer language used to create a computer programme, the instructions that drive a computer to complete various tasks. Typical languages include C, Pascal and Fortran.

Progressive proofs (progs) ➤ Set of proofs made during the four-colour printing process; also called colour proofs. Typically, there are seven different impressions in a set of progressive proofs: one for each colour alone and then the combinations as succeeding colours are added. The a final proof will show the finished colour reproduction. An example of a progressive sequence follows: (1) impression of the red plate; (2) impression of the yellow plate; (3) impression of the yellow plate on the red plate; (4) impression of the blue plate; (5) impression of the blue plate on the yellow and red plate; (6) impression of the black plate; (7) impression of the black plate on the yellow, red, and blue plate. The progs serve as a guide and are used by the printer to match up inks in the four-colour printing process. They also permit the customer to make any changes or corrections the need for which may become apparent as a result of the process.

Progs ➤ See *progressive proofs*.

Projection ➤ The display and headline treatment given to a story in the page.

Promo ➤ A promotional announcement or reference. See *trail*.

Promotion ➤ (i) As it pertains to television news, the effort of a TV station to attract more viewers by making them aware of its news, of its newsroom anchors and news programmes. (ii) Publicity material to increase sales or improve public image.

Prompt side (PS) ➤ The right side of the stage seen from the audience or camera position. (*stage left*, actor's left).

Proof ➤ Print out of part or whole page. This proof is read, corrected where necessary and the amended page (the revised) is then ready for final printing. *Galley proof* contains just columns of type

Proof copy ➤ Final sample of printed material created by the printer prior to the full print run to get final approval from the print buyer of the copy and layout. See also *blueprint, galley proof; page proof; pre-press proof; press proof.*

Proof hook ► Assembly point of galley or page proofs.

Proof press ► Machine for printing a galley or page proof. Proofs are said to be 'pulled' rather than printed.

Proofread ► Read copy, such as a proof or a typewritten text, for the purposes of checking for errors and making alterations, before the copy is submitted for further reproduction. A proofreader is a person who specializes in this process.

Proof reader ► Person who reads and corrects proofs to ensure that copy has been accurately followed; hence *proof marks,* corrections marked on a proof.

Proof reader's marks ► Standardised system of marks for correcting errors on proof.

Proof-slip ► A long *galley proof* (q.v.) Also called *slip proof.*

Props ► Properties; objects used to decorate the set or used by performer. Such devices give credence to an item during a newscast.

Proscenium ► In a theater, the space between the curtain and the orchestra ('apron'). Hence the 'proscenium arch' at the front of the stage area.

Proscriptive ethics ► Guidelines (to the press) that stress the things that should not be done by news persons.

Prospects ► See *Newsroom diary.*

Protocol ► A set of rules computers use to communicate with each other over a network.

Pro-Type ► Trade name for phototype-setting machine, mainly for headlines.

PRS(UK) ► Performing Right Society. Organisation of authors, composers and publishers for copyright protection.

PSA ► Public service Announcement. A non-commercial message broadcast by a television station.

Pseudo-events ► News incidents that would not have occurred had journalists were not there to record them.

PSTN ► (Public switched telephone Network) The regular old-fashioned telephone system for public (as opposed to closed user group), switched and voice communication. Also see *closed user group, switched network.*

Psychographics ► Criteria for segmenting consumers by *lifestyle,* attitudes, beliefs, value, personality, buying motives, and/or extent of product usage. *Psychographic* analyses are used like geographic (place of residence or work) and *Demographic* (age, income, occupation) criteria to describe and identify customers and prospective customers and to aid in developing promotion strategies designed to appeal to specific psychographic segments of the market for a product. For example, the market for shampoo may consist of various psychographic segments described by their primary purchase motives (beauty, health, grooming), usage styles (daily, weekly, salon-only), or lifestyle (frequent travelers, parents with young children, empty-nesters).

PTI ► Press Trust of India. News agency supplying wire reports and video clips .

PTO ► Public telecommunications operator, managing all or segment of a country's *PSTN*; sometimes also refers to any telecommunications operator. For example BSNL (Bharat Sanchar Nigam Limited) and MTNL (Mahanagar Telephone Nigam Limited).

Public affairs ► Programmes dealing with topical issues of public concern (political, economic, social).

Publication ► Any material that is published, in any format. For example, magazines and newspapers are referred to as publications.

Publications Division (India)
► One of the media units under the Ministry of Information and Broadcasting. It is the largest publishing house in public sector. It provides authentic information to educate and inform the public through books, pictorial albums and journals in English and Hindi and major regional languages of the country. The aims of the Division are: to disseminate information about the country in various spheres of national activity; to facilitate the task of national integration by promoting among the people greater awareness and understanding of the different regions and of the people adhering to different faiths and beliefs; and to stimulate interest to generate appreciation of and respect for the variegated patterns of life and culture in India. The Division publishes 21 journals of varying periodicity devoted to different aspects of development, culture, children and youth affairs.

Public Broadcasting Service (PBS) ► US Government-funded service founded in 1969 to provide educational, cultural, public affairs, and children's programming to noncommercial television stations. PBS was initially funded primarily by the Ford Foundation to oversee the interconnection process between stations, rather than to produce programmes. PBS now is involved in compiling broadcast statistics, conducting audience research, and promoting public television through a weekly newsletter.

Public domain (PD) ► Original material, such as art, literature, photographs, or music, that is available for use by anyone, without cost, because the material has not been copyrighted or because the copyright has expired.

Public journalism ► The new approach to journalism that emphasizes connections with the community rather than being separated from it.

Public Relations (PR) ► Form of communication that is primarily directed toward gaining public understanding and acceptance. It tends to deal with issues rather than specifically with products or services. Public relations uses publicity that does not necessitate payment in a wide variety of media and is often placed as news or items of public interest. Consequently, they offer a legitimacy that advertising does not have,

since advertising is publicity that is paid for. The practice of PR is used to build rapport with the various publics a company, or organization may have (i.e., employees, customers, stockholders, voters, competitors, or the general population). Publicity releases, employee-training seminars, and house organs are examples of instruments used in public relations. Also called *media* or *press relations*.

Public-service advertising ► Advertising with a central focus on the public welfare. Public-service advertising is generally sponsored by a nonprofit institution, civic group, religious organization, trade association, or political group. Typically, it is directed at some humanitarian cause, philosophical ideal, political concept, or religious viewpoint. Groups such as the Red Cross and Care, sponsor a great deal of public-service advertising.

Publisher ► Entrepreneur in bringing together ideas, print, and readers; but also, in some countries, the employee who sees that newspapers are parcelled correctly and put on to delivery vans and trains. The term also refers to the chief executive officer (CEO) of a newspaper or magazine, who is responsible for the overall management of the publication. He reports to the owners who publish the newspaper or magazine.

Publishing room ▸ Where newspapers are counted, wrapped and prepared for distribution.

Puff ▸ An item in a newspaper which publicizes something or somebody.

Pulitzer Prize ▸ A series of awards for outstanding achievements in letters and journalism established by the will of Joseph Pulitzer, publisher of the New York World. The awards have been presented annually since 1917 by Columbia University on the recommendation of the advisory board of its School of Journalism. A newspaper photography award was made for the first time in 1942 and an award for a musical composition for the first time in 1943. Three other categories have been established since 1970. Commentary, criticism and feature writing.

Pull ▸ Synonymous with proof. A proof is said to be pulled, so a pull of a galley or page is a proof of galley or page.

Pull back ▸ In film or video production, to dolly away from a subject or object. A pull-back technique is often used to surprise the viewer by drawing

back from a scene to reveal something that was formerly not in view. Also see *dolly shot*.

Pulling focus ▸ Changing focus to follow a moving subject.

Pull-out ▸ Separate section of a newspaper that can be pulled out, often with separate pagination.

Pull quote ▸ A quote extracted from a feature or news story and given visual emphasis by typography.

Pulp magazine ▸ A magazine specializing in the printing of sensationalised articles; any publication printed on low-quality coarse paper to economize on production costs.

Pulse code modulation (PCM) ▸ A digital coding system.

Punch ▸ To extra emphasise the most significant aspect of a news-story. Also the most compelling word, phrase or part of a news piece.

Punchline ▸ Main point of story, a "punchy" story has strong news angle.

Punch-tape head ▸ The signal from the keyboard or computer drives the punch-head to produce punch-tape for feeding into phototypesetting machine or line-caster for hot metal.

Pundit ▸ A regular newspaper columnist who dispenses opinion; expert in a field.

Put to bed ▸ To put the forme or stereo plate on the press. When a page has 'gone to bed', it is too late to make corrections.

Put up ➤ Instruction to printer to set letters indicated in capitals.

Pyramid ➤ (i) Headline form resembling a pyramid with lines succeedingly short, longer, longest. (ii) (US) pattern of arranging advertising on a page.

PZ (Pressure zone) mic ➤ See *boundary effect mic*.

Qq

Q & A ➤ (i) Question-and-answer copy, as in formal interview or court badinage. (ii) When a reporter is interviewed on air about a story he/she has been covering.

q.v. ➤ quae vide (Latin) : see; textual cross-references.

Quad, Quadrat ➤ (i) A space. A piece of blank type of equal bcdy size but less than type high used to fill spaces in a line of type. Quads are made six to a fount so that their widths are multiples of the em of the size of type used. Thus the em quads is the square of the body type; the en quad is half the body, and the smallest, the hair space, is about one-twelfth·the body. (ii) Quadraphony or Quadrasonic. Four channel sound reproduction providing front and rear, left and right coverage.

Qualitative research ➤ Dealing with reader's opinions, aspirations and feelings.

Quality press ➤ Patronising European mainly British, term for serious daily and Sunday newspapers which report Parliament, foreign affairs and court stories in addition to scandal and other frivolities. Reporters on *popular papers*, q.v., call the quality press 'the heavies'.

Quantel ➤ Makers of electronics production equipment, particularly for computer graphics .

Quantitative research ➤ Research based on demographic and statistical aspects of the readership.

Quantity print ➤ Multiple prints of a film, videotape, or photograph made at the·same time from the original master.

Quarter - cam ➤ Quarter-inch format video recording system.

Quarter track ➤ Where the recording is made over two pairs of stereo tracks. See also *Half track* and *Full track*.

Quartz lighting ➤ High intensity lighting using quartz halogen bulbs with near daylight color temperature .

Query ➤ (i) Question raised on copy or on proof, or in a message to a news agency (ii) A freelance's inquiry whether a newspaper is interested in such–and-such a story. (iii) A question-mark(?). (iv) To request information by inserting search terms into a database.

Queue ➤ Tasks fed to a computer and waiting to be processed in the sequence in which they were submitted.

Quick study ➤ A performer who can remember lines easily.

Quick time ➤ Apple Computer's PC-based digital media system.

Quire ➤ Unit of newspaper circulation, usually 26 copies.

Quoin ▶ Wedge-shaped metal device for locking type and plates in chases.

Quoin key ▶ Iron key to tighten *quoins* in locking up chase.

Quotation marks, Quotes ▶ Punctuation marks to indicate that words are those actually used by a speaker or report. Can be double ("") or single (''), "If double quotes begin, single quotes are used for `quotes within quotes' and vice-versa."

Headlines should have single quotes; books usually have single quotes in text, newspapers double quotes.

Quote ▶ Quotation; in newspapers, often means a sentence or paragraph of a speaker's words.

Queue ▶ Tasks fed to a computer and waiting to be processed in the sequence in which they were submitted.

Racks ▶ The room in a radio station containing engineering equipment.

Radial prism lens ▶ Special effects lens which gives a multiple image.

Radio ▶ Microphone with a small portable transmitter linked to it. It requires no cable connection. Radio is one of the most important means of communication. It enables people to send words, music and other signals to any part of the world. People also use radio to communicate far into space.

The most widespread and familiar use of radio is broadcasting radio broadcasts feature music, news, discussions, interviews, sports commentaries and advertising. Radio has wide variety of uses in addition to broadcasting. Aeroplane pilots, astronauts, construction workers, police officers, soldiers, taxicab drivers and others who do many other kinds of jobs use radio for quick communication.

Radio works by changing sounds or other signals into electromagnetic waves called radio waves. These waves travel through air, space and some solid objects such as walls of buildings when they reach a radio receiver, the receiver changes them back into the original sounds.

Rag content ▶ Refers to cotton or linen fiber content in high-quality paper.

Ragged right ▶ Type that is not justified, but is 'flush left' or *ranged left*. Each line is of a different length, giving a 'ragged' appearance. The opposite being ragged left, with uneven margins on the left and flush-right.

Railroad ▶ (US) To rush copy for setting.

Raj TV ▶ A satellite channel in Tamil.

RAM ▶ (Random access memory) A computer's working memory. Anything put into it is lost when the machine is switched off.

Random ▶ Composing-room table, divided into galley-widths, where galleys are assembled before make-up.

Random access unit ▶ Computer storage unit that allows for the access of information at random; also called direct access storage. With a random access unit, information can be called up by the computer operator from any position, no matter what order that information was input into storage. For example, if a particular group of information has been inputted in alphabetical order, information can be called up from any part of the alphabet at any time and does not have to be called in alphabetical order.

Random sample ► Sample group of people to be used in a research testing situation where every person in the area under study had an equal chance of being included in the sample; also called precision sample. The process of selecting this sample on the basis of chance is called randomization.

Range ► (i) The extent to which a performer can produce high to low pitch levels. Also, the extent of one's ability to perform in various capacities. (ii) The number and variety of characters available in a type.

Ranged left ► Type that is not justified but is lined up on the left.

Ranged right ► Type that is not justified but is lined up on the right.

Rate card ► Schedule of advertisement spaces/time slots available and the cost of each. Pamphlet, brochure, or single sheet that tells the costs for advertising on or in a communications medium. The rate card is usually designed to give the advertiser all the pertinent data relative to advertising with the medium. In addition to the unit costs for time or space, the card will list any and all of a

medium's regulations governing the use of said time or space, restrictions on the time or space as set up by the medium, requirements to be met for camera-ready copy (in the case of print media), copy regulations, facilities available from the medium, various discount plans, and kinds of products or services that are not acceptable for advertising in the medium. Production studios and editing facilities also publish rate cards listing their facilities and costs on a per hour or per day basis.

Rating ► Size of an actual listening or viewing audience for a particular programme or commercial as compared to the size of the potential audience. The potential audience consists of all households in a geographic area that have broadcast receivers (radios and televisions), whether or not these broadcast receivers are turned on. One rating point represents 1% of the households making up the potential audience. Thus, if a programme had a rating of 10(10 rating points), it would mean that 10% of all households in a particular geographic area had sets tuned in to that programme. Ratings and rating points are an integral part of the broadcast evaluation system, particularly television, and are used in the planning of broadcast media schedules for advertising campaigns. A programme with a high rating will deliver a large audience to advertisers for their commercials. Also see *TRP*.

RBDS ► Radio Broadcast Data Systems, a recently developed radio technology using FM subcarriers to multiplex a visual display (such as a station ID) and limit electronic scanning of stations to those channels with a required format; used extensively for traffic information to override the programme being listened to.

RDS ► Radio Data System. A data signal added to FM and digital transmissions, used for carrying text, e.g., station indent and other messages, for display by the receiver. Also provides automatic switching of car radios for local traffic information, retuning for best signal, encoding of programmes for recording, etc.

Reach ► Term used in audience measurement describing the total number of different listeners to a station or service within a specified period. Most often expressed as a percentage of the potential audience. See also *cumulative audience, penetration*.

Reaction shot ► Shot of subject's response to some part of the action often filmed as a cutaway after the master shot. See *cutaways* (see Fig. A and B).

Readability ► A story is said to

(A)

(B)

be readable and have readability if it has a compelling narrative and is easy to grasp. Readability in typography means the ease with which the eye scans the type.

Reader ► (i) Also called a *liner*, this is the most basic news script which is read, on camera by the anchor, with no other full screen picture (except that of the anchor himself or herself) while the anchor is talking. However, a picture or a graphic may or may not be shown over the anchor's shoulder on his left or right (but not on both sides) by an electronic process called keying or inserting. A reader is generally of not more than 20 or 25 seconds unless it is an extremely important late night newsbreak whose video was impossible to get on the air, e.g., the early morning newsbreak of the killings of Kashmiri Pandits in Baramulla of 'Kashmir valley. (ii) Man who checks proofs for consistency with copy and corrects errors, in setting, punctuations, etc. The 'readers' is the department where proof readers and their assistants, copy holders, do their work as correctors of the press. Now all these jobs are being handled by personal computer-equipped sub-editors themselves. Many newspapers have done away with the best of proof reader.

Reader participation ➤ Editorial material or items which involve contributions by readers, such as reader's letters, competitions and articles based on invited opinions.

Readership ➤ Something like four people read a single copy. Number of people who read newspaper as opposed to the number of copies sold; and market research to count readership is an aid in selling advertising space.

Readership profile ➤ A tabulated analysis of the sorts and ages of readers that buy a newspaper or magazine.

Reader traffic ➤ How the readers move through the paper; surveys show how long they spend on each succeeding page or part of it.

Reading-in ➤ This is when a reporter, coming on shift, reads all the copy and items produced by the previous shifts to familiarize himself with the stories the newsroom has been following.

Reading time ➤ Average length of time that the readers of a publication devote to reach issue. When comparing similar publications, advertisers may find the publication with the most reading time attractive because the target audience will have more time to read their advertisements.

Readout ➤ (US) Subsidiary headline that 'reads out' – follows and substantiates – a main *deck*.

Real audio ➤ A helper application that allows you to download sound files over web pages in real-time. The player can be downloaded as freeware without waiting for long file transfers. For example, you can listen to All India Radio's entire broadcast of Morning News on the Internet.

Real-time audio and video retrieval ➤ The ability to hear/ see a file in a computer without having to completely download it.

Real time counter ➤ A tape counter which displays the time in hours , minutes and seconds. Used for finding sequences and handy for seeing how much recording time left on a tape.

Reason-why advertising ➤ Copywriting approach to print advertising whose format is to state a fact about a product or service in a headline and then explain why the fact is true in the copy text. The idea behind this type of advertising approach is to give a reason why a customer should buy the product or service. Reason-why advertising works better in print than in broadcast, because the reader has more time to consider the message. Broadcast presents a time limitation, and the viewer may very well miss the opening headline or the reasons why the opening headline is true.

Recast ➤ To cast a new plate for a page whose content, usually editorial but sometimes advertising, has been changed; replate.

Receiver ➤ (i) An in broadcast device used to transform electromagnetic waves into images or sounds. For example, a television or stereo would be considered receivers. (ii) In general communication, person or group of people to whom a message is transmitted. The receiver perceives and responds to the message in terms of his own background and psychological processes. In mass communication, the receiver is the audience.

Recording break ➤ A period during a videotaping session when recording ceases briefly to allow rehearsal, scene changes, camera moves, etc.

Recording head ➤ The head of a tape recorder or VTR which makes the recording . It has one or more magnetic gaps which realign the magnetic particles on the tape as it passes.

Recording of (off) transmission (ROT) ➤ Tape of the output.

Recordist ➤ Member of camera crew who operates sound and/or video recording equipment.

Records ➤ Sets of information stored in a database.

Re-cut ➤ Refers to re-editing a story for a later newscast.

Redress ➤ See *rejig*.

Reduction ➤ Playback of a multitrack music recording to arrive at a final mix. Also mix-down.

Reefer ➤ (US) Slang for cross-reference line or type which directs reader to an associated story in another part of the paper.

Reel ➤ Roll of newsprint fed into the presses; the revolving drum or core which receives and winds the paper.

Reel-end ➤ Part of the paper machine where the web is reeled up;

the last few yards of a reel of newsprint.

Referee ► An expert called in to advise on a submitted article. In scientific publishing, this process is formalized as peer review.

Reflector flood ► Photoflood with a silver coating on the point where it passes obliquely from one transparent medium to another.

Reflectors ► Boards or sheets used to reflect light. In the studio, to obtain very diffused light; in open air, to reflect sunlight (as key or fill light).

Refresh ► To redisplay the contents of a Web page or window.

Regional edition ► National publication with specific news sections for readers in a particular geographic location. Many publications publish regional editions so that they may offer local advertisers opportunities for advertising in their own geographic area. A part of the editorial content in such a publication remains the same in all editions, but the rest is devoted to local tastes and requirements. For example, The Times of India, The Hindu, Indian Express, The Hindustan Times have several regional editions.

Register ► The outline of printed matter as it appears on the paper; important in colour printing where the main colours are printed separately on to the picture image; correct alignment of all four colours of ink. Printing an be 'in register' or 'out of register'.

Registrar of Newspapers for India (RNI) ► The office of the Registrar of the Newspapers for India came into being on July 1, 1956. The main functions of the Press Registrar are: (Statutory): to compile and maintain a register of certificates of registration to the newspapers; to inform the concerned authority about the availability of titles for proposed newspapers; to ensure that the newspapers are published in accordance with the provisions of the Act to watch their regularity; to study the annual statements filed by the publishers of newspapers containing information about their circulation, ownership etc; to check the circulation claims of newspapers; and to submit to the Government on or before 30th September each year a report containing information and statistics about the Press in India for the previous year, with a particular reference to the trends in circulation and in the direction of common ownership units. The other functions of the RNI include formulation of newsprint allocation policy and allocation of newsprint to newspapers and assessing and certifying the essential needs and requirements of the newspaper for printing and composing machinery.

Regulars ▶ The repeated elements in a magazine: contents page, editorials, news, letters to the editor, etc.

Regular type ▶ Standard width of a type-face, as distinct from extended or condensed versions. The preferred term, is *medium type*.

Rehash ▶ See *rejig*.

Rehearse-record ▶ Procedure most used in music recording or drama for perfecting and recording one section before moving on to the next.

Rejig/rehash ▶ Rearrangement of reporter's copy usually by sub-editor to produce better structured piece; revision of a story in the light of later information; or a change of position in the paper, often between editions.

Relay ▶ Simultaneous transmission of a programme originating from another station. Transmission of a programme performed 'live' in front of an audience. See also *deferred relay*. Electrically operated switch.

Release ▶ Glorified name for a handout such as a change of personnel in a company or a fund-raising event sponsored by a community service organization, that has been written by the company or oganization and delivered to the media to be inserted into their publications or broadcasts for public relations purposes; more properly called a publicity release or a press release; to 'okay' for production (newspaper / magazine).

Relief ▶ The degree to which texture is brought out in the form of shadows and high light. Hard directional lighting produces high relief.

Remote ▶ Broadcast production that takes place outside the studio. The simplest remote production is the type seen nightly on local or network news where a newscaster reports about an event from the place where it is taking place. The most complex remote productions are the elaborate large-scale types used to cover sports and entertainment events; live production from locations other than the studio.

Remote sensing satellite ▶ A remote sensing satellite scans and explores the earth with different instruments, including cameras. Image can highlight the Earth's physical characteristics, such as wetland acreage losses. The media have also used these satellites to cover potentially in accessible regions for news gathering.

Remote site ▶ Any place away from the location of your computer. If you can log in to your computer from another location, then you are said to have remote access.

Remote studio ► Small, often unmanned, studio some distance from the radio or TV station where guests who cannot make it to the station can be interviewed. It can be linked to the main station by satellite or cable, permitting studio quality sound and pictures for TV.

Remote user ► A person who connects to a network by using a modem and *dial-up networking*.

Removes ► The difference between one size of type and another.

Re-nose ► To put new intro on to a story, using different material or a different angle.

Repeat ► A television programme which is broadcast more than once. The term is also used by the teleprinter or telex operators for repeating some words, phrases or part of news story.

Repeater ► A repeater strengthens or boosts a signal in the course of a relay.

Repertoire buyers ► Readers who choose from a range of magazines.

Replate ► Recast a page of type for later news or corrections. The forme for the existing page on the presses is 'brought back', opened, and the type changed in large or small degree.

Reportage ► Term used for 'gritty' investigative news fea-

tures, with appropriate photography.

Reporter ► Person who gathers and writes up news. In TV, he covers the day's events with a photographer and makes sure the stories are written and edited properly for the evening news-cast. In many smaller markets, a reporter who must double as a photographer is known as a one-man band.

Report generator ► Computer programme that is used to create statistical reports based upon the information in a computer file. The simplest report generators create reports that illustrate the relationship between only two variables in the database. For example, a report generator might plot total sales to price changes.

Reprint ► Duplication of a favorable article that has appeared in a magazine or newspaper, used in an advertising display, as a direct-mail piece in conjunction with a promotion, and for public relations.

Repro ► Abbreviation for 'reproduction', meaning high level scanning of colour pictures and their reuniting with type and page layouts to make the four-colour films required for colour printing.

Repro head ► The part of a tape machine which converts the magnetic pattern on the tape into electrical signal. Reproduction or playback device.

Repro house ► also known as colour house. Facility specialising in reproduction and colour work.

Repro proofs ► Proofs of high quality, on art paper usually, to be made into engravings.

Re-punch ► Repetition of a telegraphed message by the sending station, usually for the correction of an error in transmission.

Request circulation ► Recipients of a periodical that is sent free of charge upon request. According to Audit Bureau of Circulations rules, recipients must be part of the advertiser's target market to be counted as qualified circulation. According to Business Publication Audit of Circulations rules, recipients must have completed a request form that also includes survey questions qualifying the recipient as being of interest to the advertiser. See also *bonus circulation; free circulation.*

Required readers ► Those who read only what they have to for their studies or job.

Resolution ► The degree to which fine detail in the image can be distinguished.

Resonance ► The re-enforcement of a vocally produced sound by means of physical structure, acoustics, and electronic devices.

Resume tape ► A videotape cassette showing the best work of an applicant for a radio/TV news job. The resume tape is perhaps more valuable than a written resume since it is a better indication of a person's abilities.

Retainer ► Periodic payment made to retain someone's services, as with local correspondents; see *stringer.*

Retake ► Repeating and re-recording a sequence to improve or correct performance, camera work, sound, etc.

Retouching ► Improving the quality of a photograph in the scanner or of a print by the use of a brush or pen; most questionable when photographic content is altered or inserted. Now done electronically.

Retrospective ► Feature looking back on an event.

Reusable launch vehicle technology programme ► Programme designed to create the next-generation U.S. launch vehicle.

Reuters ► Britain - based international agency, providing general , financial and television news services. Not owned by the British government.

Revamp ► (US/India) Altering a story by changing the sequence of paragraphs, but not rewriting.

Reveal ▶ The side of an opening (e.g. door, window) between the outer edge and the frame, simulating wall thickness.

Reverb ▶ Short for reverberation (echo). The continuation of a sound after its source has stopped due to reflection of the sound waves. Also see *reverberation time*.

Reverberation time ▶ Expressed in seconds, the time taken for a sound to die away to one millionth of its original intensity.

Reverse ▶ Type printed white on a black or tone background; can be done in photosetter for paste-up as *reverse video*.

Reverse angle ▶ See *cut-aways*.

Reverse cuts ▶ Editing out in which the changes of camera angle makes the subject appear to be moving in opposite direction at the end of the first shot and the beginning of the second.

Reverse indent ▶ The first line of type is full measure and the remainder of the paragraph lines are indented one or more *ems* at the beginning. This is the reverse of normal indentation where it is the first line only which is indented. Also called a *hanging indent*.

Reverse kicker ▶ (US) Same as *hammer*, q.v.

Reverse out ▶ Typically, to show white type emerging from a black background. Some times known as 'wob', for 'white on black'.

Reverse play ▶ A trick feature which runs the picture backwards.

Reverse question ▶ So called because the camera moves in the reverse direction while recording the subject in relation to the original recording. Earlier it was trained on the subject sitting one-to-one with the reporter (Fig. A). Now, the reporter's face is on-camera

(A)

(B)

(Fig. B) and he is asking the same questions as he asked during the interview proper. This is done to relieve the viewer of the visual monotony of a long interview. Also see *cutaways*.

Reverse talkback ➤ Communications system from studio to control cubicle.

Revise ➤ Second or subsequent proof incorporating corrections made from previous proof.

Rewrite ➤ Process of improving a story by making extensive revisions such as a new elad, a different sequence to the paragraphics or changing the story structure; a rewrite might involve extra information, too. Deskmen do it when the reporter seems to have hold of the loose ends of the story. Many newspapers have a rewrite man to put telephoned facts into a proper news story.

Rewrite man/rewriter ➤ A staffer who is engaged exclusively for rewriting or rehashing news stories.

RF ➤ Radio frequency.

RF adapter ➤ A modulator for converting direct video and audio signals into radio frequency for replay on a conventional receiver.

RFC ➤ (Request for comments) The name of the result and the process for creating a standard on the *Internet*. New standards are proposed and published on line, as a request for comments. The "Internet Engineering Task Force" is a consensus-building body that facilitates discussion, and eventually a new standard

is established, but the reference number/name for the standard retains the acronym RFC, e.g. the official standard for e-mail is RFC 822.

RGB (Red Green Blue) ➤ (i) The primary colours from which all other colours are derived. (ii) A type of connector used on some video equipment.

Ribbon microphone ➤ A high-quality microphone using electromagnetic principle. Bi-directional polar diagram.

Rich media ➤ Refers to interactive multimedia presentations on the Internet through direct mails, banner ads, Web pages, etc.

Rifle mike ➤ Directional microphone with long, barrel-like pick-up tube.

Right-click ➤ To click an item by using the secondary mouse button, which is typically the right button. You can display a shortcut menu by right-clicking an item.

Right of reply ➤ Procedure for correcting published errors. More a convention than a law.

Rim ➤ (US) Outer edge of copy desk where copy editors sit; the copy editors who sit there.

Rim-lighting ➤ Rear-lighting which highlights the outlines of objects.

Ring ➤ To circle a correction in copy.

Ring round ➤ Story based on series of telephones calls.

Rip 'n' read ▸ A hasty presentation of news by means of tearing copy directly from a wire machine and reading it on the air.

Riser ▸ Small, portable platform or box used to elevate a camera, object, or person in order to improve a television shot; also called apple. A half apple is used when the desired height is lower than that achieved by use of a riser or apple.

Rising initial ▸ First letter of word in large size and sometimes ornamental design which stands on the same baseline as succeeding letters but projects above the height of ascenders.

Rivers ▸ Ugly stracks. Inelegant strips of white space in a page caused by over spacing between letters and words.

RO ▸ 'Run on'; instruction on copy to set two written paragraphs as one, or treat set-out matter as a single paragraph.

Roadblock ▸ Describes a method of scheduling broadcast commercial time on local stations or networks. On local stations, a local roadblock will present the same commercial on all stations at the same time on a given day in a given area. A network roadblock would air the same commercial at the same time on the same day on all networks. Advertisers will request roadblock scheduling when they want fast, broad coverage for their product or service.

Roll ▸ (i) Graphics(usually credit copy) that move slowly up the screen, often called *crawl.*(ii) Command to roll tape or film.

Roll cue ▸ (i) A transitional statement that enables a performer to yield his or her presentation. (ii) The second's worth of copy immediately following the start-of-a-tape. Because it takes some playback machines about 2 to 5 seconds to build up to speed, the technical director orders the machine to roll 5 seconds before the tape is actually on air. Since this is a judgement call and a matter of experience, too, some amount of human error is always possible. This is why you sometimes see an anchor gazing into the camera or why you sometimes miss first few words of a sound bite. The private satellite channels may not give you such a chance so easily, but if you regularly watch the Doordarshan news bulletins produced by its own staff, you won't be disappointed. Good, to the extent it makes clear to you what the roll-cue is all about! The Lesson: do not stretch the element of judgement call above the roll-cue or be ready to get pink cards.

Roman numeral ➤ I, II, III, IV, V or i, ii, iii, iv, v instead of 1,2,3,4,5.

Roman (UK) ➤ Standard type face which is distinguished from italic by verticality and the shape of certain lower-case letters.

ROP ➤ Run of the paper, press or production. Refers to the story or advertisement that is carried in all editions of a paper. Also those stories which do not warrant upfront position. The process printing the colour text or illustrations simultaneously alongwith the black or reverse text.

Rostrum camera ➤ Camera mounted on the photographic enlarger mainly to control taping of maps and other static objects.

ROT ➤ Record off transmission. Literally, a recording of the broadcast signal via a radio tuner. Sometimes used (less accurately) to mean any recording of studio output.

Rota picture ➤ A news picture obtained under the rota system, in which limited coverage of an event by newspapers is allowed on a shared basis.

Rotary press ➤ Conventional newspaper printing press in which both printing surface and impression cylinder rotate at high speed. Rotary presses are the best choice for high-vol-ume print runs because they are fast.

Rotogravure ➤ Magazine supplement to a newspaper (usually part of the Sunday edition) that is printed using the *gravure process*.

Rough ➤ (i) Undetailed sketch of page or advertisement layout or illustration; (ii) rough proof obtained by impressing paper by hard roller with type in forme; (iii) uncorrected galley pages proof.

Rough cut ➤ First assembly of tape edited to its approximately pre-selected order and duration. The final cut, called the master tape, is prepared with some necessary additions to the rough cut.

Round-up ➤ Collation of separate items into one story or under one headline, e.g. sports and weather round-up, etc.

Router ➤ A special-purpose computer (or software package) that handles the connections between 2 or more networks. Routers spend all their time looking at the destination addresses of the packets passing through them and deciding which route to send them on. See also *network, packet switching*.

Roving reporter ➤ Reporter who travels around a lot.

RP ➤ Reprint.

RPM ➤ Revolutions per minute

RPT ➤ See *repeat*.

RSA ► Response selection amplifier – device for control of treble and bass frequencies and 'presence'. See *EQ*.

RSI ► Abbreviation for repetitive strain injury which journalists can suffer through their use of computer keyboards and mice for long hours.

Ruby ► Old name for 5½ pt. English equivalent of US *agate*.

Rule ► Type-high metal strip that prints as line or lines.

Rumble or "hum" filter ► Sound filter which cuts out low frequencies.

Run ► (i) Period of printing edition. (ii) Number of copies printed for an order; also called press run or print run.

Run down ► An out line of a segment programme or programme. Also called a face sheet. In case of news bulletins, the list of stories to be broadcast on any given day and the order in which they will run during the newscast.

Run in full ► Senior editorial instruction that copy must not be cut.

Run of paper (ROP) ► Advertising that may be placed anywhere in the newspaper. Most publishers will try to place the advertisement in the requested position if possible. Contrast this with *preferred position*. In broadcast, this same option is called *run of schedule* or *run of station*, the former allowing a

television station to position commercials anywhere in the schedule that it is convenient, and the latter allowing a radio station to do the same. Run-of-schedule and run-of-station commercial positions are charged at the lowest rate on the *rate card*.

Run of schedule/station (ROS) ► See *run of paper*.

Run on/over ► (i) Segment of story continuing from one line, column or page to the next; radio or TV broadcast crossing its allotted duration. (ii) Additional copies printed immediately after the original run. Newspapers with rising sales sometimes worry about the run-on costs.

Run out and indent ► Another term for *reverse hanging* indent.

Run round ► Setting type round irregular edges of an illustration.

Run through ► Programme rehearsal

Running head ► Caption or title that is repeated across the top of each page in a book or magazine. In a magazine, the running head is usually the anem of the publication, whereas, in a book, the running head is usually the book title, a chapter title, or a subhead.

Running order ► List of programme items and timings in their chronological sequence.

Running story ► One that is developing and constantly changing, throwing up new information that require frequent revision and updates over a number of editions or days, as in a train accident earthquake or election results.

Running text ► Main body of text on a printed page in a book or magazine.

Running time ► Total length of time that a film, programme, or commercial actually runs. For example, the running time of a particular newscast may be 30 minutes.

Running turn ► Ensuring that sentences carry on from one column to the next and from one page to the next, to discourage the reader from breaking off.

Run up ► The time considered necessary for technical equipment to become fully operational.

Rush ► (i) Urgent news agency summary of news break; (ii) A direction on copy asking the composing room to give it priority.

Rushes ► Unedited raw material from the camera .

RX ► Recording.

Ss

Sacred cow ➤ (US) Copy or subject given favourable treatment; copy which is not to be cut or changed.

Saddle-stitching ➤ A method of binding magazines by folding pages at the seam and stapling.

Safe area ➤ Most receivers cut off the edges of the picture (up to a 10% margin around the frame). So it is advisable to keep important information within the remaining central safe area. Also see *TV cutoff.*

Safety ➤ In a magazine advertisement, space between the perimeter of the advertisement and the edge of the page. The safety permits binding the pages without losing the boundaries of the advertisement. Television commercials also must be edited within a specific dimension, called a safety, to account for the various sizes of television screens.

Sampling ➤ (i) Process in which a section of digital audio representing a sonic event is stored on disk or into the computer memory. (ii) Measurements taken from a small percentage of the audience to represent the behaviour of the rest of the audiance/readers. *Television rating points (TRPs)* are a form of sampling.

Sandwich ➤ (US) Panel inset in text type cross-referring to associated material on some other page. Or a *refer* in a sideless box.

Sans, sans serif ➤ Type without serifs on the ends of the stocks.

SAP ➤ Soon as possible. 'When a correspondent or agency is asked to file sappest they do their bestest'.

Satellite ➤ Manmade equipment circling the globe, satellites have many "channels" or "paths" that receive signals from earth and then retransmit them back to the ground.

Satellite media tour (SMT) ➤ A series of interviews conducted via satellite; called a 'tour' because it replaces extensive travel should would be necessary for the newsmaker (interviewee) to be interviewed by various reporters in person. In the PR industry it is also known as *teleconference* or *video conference.*

Satellite news gathering (SNG) ➤ The process of using small, transportable satellite dishes to directly relay news stories from almost anywhere in the field.

Satellite printing ➤ Printing at subsidiary production centres by the use of page facsimile transmission.

Satellite studio ▶ Small outlying studio, perhaps without permanent staff but capable of being used as a contribution point via a link with the main studio/station centre.

Satellite truck ▶ A vehicle outfitted with the equipment necessary to send signals to a satellite. Satellite trucks are used instead of live vans when great distances must be covered or when there is no line-of-sight path to send the signal directly to the studio.

Saturation ▶ The intensity of colour in image.

SB ▶ Simultaneous Broadcast. Relay of programme originating elsewhere. Conveyed from point to point by system of permanent SB lines, or taken 'off-air'.

Scaling ▶ Method of calculating the depth of a picture to be used.

Scalpel ▶ Place material in paste-up pages.

Scanner ▶ (i) An optical/mechanical device that can be interfaced with a computer. Either desktop or handheld scanners are used to scan and subsequently input graphics or text to a computer. (ii) Radio which automatically tunes into broadcasts by the police and emergency services. (iii) Outside broadcasts vehicle. (iv) Telecine machine.

Scanning ▶ The process of converting photographs, artwork and typewritten copy into digital form.

SCART ▶ 21-way connector used in Europe for both audio and video connections. Also known as peritel and Euroconnector

Scenic projection ▶ Method of creating a set by projecting a filmed or photographed image behind the actors.

Schedule ▶ Time schedule, or sheet, listing deadlines for pages; the chief sub's or (US) city editor's schedule recording stories processed, and the headline schedule which categorises all headlines used in the paper; often to a code a time table of newspaper production from commissioning of material to printing.

Schlock ▶ (US) Slang for heavy, ugly advertising, of which there is a lot.

School TV ▶ ETV or educational television, comprising material for the school going children, and also the higher education programmes.

Scitex ▶ Equipment used at the colour house for the manipulation and enhancement of colour photographs at high resolution.

Scoop ▶ (i) An important story that is the exclusive property of one newspaper, radio or TV channel possession of which means a victory over rival. (ii) Most commonly used television floodlight. It emits a very soft light that evens out the high-light - and shadow-areas, and thus smoothly blends all the lighting on the subject, set etc. Also called basher. The most common scoop is equipped with 1000 or 1500. Watt lamp mounted in a semicircular housing of about 18 inches diameter.

Scrambler ► Device for scrambling satellite TV signals so that only authorized viewers equipped with an unscramble can receive them.

Scrambling ► A process in which a satellite's signal is rendered unintelligible. The receiving site is equipped with a decoder to return the signal to its original state.

Scratch filter ► Sound filter which cuts out high frequencies.

Screamer ► Crude, sensational headline.

Screen ► (i) Select or eliminate names or items from a list or group based upon some selection criteria, such as income, occupation, or gender. (ii) Gird device used in *halftone* and four-colour process printing to create an image, as photographed through the screen, consisting of dots that can be reproduced more easily than a continuous-tone image. Screens vary in size from 55 to 300 lines per inch, depending primarily

on the level of detail required in the print. (iii) The amount of information displayed on the computer-monitor without the need to scroll. (iv) The visual information that appears on your computer monitor. Depending on the size of the computer monitor, a screen can hold less than a page or several pages of text. (v) Where stories held in the computer are projected for reading or editing; hence screen subbing, subbing by electronic means by use of a cursor.

Script ► (i) Typefaces that imitate cursive writing, such as Palace, Script, Legend, Mistral. (ii) Complete text of a programme or insert from which the broadcast is made.

Scroll ► (i) To look at the parts of the page that fall below (or above) what you see on your screen. The long bar at the far right of computer screen is a scroll bar. The small square in it will allow you to scroll through the rest of the page. Just place your mouse pointer over the square, hold down the left click button on the mouse and move the square up or down. You will see the page move. You are now scrolling. (ii) To display material on to a VDU screen so that it can be read in seuqence.

Scrubbing ► In hard-disk editing, moving the cursor through the defined region at any speed to listen to the sound being prepared for editing; this is the hard-disk equivalent to rocking a tape by moving the spools by hand in cut-and-splice editing, and the jog mode in electronic editing.

Seal ► Wording or symbol at the top of the front page indicating the edition, i.e. dak edition, city, edition, late edition, etc.

Search engine ► A tool that searches the Web for information you want to find. You can click the search button in any window to display a list of Web-based search engines. They locate the wanted information in searches for key words, i.e, "Economy, India," could serve as keywords for information on various aspects of Indian economy. Example are www.yahoo.com, www.google.com and www.msn.-com.

Search form ► The area on the search tool where you enter the keywords and other information needed to perform a search.

Search screen ► The image that appear on your computer when you indicate to a search tool that you would like to perform a search.

Search tool ► Computer programme used for searching a database, sometimes including various categories of information that can be searched along with a search engine.

SECAM ► (Sequence Colour Avec. Memoir) French colour television system.

Second-day ► Story developing upon the one previously published; a follow-up. That is why you have a second-day lead or a second-day story, often a feature lead, but always adding something new to the original.

Section(s) ► Separately folded part of the paper. British, American and many Indian newspapers are multi-sectioned; also less properly for separate editorial or advertising areas identified in the paper with their own logo (Sport, Business, Entertainment, Travel, Review etc.). The Times of India has Delhi Times and Indian Express has Express Line, as separate sections. The Sunday Times, (London) has seven sections spread over hundred pages.

Security certificate ► A chunk of information that is used by the SSL protocol to establish a secure connection. This information is often stored as a text file. Security certificates contain information about who it belongs to, who it was issued by, a unique serial number or other unique identification, valid dates, and an encrypted "fingerprint" that can be used to verify the contents of the certificate.

In order for an SSL connection to be created both sides must have a valid security certificate. See also *certificate authority, SSL*.

See copy ► (SC) Direction to readers or composing room to check proof against the copy; 'out see copy' means that something has been omitted.

See other proof ► Indication that two or more proofs need to be combined to make all the necessary changes.

See scheme ► Direction to compositors' room to check page proof against the page scheme or layout; or to set a piece of copy according to a scheme sent to the composing room.

Segue ► In broadcast, transition from one sound source to the next without interruption, or playing two recordings one after another with no live announcement in between. It comes from the Italian, meaning "there follows"; pronounced 'segway'.
Also refers to the following of one radio item immediately on another without an intervening pause or link. Especially two pieces of music.

Selective exposure ► Individual's exposure only to those messages that are in tune with his views and avoiding those that are in conflict with his opinion. Thus a TV channel may choose to show only those programmes which suit the existing beliefs, values and attitudes of the audience.

Selective perception ► (i) A condition of attending or perceiving only those programmes which attract the attention of the audience or which come handy to the prevailing beliefs. The practice also involves ignoring or twisting other programmes to suit one's attitude. The condition is also described as Selective negligence. (ii) Individual's inclination to misinterpret messages that are not in accordance with his views.

Selective retention ► Inclination to absorb messages in harmony with one's own view and to forget messages in disagreement with one's own belief.

Self-contained ► Any item which stands by itself. A self-contained caption or picture is one without an accompanying story; a self-contained story is one without any *cross-references* or *sidebars* or *shirttails*.

Self-opping ► When a presenter operates his/her own control desk without technical assistance.

Sell ► See *stand first*.

Semantic noise ► Any disturbance in the reception of a message leading to a stage where the message received is not the same as message sent. Semantic noise occurs between people speaking different languages or by the speaker's use of technical or complex terms, not understood by the listener.

Send (a page) ▸ Dispatch a page forme to the stereo department.

Send (copy) ▸ Usually the instruction is to 'send it out' or 'send it down or 'send it up' and they all mean the same thing: send the copy to be set.

Separation ▸ Use of colour filters so that single-colour negatives can be made of multi-coloured illustration.

Separation light ▸ Back light.

Seplia ▸ (i) Film whose colour tends toward brown tones rather than shades of gray, giving the image an old-fashioned and sometimes dreamlike quality. Sepia also refers to the brownish colour itself, as in sepia tones. (ii) Brown colour (as in sepia tones) resembling sepia, a brown pigment derived from the inky secretion of a cuttlefish.

Sepmag ▸ See *double system*.

Sequence ▸ (i) Picture strip showing consecutive action in a number of pictures taken shortly after one another; a number of shots joined together is called a sequence or scene. Sometimes a long scene can contain several sequences. Also, it is a semi autonomous segment of a narrative often a scene so that the sequence ends with a change of location. In documentary programmes, a series of shots are linked thematically or logically. (ii) The order in which a story is presented (in subbing).

Serial ▸ Article/programme that is published/broadcast in installments. Generally used for fictional or biographical feature material and not for news series.

Series ▸ Size range of any design of typeface. Also number of articles pursuing same theme but in different issues of the paper. Also see *story types*.

Serif ▸ Line or stroke projecting from the end of a main stroke. Serifs are of different forms and join the strokes in different ways, and some types have no serifs (sans serifs).

Server ▸ A computer, or a software package, that manages and controls the flow of large volumes of information through a network. It provides. a specific kind of service to client software running on other computers. The term can refer to a particular piece of software, such as a *WWW server*, or to the machine on which the software is running, e.g. our mail server is down today, that's why e-mail isn't getting out. A single server machine could have several different server software packages running on it, thus, providing many different servers to clients on the network. Thus, a server is a computer that controls users' access to a network, it stores and controls shared resources that can be used by other computers or clients. See also *client, network.*

Service provider ► A company that provides Internet "service" or access.

Services column ► An advice, or consumer column.

Set ► (i) Arrangement of type for printing, to compose in type, also the width of a piece of type from side to side. (ii) The scenery (walls, landscapes, panoramas) for a production. Also called the setting. (iii) Series of books on a common theme.

Set and hold ► Set in type but do not publish without a *release.*

Set close ► Instruction to printer for minimum use of spacing.

Set flush ► To set full to the margin.

Set forme ► The last forme (of page or pair of pages) to go to press.

Set off ► Desirable and deliberate in offset printing, being the transfer of image from rubber blanket to newsprint: but accidental and undesirable in letterpress printing, being the transfer of ink from one printed page to the facing page.

Set open ► Instruction to printer that type is to be well spaced.

Set out ► Instruction to printer to tabulate the matter, setting up letters from a case of type so that wrong founts and pie can be picked out.

Set solid ► To set without line spacing.

Set up ► To compose in type; or

instruction to set in capital letters.

Setting format ► Setting of a nominated size, width and spacing that is programmed into the computer for cases of frequent use.

Setting line ► A line drawn on the studio floor showing exactly where a setting is to be built. *Also* a floor line showing the boundary limits for staging.

Set-top box ► An electronic device that decodes and decrypts a TV signal so that it can be viewed by a subscriber. Typically a pay TV device, it is a small 'box' that sits on the 'top' of or near the TV 'set'. Also see *conditional access encryption* and *pay TV.*

Set-up shots ► It is also called a '2-shot' (see Figs.) that shows both the interviewee and the reporter as they appear to be in the midst of conversation. It is better visually if the interviewee is seen listening as the reporter asks a question. That way the tape editor can make an easy cut (transition) directly to the voice (sound bite) of the newsmakers.

Suppose the narration of the reporter says:

The BJP President L.K. Advani discounts the speculations that the R.S.S. has a role to play in the portfolio distribution.

Now it is visually natural if the shot of Mr Advani listening to the reporter's question run over

Set-up shot or two-shot

Two-shot or set-up shot

the preceding narration (by the reporter) at the end of which the editor makes cut to the sound bite of Mr. Advani:

True, the R.S.S. and the BJP leaderships do discuss the matters of importance. But I don't agree that the Sangh has influenced the selection of Cabinet members.

The set-up shot is for a few seconds of narration that establishes or sets the stage for the sound bite. It is the visual equivalent of a lead-in.

Sexn ► Section.

Sexy story ► A story that has instant audience appeal. Usually light and amusing. Very occasionally sexy in the usual sense.

SG ► Signal, teletype message of service nature between two offices.

Shadow ► Typeface in which a three-dimensional effect is created, such as Cameo, Graphique, Gill Shadow.

Shadow mask ► Screen inside conventional TV tubes through which electrons are passed to hit correctly coloured phosphors.

Shank ► Rectangular main body of a piece of type; also called the *stem*.

Share ► Audience measurement term describing the amount of listening to a specified station or service expressed as a percentage of the total listening to all services heard in that area.

Shareware ► Software distributed via the honour system. You download shareware from the Internet, try it out, and if you keep it, are expected to pay a shareware fee.

Sheet ► Slang for newspaper.

Shell ► A programme allowing limited access to a UNIX computer

Shell Account ► When you log into this kind of account, the computer you log into is connected to the Internet, but your computer isn't.

Shelter magazine ► See *home service book*.

Shield laws ► Legislation giving journalists the right to protect the identity of sources.

Shirt-tail ► (US) Brief addition to a long story.

Shoot ► (i) Taking pictures of scenes to be used in a TV programme, motion picture or commercial. The term is used both as a verb and a noun and encompasses all of the work and personnel involved in a production, including camera crew, talent, lighting and sound technicians, and equipment, as wel as the caterer for any food served while the filming or videotaping is in progress. (ii) Operate a camera or cause a camera to operate in a film, videotape, or photographic session.

Shooting a page ► Term in photoset newspapers. When the bromides of type are assembled in position on the page, the page goes to the camera room for 'shooting'—it goes into negative form ready for platemaking.

Shooting schedule ► Timetable prepared from the programme script in which the scenes are arranged in appropriate group for shooting. With details of location, actors and *props* required and so on.

Shooting script ► Detailed list of shots in the order that they are to be shot.

Shopper ► Locally distributed newspaper, usually free-of-charge. Shoppers usually include sale announcements and discount coupons for local stores.

Short form ► Usually programme material in less than 30-minute lengths on television; typically upto 5 minutes for radio.

Short gun head ► (US) Multi-deck headline—two or more decks of heading on the same story, each deck consisting of one or more lines.

Short measure ► Type set narrower than the standard width of a column in a newspaper.

Short takes ► Sheets of copy of only a paragraph or two: to 'send in short takes' means to send copy urgently to the composing room a sheet or two at a time.

Shortcut ► An icon that links to a file or folder. When you double click a shortcut, the original item opens.

Shortcut menu ► The menu that appears when you right click an object.

Shorts ► Stories of a few paragraphs with small headlines intended for use down the page.

Shot ► (i) A shot is a series of pictures of an activity or happening or an action. A shot may be either minutes or only seconds in length. There are 24 frames for each second in film, but 25 frames per second in video. It is a visual unit of a programme during which an action occurs without interrupting the physical continuity by cutting and editing. Thus it an uncut, unedited strip of exposed film or videotape taken by a camera without an interruption. (ii) Particular style or angle of a photograph, e.g. a beauty shot, close-up or composite shot. (iii) Informal photograph, usually taken by an amateur, without any attention to technique, snap shot.

Shot box ▸ Switches used to pre-set the *zoom of* a studio camera.

Shotgun Pod ▸ Support fodder a camera , allowing it to be carried or braced against the shoulder.

Shot list ▸ Detailed description of each scene in raw or edited tape from which the commentary is written to match the pictures.

Shot sheet ▸ A list of the order of shots a camera is to take .

Shoulder ▸ That part of the upper surface of a type which carries no relief image itself and on which the relief image stands.

Shovelware ▸ The direct and inappropriate transfer of text from one medium to another against the requirements of genre dictates of convention, e.g. early TV dramas were shovelled from stage or early TV news bulletins were shovelled from newspaper.

Show-through ▸ Printing problem where the image printed on one side of the paper can be seen on the other side. Show-through is caused by using extremely thin paper.

Shrinkage ▸ Narrowing of the stereotype flong during moulding process, producing page fractionally smaller than original typeset page.

Shut down ▸ To use the Shut Down command, which prepares the computer to be turned off or restarted.

Shuttle search ▸ Facility allowing frame-by-frame playback of a tape, either forward or backward for editing purpose.

Shy ▸ A headline that is too short for the space available. Also see *bust*.

Sibilance ▸ An emphasis on the 's' sounds in speech. May be accentuated or reduced by type and position of microphone.

Side ▸ (US) Any department, thus feature side, city side, Sunday side.

Sidebar ▸ Story related to main story and run next to it. Sidebar story often slugged 'with..', i.e. `with Jessica murder', 'with Kennedy crash', etc. Also see *story types*.

Side-head ▸ Small subsidiary heading in the body of a story, set left instead of centred (crosshead).

Sidelight ▸ Similar to sidebar but with emphasis on personalities.

Sidesticks, Foot sticks ▸ Pieces of wedge-shaped metal or wood used to tighten type in a galley.

Sign off ▸ A sign off is the TV equivalent of a newspaper by-line and dateline. But not exactly because it comes at the end of the report unlike bylines and datelines which normally come at the beginning of a newspaper report. Also, they do not contain the date but they do contain the following: (a) name of the report, (b) name of the location and (c) name of the network. For example,... *Mahuya Chaudhary, New Delhi, Star News....Sanjay Pugalia, Congress Headquarters, Aajtak, . . . Anita Pratap, Kabul, CNN*

Signal ▸ Communication transmitted and received over the airwaves, as radio and television signals. Particularly in radio, people often speak of a strong or weak signal when referring to the clarity and audibility with which the sound is heard. In radio, the signal is actually an electrical impulse made by changing audible sounds of various frequencies into electrical waves of the same frequencies for broadcasting. In television, light waves are also produced along with the audio signal, so that an image is received along with the audio portion.

Signal-to noise ratio(S/N) ▸ The ratio between the video or audio signal and noise or interference. The higher the signal-to-noise ratio the better the quality

Signature ▸ (i) Folded sheet of printed paper constituting a set of pages in a publication. All signatures constitute a number of pages in a multiple of 4, such as 4, 8, or 16 pages. Signatures are gathered and bound, and the folds are trimmed away to produce a finished magazine, catalogue, or book. (ii) Song associated with a television or radio show or a product or service; also called theme song. (iii) The advertiser's name displayed along with the ad material, which is occasionally used inter-changeably with the logotype.

Signature tune ▸ Piece of music intended to introduce or identify a particular programme. Also called *ident* or *sig tune.*

Signposting ▸ In a news programme, this means comprehensively headlining and forward trailing the programme to keep up audience interest. During a story, it means highlighting the central theme of the story at the start, amplifying that theme in a logical manner, repeating key points where necessary, and pointing the story forward at the end.

Silhouette ▸ Pictorial style concentrating entirely on subject outline, filled in with solid colour usually black. Also see *cut-out.*

Silly season ▸ Supposedly a time (usually holiday period) when little hard news is around and the press is reduced to covering unimportant events, i.e. routine statements by politicians; intra-trade union affairs, etc.

Simulcast ▸ (i) Synchronization of an FM radio signal with the usual video and audio signal of a television programme for the simultaneous broadcast of the Programme on FM radio and television stations. Simulcasts are usually used to improve the quality of the sound in the television broadcast. (ii) Simultaneous transmission of a programme in *analogue* and *digital* form.

Single leaded ▸ Lines of body type separated by the insertion of a thin lead between each line.

Single-mode fiber ▸ An efficient and high speed, high-capacity FO (fibre-optic) line.

Single quotes ▸ These are the 'single' quotes which are preferred to "double" quotes for headline.

Single rule ▸ Rule printing one light line.

Single system (commag) ▸ Where the soundtrack is recorded optically or magnetically on to the video itself.

Siphon ▸ Term used in broadcast to describe the act of relaying a free television programme via pay-TV.

Sister paper ▸ When a company has controlling shares in more than one newspaper, each one is described as sister. Thus The Economic Times is a sister paper of The Times of India since both are owned by the Bennet coleman Co. Ltd.

Sitcom ▸ Situation comedy; weekly radio or television show focusing on the humorous side of real-life situations, often centered around a family or family situation. Among the first sitcoms to appear on Indian television was Ye jo Hai Zindagi. Other sitcoms are Ham Paanch (Hindi) Zee TV and Tu Tu Main Main on star plus, each of which deals with everyday occurrences within the family about which the show is centred. Typically, the sitcom is a 30-minute programme, where the situation is presented in the first 10 minutes, developed in the next 10 minutes, and then resolved in the last 10 minutes. The television format presents the perfect medium for the sitcom because of the visual opportunities it allows. The format has been extremely successful over the years, particularly during prime time.

Site ▸ A place on the *Internet*. Every *web page* has a location where it resides which is called it's site. And, every site has an address usually beginning with "*http://*".

Site map ► A representation of the Web site organization by using graphics or text.

Siti Cable ► A cable channel, owned by Zee TV and Star TV, mostly engaged in local programming.

Situationer ► News feature usually giving background information, as distinct from urgent or spot news, and so will probably hold until space is available or events make it topical.

Sixteen millimeter (16MM) ► Width of film used for moving pictures. Sixteen millimeter film is the industry standard for local television and film production and is also used in some commercial filming. It runs at a speed of 36 feet per minute, and shoots and projects 24 frames per second. See also *eight millimeter; thirty-five millimeter*.

Size down ► Instruction to printer to decrease the size of type to the next size down unless specified.

Size (film, video) ► The size of film or video tape is measured in length as well as width. The length of film is described in feet, hence the word 'footage' or in meters which is more common these days. From the smallest to the largest, film widths are 8mm, 16 mm, 35 mm and 70 mm. In video, the sizes are measured in quarters of an inch: 1 quarter inch, half inch, ¾ inch, 1 inch and 2-inch. The length however,

is measured in time: half hour tape, 1 hour tape, etc.

Size up ► Instruction to printer to increase the type to the next size unless specified.

Sizing ► See *scaling*.

Sked (US) ► Slang for schedule.

Skeleton (blank) ► Programme script which has gaps between the pages for insertion of new and late items.

Sketch (UK) ► Light, often witty description event, most commonly used with reference to reporting House of Commons.

Skew ► Tape tension. Incorrect skew results in distortion at the top or bottom of the picture.

Skillset ► London-based broadcast film and video industry training organisation

Sky-line (r) (US) ► Headline running above the nameplate across the top of the page; also called over-the-roof. See also *overbanner*.

Slab serif ► Typefaces with heavy, square-ended serifs with or without brackets (i.e. gentle curve) at the junction. Faces such as Rockwell, Calendar, Playbill.

Slander ► Spoken defamation.

Slant ► Emphasis or focus of a story; may also indicate that the story has a particular bias or over-emphasizes one aspect at the expense of other pieces of information.

Slide ► Colour photograph set in a frame and made on transparent film that may be projected and enlarged onto a screen for viewing by a group of people. Slides are usually made from 35mm film.

Slip ➤ (i) Special edition for particular area or event. It can involve change of more pages or whole newspaper (as in sports slip carrying sports results, news and features on a particular day); change of pages between editions hence *slip edition*. (ii) (Serial line Internet protocol) A standard for using a regular telephone line (a serial line) and a modem to connect a computer as a real Internet site. SLIP is gradually being replaced by PPP. See also *Internet*, *PPP*.

Slippage ➤ Because of a number of cues, machines, tape times involved in a newscast, it is only natural that a few seconds are lost or gained here and there. Usually, a newscast runs longer than planned, i.e. time is lost in the TV newsroom parlance. The cumulative lost time this way is called slippage, which can amount to as much as 30 seconds in a half-hour newscast, meaning that the newscast runs 30 seconds more than its allotted time. Therefore, to offset the slippage a newscast is ended with short items that can be dropped if necessary.

Slip / PPP Account ➤ When you log into this kind of account, your computer is actually connected to the Internet, and so is fully capable of all the TCP / IP services available.

Slip proof ➤ See *galley proof*.

Slogan ➤ Phrase or sentence used repeatedly in the advertising of a product or service that, through its repetition alone, eventually comes to identify the product or service. Essentially, slogans serve one of two basic functions: either to communicate an idea that manufacturers want associated with the product or service, such as "Jab Chalo Ho Jai, Cocacola Enjoy".

Slop ➤ Over-set matter.

Slot ➤ (i) (US) The centre of the inner side of the copy desk, traditionally horseshoe-shaped, the slot man or slot is the copy editor who sits here and instructs copy editors who sits on the rim; (ii) time schedule of a radio/ TV programme.

Slow motion ➤ A scene in which the objects appear to be moving more slowly than normal. In film slow motion is achieved through high speed photography and normal playback. In television , slow motion is achieved by slowing down the playback speed of the tape which results in a multiple scanning of each television frame.

Slug ► (i) The identifying word or phrase given to each story and set in one line at the top of the story and discarded when the story is complete and 'clean'. Also called *catchline*. (ii) Array of type cast on a line-casting machine. (iii) Six points thick spacing material. (iv) Blank footage inserted into a film or videotape to represent a Programme or portion thereof that is still to come. The slug will be the exact length of the forthcoming piece so that the *running time* of the footage will be the same as that of the finished product.

Slug-line ► Catchline (in US).

Small caps ► Capital letters smaller than regular capitals of a particular typeface and of the same size as the lower case letters of the same fount. They are used primarily for subheadings and running heads or to highlight certain words.

Smallsat ► A small, relatively inexpensive satellite.

SMARTV ► (Satellite master antenna television) System of sending satellite pictures to community dishes for distribution by cable .

SMDS ► (Switched multi-mega-bit data service) A new standard for very high-speed data transfer.

SMT ► See *satellite media tour*.

SMTP ► (Simple mail transfer protocol) The main protocol used to send electronic mail on the Internet. SMTP consists of a set of rules for how a programme sending mail and a programme receiving mail should interact. Almost all Internet e-mail is sent and received by clients and servers using SMTP, thus if one wanted to set up an email server on the Internet one would look for email server software that supports SMTP. See also *client, server*.

Snap ► Brief information given by news agency before main stroy is sent.

SNMP ► (Simple network management protocol) A set of standards for communication with devices connected to a *TCP/IP* network. Examples of these devices include routers, hubs, and switches. A device is said to be "SNMP compatible" if it can be monitored and/or controlled using SNMP messages. SNMP messages are known as 'PDU's" – Protocol Data Units. Devices that are SNMP compatible contain SNMP "agent" software to receive, send, and act upon SNMP messages. Software for managing devices via SNMP are available for every kind of commonly used computer and are often bundled along with the device they are designed to manage. Some SNMP software is designed to handle a wide variety of devices. See also *network*, *router*.

Soap opera ► Serialized melodramatic presentations on broadcast television of true-to-life circumstances centering around romance and family life and its problems and tragedies. Used as a slang for TV serials which are replete with cliches and stock situations It began as 15-minute segments on radio in the 1930s in the U.S., the presentations were affectionately named "soaps" (which later became "soap operas"), because they were sponsored by soap manufacturers. The creator of the format was a woman named Irna Phillips, who began the genre in Chicago in 1930 with "Painted Dreams," the story of an Irish widow and her family. Now such dramas appear on daytime TV all over the world in different languages, and are mostly sponsored by family care products. The soap opera format. has also been adapted for prime-time programming.

SOC ► (Standard outcue) Standard phrase spoken by a programme's team of reporters at the end of every contribution, e.g., Sudhanshu Ranjan, Doordarshan, Patna.

Soc, sox ► (US) Abbreviation for society or women's sections.

Soft ► (i) A shot that is slightly out of focus. (ii) Opposite of hard news

Soft lead ► A lead that uses a quote, story or some other soft literary device to attract the reader. Some special content publication called special editions are actually different versions of the same issue, such as The Times of India, featuring advertisements from local retailers. The issue name, title, price, and some or all of the editorial content are the same, but the advertising content and distribution areas differ.

Soft news ► Light news story that can be more colourful and witty than the hard news story, Television news features such as — health and nutrition specials or film reviews, added to the regular daily news to make the news programme more entertaining. Also see *story types*.

Software ► Instructional programmes to be fed to the computer for further operations. The softwares may be: Application Software, which is in a shape of written programmes, and is used to carry out special projects such as tying a text document; Systems Software, which makes the complete computer system or the hardware to operate such as switch on and control the screen; and Control Software, which comprises programmes, used to control smooth functioning of applications and system programmes.

Software piracy ▸ The illegal copying and distribution of software.

Solarization ▸ Reversal or partial reversal of the image by extreme over exposure. It is an electronic effect.

Solid ▸ Type lines without any space between them.

Solid matter ▸ See *matter*.

Solus ad ▸ The only advertisement on a spread.

Solus reader ▸ Often an ad-get feature.

SOP ▸ 'See other proof'.

Sort ▸ Letter, figure, punctuation mark, sign or other character cast as type.

SOT ▸ (Sound on tape) Video inserts complete with sound track. Also often termed sound on video (SOV).

Sound bite ▸ (*grab*, Australia) The TV equivalent for radio's actually, i.e., voice of a newsmaker or interviewee selected for broadcast. But except in foners, the sound bite in TV news run concurrently with the video of the person or newsmaker, saying those words. When a telephonic interview is aired, normally the video of the still photograph of the interviewee is shown. The sound bites are chosen very carefully and are generally five to ten second statements.

Sound bite script ▸ This is the type of script that includes no videotape (pictures) of the story (event, etc.) itself but does carry a brief videotaped interview with some one knowledgeable about the story. The anchor begins with the lead-in and then someone appears on the screen making some comments about the subject of the story, with the name identifier of the interviewee superimposed on the screen. At the end of the sound bite the anchor appears on the screen to tag the story before moving onto another. A typical story of this type is a story, say, on the woman reservation bill. If the videotape of the heated verbal exchanges are not available, the reporter has no choice but to catch hold of some well known proponents and opponents of the M.Ps to speak on the status of the Bill. If only two bites had to be accommodated, you better could take the bite of say Geeta Mukherjee (an ardent supporter and Chairperson of the committee on the Bill) and then the bite of Sharad Yadav who did not allow even the Prime Minister I.K. Gujral (of Janata Dal) to introduce the Bill.

Sound effects (SFX) ▸ Sounds, such as footsteps, ocean waves, or the squealing of automobile brakes, that are heard in a radio or television programme or commercial in accompaniment to the script and that add to the mood or atmosphere of the presentation. Sound effects are produced by playing a recording of the actual sound that has been made previously wherever the sound actually occurred, or by recreating the sound by approximating the conditions under which it actually happens, or by using special devices and props to approximate the sound itself (such as crinkling cellophane to simulate the sound of fire).

Sounder (jingle, stab) ▸ See *ident*.

Sound track(s) ▸ Area of tape on which sound is recorded.

Source ▸ The original event; a person providing information for a story; equipment picking up audio visual information.

Source code ▸ The set of commands that tells your browser how to display a page on your computer screen.

Source credibility ▸ Perception of trustworthiness and individual imparts to other people. Factors that influence source credibility are expertise and reputation for honesty.

SOVT ▸ Sound on video tape.

SP (Standard play) ▸ Normal tape speed

Space shuttle ▸ The world's first reusable piloted space craft. A shuttle can carry a variety of payloads to a low earth orbit.

Spaceband ▸ Metal wedge providing spaces of varying width to justify lines set by line-caster.

Spaces ▸ Graded units of space, less than type high, used to separate words or letters.

Spacing-in (spacing-out) ▸Composition technique for keeping line lengths uniform by reducing or increasing the width of the space between words in the line. In metal type composition, blank *slugs* of varying widths are placed between the type characters. See also *composing stick*; *letterspacing*.

S page ▸ Splash or front page.

Spam (or spamming) ▸ The Internet version of junk mail or unwanted information. Spanning is sending the same message to a large number of users, usually to advertise something. E-mail address may be collected using *cookies* or a mailing list from a *newsgroup*. The term probably comes from a famous Monty Python skit which featured the word spam repeated over and over. The term may also have come from someone's low opinion of the food product with the same name, which is generally perceived as a generic content-free waste of resources. (Spam is a registered trademark of Hormel Corporation, for its processed meat product.). For example, Supriyo spammed 50 USENET groups by posting the same message to each. See also *maillist, USENET*.

Special ► Programme that is not part of the regular broadcast schedule and is presented on a one-time basis. Usually is of special interest to the listening or viewing community, it may also be a dramatic showcase for known talent, or a spectacular production such as an awards presentation or a musical variety show. Because of the special nature of the programme, a large audience is usually expected. Therefore, commercial time will sell at a premium throughout the length of the presentation. See also *one-shot*.

Special effects ► Animated graphics representing a very wide range of physical illusions, including catastrophes, destruction, fire, gimmick apparatus, 'impossible' monsters, etc.

Special effects generator (SEG) ► Unit in video production to mix, switch or process video signal.

Special feature ► Often an adget feature aimed at getting advertisers' participation. The message is : say, what you want editorially and pay for it.

Spectacolour ► (US) Form of preprinted colour advertising.

Spectacular ► (i) Elaborate television show, motion picture, or live stage presentation that usually features a very large cast, unusual costuming, and many Special Effects, and costs vast sums of money to produce. (ii) Outdoor advertising display that features neon or electric lighting, some moving parts, lavish colours, and/or unusual special effects as a part of the advertisement. Located in or around large metropolitan areas, spectaculars are usually custom-made to fit special high-traffic locations and are the costliest of all outdoor advertising display. Typically, they are leased by an advertiser on some long term arrangement.

Spectrum scarcity ► Theory based on the belief that since the electromagnetic spectrum is finite only a limited number of individuals could receive a license.

Speech recognition ► A subset of natural language processing, it allows a computer to recognize human speech or words.

Speed (lens) ► The f-number of the lens aperture when it is fully open. A fast lens is suitable for shooting in low-level lighting . The lower the f-number, the faster the lens.

Spider ► Device which holds the legs of a tripod in fixed relative positions on a slippery floor.

Spike ► To shelve copy or other information (e.g. press release); 'spike it' means `do not use it but keep the material available'. This is different from a story being 'killed', which means the story must not be used.

Spill light ➤ Accidental illumination (e.g. light falling on to adjacent walls as distracting streaks or blobs).

Spin-doctor ➤ Organisation or person hired to promote positive aspects of policy and events, and to suppress the negative.

Spinoff ➤ Television programme derived from situations or characters in another television programme.

Splash ➤ (i) The main story on the front page; (ii) The front page itself. (iii) A web page that usually contains only a graphic, logo, quote, or brief text ("Click Here to Enter") that links to the "real" home page.

Splice ➤ The word splice is used as a verb when using video and film, e.g., 'splice these two shots together' means to cut these two shots together.

Splicer ➤ In film the footage is physically cut with a small machine called a splicer and the pictures are spliced together with glue or special sticky tape.

Splicing tape ➤ Sticky tape used to join physical edits made by cutting the shot film.

Split-field diopter lens ➤ A close up lens which has been divided into two halves, the lower half usually has greater magnification.

Split fractions ➤ Type cast for setting fractions in two parts, one bearing the top figure, and the other the bottom figure with the horizontal line over it.

Split page ➤ (i) First page of the second section of a paper printed in two sections; e.g. first page of the Delhi Times which is published as a separate section in The Times of India, Delhi edition. (ii) The standard TV news script; the left side of the page is used for video directions and the right side is for the script and audio cues.

Split screen ➤ (newspaper) The use of a terminal to display two stories at once.

Split screen ➤ (video) Picture composed of two separate elements , each occupying half of the screen area (see Fig.). (A picture with more than two elements is known as a multi-screen). See *composite shot*.

Andhra Pradesh

Split screen

Split-run ➤ Division of a printing (advt. etc.) into two or more editions of the same newspaper. The differences may be in appearance or number of pages; an advertiser may ask for a split run to try the effectiveness of two presentations of the same advertisement.

Split-run editions ➤ Slightly changed versions of the same newspaper or magazine, as in *regional editions*.

Splitter box ➤ Device used to feed one input signal to more than one output; commonly used at news conferences to avoid a jumble of microphones by splitting the feed from one mike to all those covering the event.

Spokesperson ➤ Individual who speaks on behalf of an organisation or a product or service. In advertising the spokes person's name becomes associated with the product or service, as, for example *tabla* maestro Zakir Hussain with Taj tea. See also *personality; testimonial advertising*.

Sponsored magazines ➤ Refers to magazines published by associations or organizations, e.g. national geographic.

Sponsored programme ➤ A radio or TV programme for which a sponsor foots the bill.

Sponsorship ➤ Generating revenue by selling to one or more advertisers the right to associate themselves with some editorial area or event.

Spool ➤ (noun) When the footage is wound on to tape or film

from one spool to another i.e., spool on is to go forward on the tape or 'spool back' is to go backwards.

Spot ➤ (i) General term for spotlight. *Also* concentrated area of light emphasizing the main performer. (ii) Adjustment of a spotlight to provide a narrow light beam. (iii) Time slot set a side for a commercial or public service announcement. (iv) A place in the organisation of a programme is referred to as a spot.

Spot colour ➤ (i) Non-process colour. With no special plate prepared, colour is applied during the run to selective parts of the page, usually one place and one small amount of colour, as in a coloured seal or couloured fudge. (ii) Single colour (in addition to black).

Spot Fx ➤ Practical sound effects created live in the studio.

Spotlight ➤ Lamp designed to give a very powerful and narrow beam of hard light.

Spot news ➤ News about which there is no prior information, e.g. accidents or fires, as distinct from scheduled news (court cases, speeches). Also see *story types*.

Spot radio ➤ Local radio time set aside for Spot commercials. When advertisers speak of spot radio, they are speaking of the purchase of commercial time in a market-by-market buy.

Spot story (US) ▸ An item of breaking news, such as a fire or a train-collision. See *spot news*.

Spot television ▸ Local TV time set aside for 120 *spot commercials*.

Spread ▸ (i) Two facing pages; a major display covering part of two facing pages. (ii) (US) An advertisement covering full page or almost. (iii) In television filming, to focus the lens on a lighting instrument to its widest opening in order to give maximum width to the light distribution, as, for example, in opening the fresnel spotlight (spotlight with an adjustable lens that allows for the variation of transmitted light) to its flooded capacity.

SQL ▸ (Structured query language) Specialized programming language for sending queries to databases. Most industrial-strength and many smaller database applications can be addressed using SQL. Each specific application will have its own version of SQL implementing features unique to that application, but all SQL capable databases support a common subset of SQL.

Squares ▸ Black or open, a species of type ornament used to mark off sections of text.

Squelch ▸ Means of suppressing unwanted noise in the reception of a radio signal. See *Noise gate*.

Squib ▸ (US) Filler or short, q.v.

SS ▸ Same size: instruction to make engraving the same size as the original.

S/S ▸ Abbreviation for 'same size'.

'S' signal ▸ The difference between left and right stereo signals, i.e. the stereo component.

SSL ▸ (Secure sockets layer) A protocol designed by Netscape Communications to enable encrypted, authenticated communications across the Internet. SSL is used mostly (but not exclusively) in communications between web browsers and web servers. URL's that begin with "https" indicate that an SSL connection will be used. SSL provides 3 important things: privacy, Authentication, and Message Integrity.

In an SSL connection each side of the connection must have a security certificate, which each side's software sends to the other. Each side then encrypts what it sends using information from both its own and the other side's Certificate, ensuring that only the intended recipient can decrypt it, and that the other side can be sure the data came from the place it claims to have come from, and that the message has not been tampered with. See also *browser, server, security certificate, URL*.

Stab ▸ Short, emphatic jingle. See *ident*.

Stadium microphone ► See *filter microphone*.

Staggered head ► Headline in which each line is set with an indention on the previous line. For opposite effect centred headline setting is used.

Standard outcue (payoff) ► See *outcue*.

Standards ► The technical parameters that govern the operation of a piece of equipment or an entire industry. A standard may be mandated by law, voluntarily supported, or de facto in nature.

Stand-by ► (i) A warning cue for any kind of action in television production. (ii) A button on a video tape recorder that activates the rotation of the video heads or head drum independently of the actual tape motion. In the stand - by position , the video heads can come up to speed before the videotape is started.

Standfirst ► Few brief sentences to introduce a news or features, text intended to be read between headline and story which can elaborate on point made in main headline. Add new one, raise a question which will be answered in story(a teaser). Sometimes contains by-line. Helps provide reader with a "guiding hand" into reading large slice of copy thus mainly used for features and occasionally for long news stories. See also *blurb, precede*.

Standing artwork ► Graphic material used in every issue.

Standing matter ► Text elements used in every issue. Also see *matter.*

Standing type ► Composed and stored type awaiting use.

Stand-up drop ► An initial letter in large type that stands above the line of the text at the start of a story.

Standuppers ► A report is called a 'stand upper' when it is entirely delivered by the reporter on-camera. This term is derived from the typical shot of the reporter at the scene of the action – standing up and delivering his copy directly into the camera. Full length standuppers are rare in TV news these days. In the normal course of day-to-day reporting stand- uppers are divided into: (a) Openers, (b) Bridges and (c) Closers. And either all these three elements or any one or two are used in a story, but mostly as a part of the whole story package, i.e., the reporters's face is not on the screen from the beginning to the end.

Openers: An opener is a shot of the reporter on-camera at the very start of a report. Of all the stand uppers, an opener is the rarest. This so because what a reporter wishes to say by an opener, i.e., scene setting for the report, is better done by a lend-in read by the anchor. An opening picture of a location is a better visual way of setting the tone of a story. However, in a feature report, in which the reporter's presence plays an important part throughout, an opener establishes that close relationship immediately. Example: *Here, you see the outer gate of the Jhansi Fort overlooking the Muharrum Procession that is led not by any religious replica but by the replica of Rani Lakshmi Bai... Do you know, why?...* The reporter opens his story setting its tone – the procession being led by the replica of the Rani. This is an exceptional element of the Muharram procession in Jhansi and this a tradition which has its origins in the rule of Jhansi by Rani Lakshmi Bai before 1857. Thus by setting the tone of his feature report, the report might go on to detail the way Muharram processions are taken out in the city.

But now the reporter wishes to *connect* the history with some current incident which is not in keeping with the spirit of what the Rani had envisaged, i.e. the communal amity. Therefore, he again appears on-camera, this time with the *Bridge*:

... That was the genius of Rani Lakshmi Bai to find a unique way to maintain and strengthen the communal harmony in the city.

But that was not all. Her Commander-in-chief was an Afghan warrior who lies buried here, in the inner circle of the fort... This grave under the banyan tree was damaged by vandals last week...

The reporter has not only talked about the preceding section of his story but also informed the viewers what is going to come next on the screen. His last sentence alerts the viewers that all is not so well with the communal harmony of the city of Jhansi at present. This way he has linked the two sections of his feature story that reviews the state of communal harmony in retrospect.

Following this bridge, the reporter might narrate how the vandals damaged the grave of a great soldier and how the administration dealt with those unsocial elements. Now before we go on to closer, let's define what a bridge or stand-up bridge is: A bridge or a *stand-up bridge* links the two story elements or locations.   *Closer*: In the preceding example of Muharram procession story, the reporter might have talked to a professor of history (who did his Ph.D. on Lakshmi Bai) and before ending the story he might include the professor's should bite to give an element of authenticity to this story. He might have already narrated the current status of communal tension in the city. Now he wants to end the story with a perspective. He might give a closer like this:

..*That was Prof. R.K. Khanna on the Rani of Jhansi, Lakshmi Bai – as a ruler, as a warrior and as the caretaker of her subjects. But will the present administration of Jhansi take any leaf from what Lakshmi Bai did to maintain communal peace in this city about hundred and fifty years ago?*

With this we can now easily and briefly define a closer or *stand-up closer*: A closer concludes the report coming at the tail end of it and includes the reporter's sign-off (the TV equivalent of the print's byline and dateline). Closers are the most frequently used type of stand-up element. Why? Because after the short is over the reporter has fitted together the pieces of his electronic equipment and course of the story. He is now in a position to say a sentence or two in perspective. Something like the 'moral' of the story.

Star ▶ Type ornament; hence *star-line,* a line of stars.

Star-burst ▶ Headline or slogan enclosed in star-shaped outline, used in blurbs and advertising.

Starburst filter ▶ Special effect lens which dramatises highlights by creating star shaped flares of light.

Stare decisis ▶ Similar cases should be decided in a similar way.

Stars ▶ Common symbol for newspaper editions-one star , two star, etc. –often apparent only to the insider.

Start-up ▶ When the presses begin to print.

State editor ▶ (US) Senior deskman who supervises coverage of state or that part nearest the publishing area.

Status   Conferral ▶ Mass media's ability to confer status or single out a person, institution or an issue by focussing attention on it constantly.

Stay tuned! ▶ It is designed to tease you. How? By exciting your desire for a story and make you stay tuned to hear it (the story), usually through a commercial break, then tell the story itself as the first item following the commercial break or as the case may be. For example: *"The latest on the election results from Bihar in a moment..."*

There are two types of teasers. The first tells the one sentence 'headline' containing the crux of the story: *"The BJP gains three seats in Tamilnadu and loses many more in Rajasthan..."* The second type pricks the listener's mind without telling the crux of the story: *"The BJP's gains in the south are significant, but the losses in Rajasthan are heavy... More about this after the break...".*

The choice of the type of teasers is a matter of journalistic ethics. The first type by telling the crux of the story emphasizes the need to be accurate and be first with the news. The second type, though more innovative, appears to say, "Hey, we have not got the news, but we are not going to share this with you just now". This looks like equating news with entertainment. Also see *teasers.*

Stem ▶ See *shank*

Stepped head ▶ See *staggered head.*

Stereo ▶ A recording made using left and right channels to separate and spread the sound.

Stereotype ▶ Duplicate printing plate cast from a paper matrix used in letterpress. Newspapers or other print media who use the letterpress printing method require advertisers to provide a plate of their ad.

S-Terminal (Separate video) ▶ Also known as a Y/C connector. A connector used by high quality picture formats (such as S-VHS) which keeps the chroma (C) and luminance (Y) signals separate for improved picture quality.

Stet ▶ Latin for 'let it stand': a sign on copy that a correction or deletion has been made in error and should be ignored. The words affected are underlined with dots and the word 'stet' written on the margin.

Stickiness ▶ Refers to a measure used to gauge the effectiveness of a Website in retaining individual users. 'Never mind the quantity, feel the stick'. 'Stickey' is a website people want to stay on and visit frequently.

Stick mike ▶ Stick shaped microphone much favoured for news work for speed of preparation and ease of use.

Still ▶ A single picture, slide or painting showing an individual or a scene frozen in time.

Still video ▶ An electronic version of the conventional camera . Still video pictures are recorded on to a magnetic disk or chip and can be replayed on a TV set or printed out like a photograph.

Sting ▶ (i) The central and most damaging allegation in a libel case. (ii) Single music chord, used for dramatic effect.

Stock ▶ Raw unused video tape.

Stock bills ▶ Newspaper display bills on fixed subjects such as 'today's TV', 'latest scores', etc.

Stock footage ▶ Previously shot scenes of all kinds found in stock footage libraries. The initial charge is for making an examination print or tape of the footage requested, plus a perfoot charge for the footage that is actually used in a commercial . Stock footage includes historic newsreel footage, scenic locations in all types of weather, as well as every imaginable type of sports or stunts.

Stock music ▸ In-house library of recorded music.

Stock shot ▸ See *library shot, stock footage*.

Stone ▸ The imposing surface on which pages are made up it is now a misnomer as steel has replaced stone.

Stone sub ▸ Usually a senior deskman (deputy news editor, chief sub-editor etc.) who works at the stone in the composing room, seeing that the make-up is followed, cutting stories which run too long in type, and ensuring that deadlines are kept.

Stonehand ▸ Print worker who arranges type in page forme often called comp (compositor).

Stop ▸ Any of the range of fixed aperture setting. Opening the aperture by one stop allows twice the amount of light into the camera as the previous stop.

Stop motion ▸ See *freeze frame*.

Stop press ▸ Column on front or back page of newspaper left blank and allowing for slotting in of news which had broken just before publication; news item inserted after the commencement of printing.

Stop-pull ▸ Technique of altering the course of a shot.

Stop words ▸ Words such as 'and', 'in', 'the' 'a', 'or', 'of' that are often ignored by *search engines*.

Storecast ▸ Broadcast of radio programming in a retail store. A storecast may be an actual radio station broadcast over loudspeakers positioned throughout the store, or it may originate from a wired service that simulates radio broadcasting. Special announcements of sales or featured items may also be considered storecasts.

Store-distributed magazine ▸ Magazine not offered by subscription its circulation depends primarily on sales in retail outlets.

Story ▸ Any news or editorial item in a newspaper other than leading articles; (US, editorials): features, letters and illustrations. The Panchtantra stories are fictional while newspaper stories are intended to be real.

Story board ▸ A series of either art frames or photos which depict the planned for video and audio (the storyline) of a commercial or *PSA*.

Story types ▸ Depending on the nature of content and their treatment, stories can be divided into: (a) Spot News, (b) Hard News, (c) Backgrounder, (d) Side Bar, (e) Series, (f) Documentary, (g) Feature, (h) Kickers and (i) Follow-up.

Spot News: It usually refers to the stories of events that occur suddenly with no warning, such as a fire, bank robbery, boat-capsizing, bus accidents, etc. These are the events about which their is no prior information.

Hard News : This is almost always a spot news. A boat mishap or bus accident occur suddenly making it a spot news. But a hard news also involves such stories as the former Prime Minister Narsimha Rao going for trial in a case of forgery. This event was scheduled yet a hard news. Thus a hard news is not necessarily a spot news, which by its very nature is unscheduled.

Backgrounder: This is a story about the background of a group, persons, an object or a place. A backgrounder throws light on the different hidden events of the main story. For example, after the withdrawal of support by the Congress, the UF government Prime Minister I.K. Gujral sent in his Cabinet's resignation to the President. Of course, the resignation is the main story. But a backgrounder could be on the previous withdrawal of support to the U.F. government led by Mr. H.D. Devegowda. Furthermore, this backgrounder could also talk about the history of Congress-withdrawals of support to various governments at the centre – i.e. from the government of Chaudhary Charan Singh

(1980) to government of I.K. Gujral. Shown together, the two stories – the resignation by the Prime Minister I.K. Gujral and the history of Congress-withdrawals of support – from a well-rounded and complete report that can very well compete with a newspaper story on the same issue. This is so because newspapers usually give backgrounders with the main stories unlike a television newscast that has to cover every importa0nt event within a very short time – usually between 5 and 30 minutes.

Side bar: A sidebar is a strong done in relation to another – an off-shoot of the first. It could be a backgrounder (as in the preceding example), but not so always. Now, suppose a debate is on in Parliament on the issue of whether to allow the Union Carbide Company of the U.S.A. to continue its operations in India after a gas leak from its plant killing over four thousand people in Bhopal. The debate over the issue of whether to allow the company to continue to operate in India, is of course, the main story. However, a sidebar could be on the fail-safe system in the company's plants operating in other countries. If the gas leak incidents are unique to the company's operations in India, it means that the company has deliberately ignored the installation of in-built production systems in its India-based plants. Thus sidebars help the viewers understand and the complex or controversial stories. However, such sidebars are a rarity these days.

Series : A group of stories on a topic of interest to a large number of people is called a series. It might consist of just two consecutive reports spread over two consecutive telecasts or a dozen reports telecast during a three-week period. Most series are aired, for less than a week, especially during a rating period to draw the maximum audiences. For example, a series on the nexus between crime and politics shown on your favourite network during the first week of say, November, 1997.

Documentary : A documentary is similar to a series in that it is a relatively long duration report on a serious subject. Sometimes a documentary is made on a 10-part series. The typical length of a documentary is half-an-hour and occasionally one hour. Created from interviews, analysis and audio or visual presentation of facts selected by the producer, a documentary provides a personal view of real events but NOT to the total exclusion of alternate opinions. A documentary takes a variety of

forms and it is only the news documentary that is of concern to journalists, as far as their professional work is concerned. A full discussion on the genre of documentary requires a separate treatment and as such, falls beyond the purview of this book.

Features: These are stories usually done on lighter subjects and one of the same duration as news stores. Sometimes, they cover serious subjects, too, but often they require a clever writing and are shown before the end of a newscast. For example, a story on the first sheep-cloning in UK or what the villagers of Latur (Maharashtra) think about the impending elections after a decade of the earth-quake that razed the village to the ground killing almost two-third of its population. But such a feature would befit when elections are round the corner.

Kickers : A kicker is a lighter item at the end of a newscast or just before the recap of the headlines or before the weathercast. Here is an imaginary example: *Tonight we have for you a strange case of love and affection... that is between a group of monkeys and a five-year old child... Our reporter Ashwini Gadoo has traced the child who says... The monkeys fed him with bananas, mangoes and even Leher Pepsi. More on this from our reporter in Jammu...*

Now take another example:

A new weapon in the age old battle between man and mosquito: two scientists in New Delhi say garlic not only fights bacteria but also kills mosquitoes. But about the prescribed dosage of garlic... the socialites say that could kill your social life as well. (Quoted in Broadcast Journalism, D.K. Cohler, PHI, 1985). Almost all the kickers are features but not all the features can be termed as kickers because features are also, sometimes not always, on serious issues. Why Kickers? By its very nature a newscast is largely devoted to serious stories. Seldom is there much scope for human interest and light stories assuring the audiences that 'despite all the bad things you have heard and seen there is something good as well? Thus kickers are important psychologically, too, for the viewers. And for the news writer writing kickers is a sort of release from the tension of writing issue-oriented serious copies all the day. However, kickers should never: (a) Treat serious issues lightly (b) Make fun of people or their beliefs (c) Be cruel to people, animals or religious institutions. In fact, a kicker should always be in good taste while being mostly funny. Also, a kicker should not stretch itself too far so much so that viewers have to make ex-

tra effort to make out the story. As a matter of principles, kickers should suggest themselves at once.

Follow-up: Also called folo, it refers to the updating of stories. It gives the regular viewers a feeling that the news people go beyond covering the events of just one day. Such an updating of a previous story that was aired a day, week or even a year before is called a follow-up. For example, you did a story on a Kolkata girl who is suffering from blood cancer and was denied permission to appear at the matric examination because she was short of the attendance requirement of her school. Now you can do a follow-up after a month or so on whether the school authorities have relaxed their rules to allow for such an exceptional case on human grounds and if not, what the student, who is everyday inching towards an early death, plans to take on the rigid attitude of the school authorities. Follow-ups are very helpful on slow news days. Therefore, alert reporters are always on the look out for such stories and develop a list of potential folos in their representative beats or otherwise.

Straight matter ▶ Ordinary editorial setting in regular column width without illustrations. Also see *matter.*

Straight news ▸ Story without colour or interpretation of any kind.

Strap ▸ Subsidiary headline in smaller type; over main headline. See *overline* and (US) *eyebrow, kicker*.

Streamer ▸ Headline running across top of all or most of the columns.

Streaming ▸ Video, audio, text and graphics available for viewing on your computer even as these are in the process of getting downloaded to your system (computer) from a *website*.

Strict liability ▸ A type of contempt of court that can be committed accidentally.

Strike ▸ To remove objects no longer needed in the show; to take down scenery.

Stringer ▸ Freelance, either in district, in the Capital or overseas, who has come to arrangement with news organization to supply copy on agreed basis. *Super stringer* will contract to devote most of time working for one organization but still be free to work for other media outlets for the rest of time.

Stripe filter ▸ A single- camera tube that can produce three-colour output.

Strobing ▸ See *line beating*.

Studio ▸ A specially equipped room in which a performer rehearses or presents his or her act.

Studio camera ▸ Heavy high quality camera and zoom lens that cannot be manoeuvred properly without the aid of a pedestal or some other type of camera mount.

Studio spot ▸ Usually a contribution made live in a studio by a journalist other than the main presenter (s).

Style ▸ Set of rules, conventions, or usage adopted by newspapers, radio and TV news channels relating to spellings, punctuation, abbreviations. Often contained within a *style book*, though increasingly carried on screens. Many newspapers and TV channels somehow now manage without them. Also see *house rules*.

Style book ▸ The repository of *house style*.

Style sheet ▸ (i) A style sheet defines the attributes of a document's different elements, such as a headline and body text. A headline may be centered and set in specific typeface. To use this style, you just have to highlight the appropriate word(s) during editing, select the headline style, and the text will be automatically reformatted; in desktop publishing programmes, a style sheet refers to a stored set of type specifications to which incoming text can be made to conform. (ii) A shorter version of a *style book*. (iii) The instructions which enable a browser to produce a web page in full (e.g. layout, colours, founts, text, etc.) from a marked-up document. Also see *browser*, *web page*, and *HTML*.

Stylist ➤ The person responsible for organising a photographic shot, especially if models are involved.

Stylus ➤ Small diamond tipped arm protruding from gramophone pick-up. In contact with the record surface it conveys the mechanical vibrations to the cartridge for conversion into electrical energy.

Sub (UK/India) Sub-editor ➤ to edit a story and write the headline. Hence the word subbing.

Sub-carrier ➤ The frequency on which colour information is modulated in a colour TV system.

Subedit ➤ The process of amending copy for style, readability, legality etc. Distinct from editing, which is the process of deciding whether the work is worth publishing in the first place.

Sub-editor ➤ Editorial deskman responsible for amending reporter's copy, writing headlines, captions, laying out pages, etc. Stone-sub makes final corrections and cuts page proofs. (US) *copy reader.*

Sub-head ➤ Small subsidiary heading in the body of a story, usually centred for giving a break and arousing interest in

a long or complex story. See *cross head, cross-line*.

Subject heading ➤ A term in a library database or reference that categorizes items that are similar to one another.

Subjective expectation of privacy ➤ The right to expect that personal workplace items such as a briefcase, personal mail, desk, files and wastebaskets will not be subject to an unreasonable employer search.

Subjective track ➤ Tracking shot in which the camera moves in place of a character in a movie and reveals what is supposed to be the scene through their eyes.

Subliminal advertising ➤ Advertising messages presented below the level of consciousness, such as words flashed across a television or movie screen at intervals of no more than 10 seconds in length, during the presentation of regular programming or a feature film.

Subscription TV (STV) ➤ Television programming that is transmitted over the airwaves through a scrambler. Subscription TV (popular in US, Europe) can be viewed only by households subscribing to the service. For a monthly fee, subscribers receive a special device that is attached to their television sets and decodes the signal, allowing viewers to see the programming. STV broadcasts over standard broadcast channels that, for the most part, are independent stations featuring regular syndicated or local programming during the day, switching over to STV programming in the evening.

Subsology ➤ Study of the TV soap operas.

Subst ➤ Substitute the story so marked to run in place of another.

Suite ➤ This is the number of video tape players and recorders needed for editing . Sometimes the room itself is called the edit suite.

Summary ➤ News programme or bulletin rounding up the most important news events; a prepared statement with which a moderator closes a programme; precis of a story. Also see *news lead, headline.*

Summary lead ➤ The first paragraphs of a news story in which the writer presents a synopsis of several actions rather than focusing on one specific angle.

SUN TV ➤ Satellite channel in Tamil.

Sungun ➤ Hand-held rechargeable battery light.

Super ➤ Also called titles, supers are names of places, persons or other bits of information superimposed on the TV screen. They are broadly of two types: (a) Locators and (b) Identifiers. Locators indicate the location where

Super (locator)

Super (Identifier)

the story or a part of it was shot (see Fig.), while Identifiers (see Fig.) show the name of the person being interviewed or seen talking on the screen.

Super caster ➤ Trade name of monotype machine which casts large sizes of type for headlines, borders, rules and leads.

Supercomputers ➤ Extremely powerful computers used primarily by scientists and often shared with others who log in from remote sites.

Superimposition (SOS) ▸ Facility in some tapes for recording one sound on top of another.

Super stations ▸ Local TV stations using satellites to deliver their signals to cable systems.

Super VHS (Super Video Home System, S-VHS) ▸ An enhanced version of the VHS format. Also the name of a full-sized camcorder format.

Super VHS-C (Super Video Home System Compact, S-VHS-C) ▸ A miniature camcorder format that offers Super VHS picture quality.

Superior letters or figures ▸ Small letters and figures cast on the shoulder of the type so that they print above the level of primary letters, as in P.

Supplement ▸ Section added to a newspaper, particularly the Sunday edition, that enhances the content of the newspaper. Supplements are typically composed in a magazine format and contain fiction and nonfiction articles of a general or family appeal. Some supplements specialize in their content- for example, comic supplements, book supplements, or the broadcast-schedule supplement. Others may be marked "supplement," but are actually printed by an advertiser and inserted in the paper as a form of advertising. Supplements may be locally edited or nationally syndicated, but are never sold separately from the newspapers that carry them. Two examples of nationally syndicated magazine supplements in the U.S. are Family Weekly and Parade, which are sold to and carried by local newspapers throughout the country. The syndications edit and print their supplements, and then imprint each with the masthead of the individual newspapers that will feature them (as per newspaper postal requirements). In India, HT City (Hindustan Times) and Delhi Times (The Times of India) are daily supplements circulated to the readers in Delhi and adjoining areas.

The advertages of advertising in a supplement are (1) the longer ad life, due to the fact that people tend to keep something in magazine format longer than the rest of the paper, and (2) the fact that the limitations on the closing dates are not as stringent nor as long in advance as those of most magazines. In addition, advertisers in a syndicated supplement are afforded the capability of reaching a mass audience.

Surfing ▸ The process of "looking around" the *Internet*. When you search for a piece of information on the Internet, you are *surfing* the Net. The term is also used to describe the act of moving rapidly from site to site on the *web* or channel to channel on TV.

Surprint ► Superimpose one photographic negative over another and print the assemblage as one piece. This is most commonly done when an advertisement calls for a line of type to run across a picture, such as an image of a product with the headline "Final Sale!" running across it.

Survey ► A research technique for asking questions of a particular group of people. It may be written or recorded. Interviews must be cited in your works cited or reference section.

Sustaining programme ► Programme supplied by a syndicating source or elsewhere to maintain an output for a station making its own programmes for only part of the day.

Swash letters ► Those embellished with tails and flourishes in the manner of sixteenth-century capitals.

Sweep ► The process of audience survey for a particular station or service within a given timescale.

Sweepstakes ► Popular type of sales promotion where lavish prizes are offered to entrants who have only to submit entries with their name and address by return mail or at a location determined by the sweepstakes sponsor, usually in a retail outlet where the sponsor's products are sold. Winners are chosen at random from among the entries, and no purchase is required in order to enter (a legal condition of a sweepstakes, allowing it to create consumer involvement with a brand or product and thus encourage consumption of the product.

Swelled rule ► A rule that is thicker in the centre and tapers to each end.

Swish pan ► See *whip pan*.

Switched broadband network ► Describes a network that allows two way, point to point communication at band widths that can support video traffic, also called full service network or video dial tone. Also see *bandwidth* and *point to point*.

Switched network ► Refers to a network that is capable of officient routing of signals from one party to another.

Switcher ► A device for cutting from one video input to another. Also, the engineer or production team member who does the video switching (usually the technical director); also , a panel with rows of buttons that allows the selection and assembly of various video sources through a variety of transition devices, and the creation of electronic special effects.

Switching ► A change from one video source to another during a programme or programme segment with the aid of a switcher.

Switching pause ▸ Short pause in transmission before and after the network bulletin to permit local station to opt-in and out cleanly.

SWOT ▸ Strengths, Weaknesses. Opportunities, Threats. A fashionable way of analysing a magazine's position in the market.

Symmetrical make-up ▸ Balance in display elements in a page on either side of a given central axis.

Sync output ▸ Programme replayed from the record heads of a multi-track recording machine heard by performers while they record further tracks.

Sync ▸ Synchronisation, i.e. accurate correspondence between sound track and vision.

Synchro edit ▸ An editing feature which enables two pieces of video equipment to be linked together (e.g. VCR and camcorder) and controlled by a single machine.

Synchronize ▸ With regard to offline favorites, to ensure that the files on your hard disk are the latest version. See also *offline favourite.*

Syndicate ▸ Organisation selling and buying feature or news material; group of newspapers; to sell editorial material to group of newspapers, etc.

Syndicated tapes ▸ Tapes sent out to radio and TV stations by PR and advertising agencies to promote a company or product.

Synectics ▸ Idea-generating technique, similar to brainstorming, where the discussion is centered around a general idea that is related to a problem, rather than the problem itself (as in brainstorming); also called *blue sky*. Synectics is often used by the creative department of an advertising agency when designing an advertising campaign. The method is based on four concepts: (i) the identification of a specific leader, (ii) the knowledge of a common understanding of the problem or situation, (iii) the common belief that all ideas have some good qualities, and (iv) the equal importance of all participants and their ideas.

Synopsis ▸ A brief summary of an article.

Sy Quest ▸ An optical disk used for storing and transporting large volumes of digital material, e.g. scans and completed pages.

Sysop ▸ (System operator) Anyone responsible for the physical operations of a computer system or network resource. A system administrator decides how often backups and maintenance should be performed and the system operator performs those tasks.

T-1 ➤ A leased-line connection capable of carrying data at 1,544,000 bits-per-second (1.544 megabits per second) A maximum theoretical capacity, a T-1 line could move a megabyte in less than 10 seconds. That is still not fast enough for full-screen, full-motion video, for which you need at least 10,000,000 bits-per-second. T-1 is the fastest speed commonly used to connect networks to the Internet. See also *bandwidth, bit, byte, ethernet, T-3*.

T-3 ➤ A leased-line connection capable of carrying data at 44,736,000 bits-per-second. This is more than enough to do full-screen, full-motion video. See also *bandwidth, bit, byte, ethernet, T-1*.

T: 10 # ➤ Scriptwriter's notation for 10 seconds, often used to indicate a 10-second broadcast commercial.

Tabloid ➤ (i) Newspapers whose pages are roughly half size of bradsheet. e.g., Evening News, Sandhya Times, Blitz. They refer to sensational newspapers & opposed to heavies such as The Times of India, The Hindustan Times, The Hindu, etc. Often used as term of abuse when press is collectively criticised. (ii) Newspapers characterized by abundant illustrations, especially photographs, and sensational or non-serious approach to new. Also see *broadsheet*.

Tabloidese ➤ Shoddy, over sensational, cliche ridden copy which is most commonly associated with the tabloids.

Tag ➤ It is a concluding statement by an anchor to end a story. It is important for packages because it makes the anchor a concerned party in the story rather than just its introducer. If an anchor goes directly from one to another story of the newscast, viewers may confuse the preceding story with the one that has just begun. But with a tag they will realize that the story has ended making way for the next item of the newscast. Tags are especially helpful in stories that include sound bites or VO-sound bites. These days some newsrooms do not end every story with a tag from the anchor. The tag itself may be the concluding part of the narration and the anchor appears on the screen with the next story, without any resulting confusion to the viewers. This is possible with the change in visuals mounted with the attention – grabbing music just after the concluding item or sand-witching a commercial between the two consecutive stories. A tag should be giving some additional information or a perspective to the story, not just a quickie wrap-up.

Tag line ➤ Smaller line attached to a headline to attribute source of statement there:
'Freedom is out birth right' - Balgangatdhar Tilak.

Tailpiece (kicker, and finally) ➤ Light hearted story at the end of a bulletin or newscast.

Take ➤ (i) Signal for a cut from one video source to another . (ii) Any one of similar repeated shots taken during videotaping and filming . Some times take is used synonymously with shot. Each time a shot is filmed or recorded it is called a take . But a shot may have to be repeated a number of times before it is done perfectly, so each time it is made, it is given a take number. For example, scene 4 , shot 16 take 3. (iii) Page or number of pages comprising a section of some longer piece.

Take copy ➤ Copy dictated over the telephone and meant for typing.

Take in ➤ Instruction to typysetter to thin-space a line or lines to get in an extra syllable or words; direction on proof to incorporate insert matter at that point.

Take up ➤ To pick up type and move it to the page chase or random.

Take-up reel ➤ Blank reel used in conjunction with a reel of film or audio tape in a projection or playback system. The take-up reel actually pulls the tape through the system and holds the film or audio tape that has already been played.

Talent ➤ A collective or individual name for television and radio announcers, performers and actors.

Talk ➤ A radio or television format consisting of information, news, discussion, and interviews.

Talk show ➤ Broadcast show with a format arranged around interviews conducted by a host. The interviewees may be celebrities, or members of the viewing or listening audience. The Hard Talk on BBC is a familiar example of a television talk show.

Talkback ➤ Intercom device for talking to station staff on location or in other parts of the buildings.

Talking head ➤ Disparaging term used for an story which features dry expert opinion rather than the views of 'real' or ordinary people; any interviewee.

Talks table ➤ Specially designed table for studio use, often circular with an acoustically transparent surface and a hole in the middle to take a microphone.

Tally light ➤ The light on a camera which indicates to the subject that it is in use at a given moment. Also called cue light.

Tape ➤ (i) Strictly, ribbon of paper with perforations which actuate a teleprinter to type copy or a line-caster to set copy in metal. Also loosely used to refer to news agency or wire copy. (ii) Several strips of plastic cut in various gauges and coated for different purposes such as recording sounds and picture, filling blanks, mending, and providing leader. To tape means to record. (iii) Record on audio or video tape.

Tape copy ➤ Process of creating a duplicate magnetic tape file. Tape copies are made to prevent the loss of data due to damage, loss, or theft of the *master copy* or to transfer data from one computer system to another, such as for a subscription file conversion or a list rental.

Tape library ➤ Facility used to store and maintain *magnetic tapes*. Tapes are usually stored on racks from which they hang vertically. A serial number and identification information is placed on each tape. Many facilities use computerized systems to assign serial numbers and tape locations. Random assignment can be used to make it more difficult for an intruder to find and steal a particular tape.

Tape synchroniser ➤ Device used during editing and viewing to keep a tape recorder and VCR locked together, adjusting the speed of one to match the other.

Tapeless systems ➤ An umbrella phrase describing equipment that doesn't use tape as the primary recording and/or playback medium.

Tape time ➤ It refers to the running time between the beginning and end of an unbroken length of tape.

Target ➤ The face of a camera pickup tube or chip.

Target audience ➤ Audience to whom the advertising is directed the target audience is defined in terms of *demographic* (and sometimes *psychographic*) characteristics, such as age, sex, education, income, buying habits, and the like.

Taskbar ➤ A tool you use to open programmes and navigate your computer. Usually positioned at the bottom of your screen, the taskbar contains the Start button, toolbars, a clock, and other features.

Tass ➤ News agency of the former Soviet Union.

Taste ➤ To scan a story or stories in copy and assess their editorial value.

Taster ➤ Abbreviation for *copy taster*. Journalist who checks copy, selecting good and removing the unwanted material. The process is known as tasting.

TCP/IP ▶ (Transmission control protocol/Internet protocol) This is the suite of protocols that defines the Internet. Originally designed for the UNIX operating system, *TCP/IP* software is now available for every major kind of computer operating system. To be truly on the Internet, your computer must have TCP/IP software. See also *IP number*, *Internet*, *UNIX*.

TD ▶ The technical director or switcher, who operates switching controls changing from one camera to another by cutting, dissolving, fading.

Tear sheet ▶ Single newspaper page to show article or advertisement to contributor or reader or advertiser; pronounced 'tare' sheet.

Tearing ▶ A distortion caused when horizontal sync is lost or distorted.

Teaser ▶ (i) Overhead material strip used to hide lights and studio and avoid overshooting. (ii) Snappy, one line headline, usually at the start of a programme (see *menu*), designed to tease the audience into wanting to find out more. It may include a snatch of actuality. Also see *Stay tuned*.

Teaser ad ▶ Brief advertisement designed to tease the public by offering only bits of information without revealing either the sponsor of the ad or the product being advertised. Teaser ads are the frontrunners of an advertising campaign, and their purpose is to arouse curiousity and get attention for the campaign that follows. In order for a teaser campaign to be effective, the ads must have great visibility in print, broadcast, and *out-of-home* media so as to reach a great many people. Teaser ads are often used in the introduction of a major new product.

Teeline ▶ A shorthand system favoured by journalists.

Telecast copy ▶ See *dubbing*.

Telecine (film chain) ▶ The total system for transferring film on to video tape or on to a live-output video system.

Telecommunications Act of 1996 (US) ▶ Known as the 1996 Telecom Act, this is comprehensive legislation that will greatly influence the communications industry. This inludes telco/video operations.

Telecommuter ▶ An individual who works at home and maintains contact with the office by computer.

Teleconference ▶ An umberlla term for the various categories of electronic meetings and events, ranging from audio conferences to videoconferences.

Telegraph editor ▶ (US) Editorial desk man who deals with wire-service news. On a smaller newspaper he may edit it all by himself; on larger papers the duties will be shared. Also called *wire-editor*.

Telemarketing ► Use of the telephone as an interactive medium for marketing as a response vehicle includes receiving orders, inquiries, and donation pledges in response to print and broadcast advertisements, catalogues, and direct-mail promotions, and also receiving customer inquiries and complaints. Incoming telephone callers are usually given access to an *In-wats* number but may also call collect or call at their own expense. Outbound telephone is used to follow-up on inquiries, to sell products or services, to clarify or Upgrade an order, or to gather information about consumers or other aspects of the market.

Telephone balancing unit (TBU) ► Device used in the making of recorded telephones interviews. It permits interviewer to use a studio microphone and balance the levels of the two voices.

Telephoto ► Photograph transmitted telegraphically. Also, loosely, to send a picture by wire, or a photograph taken with a telescopic lens.

Teleport ► A satellite dish farm.

Telepresence ► The subjective experience of presence in a technologically mediated environ-ment, e.g. video conference using Internet or *IRC*. Also see *virtual reality*.

Teleprompter ► This is an electronic prompting device which enables newscasters to read a script while directly looking into the camera. However, the newscaster do keep the typed script copies as a back-up in case the teleprompter goes wrong or the operator types unwanted words on the teleprompter when the newscast is on air. Also, the brand name for an electronic prompting device. Also see *autocue*.

Teletex ► Broadcast videotex. On-screen text information transmitted on unused lines within the television signal. Used to broadcast stock quotes, news, weather, sports results and so forth. Teletext system is not capable of broadcasting charts, illustrations, or other pictorial images. See also *videotex*.

Teletext magazine ► An electronic magazine that appears on a television screen. It is a spectrum-efficient communications service.

Teletype ► (Telex, TWX) Machine that types out news coming from a news agency—too often in capital letters that hinder readability. The machine is also capable of deliveriing typewritten messages. The tletype system is a worldwide network and is available through a subscription service. Subscribers from one network can communicate with subscribers, from anyother network through the use of telex numbers. Also called a *teleprinter* or *ticker*, or just 'the wire'.

Teletypesetting ➤ System in which line casting machine is operated from code in perforated tape. Tape may be punched at the local plant commonly supplied to newspapers all over the country by central news agency. Now getting out of use with the coming of computers which give on-line view of the news on their screens.

Television household ➤ Household with at least one television receiver, regardless of whether the set is operational. See also *households using television*.

Television (TV) ➤ Medium of communication that operates through the transmission of images and sounds over a wire or through space by means of an electronic system that converts light and sound into electrical waves and then reconverts them into visible images and audible sounds. As an advertising medium, television is the youngest and has grown faster than any other in history. No other medium has the unique creative capabilities of television. The combination of sight, sound, and movement,

the opportunities for demonstration and the believability of seeing something happen right before one's eyes, the potential for special effects - all these have contributed to television's successful impact. See also *cable television*.

Television support ➤ Advertisement broadcast on television to serve as a secondary part of a multimedia campaign. For example, the television medium is sometimes used to announce a newspaper insert and/or to remind the viewer to read the insert. The insert will contain detailed information on the product or promotion not provided in the television broadcast and may include a reply form. Television-support advertisements are usually broadcast in specific areas that correspond with the locations where the newspaper insert will be distributed.

Telex ➤ See *teletype*.

Telnet ➤ Term coined from the word "telephone" and "network". Telnet software enables you to use phone lines or other Internet lines to log into computers at other sites around the world, provided that you have a login name and a password.

Ten add ➤ (US) Method of sending story to be set before the intro or news lead is ready. Then initial take is marked 10-add, plus the catchline, hence

10-add Parliament. The next is 11-add Parliament and so on.

Ten code ► The spoken communication code used by the emergency services, where the word 'ten' indicates that the code is being used, and the number spoken after it carries the message, i.e. '10 31' means crime in progress. The code numbers used will vary.

Terabyte ► 1000 gigabytes. See also *byte, kilobyte.*

Terminal ► A monitor and keyboard that interacts with another computer. When you log into computers at remote sites, your computer becomes nothing more than a terminal or transfer device for viewing or interacting with information on the remote computer.

Terminal server ► A special purpose computer that has places to plug in many modems on one side, and a connection to a LAN or host machine on the other side. Thus the terminal server does the work of answering the calls and passes the connections on to the appropriate node. Most terminal servers can provide PPP or SLIP services if connected to the Internet. See also *LAN, modem, host, node, PPP, SLIP.*

Terrestrial ► Refers to television signals broadcast from a ground based transmission site. Also see *cable network* and *DTH.*

Text ► (i) Body matter, as distinct from illustrations, headlines, and white space. (ii) Class of type - roman, italic, script, gothic, and text.

Text-based interface ► A computer screen display that requires a user to type commands rather than use a mouse to point and click to select actions. When you Telnet to an Internet site (such as a library), you are in a text-based environment rater than a graphical one.

Textsize ► A broadsheet, or full-size newspaper page.

Text type ► Type in which the body of the paper is set, as distinct from headline or display type.

Theme ► (i) Primary topic, subject, or idea around which a book, motion picture, television show, recording, or the like is organized. (ii) Recurring melody that characterizes a personality, television show, movie, radio broadcast, or theatrical presentation. See also *signature.*

Thesis journalism ► The term refers to a practice adopted by Press in which an opinion or thesis precedes its substantiation.

Thick lead ► 3 pt. lead (pronounced led)

Thick space ► Space of 3 points.

Think piece ► Item of opinion or interpretation rather than straight news reports.

Thin lead ▸ 1 or 1½ pt. lead (pronounced led)

Third Cover ▸ See *inside back cover*.

Thirds rule ▸ Principle of composition which states that strong horizontal or vertical lines should cut the picture in thirds rather than in halves.

Thirty, 30, 30-dash ▸ Sign at the end of a story, either in type or copy written '30' in metal, it is a dash of about six picas. Also see *endmark*.

Thirty-five millimeter (35MM) ▸ (i) 2" x 2" slides used in a slide chain (35mm slide projection). (ii) Film format used in the production of most motion picture. It is also used in the production of network television shows and for some nationally produced commercials. However, only the networks and the largest television stations are equipped to project 35 mm film; therefore, it is rarely used in other television productions. Thirty-five millimeter film has a running and projection speed of 90' per minute, 24 frames per second. Because of its size, the film produces exceptionally beautiful pictures. (iii) Print film used in 35mm cameras.

Three-D ▸ A technique, used in films, which provides illusion of three dimensions – length, breadth and depth. The usual practice is of two-dimensional films, which contain two dimensions of length and breadth.

Three-line cap ▸ See *two-line cap*.

30 # Scriptwriter notation for 30 seconds, often used to indicate a 30 second broadcast commercial.

Three-shot ▸ Mid or long shot in which three people appear. Also see *establishing shot*.

Through-the-lens ▸ A variety of meter in which some of the light passing through the lens is diverted to a light - sensitive cell. This measures the intensity of the light that will reach the chip, and in some cameras controls the automatic adjustment of the aperture.

Throw away ▸ To underplay a line or scene.

Thumbnail ▸ (i) Half-column portrait block, also called porkchop. (ii) Rough miniature dummy of a page for advertisement or any text. (iii) Single quotation mark or apostrophe.

Ticker ▸ See *teletype*.

Tie-in ▸ A story that is connected with one alongside.

Tie-on ▸ A story that is connected with the story above.

TIFF ▸ A format for storing images in digital form.

Tight line ▸ Inadequate space between words, in a line or, in headlines, between that line and the next.

Tight paper ▸ Newspaper with too little space for the news.

Tight story ➤ The term refers to a story written so concisely it cannot be cut without damage to its message and style.

Tight sub ➤ (UK) Sub-editor expert at slicing away the unnecessary details from a story.

Tile-back ➤ (US) Background information in a story to help the reader understand it in perspective.

Tilts ➤ (tilt shots) A tilt shot is obtained when the camera moves up or down on a fixed axis – as in the tilt-up or tilt-down. It is a vertical panning movement of the camera. Both pans and tilts are mostly used while shooting conferences, meetings and rallies. They are also used when shooting stills for TV news, otherwise only in exceptional cases when the news value of a picture is paramount, not its quality. Like zooms, both pans and tilts cause editing problems. A TV news tape is to be edited swiftly to meet the newscast deadlines, not to do artistry or to ponder over the ways to edit the pans and tilts that do not look like visual jumps to the viewers. Also see *pans*.

Time ➤ A term that means the segment is over. *Running time* is the duration of any programme or segment, often measured in seconds. Timing refers to a performer's judgement in the delivery of material to receive maximum impact on the audience.

Time code ➤ An electronic device that gives frame-by-frame time reference recorded on the spare track of a video tape. This is needed because you cannot physically see where you are on a piece of tape. This tells you exactly where you are. It manifests itself as a series of numbers, shown in pairs, giving the hours, minutes, seconds and frames that have elapsed since the time code started at the beginning of the spool or cassette.

Time code editor ➤ A device that uses the time code recorded on a tape as the reference for editing.

Time copy ➤ Practically 'anytime' copy, meaning copy—or type matter—without a deadline and can be run at any time.

Time lapse ➤ Technique of exposing in short bursts at regular intervals so that the event filmed appears greatly speeded up when played back as normal.

Time line ➤ The specific time, measured cumulatively from the start of a tape, at which a sound bite, graphics or super appears during the tape play.

Time signal ➤ In broadcast, a public service announcement of the exact time, sometimes accompanied by a buzzer, beep, bell, or other sound that signals the exact moment of the time.

Some stations will offer the time signal for sponsorship by an advertiser. In that case, the time would be announced and an announcement would be made that the time signal was "brought to you by so-and-so company" followed by a *tag line* or *slogan* that represents the company.

Time-base corrector ▸ A device that corrects mechanical and electronic errors in a video system for purposes of transmission.

Time-sharing ▸ Shared use of a *mainframe* computer by various individuals or organizations who do not have the need or resources to own and operate their own computer. The mainframe is usually accessed via a remote terminal—that is, a terminal in a separate location from the mainframe, typically located in the user's office. Time-sharing is made possible by the computer's ability to process several jobs simultaneously. The fee for a time-sharing service is usually based upon some combination of a flat fee for the service, a variable fee for the number of times the computer is accessed, and a variable fee for the duration of each access. See also *CPU time*.

Time-shift viewing ▸ This is a facility, introduced by the arrival of video technology, relieving the viewers of the compulsion to watch the programmes when they are on air. Many viewers are not free during the broadcast of their favourite shows. The new facility records the programme for a later replay.

Time slot ▸ In broadcast, a period of time slated for a particular Programme or commercial.

Tint ▸ Shades of colours - plain or decorative from palest grey to near-black, to superimpose on a picture, type, or background.

Tint block ▸ Block or surface used for printing flat background colour.

Tinted headline ▸ One in which the black of the type has been softened to a grey.

Tip ▸ Hint or information which, if proved correct on checking, may lead to a news scoop. Such an information is usually paid for.

Tip-in ▸ Insert placed in a publication, such as an extra page advertisement.

Tip off ▸ Call from a stringer, *tipster* or member of the audience to let the station know that a story is breaking.

Tipster ▸ See *tip off*.

Title ▸ (i) Name of a specific publication or film or, generically, any publication or film, such as the titles carried by a newsstand or by a film distributor. (ii) Prefix or suffix used with an individual's name to properly address him or her according to standards of etiquette, such as Mr., Miss, Pt., Md., Mrs., Jr., Sr., and so forth. (iii) Brief text shown at the beginning or end of a film or television programme, such as the *credits* indicating who produced the film. A title may be used to identify the primary sponsor/advertiser of a programme. (iv) Caption describing an illustration.

Titlepiece ➤ The magazine's title in the typographical form used on the cover.

Titling ➤ Fount of type without lower-case letters and usually minimal beard.

Toby man ➤ (UK) He travels round retail outlets on day of publication to check if they have enough copies after initial deliveries and sales.

Toenails ➤ Parentheses, quotations marks or apostrophes.

Tombstone ➤ Newspaper display in which a page was made up of single-column headlines in identical type side by side. A practice of the bygone era.

Tone ➤ (i) The amount of reflected light; the contrast between the areas of light and dark on a printed page. (ii) A test or reference signal of standard frequency and level. For example, 1 khz at 0 db.

Toner ➤ (i) Pigment used to lend colour or body (viscosity to ink). (ii) Chemical used in photocopy (electrophotography) machines.

Toolbar ➤ A set of buttons you click to perform common tasks, usually at the bottom of the computer screen.

Tool tip ➤ A brief description of a screen object. Tool tips appear when you position the mouse pointer over objects.

Top and tail radio ➤ A shortened programme rehearsal where only the openings and closing of inserts are played. Also, adding the opening and closing to a package.

Top deck ➤ The first deck or bank of a headline of several decks.

Tops ➤ Originally stories meant for the top of a page, and hence carrying a certain minimum size headline. Now, with the development of horizontal layout and also the use of below-the fold display, any story having a headline over a set minimum size wherever it appears.

TOT ➤ Triumph over tragedy. an emotional story built on human suffering but with a happy ending.

Total audience rating (TA) ➤ Percentage of the population in a given geographic area that has viewed a particular television station for a given interval of time, or a specific Programme on a given station for a minimum of six minutes. Typically, the total audience rating is higher than the average audience rating, which is measured on a minute-by-minute basis. See also *Nielsen rating*.

Total market coverage (TMC) ▸ Describes the market penetration that is realized by delivering a newspaper, on payment or free, to all or nearly all homes in a market to satisfy the household reach as required by advertisers.

Touch screen studio ▸ A studio where all the equipment is controlled electronically by touching part of the screen of a computer.

Track ▸ The portion of a film strip or tape that carries the sound impulse. Sophisticated sound uses multi-tracks. See *sound track*.

Tracking ▸ (i) Moving the camera horizontally across the ground while filming a shot. (ii) Making an audio recording (sound track) by moving a *stylus* along a track in a record. (iii) Monitoring a process or the results of an action.

Tracking weight ▸ The downward pressure of a gramophone pick-up transmitted through its stylus.

Trade book ▸ General interest books fiction as well as no fiction, sold to the general public.

Trade magazine ▸ Magazine with editorial content of interest only to persons engaged in a particular industry, occupation, or profession; also called

business publication. A trade magazine may be as wide in scope as manufacturing, management or sales, or as narrow in scope as patio-furniture manufacturing or used-car sales. Trade magazines are frequently, but not always, controlled circulation magazines, because the publishers derive more revenue from selling advertising space that reaches a large audience of targeted readers than by selling single copies or subscriptions to the readers. In India, PC world, MIS, TV world, etc. are trade publications. See also *consumer magazine*.

Trade publications ▸ Periodicals dealing with matters of interest to a particular trade or industry and are considered essential reading for people in that industry.

Trade show ▸ Exhibition of goods and services for the benefit of individuals or companies involved in a particular trade. Generally, a trade show is held in an exhibition hall, and each exhibitor is allowed to rent space to display goods and services. Many trade shows are accompanied by seminars and lectures where the newest trade information can be presented and new trade ideas and concepts may be exchanged.

Traditional media or folk media ▸ Indigenous forms of communication which have their roots in the cultural tradition of the country like *jatra, videsia nautanki, burrakatha, yaksha-gana, jatra, kabigan,* puppetry, etc.

Traffic ➤ The department in an independent broadcast station which allocates commercials for transmission.

Trail (or promo) ➤ A short item telling the audience about items which are to follow.

Trailing ➤ Picture defect in which a smeared image persists behind a moving object.

Tramlines ➤ Two rules running close and parallel giving a sober and subtle look.

Transcribed programme ➤ Prerecorded radio or television programme available for syndication (meaning that it can be sold to any number of sponsors and stations throughout the country, although, in any one market, it will be sold on an exclusive basis). See also *syndicate*.

Transcript ➤ The text of a broadcast as transmitted, often produced from an off-air recording.

Transcription ➤ A high-quality recording of a programme, often intended for reproduction by another broadcasting service.

Transducer ➤ A transducer changes one form of energy into another. They are the cores of our communications system

and include microphones and video cameras.

Transfer files ➤ To move the files from one computer to another, usually using software such as Xmodem or Kermit.

Transient response ➤ The ability of a microphone or other equipment to respond rapidly to change of input of brief energy states.

Transit advertising ➤ *Out-of-home* advertising on transportation vehicles such as buses, taxicabs, subways, commuter trains and ferries, as well as in transportation vehicle terminals. There are three major types of transit advertising: car cards, found inside the vehicles in a fleet; outside posters, located outside the vehicles in a fleet; and station posters, located in carrier terminals. Transit advertising is offered at relatively low cost. Transit advertising reaches a mass audience with a high rate of repetition and can be geographically selective.

Transition ➤ Writing device that takes the reader smoothly from one aspect of a story to another loosely-related topic area.

Transitional ➤ Typefaces in which the axis of the curves is vertical or inclined slightly to the left; the serifs are bracketed, and those of the ascenders in the lower case are oblique. They are mid-way between old style and modern.

Translators ► These electronic devices receive a station's signal, strengthen it, and retransmit it to a rural area that otherwise might have no television reception. Since the signal is retransmitted on a different channel, it won't interfere with the main station's signal, even if it's weak.

Transmission ► Process of broadcasting electronic signals.

Transmission stop ► *T-stops*.

Transparency ► A single frame of positive photographic film or glass that represents the actual colour values of the original subject.

Transparent copy ► Illustration or text printed on a transparent medium such as plastic or film through which light must be projected for the image to be seen; also called *transparency*.

Transparent GIF ► A GIF that has one of its colors set to be transparent. When displayed against a background tile or color, the image will appear to float above it.

Transponder ► (Transmitter / responder) On-board satellite equipment which receives and passes on a telecommunications signal. It also acts like a repeater in the sky.

Transpose ► Mark on proof (*trs*) asking the printer to change the order of the lines, words, or letters as instructed.

Trapping ► Method of printing by layering various colours of ink on the same sheet of paper. This is used in multicolour printing (creating a printed image with as many colours as the colours of ink used) and four-colour process printing (creating a printed image with a full Spectrum of colour created from three colours of ink). It is important that each successive layer of ink have less *tack* than the previous layer, so that the ink can be applied smoothly without damage to the previous layer of ink. *Dry trapping* is the application of ink to a dry ink surface. *Wet trapping* is the application of ink to a wet ink surface. See also *transparent ink*.

Treatment ► Written reinterpretation of a story, an idea or a theme in terms of video.

Trial balloon ► A leak which reveals that some action is under consideration in order to test public feeling about the action before going ahead with it.

Trim ► (i) To cut a story (audio, video or text) a little. Also called edit. (ii) Final process in book, catalogue, or brochure production that involves cutting off folded edges to make separate pages or cutting of excess or uneven edges to produce pages that match the desired dimensions. In some cases, trimming is necessary to separate two or three magazines or catalogues that are printed and bound 2-UP or 3-UP.

Tripod ▸ Adjustable three legged stand fixed to the base of a camera to keep it steady .

Trojan horse ▸ Like the mythical Trojan horse, Trojan horse *viruses* pretend to be one thing when in fact they are something else. Typically, Trojan horses take the form of a game that deletes computer files while the user plays.

TRP ▸ Television rating points. These are indices to express the viewers' preferences for various TV programmes – news, current affairs, fiction and so on. These ratings are taken virtually throughout the year but depending upon markets different months of a year are chosen to do focussed surveys on the viewers' preferences. For example, serials like the Ramayana and the Mahabharata had very high TRPs – crossing 60 points while the Aap Ki Adalat on Zee TV usually did not cross the TRP of 2.5. As opposed to this, the newscast of South Indian channels – SUN, RAJ, EENADU, etc. – score an average TRP of 50. The TRP of any programme is in relation to a market, which in television parlance, refers to an area served by different competing TV channels. For example,

Delhi is a market for almost all the major networks beaming their programmes in the Indian skies – Doordarshan, Zee, Discovery, Star Plus, Sun, Eenadu, Asianet, etc. But Delhi is also a market for Siti Cable which tailors its programming to meet the specific demands of Delhi viewers – something like a local newspaper or local radio station. But a small town like Muzaffarpur in Bihar may be dominated by Doordarshan because of a limited demand for or a limited reach of the satellite channels in that town.

Trs ▸ Abbreviation for *transpose*.

Truck ▸ To move the camera and dolly laterally, left and right.

T-stops ▸ System of lens calibration which makes allowance for the varying transmittance of light lenses after absorption and reflection; replaces theoretical t-stop/number system as the T-stops: indicate actual transmission of light.

TTS ▸ Teletypesetter, the trade name for machine which does *teletypesetting* (q.v.).

Tube ▸ Suction tube, common method of delivering copy around a newspaper.

Turn arrow ▸ A symbol at the end of a page of type telling the reader to turn the page.

Turn head ▸ Headline on an inside page identifying resumption of story continued from some preceding another page. US term is *jump head*.

Turn line ➤ Words, usually bold or italic, directing the reader to the continuation of a story on another page ('continued on page ten'); also the line on the inside page indicating the beginning of the continuation ('continued from page one').

Turn ➤ Part of a story running over to another page; (US) *jump*.

Turn up ➤ Direction to printer to turn over a *slug* (q.v.) in the galley or page as an indication that an insert or correction must be made at that place. The turned slug shows up as a rough black line on any subsequent proof.

Turnover ➤ Number of people tuned to a television or radio programme at any one time, divided by the total number of people who tuned to it at all. For example if 100 people watched part of a television programme but only 50 watched it at one point in time, the programme has a turnover rate of 50%, indicating that it was not able to hold the viewers' attention to any great extent.

TV (Television) ➤ It is humanity's one of most important means of communication. It brings pictures and sounds from around the world into millions of homes. Through televison home viewers can see and learn about people, places

and things in faraway lands. Furthermore, TV brings to its viewers a steady stream of programmes that are designed to entertain. The programmes include soap operas, action-packed dramas, light comedies, sporting events, cartoons, variety shows and motion pictures. The name television comes from Greek world 'tele' meaning far, and Latin world 'videre', meaning to see. Most pictures and sounds received by a TV set are beamed from a TV station on electronic signals called electromagnetic waves. The TV set changes these signals back into pictures and sounds.

Because of its great popularity, TV has become a major way to reach people with advertising messages. Most TV stations carry hundreds of commercials each day. The use of TV advertising has greatly changed the process of getting elected to public office. Today most political candidates for high offices reach many more people through TV than they do in person.

TV cut off ➤ Do you remember watching old movies like '*The Great Dictatorr*', '*Aawara*' and '*Sri 420*' on your television set? When you again watch an old movie on TV, pay attention to the credit titles which seem to be off-centre, either to the left or right. You will find that the entire lines of credit titles are not completely visible on your set. Some lines appear to be lost at the top or bottom of the frame. This is because the movie you are watching was made to be screened in a movie theatre, not on TV screen.

In film medium, every bit of the picture-frame is projected onto the screen. However, in TV, the signal passes through many different steps (from transmission tower to satellite, from satellite to dish antenna and from dish antenna to home screen, etc.) before finally reaching the screen of your TV set. And, at each step, a little bit of image is lost along its outside edges.

Also, as a TV set gets older, its picture tube deteriorates, resulting in more picture loss along the outside perimeters. This picture loss on the edges of the TV Screen is called TV cut off and is estimated to be 10 percent of the total frame. Thus, this loss must be compensated for during shooting and later in shot selection before editing the news story. The modern movie makers realize that some day their films would be screened on TV also, so they take into account the limits imposed by the technical considerations of TV cut off. A TV cameraman must frame the picture about 10 percent smaller than what the frame permits. That is, the TV cameraman should frame his shots 10 percent smaller than a movie cameraman. Also, the tape editor must not choose shots that contain important scenes too near the edges of the frame, where they may not be seen on the home screen after 10 per cent loss. But where alternative shots are not available, as may be the case often in TV news, the constraint of TV cut off has to be waived. Also, the tape editor must pay attention to this lost area, as it is possible that the very part of the picture which is of interest to the director may be too close to the frame to be actually seen in the home. This does not apply directly to cinema, but does if the film is transmitted on TV, which is the case most of the time. The editor can do little about domestic cut off, but to accept the fact that it exists and choose shots accordingly.

TV-Q ► A measurement of audience response to a performer in terms of whether a performer is known or liked.

TVRO ► Television receive Only. 20 # Scriptwriter notation for 20 seconds, sometimes used to indicate a 20-second broadcast commercial.

Two-colour process ► Printing process utilizing two colours of ink. Two-colour printing is less costly than four-colour process printing. The two-colour printing is less costly than Four-Colour process printing. The two-colour combinations most often used include yellow-*magenta, yellow-cyan, cyan-magenta, yellow-black, magenta-black*, and *cyan-black*. The colours are combined in varying proportions to achieve different hues. See also *four-colour process*.

Two-decker, Three-decker ➤ Headline composed of two or three decks, i.e. self-contained units which may each have several lines.

Two-line cap ➤ Capital letter, generally at the beginning of text as a rising initial having the depth of two lines of the following text. Similarly, *three-line cap* and so on.

Two-line double pica ➤ Old name for 44 pt. type.

Two-line English ➤ Old name for 24pt type.

Two-point (2pt.) lead ➤ Lead (led) which is two points thick, the commonest.

Two-shot ➤ A shot of two people used as an establishing shot for an interview (see figs. on Set-up shot). The shot (medium close-up or wider) comprises the interviewer and the interviewee. Also see *picture composition*.

Two-step flow theory ➤ A theory that takes into consideration the role of interpersonal communication in the dissemination and flow of media messages. According to this theory, information disseminated by mass media is i) received by a direct audience and then ii) relayed to other persons second hand for its contrasts, i.e. *bullet theory*.

Two-way ➤ A discussion or interview between studios remote from each other. Frequently used to mean a reporter questioned on air about their story. In commercial radio, this type of reporting is called a *Q&A* (question and answer). In generic terms, it refers to a mode of communication where all parties are able to send and receive messages.

Two-way Cable ➤ An interacting, two-way cable system.

TX ➤ Transmission.

Type ➤ (i) A piece of metal or wood bearing a relief image of a letter of character for printing. (ii) Instruction on proof indicating typographical error.

Type area ➤ The amount of space on a page to be filled with type.

Type book ➤ Catalogue of types held.

Type chart ➤ A tabulated list giving character counts for given types.

Typeface ➤ Particular style and design of letters, numerials and symbols that make up a font; its appearance when printed. Usually defined by name of type family (e.g. Bodoni, Century, etc.), style (Roman, Italic, etc.) and point size.

Type guage ► Device used by typographers and in *copyfitting* to measure the size of the type in terms of *picas* and *points*; also called *pica gauge*, line gauge. See also *typography*.

Type high ► (i) Size of a type *slug* measured from the nonprinting back surface to the front printing surface; usually 0.918 of an inch. Slugs used to create spaces between letters or words are less than type high so that no impression is made by them when placed along with typhigh slugs against the printing surface. (ii) Of the same height as type: English type is 0.918 an inch high.

Typesetter ► Trade name for photographic machine producing cold display type.

Typesetting ► See *composition*.

Typo ► (US) Name given to compositor. Elsewhere abbreviation for *typographical error*.

Typographer ► Person trained in the use and design of type.

Typographical error ► Mistake in setting the copy (as distinct from editorial error).

Typography ► Planning of printed work, (choice of typeface and its size, and the layout of type and illustrations) appropriate to the content of the material to be printed and to the ink and paper used.

Uu

U C ► Upper-case or *capitals*.

UDP ► (User datagram protocol) One of the protocols for data transfer that is part of the TCP/IP suite of protocols. UDP is a "stateless" protocol in that UDP makes no provision for acknowledgement of packets received. See also *TCP/IP*.

Uher ► Trade name of portable tape recorder.

UHF ► Ultra- high frequency radio or TV transmission in the range of 300 to 3000 MHz. Also used to refer to coaxial cable connectors. All channels numbered 14 to 83.

Ultra-violet filter (UVF) ► Filter designed to cut down ultra-violent light, which , while invisible to the human eye, produces a blue haze on reproduction.

U-matic ► Three quarter inch videotape recording system first introduced by Sony.

Umbrella competition ► Refers to a competitive situation in a metropolitan market where newspapers and magazines compete under the umbrella of a large metropolitan paper.

Umbrella story ► A single story incorporating a number of similar items under one banner. See also *multi-angled story*.

Undated story ► (US) A pull-together or round-up in which material from several sources is presented in one story; (India) copy to be used when convenient.

Under-dash matter ► (US) Background material which is released when the main issue makes news, i.e. when the material becomes topical, it is published underneath the main story but separated by a *dinky* or *jim dash*.

Under measure ► Typeset that falls short of the standard column measure.

Under-exposure ► The effect of allowing too little light into the camcorder; giving an excessively dark image.

Underground press ► Publication supporting many activities that are illegal, such as demand for a sovereign Bodoland in the north-eastern region of India; *alternative* newspapers of the 1960s and 1970s in the US that supported activities (abortion, etc.) which were illegal those days.

Underlay ► See *overlay (i)*.

Underline ► Wording about an illustration and written beneath it. Also called *legend* or *caption*.

Underscore ► To underline a word or letters in copy or in type.

Uneven folios ► Odd page numbers 3,5,7,9,11,etc. Also called *odd folios*.

Unfair dismissal ➤ Any dismissal that is not in accordance with employment law.

UNI ➤ United News of India , a news agency providing various types of wire services political , economic and social. Its Hindi language service is UNIVARTA; headquarted in Delhi.

Unidirectional ➤ A type of pickup pattern in which the microphone picks up sound from only one direction.

Unilateral ➤ Exclusive use by one broadcasting organisation of communications satellite, etc.

Units ➤ Standards of measurement, the point being the unit of measurement for type size, the pica (12 pts) for area of type lines, white spaces, pages, etc.

Universal access ➤ Describes a common regulatory principle which allows connection to any party willing to be connected to a network, based on the notion of service obligation that involves connecting geographically distant and economically unviable customers.

Universal desk ➤ (US) A copy desk which receives and examines all copy: wire copy, city copy, state copy and so on; (India) *general desk*.

Universal serial bus (USB) ➤ A hardware standard for external device connections (such as a mouse, modems, game controllers, and keyboards). USB supports Plug an Play installation so that you can easily add new devices to your computer without having to add an adapter card or shut down.

UNIX ➤ A computer operating system (the basic software running on a computer, underneath things like word processors and spreadsheets). UNIX is designed to be used by many people at the same time (it is multi-user) and has *TCP/IP* built-in. It is the most common operating system for *servers* on the *Internet*.

Unjustified ➤ Type which has not been made flush at both ends of a line.

Up-and-over ➤ Direction given to the sound effects person to bring up the volume on the sound so that it plays over the dialogue, rendering the latter inaudible.

Upcut ➤ US term for the accidental overlapping of two sound sources (e.g. live commentary running into recorded sound.)

Update ➤ To include later information in a story to make it more timely; a type of follow-up story that gives newer developments to an earlier story. That is why some stories are updated from edition to edition as new information becomes available.

Upgradgracking ➤ See *digitize*.

UPI ➤ United Press International, syndicated news service.

Uplink ➤ Transmission path from an earth station up to a satellite; sometimes used to describe the ground station capable of sending a satellite signal. Also used as a verb.

Upload ► The process of transferring information from your computer to another computer through the *Internet*. Every time you send e-mail to someone you are uploading it.

Upper case ► Capital letters when used alongside small (lower case) letters. When just capital letters are used (as in headline) they are known as *caps*.

Upper-and-lower ► A headline regime in which upper and lower case letters are used as sense requires: as opposed to 'all capitals' or 'initial capitals'.

Upstage ► Area near the black walls of a setting. In TV, usually indicates a position further from a particular camera. Thus 'Go upstage a little' means 'Move away from the camera'.

Up style ► Writing style that favours capitalization of letters if these is a choice. In newspapers, magazines or other print channels, there is a compromise between up style and *down style*.

URL ► (Uniform resource locator) The standard way to give the address of any resource on the *Internet* that is part of the *World Wide Web (WWW)*. A URL looks like this: http:/www.timesof-india.com: or http://www.eth.-

net. This is also known as website address.

The most common way to use a URL is to enter into a *WWW browser* programme, such as Netscape, or Internet Explorer. See also *browser, WWW*.

Usenet ► A collection of so-called newsgroups that have nothing to do with news. Usenets are ongoing discussion groups among people on the *Internet* who share a mutual interest. Subjects range Internet to moustache care. The network extends beyond Internet, too.

User ID ► This is the unique identifier (like your logon name) that you use to identify yourself on a computer. You probably typed your User ID (and password) when you logged onto the *Internet* to check your *e-mail* box.

Uses and gratification theory ► That explains media effects based on the ways in which media consumers actively select and use media to meet their own needs.

Utility programme ► Computer Programme that performs one of the routine operating functions of a computer, such as file storage.

UUENCODE ► (Unix to unix encoding) A method for converting files from binary to *ASCII* (text) so that they can be sent across the Internet via e-mail. See also *binhex, MIME*.

Vv

Vanity press ▶ Publishing entities that publish only books for which the author pays the full cost of publication.

Variable direct ▶ Costs which increase with the print run and pagination.

Variable shutter ▶ Video cameras do not have mechanical shutters, but some models can vary the duration of the individual scan down to thousandths of a second and beyond.

Variance ▶ Departure from an agreed budget.

Varityper ▶ Trade name for electric automatic-justifying machine with great facility for altering typefaces.

Varta (UNI) ▶ An offshoot of the Indian news agency *UNI*, providing news services in Hindi. Also called UNI-VARTA.

VCR ▶ See videocassette recorder.

VDT ▶ See *VDU*.

VDU ▶ Visual display unit, a device with a screen and keyboard used to display and enter text into a computer; also VDT, visual display terminal.

Verite (radio) ▶ Actuality programme or feature made without accompanying commentary or narrative.

Vernacular Press ▶Newspapers, magazines or any type of journals which are published in a native language. Also called Language Press, it was a derogatory term first used by the English to differentiate the English newspapers and magazines from those of the Indian languages which they wrongly considered undeveloped. The term is still in use and denotes only Indian languages press.

Veronica ▶ (Very easy rodent oriented net-wide index to computerized archives) Developed at the University of Nevada, Veronica is a constantly updated database of the names of almost every menu item on thousands of gopher *servers*. The Veronica database can be searched from most major gopher menus. See also *gopher*.

Vertex ▶ Junction of two diagonal strokes at the bottom of a letter such as w, v, y.

Vertical blanking interval (VBI) ▶ The component of the television scanning process that makes it possible to insert teletext information in a conventional television signal.

Vertical interval time code (VITC) ▶ Time code that is recorded vertically on videotape within the video signal but outside the picture area so that it is visible.

Vertical make-up ► Page make-up with no display element crossing a column rule, i.e. all single-column headlines or pictures, or an emphasis in that direction. Now, out of practice.

Vertical publication ► Publication whose editorial content is written for the benefit of a single business, industry, trade, or profession. Examples of vertical publications are MIS for the benefit of the IT industry, Screen for film industry. Every industry has several of these publications available for interested parties and for advertisers.

Vertical wipe ► See *wipe*.

Very small aperture terminal (VSAT) ► A small satellite dish and the complementary electronic components. The equipment is transportable and is capable of relaying messages (news, etc.) from almost anywhere in the field. A VSAT system is cost-effective too.

Vet ► To check the story for legal wrongs which otherwise could lead to libel suites, etc.

VHF ► Very high frequency. Channels 2 through 13. Radio or TV transmission in the range of 30 to 300 MHz.

VHS ► Video home system, the ½-inch cassette format.

VHS-C ► This is the video home system compact cassette, which runs for up to 45 minutes at standard play on ½ inch tape.

Video (tape) cassette ► A plastic container which holds videotape and allows it to be threaded automatically into cameras and recorders.

Video ► Picture information that is obtained and displayed electronically. Also generic term for all matters that are televisual.

Video 8 ► The smallest tape formats currently available - only 8 mm wide with a running time of 90 minutes at standard speed, or three hours at long play settings. Also called *high-8*.

Video archivist ► Found in larger stations, the person responsible for saving and keeping track of all videotape stories used in every newscast.

Videocassette recorder (VCR) ► Magnetic tape machine that when attached to a television set, can record television broadcasts on videotape cassettes to be viewed later. The machine is also capable of playing prerecorded videotape cassettes, such as movies or concerts, that have been made professionally and are available for sale or rent. The video-cassette recorder was first introduced for the home market by Sony in 1976 (Betamax) and was closely followed by Matsushita with the VHS (video home system). The formats for these two machines are mutually incompatible but remain as the two principal formats for the unit.

Videoconference ▶ A teleconference wherein, as implied by the name, video or visual information is exchanged.

Video disk (disc) ▶ Replay system for pre-recorded video information (in digital format) on high - speed rotating disk. It is scanned optically by laser. Typically suited to interactive training applications and movie distribution to consumers. This is similar to a videocassette system except that the disk system has no recording capacity and can be used only for playback. Also, videodisks have generally better fdelity (due to the use of lasers) than videocassettes, and is for less expensive. Also see *Videocassette recorder.*

Videodisc kiosk ▶ Viewing station providing public access to a videodisc recording and operated by the viewer. Videodisc kiosks advertise goods available for sale from one or several sellers and may include a keyboard or telephone for ordering the goods via credit card. Videodisc kiosks are placed in a variety of locations including the public areas in shopping malls and other retail areas, inside stores, and in other locations likely to draw consumers of the products advertised. For example, a major shoe manufacturer displays its entire product line via videodisc kiosks set up inside its retail stores. If a particular shoe is not in stock, customers can order it, using the kiosk, for delivery to their home. This medium can be expensive if owned and operated by one advertiser, but suppliers will provide the equipment on a leased basis at a significantly lower cost. See also *teletext; videotex.*

Video dub ▶ An editing feature which replaces the picture but leaves the original soundtrack intact.

Video for windows ▶ (VFW) Microsoft's first PC-based digital media system.

Video heads ▶ Heads which record and play back the video signal. Home VCRs have two or four video heads mounted on a head drum.

Video journalists ▶ Solo act by a reporter with a video camera who shoots, interviews and edits.

Video-on-demand (VOD) ▶ System that will be able to deliver entertainment and information to users on demand; will work in conjunction with a set-top computer storage device to hold programming in memory for instant recall. See also near-video-on-demand.

Video recording ▶ The process of recording still or moving images electronically rather than photochemically as in photographic film. Electrical signals from a television camera are stored as patterns of magnetized regions of iron oxide on magnetic tape. When the recorded tape is played back, the original signals are generated. These signals can be disseminated by broadcast antenna or by cable TV receivers that transform the signals into images and sounds. Video tape recorder/playback systems for domestic use are connected to a TV receiver. Unlike motion picture film, Video tape doesn't require processing and so may be played back immediately. This makes possible the so called instant replay common to televised sporting events.

Video server ➤ A high-speed and high capacity information processing/ storage device geared for a video relay. Applications include Video on demand VOD and commercial playbacks(by a television station).

Video tape ➤ A plastic, iron-oxide coated tape of various widths (from 8mm to 1 inch) for video technical code and audio recording. It looks like a roll of black plastic tape, dull on one side and shiny on the other. The shiny side is a very thin coat of metal oxide which is responsive to magnetic impulses. The tape, unlike film, can be instantly replayed and re-used.

Videotex ➤ Interactive system for transmitting text and graphic information to consumers via a personal computer system, consisting of a *keyboard, modem*, cathode-ray *tube* display, and telephone line. This system has been extremely successful in France, where the hardware is provided to users at no cost, but it is growing slowly in other countries like U.S. and U.K. Videotex systems are also available for public access via videotex kiosks in airports, shopping malls, and so forth. Videotex can be used to bank, shop, receive news and stock market quotations, send and receive mail, make travel and theater arrangements, review restaurant listings, run credit checks, and for a variety of other applications. Home access to videotex services is usually sold to consumers on a subscription basis, with an additional charge based on the amount of usage. Advertisers pay a fee based upon the quantity of information and graphics they have available for viewing on the system. See also *teletext; videodisc kiosk.*

Viewdata ➤ Non-broadcast videotex accessed over the telephone.

Viewer ➤ (i) Individual who view a television broadcast. (ii) Optical instrument designed to aid in the viewing of artwork, slides, photographs, transparencies, or the hike. (iii) Viewers per viewing household (VPVH) Estimated number of individuals who comprise the viewing audience within any one household where the television is tuned to a particular programme or station, or where the television is turned on during a given time period. The viewers per viewing household are usually classified by sex and age, such as women, 20-35.

Viewfinder ▸ The system through which the subject is viewed by the camera operator.

Vignette ▸ Small illustration or decoration not enclosed by a border and which appears in the bodytext of an advertisement; camera lens covering that will fade off the edges or background of a shot; advertisement technique where several situations emphasizng the product-qualities are shown in rapid succession. Each situation shows a group of people enjoying the product as they enjoy life often accompanied by lively music; a photograph that fades away at the edges.

Vignetting ▸ Fading of the image towards the corners of the frame. It is sometimes produced by an aberration or fault in the lens, but it can also be introduced as an optical special effect.

Virtual office ▸ Instead of working in a traditional office, you are equipped with a PC and mobile communications tools so that you can work/communicate from the field. Sites have also been designed to serve this workforce when not in the field(for example, a place to plug in your PC).

Virtual reality ▸ A complex graphics and optics system, in which someone can "walk through" a three dimensional computer generated (graphic) environment. All the virtually real factors exist only in the computer, and complete the illusion of a real environment by monitoring users' action and responding to them.

Virus ▸ Describes a computer programme designed to infect, affect and may be destroy other programmes, data and even the computer hardware. It is so called because it can replicate itself like a virus. Computer can get a virus just like your body can be invaded with a virus making you (or your computer) sick. Viruses usually originate from malicious people. You can unintentionally download virus from a web site or get it from a disk that someone has lent you. There are virus-checking programmes, but there are new viruses poping up every day. So the best defence against a virus is to be very careful not to *down-*

load programmes or data from a site you're not familiar with.

Vision story ▶ See *in-vision* / on-camera (story).

Visual production effects machine (VPE) ▶ Computer graphics system used in TV.

Visualize ▶ To plan and work out how a page or display will look.

Visuals ▶ The visual element of a TV report: photographs, film or tape footage or graphics.

VJ ▶ (Video Jockey) The term refers to a person anchoring a light musical programme on television.

VNR ▶ (Video news release) Video version of written press release.

VO-bite script ▶ As the name suggests, a VO-bite script is a combination of Voice-Over and sound bite. The story begins like a VO story but at some point the anchor stops reading behind the TV screen and a sound bite or someone involved in the story or having knowledge of it (e.g. a passer-by who was present at the time of occurrence of the news, say, fire) appears on the screen. After the sound bite there may be more footage of the same story. With the anchor continuing to narrate or he may be back on the screen immediately after the bite to conclude the story. A VO-bite script should always conclude with anchor's tag. Both a locator su-

per and a name-identifier super will be done in a VO-bite story.

Vocal quality ▶ The audible characteristics of a voice including all its nuances. A voice displaying a broad range of clear tones is considered to have high quality. A voice having excessive or unpleasing nasal, breathy, harsh, or strident characteristics has poor quality.

Voice over ▶ Commentary recorded over pictures by an unseen reader. See also *OOV*.

Voice over script ▶ Voice-over or anchor voice-over (AVO) script is like the *reader* to the extent the complete narration is done by the anchor himself but it includes pictures of the story, say of the press conference by a minister to outline the priority areas of his ministry. Soon after the anchor begins a story on camera, pictures or videotape of the story appear on the screen, while the anchor continues to read out. The name is possibly derived from his 'voice over the pictures'. When the tape (pictures) first appears on the screen, you will see the locator super, i.e. the name of the place where the story was shot. For example, the word 'New Delhi' if the pictures were shot there. If the story is edited properly, the videotape images will match what the anchor is talking about. Shortly before the end of the story the anchor is back on the screen with a concluding sentence to wrap the story. This is called tagging the story. Sometimes the video used on VO consists only of graphics and charts (especially in case of stories on budgets and election-analysis) as opposed to the moving pictures showing people, places or things. Such a story may also consist of visuals put on the screen by the C.G. – i.e., numbers and words – especially in case of price movements and share indices.

Voice-over credits ➤ Acting and production credits presented by an announcer whose voice is heard but who is not on camera. Voice-over credits are an alternative to an opening or closing billboard and are used solely at the discretion of the repoducer or director.

Voicer ➤ A prepared presentation by an identified reporter. Also see *voice report*.

Voice report (voicer) ➤ Details and explanation of a story by a reporter or correspondent within a bulletin. More expansive than a copy story. Permits a change of voice from the newsreader.

Voluntary pay newspaper ➤ A newspaper, generally a *shopper*, delivered free but for which payment is later requested. However, its delivery continues whether or not a payment is received.

Vortal ➤ A subject specific portal is called vortal. For example www.ecomready.com is a vortal dedicated to e-commerce.

Vox pop ➤ (Vox populi) A series of usually very short interviews on a specific topic, often with people selected at random, and edited together to give a cross section of opinion. The word Vox populi (Latin) means voice of the people.

VPVH ➤ Viewers per viewing household. Also see *viewer*.

VRML (virtual reality modeling language) ➤ A language used to create 3-D interactive Web graphics, similar to those found in some video games, where the user can "move around" within a graphic image and interact with the objects.

VSNL ➤ Videsh Sanchar Nigam Limited, a joint venture of Indian government and the Tata Sons authorised to provide satellite uplinking facilities from India.

VTR ➤ A videotape recorder.

VU meter ➤ Volume unit meter. A device to measure sound levels. It is a less professional equipment than the PPM (*peak programme meter*), being more inaccurate at some frequencies.

Ww

WAIS ► (wide area information servers) A commercial *software* package that allows the indexing of huge quantities of information, and then making those indices searchable across networks such as the Internet. A prominent feature of WAIS is that the search results are ranked (scored) according to how relevant the hits are, and that subsequent searches can find more stuff like that last batch and thus refine the search process.

Wait order ► Instructions to a publication, usually a newspaper, to wait until subsequently notified to insert an advertisement. The advertisement referred to in the wait order has already been typeset and is ready to go, upon further notification. A rainwear manufacturer might use a wait order with an ad for raingear and then notify the newspaper to run the advertisement on a date when the forecast calls for rain.

Wall brace ► Scenic brace used to support scenery. Attached to a fitting in the studio wall.

Wall newspaper ► News paper, usually hand written, stuck on walls. Journalism training schools often produce wall newspapers when final pages are produced but not sent away to be published. Simply stuck on walls. In some countries (e.g., China) newspapers gained most of their readership through being pinned to walls at public places.

War ► Word beloved of reporters and subs, used often in relation to press: hence tabloid wars, circulation wars.

Wallpaper ► The background on your desktop. You can select a background from bitmaps and *HTML* documents included in Windows 98, or you can choose from your own files.

Warming filter ► Filter which reduces the proportion of blue in the light entering the lens.

Warm-up ► Three-to-five-minute period prior to a live television (or radio) show when someone affiliated with the upcoming broadcast spends time with the audience telling jokes, relating information about the show, or explaining some production elements in the show. A warm-up is done to make an audience more at ease and to make them feel as if they are part of the production, so that they will be in a responsive mood when the show comes on.

Wash drawing ► A sketch with more tonal scale than simple black and white, and hence suitable for half-tone reproduction.

Waste copies ▶ Copies of a newspaper at the beginning of a run when ink and registration are being adjusted to start the actual printing.

Watchdog ▶ It refers to the role of Press in India as it is supposed to raise a voice against injustice, corruption and all types of wrong doing which are harmful to the society.

Waveform ▶ Digital speech is displayed on a computer in the form of zigzag waves of sound. These can be edited on-screen.

Wavelength ▶ Expressed in metres, the distance between two precisely similar points in adjacent cycles in a sound or radio wave. The length of one cycle. Used as the tuning characteristic or 'radio address' of a station. See also Frequency.

Wavy rule ▶ Rule that prints undulating line.

Waxing ▶ A process in photoset newspapers. Each bromide of type is fed into a heated roller machine which coats the opposite side of the bromide with an adhesive wax so that the bromide can be stuck down on paper.

Web ▶ (i) Roll of paper threaded through the printing presses. (ii) See *world wide web*.

Web browser ▶ The tool or programme that allows you to *surf* the *web*. You mostly use your browser to locate a web page. The most popular web browsers are *Internet* explorer and Netscape Navigator.

Web editor ▶ A computer programme used to create web pages.

Weblog ▶ The term describes a regularly updated web site that points to links on other sites and has commentaries about the links. You can create a Weblog that relate to your field, say journalism, and can attract potential readers of your write-ups. For more information on the Weblogs, log on to: *www.weblogs.com*.

Web master ▶ Person who maintains either content or systems for large *Web sites*.

Web offset ▶ A system in which printing is done not directly from the plate (by relief impression) but from a rubber-blanket which has picked up the images from the inked plate. See *offset*. Mr 'Webb', who does not exist, is often credited with this invention through an error in spelling.

Web page ▶ An individual document in world wide web format usually a part of a website. It includes words, photographs and graphics. May also include sound, moving pictures and animation. The term is sometimes used to descrbe any HTML documents.

Web ring ► Collections of related Web sites by a ring master who chooses each site for its quality as a resource on a particular topic.

Web search mechanisms ►Software tools used to identify and locate web-based resources (for example, keyword search).

Web site ► A set of related Web pages (usually connected by hyperlinks), arranged on the *World Wide Web* under a common address, and allow retrieval via a *Web browser*. A website is built around a company, organization or person. For example, the Website of Indian Institute of Mass Communication (IIMC) is: www.iimc.-ac.in.

Web style ► A desktop display option. In web style, you can navigate your computer by using such Web conventions single clicking

Weight ► (of type) The degree of blackness or thickness of colour of a typeface.

Wet printing ► Four-colour process printing technique that layers ink over previously printed surfaces that have not yet dried. Most web presses and a few sheet-fed presses operate too quickly to allow drying time between ink colour impressions. If we printing is to be used, the Proofs should also be created using wet printing, to accurately represent the appearance of the final product. Four-colour process printing can also be done with a combination of wet and dry printing on a two-colour press that allows drying time during washup and press preparation for the next two colours. See also *transparent ink*.

Wf ► Abbreviation for *wrong fount*.

WHAT formula ► Essentials of story construction: what has happened? How did it happen? Amplification; Tie up loose ends.

When room ► An indication that story will hold for a few days, waiting to be published when space is available.

Whip pan (Swish pan) ► Very rapid pan which completely blurs the subject and the background. Also called *whiz pan* or *blue pan*, it is used as a transition from one scene to another in a commercial or other motion picture film or in TV news out of necessity to shoot a moving subject.

Whistle blower ► Person revealing newsworthy and previously secret information or material.

White balance ► The system for calibrating colour balance on a domestic colour camera.

White out ► To increase spacing in the page where indicated.

White space ► Unprinted areas used by a designer to direct the eye. Manufacturers of expensive or prestige products, use this to create a concept of luxury or elegance. On the other hand, advertisements for discount products seldom use any white space.

Whiz pan ► See *whip pan*.

Wide angle lens ► A camera lens with a short focal length which provides wide coverage (e.g. >45°). In the shot, subjects look further away than normal; space and distance appear exaggerated; depth and thickness emphasize.

Wide leaded ► Lines of type separated by more than one thickness of lead.

Wide-screen TV ► Transmission and reception format providing a wide-screen image, available to viewers owing TV sets equipped with appropriate receivers.

Wide meas ► Wide measure. Lines of type longer than normal for the newspaper or for the size of type used, e.g., setting across 24 pica ems would be wide measure for a type as small as 3pt.

Wide open ► A situation when there is more than enough space in the newspaper for the news available. This situation is a rarity.

Wide shot ► see *long shot*.

Widow ► A short line or a few words making up a line at the end of a paragraph appearing at the top of column; also *jackline*. They are best avoided.

Width ► Typefaces vary in width ranging between ultra-condensed and ultra-expanded.

Wild ad ► Run of paper ad which can go any where.

Wild copy ► A copy which can go anywhere in the newspaper or news broadcast.

Wild shot ► Shot taken by a television or motion picture camera that has not been synchronized with sound. Sometimes in the making of a motion picture, television show, or commercial, directors will have the camera crew take a series of wild shots that will be viewed during the editing process and used as the director and editor see fit.

Wild track/wild sound ► Recorded sound which is related to but not synchronised with the picture. It is recorded for dubbing later as background sound for a report. Recorded for the same reason as *wild shot*.

Wind screen ► A sponge rubber or latex sound-absorbing shield wrapped over a microphone to reduce extraneous noise.

Window ► The rectangular portion of your screen that displays an open programme or the contents of a folder or disk. You can have multiple windows open at the same time.

Windows explorer ► A feature you can use to view the contents of your computer and network drives in hierarchical structure.

Windshield ▶ Protective over of foam rubber, plastic, or metal gauze, designed to eliminate wind noise from microphone. Essential on outdoor use or close vocal work.

Wind up ▶ A signal to end a segment, commonly the final 30 seconds. Also, called wrap-up.

Windy line ▶ Line with excessive white space.

Wing ▶ Working space offstage to left and right of main stage or acting area. This space lies on either side of the mainstage and is intended to conceal wings.

Wing copy ▶ Additional matter enhancing a feature, appearing in a box or panel to one side. Also see *sidebars* in *story types*.

Wing in ▶ To place a headline within the top rule of a panel or box, leaving a piece of rule showing on either side.

Wing it ▶ A term for doing a programme without a rehearsal.

Wipe ▶ (i) An effect in which one shot (film/TV) appears to wipe the preceding image from the screen. Wipes are used most frequently and most effectively when a rapid succession of scenes is desired. There are several different types, including a *flip wipe* (in which the entire scene appears to turn over like

the front and back of a postcard), a *horizontal wipe* or *vertical wipe* (in which an image moves from side to side, or from top to bottom or bottom to top), a *diagonal wipe* or *closing door wipe* (in which an image comes both sides), a *circle wipe* or iris wipe (in which a new image comes in, in a circle that grows bigger and bigger, or an old image moves out, in a circle that grows smaller), or a *clock wipe* (in which images sweep around the screen in a clockwise or counterclockwise motion). (ii) To erase tape.

Wire ▶ A means of transmitting copy by electronic signal which requires a receiver or decoder.

Wire editor ▶ See *telegraph editor.*

Wireless LAN ▶ As implied, you can tap a LAN's resources without a direct physical connection. Also see *local area network*(LAN).

Wireless network ▶ A network where the user's device, for example, a handset doesn't have to be physically connected to the network. Cellular and wireless-in-local-loop telephony are wide spread example of this technology.

Wirephoto ▶ Telephonic photo transmission system operated by PTI / AP / AFP. See also *Telephoto*. Now, the photo transmission is done through satellites, yet the name *wirephoto* persists.

Wireroom ► Department which receives teleprinted copy and photographs from the news agencies and correspondents on distant assignments.

Wire service ► News agency which sends copy out to newsroom along landlines (wires) where it is received by teleprinters or directly into computers. These days satellite links have replaced landlines, yet the name 'wire' continues. Reuters, AP, PTI are wire services.

Wizard ► A tool that walks you through the steps of a complex task.

WOB ► White on black type.

Womb-trembler ► A highly emotional or disturbing story or feature, usually involving children, childbirth or fertility.

Women's service magazine ► Magazine the editorial contents of which are designed to appeal to homemakers; also called service magazine. Articles contain information about child rearing, cooking, household management, home decorating, and other home-related subjects. Care and the Ladies' Home Journal are examples of women's service magazines.

Woodcut ► Ancient printing technique utilizing a carved wooden block or board as a relief image carrier; also called black-line engraving. In a wood engraving, the image areas are recessed below the surface of the board; in a woodcut, the nonimage areas are carved away. Woodcuts can be used with one or several colours of ink. Although they have largely been replaced by modern photographic and printing techniques, woodcuts are still in use as an artist's medium and are employed in advertising for their unique character as a fine art form.

Word processor ► Programmemable typewriter or computer Programme used to compose, format, sort, and rearrange text upon command and sometimes perform other related functions such as correcting misspelled words. Word processors are commonly used to compose copy and to create personalized computer letters to customers or prospects using standard formats with spaces for inserting information specific to that customer.

Word-rate ► The fee for freelance contributions.

Word-spacing ► The amount of space between words. Controlled by software, e.g. Word, Page Maker, etc.

Workgroup ► A set of networked computers that typically share the same resources, such as printers. A network can be comprised of many workgroups. See also *network*.

Working light ► Any light introduced to enable craftsmen, performers, etc. to see what they are doing when there is insufficient lighting (e.g. behind scenery).

Work print ➤ (i) Dub of an original film that is used for editing so that the *master* will remain intact. (ii) In TV, assemblage of scenes that have been selected from the *assembly dailies* and placed in proper sequence without the opticals (*Dissolves*, *Wipes*, etc.), titles, or any *Supers*; also called rough cut. As the name implies, this is the print to which scenes will be added, deleted, or substituted and on which other changes will be made until the director feels that the footage is right and the other elements can be added. When the work print is complete to the director's satisfaction, a composite print will be made. See also *final print*.

Work station ➤ A special video display terminal used at a distance from the main computer, with access and facilities to enable work to be done over a telephone line (or any other communication network) away from the main centre.

World Wide Web (WWW) ➤ The graphical, multi-media portion of the Internet. The web is comprised or millions of web bages. To explore the web you use web *browsing* software. These web pages are lossely knit by *hyperlinks*. The term is frequently and incorredtly used to mean the Internet, while it is just a facility provided by the Internet.

A product of the Swiss-based CERN research centre, it was pioneered by Tim Berners-Lee to help facilitate the exchange of information. You use the Web to travel across the Internet and to retrieve and exchange information ranging from text to digital video. Also see *Internet*, *web page*.

Worldwide Television News ➤ (WTN) UK-based international television news agency.

WOT ➤ White-on-tone type.

Wow ➤ Slow speed variations discernible in tape or disc reproduction..

WPB ➤ The ultimate destination of 90 per cent of a newsroom's incoming mail—the waste paper bin.

Wrap ➤ Radio equivalent of package in TV reporting. See *package*.

Wraparound ➤ (i) Publishing device in which the normal newspaper is enclosed within four extra pages, e.g. Punjab Kesari (India). (ii) A TV news story around which a reporter appears for a lead-in and a final statement.

Wraparound plate ➤ Cylindrical relief (raised image area) plate used in direct (to paper) and indirect rotary press printing. Wrap-around plates reduce preparation time and expense, compared to other relief printing methods in which a cylindrical duplicate has to be made from a flat plate. Wraparound plates do not have to be etched as deeply as other plates, also saving expense. They are most often used for long press runs, such as for newspaper and magazine printing.

Wrapped up ➤ Indication that all the copy has been sent to the composing room, all the blocks to process, and the make-up completed.

Wrinkles ➤ Print problem caused by a crushed or irregular paper surface that can ruin the print product. Wrinkles can be caused by many factors, including moisture damage, sloppy packing or handling, or incorrect paper feed to the printer.

Write once, read many (WORM) ➤ A non-erasable but user-recordable optical disk.

Wrong fount (wf) ➤ A mistake in composition by using a letter of inappropriate size or not of the same design as the rest.

Wrongful dismissal ➤ A dismissal without proper notice.

WSTV ➤ (World Service Television) BBC-owned news and entertainment service.

Wysiwyg ➤ What You See Is What You Get (acronym).

Xx

Xerography ▸ Electrophotography technique that produces an image on paper, using electrically charged particles. Electricity is projected onto the paper in the form of the image to be printed. Particles of pigment bond to the charged area. The pigment is then made permanent by the application of heat. See also *laser printer*.

X-height ▸ The average height of ordinary lower-case letters without ascenders or descenders, for example, a,c,e, etc. It determines how large a typeface of a given size actually appears.

X-prize ▸ Echoing back to an earlier era, a proposed monetary prize to advance reusable launch vehicle technology (for example to develop space tourism).

X-ref ▸ *cross-reference*.

Yy

Yellow journalism ➤ The practice of giving sensationalized stories often bordering on scandalous, scurrilous and personal slander. The motto is 'never let the facts stand in the way of an invitng story'. The term derived from a popular comic ship, The Yellow Kid and first applied to Hearst-pulitzer circulation wars in New York newspapers of the 1890. Later the same Joseph Pulitzer, owner of the New York World that engaged in yellow journalism, founded the prestigious *Pulitzer Prize* in 1917.

Yesman journalism ➤ The practice of or highlighting the accomplishments of the ruling party or the establishment and ignoring its wrongdoings. Also called *yours faithfully journalism*.

Yours faithfully journalism ➤ See *yesman journalism*.

Zapping ► Practice of skipping or avoiding commercials while videotaping through the pause button.

Zero level tone ► A standard reference level signal (0 dB or 1 mw in 600 ohms at a frequency of 1 kHz) used to line up broadcasting equipment.

Zinco ► Half-tone plate that is engraved on zinc, but commonly used for all photo-engravings, whatever the metal.

Zines ► Low cost magazines put out by volunteers on a variety of topics.

Zip-A-Tone ► Trade name for tinted sheet added to line drawings or headlines.

Zipping ► Skipping advertisements in a TV programme while playing back a videotape by fast-forwarding through them.

Zombie ► Body –type setting which splits words near the end of the line for the convenience of the line-caster, not the ease of the reader.

Zone ► Section of a publication, which is changed to cater to the needs or interests of various geographical zones in respect of news or advertisements. In a zoned edition of a newspaper, you find some special content for that zone which doesn't appear in other editions of the newspaper.

Zoom-in ► Reducing the angle - of - view by increasing the focal length of a zoom lens during the course of a shot. The result is that the subject becomes larger in the frame.

Zooming ratio ► The ratio of the longest to the shortest available focal length of a zoom. For example, a 10 mm to 50 mm lens is said to have a zooming ratio of 5:1.

Zoom lens ► Lens of variable focal lengths. This means that an object can be held in focus while the angle-of-view and magnification of the image is varied during a shot between certain limits (e.g., 10-30; a 3:1 ratio).

Zoom-out ► Widening the angle - of - view by shortening the focal length of a zoom lens during the course of a shot. The result is that the subject becomes smaller in the frame.

Zooms ► A zoom shot of a subject is a picture that is obtained by either moving the lens closer or away from the subject. The name 'zoom' is derived by the lens called Zoom Lens, which is capable of giving a close or distant shot of the subject without actually moving the camera. To 'zoom-in' means to come closer or 'tighten' on the subject. To 'zoom-out' means to move farther away or 'widen' from the subject. In TV news, zooms are rarely used except when it becomes necessary while shooting some unpredictable events – a star cricketer all on a sudden surrounded by his fans and the police trying to rescue him to a place out-of-bounds for the uncontrollable crowd.

Why is it that the zooms are used so rarely in TV news? First, because the zoom shots are not as revealing and communica-tive as the static shots of an action and second, because they (zoom shots) are difficult to edit – in terms of time as well as skills especially if the shots are too long. And, a newsroom cannot afford the luxury of spending so much time on a few shots except when they are exceptional because of their news value: zoom shots of a passenger plane that caught fire in mid-air and is falling into a sea. Who captured such shots? Well, a holidaying couple with a Video-8 camera.

Extended Reference

AIR Style Book. (1991). Delhi.

Albarran, Alan B. (1996). Media Economics- Understanding Market, Industries and Concepts. ISUP (USA).

Alexander, Pat. (1989). Broadcasting Glossary. AMIC. Singapore.

Andrews, Deborah C. and Andrews, William D. (2004). Management Communication: A Guide. Houghton Mifflin Company. Boston.

Bell, A., Joyce, M. and Rivers, D. (1999). Advanced Level Media. Hodder & Stoughton. London.

Biamant, Lincoln. (1991). Dictionary of Broadcast communications. 3rd edition. NTC Business Books. Illinois.

Bielark, Mark. TV Production Today. 3rd edition. National Textbook Company. Illinois.

Bly, Robert. (2002). The Online Copywriter's Handbook. McGraw-Hill. USA.

Boyd, Andrew. (1997). Broadcast Journalism. 4th edition. Focal Press. London.

Bromley, Michael. (1994). Teach yourself Journalism Hodder & Strughton. U.K.

Burns. L.S. (2002). Understanding Journalism. Vistaar Publications. New Delhi.

Callahan, Christopher. (1999). A Journalist's Guide to the Internet. Allyn and Bacon. Boston.

Cheshire, David. (1990). The Complete Book of Video. Dorling Kindersley. London.

Chopra, Deepti and Merrill, Keith. (2002). Cyber Cops, Cyber Criminals & Internet. I. K. International New Delhi.

CNN International Writing Guide. (1995).

Cohler, David Keith. (1985). Broadcast Journalism. Prentice-Hall Inc. New Jersey.

Defleur & Dennis. (2002). Understanding Mass Communication: A Liberal Arts Perspective. Houghton Mifflin Company. Boston.

Dennis, E. E. and Merrill, J. C. (2002). Media Debates: Great

Issues for the Digital Age. Wadsworth. Ontario (Canada).

Evans, Harold. (1979). Editing and Design, Book-III News Headlines. Heinemann. London.

Everett, Anna and Caldwell John T. (editors). (2003). New Media: Theories and Practices of Digitextuality. Routledge. New York.

Flemming, Dan. (1993). Media Teaching. Blackwell. Oxford.

Garrison, Bruce. (1992). Advanced Reporting Skills for the Professional. LEA. New Jersey.

Gauntlet, David (editor). (2000). Web. Studies. Arnold. London.

Ghosh, Subir. (2001). Public Relations Today. Rupa & Co. Delhi.

Hall, Jim. (2002). Online Journalism: A Critical Primer. Pluto Press. London.

Harper, Christopher. (2002). The New Mass Media. Houghton Mifflin Company. Boston.

Hicks, Wynford Holmes, Tim. (2002). Sub-editing for Journalists. Routledge. N.Y.

Hicks, Wynford, Adams, Sally and Gilbert, Harriet. (2000). Writing for Journalists. Routledge. N.Y.

Hodgson, F.W. (1998). New sub-editing. 3rd edition. Focal Press. Oxford.

Hough, Geroge. A. (1988). News writing. Houghton Mifflin Company. Boston.

Jethwaney, J. (1994). Public Relations: Concepts, Strategies and Tools. Sterling. New Delhi.

Keeble, Richard. (2001). The Newspaper Handbook. 3rd edition. Routledge. N. Y.

Kumar, Keval. J. (1994). Mass communication In India. Jaico. Delhi.

Ma Ciuba-Koppel, Darlene. (2002). The Web Writer's Guide: Tips and Tools. Focal Press. N.Y.

Marjoribanks, Timothy. (2000). News Corporation, Technology and the Workplace: Global Strategies, Local Change. Cambridge University Press. UK.

Mayo, Don and Barkemeyer, Kathy. (1998). Internet in an Hour for Beginners. DDC Publishing. USA.

McMahon, E.D. (2001). Bricks to Clicks. Macmillan. New Delhi.

Millerson, Gerald. (1995). The Technique of Television Production. 12th edition. Focal Press. London.

Mitchell, Wanda. (1974). Televising Your Message. National Textbook Company. Illinois.

Morrish, John. (1996). Magazine Editing. Routeledge. London.

Paul, Nora M. (1999). Computer-assisted Research: A Guide to Tapping Online Information for Journalists. Bonus Books. USA.

Picard, Robert G. and Brody, Jeffrey H. (1997). The Newspaper Publishing Industry. Allyn & Bacon. MA (USA).

Rau, M.Chalapathi. (1975). The Romance of the Newspaper. NCERT. Delhi.

Rodman, George. (2001). Making Sense of Media- An Introduction to Mass Communication. Allyn & Bacon. Boston.

Rodrigues, Dawn. (2000). The Research Paper and the World Wide Web: A Writer's Guide. Prentice Hall. USA.

Sanjay, B. P. (2002). Communication Education and Media Needs in India. AMIC- India with support from UNESCO-IPDC. Chennai.

Schultheis, Robert and Sumner, Mary. (1999). Management Information Systems: The Manager's View. 4th edition. Tata McGraw-Hill. New Delhi.

Shrivastav, K.M. (1992). Media Issues. Sterling Publishers, New Delhi.

Singh, C. P. (1999). Before The Headlines- A Handbook of TV Journalism. Macmillan. Delhi.

Stein, ML & Paterno, Susan F. (1999). The News Writer's Handbook: An Introduction to Journalism. ISUP (USA).

The Internet Handbook for writers, Researchers, and Journalists. Guild Ford Press. London.

Turow, Joseph. (2003). Media Today: An Introduction to Mass Communication. Houghton Mifflin Company, New York.

Vizjak, Andrej and Ringlstetter, Max (editors). (2001). Media Management: Leveraging Content for Profitable Growth. Berlin.

Ward, Mike. (2002). Journalism Online. Focal Press. Oxford.

Whittaker, Jason. (2002). Web Production for Writers and Journalists 2nd edition. Routledge. London.

Yadav, J.S. and Mathur P (editors). (1988). Issues in Mass Communication. IIMC. New Delhi.

Yorke, Ivor. (1995). Television News. Focal Press. Oxford.